Dress Whites,
Gold Wings

Daniell M. Brown

10-10-06

For: Dwyane
 - Good Times
 - Good Friends
 - Good Memories
Best Wishes always -
 Dan Brown

Now you can tell Folks
you know "Dan Brown"
 the author

Note for Librarians: A cataloguing record for this book is available from Library and
Archives Canada at www.collectionscanada.ca/amicus/index-e.html
ISBN 1-4120-6762-6

*Printed in Victoria, BC, Canada. Printed on paper with minimum 30% recycled fibre. Trafford's print
shop runs on "green energy" from solar, wind and other environmentally-friendly power sources.*

TRAFFORD
PUBLISHING™

Offices in Canada, USA, Ireland and UK
This book was published *on-demand* in cooperation with Trafford Publishing.
On-demand publishing is a unique process and service of making a book available for
retail sale to the public taking advantage of on-demand manufacturing and Internet
marketing. On-demand publishing includes promotions, retail sales, manufacturing,
order fulfilment, accounting and collecting royalties on behalf of the author.

Book sales for North America and international:
Trafford Publishing, 6E–2333 Government St.,
Victoria, BC V8T 4P4 CANADA
phone 250 383 6864 (toll-free 1 888 232 4444)
fax 250 383 6804; email to orders@trafford.com
Book sales in Europe:
Trafford Publishing (UK) Limited, 9 Park End Street, 2nd Floor
Oxford, UK OX1 1HH UNITED KINGDOM
phone 44 (0)1865 722 113 (local rate 0845 230 9601)
facsimile 44 (0)1865 722 868; info.uk@trafford.com
Order online at:
trafford.com/05-1673

10 9 8 7 6 5 4 3 2 1

Dedicated to:

Becky and Beth, my two girls,
my wife and our daughter,
thank you for loving me

and

the memory of my parents, Julian and Wilma Brown,
my role models, my heroes

and

the memory of Mrs. Mary Knight, Becky's mom, who
helped proofread the original manuscript, and Mr. Earl
Knight, her dad, who accepted me like a son

and

Mrs. Jane Adams, a charming friend, 87 years young, who
proofed a late manuscript

And

Nicola Fantei, my Italian friend, the world's greatest
computer guru who formatted and paginated this book, and
also designed the cover

and
to

great memories of Billy Fridell, Richard Fortuna, Wes
Woolf, Dick Bright, John Huber, Tom Brandstetter, and
Harris Marshall, all wonderful guys gone but remembered in
these pages

NOTE: Famous personages mentioned herein are real. Likewise, the author has used actual real life names for himself and all immediate and extended family, including son-in-law Doug. All other names have been changed to protect privacy rights. Dates and events are generally correct.

CONTENTS

PREFACE

Think storytelling.....The book has a beginning to ending connective thread, sometimes thinly veiled, but each chapter could be and is a stand-alone story

September, 2005
Age: 70

People often ask, "What's your book about?" Feinting abject surprise, I might project utter naiveté that such a query was necessary as I replied, "Why me, of course." Actually, my response was gauged in witticism to elicit an all-knowing smile from the source of the question. And their reaction was predictable: "I guess *you would* write a book about yourself." The fact is my answer was true in large part but not in the manner they were thinking. Admittedly, this book could be labeled an ego trip of sorts, chronicling the minor achievements of yours truly. But to my mind, it's more a book about *life*. **Dress Whites, Gold Wings** is a compilation of short stories about real events and real people. "Me, myself and I" as an All-American hero was never intended to be the genre of this written offering. But we all have narratives, tales, yarns, anecdotes, and punch lines that we tend to tell over and over again, most of which include personal touches. Cocktail parties, dinner conversations, campfire reverie, joke telling around the water cooler, any of many venues are magnified and enhanced by recollections we love to relate about ourselves and others. In these pages, I have shared my favorites. And as noted below, the stories are true, therefore necessarily experiences centered on or around my life and those of friends and acquaintances of which I have first-hand knowledge. By default I become the main character, yet I don't think of my book as an *autobiography* since the very word seems to connote status, noteworthy achievements, financial import, political power, etc. I fall into none of those categories. So while necessarily autobiographical in content, I think of this book as *True Short Stories.*

I *believe* it was Samuel Clemens (or was it Lord Byron?) who surmised, "Truth is stranger than fiction". They might be right. Look at the real life dramas of Lorena Bobbitt, John Gacey, Tonya Harding, Amy Fisher, the Menendez Bothers, Michael Jackson. Even sports stars at the highest level encounter unbelievable real life complications - O.J. Simpson being the epitome of real life scenarios that fascinates our innate curiosity. Yes, Clemens or Byron may have been absolutely correct. In my case, in justifying why you should read, no, not only read but devour, **Dress Whites, Gold Wings**, I feel <u>truth is exactly the ingredient</u> that makes the stories unique and worthwhile reading. Let me reiterate: the experiences recited herein actually happened to the author or his immediate friends as principals. How does that John Lennon quote go? Something like, *"Life is what happens to us while we're making other plans"*. These chapters and verses are about 'what happened' along the way to a 'country boy gone to town'. Very few of the incidents related were in *'the plan'* I had in mind. Plan or no plan, I think the stories are interesting and worthy of your time to read.

Let me expand on my version of *truth* as used herein. One of my major disappointments in life is that I did not keep a diary. I had no written reference to use, just experiences tucked away in gray matter. My friends and I have told many of these stories over and over again. The bottom line, the stories are true *as I remember them.* Let's recall, truth is not always readily apparent or easily identified. The Clinton presidency has taught us that perception is the true reality. In this book, truth is how I remember, i.e., *how I now perceive after several years,* both the big picture and the related details. I did look up a few things on the Internet and I used various other sources to keep dates and events in context. Of necessity, most names and many geographical locations have been changed to protect other's privacy.

Just a word or two on style. I write stories as I would tell them. I'm not into routinely describing clothing or hair color, facial features, etc., unless the detail is important to the storyline. Most facts not germane to the point are omitted while other seemingly insignificant details are included in the telling simply because I thought them scintillating. Names, especially that of the storyteller (me – I have an aversion to the pronoun 'I'), are repeated in every account as each story event ends with that chapter. Thus, each chapter could conceivably be dissected from the whole and used as a stand-alone story. Conversely, I do not repeat footnote information so you might have go back to a previous chapter to decipher unfamiliar "Navy-isms."

Yes, there is a general plot ribbon, as collectively, all the chapters contribute to the author's journey from childhood to senior citizen. The storyteller is continually reminded by events beyond his control that some, if not many, answers to life's questions are evasive or unanswerable. That seriousness is peppered with fun and zesty, sometimes provocative or suggestive, sub-plots that tantalize the imagination. I hope the reader will be mindful of this background information. The story backdrop is especially poignant as you read about the bird, the vision, and the cancer. I have strived diligently to construct those special scenes and events as realistically as possible.

I love the title, *Dress Whites, Gold Wings,* which in and of itself connotes a military theme. But these pages are more than an all-Navy treatise. The few before April, 1955, set in motion the general storyline thread while the several after June, 1976, are crucial to finalizing the book's hunt for answers to some of life's difficult questions. Forty middle chapters comprise the Navy years ending June 30, 1976.

After drafting many of the accounts recreated herein, I saw a need for some sort of form. Since the storyline covers a period of about 65 years, many of the episodes deal with topics that were cutting edge *'back then'* but are second nature to us as we enter the third millennium. For example, the prostate cancer scare of Chapter 51 was a big deal in 1979. Surgery was almost always immediate, and unfortunately a final solution to the virility of many men. Today, prostate cancer when caught early is one of the least feared malignancies. The event that set the stage for *The Right Stuff* was a humongous happening in 1962. Today, space exploration is old hat - we talk of new planets being discovered and expanding galaxies. I felt historical perspective might help the reader more easily identify with the context of each story. I decided upon three specific aids. First, chapters are compiled chronologically. Secondly, by annotating the specific calendar year an event occurred. Last, the storyteller's age (mine) at the time is confirmed at the outset of each chapter.

Sorry, but *Dress Whites, Gold Wings* may not be deemed appropriate family reading and entertainment. I tried to keep events, circumstances, and language within the confines of a PG 13 rating but in the end, could not. It's definitely NOT "X" material. There is only one use of the "F" word in a situation where no substitute is available (but even there, dashes are used as camouflage). "G.D.", a favorite of sailors since the invention of sails, doesn't see the light of day in these pages except for a quote by a three-year old. There are other expletives employed, but I assure you it's mild stuff compared to the sex and language in today's novels or TV scripts. Since the PG 13 envelope is pushed aside occasionally I guess certain dialog puts it in the "R" category. **Warning! Several episodes include bathroom incidents and humor**. Again, the stories are no more risqué than we are finding on today's prime time family sitcoms and not nearly as descriptive as filmmakers offer moviegoers.

Ladies, women, girls, *please note!* There are a few chapters wherein the story unfolding is probably set on an unfamiliar stage: Flying. I'm afraid there will be a tendency for the fairer sex to skip those episodes. My gut instinct tells me that females feel about flying stories the same way they feel about professional football on Sundays: *they either love it or can't stand it.* I hope you will lay any prejudices aside and look at the *real* story being told as flying in most cases is just the background vehicle. Or, go to the next chapter for a totally different story. By the by, military flying movies of late have the pilot's using code names, like 'Maverick' and 'Iceman' in *Top Gun.* It was different in my day as you will see. The squadron's code identifier plus the side number of the aircraft being flown was the call sign, i.e., *Mustang 022.*

Some of the major events occurring to yours truly left me pondering the deeper issues of life and death, fate, predestination. I don't think I am unique in desiring to find sum and substance in life beyond the fleeting experiences of the day. Mankind's eternal quest for the meaning of life has intrigued me since my youngest memories. We were an economically poor rural family but compared to the black sharecropper widow and children who lived only a quarter mile away, we were rich. I'm sure the conflict in my immature mind over the fact that we were simultaneously lacking in material niceties and yet wealthy by comparison to the less fortunate, fertilized my questioning nature about the great scheme of things. I love cartoons showing the aged Hindu sage sitting atop the mountain waiting for the weary traveler who comes seeking the "Why" of life. In the world of comic characters, he can only dispense humor…that's the whole point of the "B.C." strip. Ahhh, but our real world deals us the same question, "Why"? The mysteries of life and death and heaven and hell continue to dominate the pursuit of ordinary men as well as learned thinkers. The ultimate puzzle, the meaning of life, as yet, remains unsolved for most of us. The egotistical search for clues to our beginning and to our destiny continues now and will endure long into the twenty-first century. Some see in this an inane sense of humor by a Supreme Being. Others would say that humanity is obsessed with trying to know the will of God, an incongruity in itself. How can God be God if we can discern His will? It seems to me that, we, the human race, have a propensity for attempting to bring God down to our level. I wish we would solve the dilemma by raising mankind up to God's expectations through personal moral courage. **Wait! Please read on!** Not to worry, that's a tangent these chapters do not pursue. Yes, I thought it meaningful for you to know where I'm coming from in the great search for the essence of life but by and large this is a secular book (that means *non-religious*, you redneck buds). The salient point is to say that while the main character struggles introspectively with destiny and fate, I endeavored to keep his sixty-odd year sojourn free of religious connotations. The cancer scare previously mentioned and the conclusion in Chapter 62 where Dan wrestles with *why* many of his friends are gone while he reaches Medicare age happy and relatively healthy, are rare and reasonable exceptions. Again, simply injections of truth. I know, I was there. For my religious friends, especially the *Walk to Emmaus* zealots, let's understand that my statements above do not impugn or deny my faith. I'm not ashamed of God, but I feel that once Faith is injected into an open discussion, give and take dialog disappears and intelligent conversation degenerates into argument. I wanted to do this book using secular thinking, which in a convoluted way gives greater credence to the faith of the faithful. As the guy with the bad haircut (Ross Perot) used to say, 'Follow?'

My main objective in writing this book is to leave something of myself to the grandchildren I might not get to know, the great-grandchildren I will never see. I hope that my efforts are not perceived as a written monument to the great Ego-god. O.K., so it might be a small exercise in vanity. Narcissism not withstanding, I know in my heart these core stories are worthy of being retold on paper. Frankly, when the lid on my casket is closed, I'd like for many of these remembrances to live on to be enjoyed by my heirs. I love recalling anecdotes, stories, and yarns handed down by my father and grandfather. Maybe, just maybe, some of the happenings enunciated herein will be judged interesting enough to be retold by family progeny decades from now. Look at *Forest Gump*, the perfect example of little stories being woven into a successful larger-than-life scenario. Hopefully, Daniell Brown won't be portrayed quite as intelligently challenged as Winston Groome's hero.
By the way, have you read best-selling author Dan Brown's *The Da Vinci Code* and *Angels and Demons*?[1] Aren't those books interesting and fascinating? I hope once you finish *Dress Whites, Gold Wings* you will say, "Those Dan Browns can really tell stories!"

---

[1] And *Digital Fortress* and *Deception Point*

Yes, Lord Byron, Mr. Clemens-Twain, truth *can be* stranger than fiction.

Daniell M. Brown
the other, older Dan Brown

Chapter 1

Before I begin at the beginning, let me explain -

MY OTHER LIVES

December, 1955 – July, 1961
Ages 20 – 26

*No, the author is not a devotee of L. Ron Hubbard or Shirley
MacClaine. Perhaps the teasingly incongruous title above requires
explanation. The chapter title reflects the author's affable affinity of
referring to a six-month engagement to first love Ann, then later an
almost nine years marriage to Eleanor, as 'my other lives'.*

**...But love is blind, and lovers cannot see
the pretty follies that themselves commit.**
                    The Merchant of Venice   Shakespeare

The batter at the plate imbued fear in the heart of every
Kansas City *Athletics*[1] fan. Pitcher Rip Coleman looked into
his catcher, wound up and delivered a nasty slider,
down and in to the switch-hitter, batting right-handed
against the southpaw. The hitter waited, then swung
smoothly and confidently. **CRACK!** The sound of
hardwood on horsehide resounded throughout Municipal
Stadium. Mickey Mantle had hit another one, a towering,
cyclopean home run to deep centerfield. The partisan crowd
quieted as the Yankee star slowed to his signature trot for a
circuit of the bases. Dan Brown picked that memorable
moment to propose marriage to Eleanor Woods. He leaned
toward her, and said simply in a straightforward and earnest
manner, "Let's get married." His attractive companion
immediately turned and looked at him. Surprise was plainly
visible in every pore of her countenance. Her head tilted
slightly and a quizzical half-smile formed, suggesting
genuine shock at his offer of marriage. Eyes, wide and alive,
manifested further evidence that his unorthodox proposal
had caught her unawares. She found her voice, "Did I hear

---

[1] Yes, Kansas City had the *Athletics* before the *Royals*

you correctly?" Apparently, body language had failed her momentarily, but just as quickly those spontaneous facial features dissolved. Now she became stoic and serious. She focused directly on his eyes and slowly, aimlessly, shook her head in disbelief. In recalling the events of that night, he imagined that a smorgasbord of feelings coursed through her mind at that point. She would later explain her feelings this way. She knew he was infatuated with her but *this*, this impromptu attempt at a proposal was unprecedented in her dating life. He was so young, was he that immature too? In the short time she had known him, she found him to be gregarious, completely outgoing. Most pilots were, if they were any good, it seemed. So she could imagine that he was impetuous to a fault, but this was crazy. He had casually and offhandedly asked her to be his wife.

Dan sensed hesitancy building in Eleanor's demeanor. He countered with "O.K., I'll do it again, in the more conventional manner." Taking her right hand and dipping a knee toward the concrete, he asked, "Will you marry me?" He added, "I think I'm just the right guy for you." His mind was racing, too. Thoughts of what he was suggesting consumed every fiber of his being. "Why shouldn't I want to marry her and why shouldn't she accept? I'm almost twenty-three years old. Soon I'll be wearing full lieutenant's double bars, and along with flight pay, life will be very livable. Topping that, I have orders to Key West, Florida. Doesn't every woman fantasize about honeymooning in a tropical setting? O.K., so it is only our second date, perhaps I am rushing things. But what's done is done. My mouth overruled my mind again and the marriage bit just sort of popped out in the excitement of the homerun."

The mind games in play were given momentarily respite as both Dan and Eleanor returned their gaze to the game on the field. 'The Mick' jogged easily, finally touching home plate. New York 2, Kansas 0, third inning.

Now he waited for a verbal response to his question. The slow, unhurried side-to-side head movement previously observed had not been construed as rejection in and of itself. Dan knew many individuals who involuntarily shook their head when surprised or caught off guard. Looking at her, eagerly waiting for her decision, he was again engulfed in her beauty and poise. Her game wear consisted of a dove gray pantsuit, complimented by a silk bandana encircling the neck. Emerald hues in the neckerchief appeared to shimmer, illuminated by the numerous lighting arrays found in major league ballparks. The word of the day for describing women's wear, he remembered, was 'sheik'. At that point in his life, he had little experience in judging women's apparel, but he could recognize a perfectly coordinated outfit. And he knew fashion in her mind was about highlighting that cascading red hair now touched by a slight breeze. Again, he marveled at how good she looked. He felt ten feet tall just being with her, being seen as her escort!

The enormity of the question evidently sobered Eleanor from her transfixed gaze. He was serious, no doubt about it. She told him later that once she could think straight, she tried hard not to laugh at his ridiculous efforts at proposing. She said somewhat irritably, "Dan, we're still in the first hour of our second date. You're impossible! And don't you think you're a little young for marriage? You're not even twenty-three years old." She had continued looking at him and now he saw the very serious look on her face deteriorate further into a frown. She offered one additional note of resistance to his improbable question. "Did Carlton tell you that I'm two years older than you? That I'm an addicted 'clothes horse'? And you know about my two little girls. Too many obstacles, Dan." Abruptly, she changed gears and commented on the homerun and the deficit score the *Athletics* now faced.

Dan could not let go so easily. "I'm getting a picture of rejection but you haven't answered my question with a direct 'Yes' or 'No'. Will you marry me?" he asked again. This time her answer was short, simple and definite.

"No, we barely know each other. Besides, you'll be leaving Olathe in less than two weeks. Two or three days after that you'll forget all about my kids and me. Now, let's enjoy the game."

Final score: *Yanks* 6, *A's* 2.

They were returning to her mother's home to pick up the
girls when Dan brought up the topic a third time. He
reviewed his case from *A* to *Z*: the forthcoming promotion,
the advantage and fun of Florida living, the pounding of his
mind and heart when he thought of her. He implored her to
re-think her answer. Eleanor studied his youthful and
masculine profile as he worked the Ford *Fairlane* through
traffic. Dan wondered if she was thinking that perhaps she
was making a mistake in rebuking his offer out of hand. She
countered with her own reasons. "You're another pilot –
which I don't need for obvious reasons. I know the drill.
Pilots are a breed of their own and have this strange habit of
being sent to far-off places unaccompanied with little or no
notice. No, it's better to nip this in the bud. Leading you on
serves no purpose." She shook her head slowly. She added,
her words tinged with sarcasm. "Dan, what is there about
'No', that you don't understand?"

The *Ford* had gone half the forty miles back to Naval Air
Station, Olathe, before he realized that neither he nor
Eleanor had mentioned *love*. And, of course, he had not yet
kissed her.

Her brother had fixed them up. He met Carlton while
waiting in line at *Joey D's*, a very popular steak house in
downtown KC. Then there was the mix-up in arrival time
and Dan showed up a half-hour early for their date the
following evening. Eleanor was showering when he rang
the bell. Soon a little girl cracked the door just enough to
peek out to see who was there. The suitor was left standing
looking through a screened door into a hallway foyer as two
little feminine voices ran for their mother. Eleanor was
forced to exit her bath and make a hurried appearance at the
front door. She arrived, dripping wet hair bundled and
hidden in a makeshift turban fashioned from a white towel.
She had donned a short terry robe belted tightly at the waist.
A few water droplets that had escaped hurried toweling now
beaded and ran like tears down bronzed legs. A deep
summer tan contrasted with and accentuated the snowy
whiteness of the towel guarding her hair and highlighted the
muted yellow of the robe. The length of the robe, that is its

hemline, warrants additional descriptive discourse. The robe certainly afforded sufficiently adequate coverage for a lady to feel comfortable in the familiar, secure surroundings of her home. That same length, when viewed by a member of the opposite sex as it cut across soft, mid-thigh loveliness, can evoke a totally different mindset. We all know the male mind is known to beat to a different drum. Identical clothing seen as 'safe, secure' attire by feminine rationale often equates to 'sexy' or 'inviting', in the minds of virile, young (and old!) men. Provocative, even racy, thoughts have been known to invade the minds of healthy, heterosexual young men faced with far less visual stimulus. In this case, the lady had no way of knowing that the young man standing beyond the door had just spent nearly two years in Newfoundland where compatible members of the fairer sex were almost non-existent.

Despite the inconvenience of an interrupted bath, she smiled cordially, confirmed that she was indeed Eleanor Woods and introduced her two daughters. Then as gently as possible, she explained he was a little earlier than expected. "You can see I'm not quite up to receiving gentlemen callers." She suggested hanging out at a nearby drugstore for approximately thirty minutes. "Will that be all right? Can you come back in a little while?"

Outside, one foot in the grass, the other resting on a porch step; the young pilot was in a trance. He had not yet spoken. In a word he was mesmerized. Another word, awestruck. Another, tongue-tied. For long seconds he seemed to be virtually spellbound. He was looking, no, he was staring, at the most beautiful, tantalizing woman he had ever seen. A semblance of composure eventually returned and he realized he was probably grinning like an idiot. Some sort of reply was stammered and he tried his best to apologize, to salvage the date, and to beat feet all at the same time. Walking dolefully down the driveway back to his car, he could feel the burn on his face and ears, and he felt like a fool.

Memories of teenage insecurity flooded his mind and senses. Somewhere within his being was an almost overpowering urge to run away, to leave this place, to return to base. He nearly succumbed.

Pacing up and down in front of the drug store offered an opportunity to readdress the situation. Stress was not an overused word in 1959 like it is today but perfectly describes the situation at hand. A better term for the anxiety Dan Brown experienced is not to be found in *Webster's*. So, the wait, while beneficial for calming a case of the jitters, still seemed interminable. "Will thirty minutes never pass?" he repeated several times. Thankfully, time marches on and 6:30 finally came.

Conversely, the next four hours with Eleanor and girls sped by at mach speed. Already smitten in the initial encounter, Dan offered no resistance to the little cherub with a bag of arrows. Cupid had skewered, dead center, one of Uncle Sam's finest.

"My first time to see a major league baseball game, and those damn *Yankees* had to win. And I, Lieutenant Junior Grade Daniell M. Brown, struck out just like the *Athletics*. Hey, now I'm 'O' for two. Two gals up, two strikeouts. Eleanor meet Ann, Ann meet Eleanor."

Over the next few days Dan Brown's cognitive reasoning tried to talk sense with Dan Brown's heart and libido. The analytical left side of the Georgia boy's brain teamed up with the emotional right half and convinced him that he was immune to sophomoric infatuation, that his feelings for Eleanor were real, that he was thinking with both his heart and his brain, that testosterone was not a factor. Hadn't the engagement to Ann proven Shakespeare in error? He was neither blind nor blinded. His love for her had certainly been real, otherwise, why had it taken a year to get over the hurt? That was *another life*, past history, even though he knew he would never forget Ann Collins Dixon.

The magic of first love is our ignorance that it can ever end.
Henrietta Temple, Benjamin Disraeli (1804-1881)

Ann Dixon was his first love, the only sister of a roommate in flight training. Tommy "D" had invited Dan home to Connecticut for Christmas holidays when they were still in

Pensacola as cadets. Ann, at seventeen, was just a kid that year in the eyes of the visitor. Definitely cute, but still too much a child for the likes of a twenty-year old man of the world, a pilot in flight school. Tommy insisted Dan return the following Thanksgiving after they had graduated and received commissions and wings (Graduates were designated Naval Aviators but could choose to become either Navy or Marine Corps officers). Dan went Navy, Tommy opted for the Corps. Back in Connecticut for a second time, Dan found little sister had grown up. Within the seven days comprising holiday leave, two young people found each other again and fell madly in love.

There followed a time of long distance dating but Navy training flights and free military air privileges fueled the romance. A young man in love for the first time! The emotions inside him were new and invigorating. An awareness grew that let him know all previous boy-girl relationships had been *puppy love*, feelings no more, no less than growing pains. There was no doubt this was the real thing. When he wasn't flying, he was thinking of her or writing to her. Sometimes, pay of a very junior officer permitted phone calls which eased the pain of being in love with the most beautiful girl in the world exactly 1000 miles away. LT Charlie Fisher, an officer in the squadron, offered to bet Dan that the distance factor would eventually kill the romance – that they would never be married. While an enormous sum – heck, he didn't have that much in the bank - Dan took the hundred-dollar bet in a heartbeat.

Occasionally, Tommy would also get home at the same time and the relationship appeared well on its way to consummation at the altar. A ring was on her finger by Christmas, 1957.

The Marine Captain briefed the young second lieutenant who would be flying as his wingman. "Tommy, I'll be towing a gunnery banner several yards behind me. I know you've fired at tow targets before but have you ever flown safety wing on one?"
1stLt. Thomas Dixon shook his head, "No."
Captain Tim Evans continued. "O.K., just a quick review of what we're going to do. The textile target that the flight behind us is

going to shoot at is in a frame a little over 7 feet high and about forty feet long. Piano wire attached to the banner is reeled out to approximately 1800 feet behind my plane and is impossible to see close up much less from any distance. Also, the banner itself is a hazard since it is too small to be seen by other aircraft until they are so close they might not be able to miss it. Your job will be to fly wing on the banner just as though it were an aircraft. That way, other pilots will see me ahead, and you following behind, and whether or not they see the banner trailing on piano wire, they will not cut between us. They will circumvent us by passing in front of me or passing behind you. Or fly over us or under us. Got it? You fly wing on the banner. Once I climb out and level off, my initial speed will be 220 knots. I want you take off first, circle overhead, and wait for me. The banner can't be wired and rigged until after I taxi onto the runway. So I will be sitting dead on the runway for a few minutes while the ground crew hooks up the reel. After takeoff I'll climb to 2000 feet overhead before you join up. OK?" Second Lieutenant Tommy Dixon nodded his head in agreement with the details as briefed by Captain Evans.

At the Maintenance desk, Tommy Dixon was assigned an FJ3 Fury, the Navy/Marine's version of the more familiar F-86 Sabre flown by the Air Force in Korea. Soon, in Fury #503, he taxied and took to the air. Normally, Fury flights climbed out at 300 knots. Tommy checked airspeed. Right on 300! The flight leader released brakes and screamed down the runway. Leaping into the air, the banner streamed behind. Looking high and left, he saw Lt. Dixon in an oval orbit. He keyed his mike and advised the young pilot he too would be at 2000 feet shortly, to adjust orbit accordingly, to be ready to join. The leader leveled off at pre-briefed altitude. After trimming the aircraft for 220 knots, an appropriate speed for a Fury full of fuel and pulling a banner, he looked for Tommy in his rearview mirror. A critical difference in airspeeds between the tow plane and the joining Fury was not apparent to either pilot until too late.

When Captain Evans finally saw the wingman closing for join-up, he knew the junior pilot was much too fast. "Jukebox 503, you're too fast! Slow to 220!" By then, Tommy had seen the disparity, reduced his throttle to idle but was still overtaking the banner. Momentarily, 503 was easing past the banner, his head on a swivel to keep clear of the tow plane and to keep the banner in sight. Captain Evans could see his young counterpart looking backward at *the banner while continuing to lose airspeed. The uninitiated reader must understand that to close and join on another plane or an object like a banner flying at X knots airspeed, the joining plane has to reduce speed to slightly <u>less than X</u>, and then add power and move into position slowly. In this scenario, the swept-wing Fury, with a full fuel load, throttle at idle, flaps up, required airspeed in excess of 190 knots to continue to fly. To reduce speed to something less than 190 knots would jeopardize controlled flight. The wingman continued to ease ahead of the tow reaching a point abeam the slower flight leader who had increased speed to help alleviate the excessive closure problem. Now cruising around 235, Captain Evans saw that the other plane was no longer passing him by but that the pilot was still looking backwards at the tow.* He had *no idea how long the junior pilot had been away from scanning his instruments which would warn of RPM (engine revolutions per minute) and air speed shortfalls, which, uncorrected, could lead to disaster.*

Suddenly, 503's left wing dipped erratically. Immediately, the Fury entered a full downward spiral. Again for the benefit of non-flyers, jet aircraft and especially those with sweep built into the wings, cannot recover from a spin at a low altitude. 503 crashed into the ground just outside the perimeter of the field. There was no ejection, no parachute. The aircraft burned for over fifteen minutes before firefighters could secure the crash scene. Over-zealousness and inattention to detail had killed twenty-three year old Tommy Dixon.

A simple phone call brought word of tragedy that set in motion collateral events that ended Dan Brown's short engagement. It was the hour of the evening meal at the BOQ[1], Naval Air Station Cecil Field, Jacksonville, Florida. Dan was having dinner with several other pilots when his name was called over the intercom system for an emergency call. Mr. Dixon, Ann's dad, was on the other end explaining that Tommy had been killed in an aircraft

---

[1] Bachelor Officer's Quarters

accident that afternoon in North Carolina. Could Dan go to Cherry Point and escort the body home?[1]

Two months later, Ann issued her ultimatum. Dan would have to get out of the Navy as soon as he could. He would go to work for her father manufacturing refrigerated truck bodies. She was not going to have him flying jet airplanes after losing her favorite brother in a fiery crash. The *Bard* knew his love stuff, youth is so uncompromising. She was adamant, he was stubborn. There were tears in two sets of eyes as she removed the diamond from her finger. Reluctantly, he put the ring in his coat pocket.

The March wind felt bitterly cold against the wetness on his cheeks as he waited for a train. A few minutes later he boarded the New York/New Haven commuter that would remove him from her life forever. The next morning LTJG Brown boarded a transport plane bound for Newfoundland, a new duty assignment. An unhappy young man climbed the boarding ladder into the cavity of the twin engine C-117. The seat was as uncomfortable as his thoughts, 'Exiled to staff duty in the forever-forsaken north woods of Newfyland, and shit-canned by my gal. Dammit it all to hell!'

Now in June 1959, unexpected but appreciated orders had reassigned him to Key West, Florida, via Olathe, Kansas, for refresher jet training. An understanding Admiral, a former jet pilot himself, pushed the right buttons for Dan's cold, lonely tour in Newfoundland to end early. Sixteen months in Canada's stepchild province equated to sixteen months of psychological self-abuse over the breakup with Ann. New orders had given him new hope. And he was convinced that he was finally over his first love. With her out of mind, out of heart, he was ready to move on with his life. Stateside in Kansas City area for a couple months and then several more in the Keys would be great places to resurrect his career and reacquaint himself with the American female. Eleanor Woods has complicated the plan. Thinking about the situation was perplexing. 'Now

---

[1] In fact, Dan did not accompany the coffin to Connecticut. Tommy's squadron insisted on that honor, providing full military escort.

here I am in Missouri - and Kansas, Toto, and I can't get to
first base with Eleanor. Is it love or is it testosterone? *Is it
love with being in love?* Whatever, this is the thing books and
songs are made of, *love at first sight.* If I were an artist, I
could paint *Wet Woman in Short Terry Robe, framed by screened
door.* Just for fun, how many women get asked for their
hand in marriage while the great Mickey Mantle is rounding
the bases after a gigantic home run?' He continued debating
himself. 'And Eleanor needs me, right? She's a widow with
two small girls, Diane and Tanya, nearly five and almost
two. Tanya wasn't even born when Eleanor's husband, an
Air Force jockey, was lost when his plane flamed out over
an icy North Sea off the coast of England. Heck, she admits
she still loves military life. And traveling. Maybe she'll
wake up and smell the roses someday in the next two
weeks.'
Fifteen days passed quickly. Training course completed,
one retrained and refreshed jet pilot was packed and ready
to head south. 'Impasse' was a word as well as any that
described the status of the romance. An occasional kiss,
absolutely no farther along physical lines, was where the
relationship had progressed. To his credit, Dan had not lost
hope at that point. "O.K., off to Key West tomorrow. Well,
I'll just have to write convincing letters to a certain redtop
and show my intentions are long term. And honorable.
Well, maybe not totally honorable. I guess I'll always wonder if
she's a real redhead? Who knows what eloquence lurks in
thy pen, Lieutenant Brown? Maybe, just maybe, absence
will make the heart grow fonder."

A rush of letters to Missouri followed but when no replies
were forthcoming after several weeks, reality set in.
Absence was not working. Eleanor was not going to
respond. She had not even sent a post card acknowledging
his birthday. To his surprise, flying became a passion once
more. He was back in jets. He was a *Tophatter*, a member of
one of the Navy's oldest and most elite fighter squadrons.
VF-14 flew the F3H *Demon*, an old and accident-prone jet
serving out its last days in the Navy inventory. All the
squadron pilots wished for a newer, faster, safer bird to fly.
Yet knowing they were flying and handling second-hand,

second-rate (perhaps third-rate?) *Demons* and still winning safety and performance awards gave great satisfaction. Sometimes at night, before sleep, he wondered if Lady Luck had intervened on his behalf. Many moons had passed since watching "The Mick" blast that tremendous homer. 'Gosh, it's been over a year now.' He acknowledged, sometimes reluctantly, he had not needed the responsibility of a family. Mastering the *Demon*, especially for shipboard operations, had demanded total dedication to the job at hand. Three beautiful girls waiting at home would not have permitted the freedom to use his time as required. Now, mission accomplished. In just a few weeks the squadron would be deploying to the Mediterranean Sea area for a six-month stint of duty with COMSIXTHFLEET. He would be flying and nursing that old *Demon* on and off those little *postage stamp* carriers.

Sometimes, Cupid, like God, works in strange and mysterious ways. Just before Christmas, 1960, about eighteen months after their abbreviated relationship, Eleanor was moved to mail him a Christmas card. Inside, she scribbled a succinct note:

> *I've been thinking of you a lot lately. Why not give me a* call? *Eleanor & girls*

The "No" that Dan didn't understand those many months previously became a belated "I do" at the Navy chapel altar when they were married nine months later.
More than two years had passed since that baseball game so long ago. She met USS FRANKLIN D. ROOSEVELT (CVA-42) in Florida when the ship and squadron returned from the Med. Six days afterwards, Mrs. Eleanor Woods became Mrs. Daniell Brown. Within a year, Dan had adopted Eleanor's two daughters. A son would be born in their second year of wedlock.

Postscript. A few years ago the author heard that Anne was happily married with two wonderful children. Dan's first marriage lasted eight and a half years during which he completed three lengthy at-sea tours to Vietnam, mixed around still another to the

Mediterranean, one to the North Atlantic, and numerous training exercises off the coast of Florida, Cuba and California. Eleanor remarried again, to another aviator, and they were blessed with a baby boy after a year or so.

Now, Let's begin the stories of **Dress Whites, Gold Wings:**

Chapter 2

THE FOURTH HORSEMAN

Winter, 1941
Age: 6

......"Jimmy died this afternoon."

They were not "buddies", at least not in Jimmy's mind. He
was three years ahead of the new first grader. But in the
eyes of Danny Brown, the older boy was the best friend a
guy ever had. At least for a few months..........

School began as usual in that part of the South, early in
September. Built in the late 1800's, the one-room school,
one teacher, concept had somehow survived into the mid-
twentieth century. Now accommodating classes first
through eighth,[1] the rural schoolhouse with its single large
classroom was seeing the end of an era. Students going on
to ninth grade and beyond were bused to the countywide
high school in Douglasville.

Danny, as most kids probably do, would always remember
his first day of school. In a new plaid shirt and almost new
overalls, his mother walked him out to the mailbox where
they waited for the bright yellow bus. Not many minutes
passed before a cloud of dust down the long dirt road
announced an oncoming vehicle. Then the huge, long,
yellow school bus was stopping in front of them. The driver
activated a handle that opened the hinged double doors. At
the last moment, two or three tears trickled down the young
boy's face as he took two giant steps forward and upward
that put him inside. His mother smiled and called after him,
waving tentatively. Then came the long walk down the aisle
of the bus looking for an open seat. He found a vacant bench
other students never selected voluntarily, the one housing
the rear tires. He rubbed the wetness from his eyes as he
anticipated the unknown. He wished he had a friend sitting
next to him. He had to stop the tears! This was his first day

---

[1] There was no kindergarden in rural Georgia schools in 1941.

of school! Still, not knowing what awaited him at school fueled inner feelings of inadequacy. Finally, an older girl student smiled at him and offered a hankie. He declined, using his hand to wipe his nose and then rubbing his hand on a pants leg. He looked out the window so he would not have to look the girl in the eyes. Then the bus jolted to a stop.

Mrs. Sarah Turner, Fairplay School's only teacher, met the bus and Danny felt welcome as she walked the newcomers through the initial routines of starting school. There was one other boy beginning first grade. Leon Haslett had a friendly but shy smile. The four or five girls entering first grade all seemed to know each other.

Danny was acquainted with two of the girls as well as a few of the older students who attended the same little country church as the Browns. He recognized many of the other students, having seen them at movies in town, at the crossroads country store, or occasionally, at the cotton gin when he went with his cousins. When seating arrangements were finally completed, only Jimmy Frazier, three years older and in third grade, came over to Danny's desk to say hello. Danny's dad and Jimmy's dad were remotely related and the families were very good friends. They all attended Flinthill Methodist Church. Somehow, Jimmy's open acceptance of the younger boy made the first grader feel better. He was getting over his first day fears.

An old-fashioned bell announced morning recess. As the two first year boys descended the front steps to the large front yard, several older youths awaited them. Danny and Leon were easily enticed by friendly smiles and ushered to the back of the school. Out of view of Mrs. Turner as well as the other children, the newcomers were welcomed to a harsh and bitter reality. The older boys dropped all pretense of friendliness, pushing and shoving them roughly against the back wall of the building. Danny looked for Jimmy without success. These boys were five, six and seven years older; evidently Jimmy wasn't old enough to participate in whatever was about to happen. Danny guessed he and Leon were about to be beaten in some way.

An eighth grader who seemed to be the leader lit a cigarette and did most of the talking. "O.K., you two, undo those britches and pull your pants down. You gotta show your dicks or we'll show them for you. And don't think about telling the teacher. You tell on us and we'll beat the stew out of you after school. It'll be our word against yours. · Now pull down your britches." He inhaled smoke from the Lucky Strike and blew it out his nose. "Let's see those little worms." Grinning, he continued to tease the confused and anxious boys. "Hey, don't worry, it's a Fairplay School tradition."

Tears again filled Danny's eyes as he fought back the urge to cry outright. Leon seemed mesmerized and began bawling. Suddenly, several of the more physical and older youths grabbed and held the younger boys. Others loosened the gallowses of Danny's bib overalls while Leon's belt was unbuckled. The victims were then thrown to the ground where unseen hands pulled clothing, including jockey shorts, down to their knees. Once their privates were visible, the ordeal was over except for the taunting. "It's the same every time." "Look at those weenies. There ain't a real prick in the crowd." "First graders don't have nothing to show yet." The cigarette still dangling from his lips, the self-professed leader flicked his wrist in apparent disdain indicating to the others to turn the two kids loose. As an afterthought, he added sarcastically, "Maybe we'll call them the 'Little' brothers: Danny and Leon."

Whatever the test was intended to prove, it was over. It appeared they had passed. Once the older boys had mortified the two young newcomers by exposing their genitals, interest quickly waned. Perhaps the charade of force was simply to see if the six-year olds would tattletale. For whatever reason, after that first day experience, the older boys ignored the new students. While not accepted as peers, they were simply tolerated because they were there. When Danny had a chance to ask Jimmy about what happened, Jimmy just cast his eyes downward, kicked at an imaginary pebble, and said, "Forget it. They do it to all of us just to see who will cry. Then they laugh at you anytime something happens to make them remember it."

Danny felt he could trust Jimmy and told him, "I didn't really cry but I had tears in my eyes."

Jimmy again looked away. "I didn't cry until one of them tore my new shirt. I couldn't help it then because I knew Mom would want to know what happened."
Danny: "What did you tell her?"
Jimmy: "I told her I caught it on a nail in the boy's toilet out back."

In late November of that year, Jimmy caught a severe chest cold. Accepted normal procedure in those years, he continued to go to school daily. After two or three days, he coughed incessantly. His throat became so hoarse he could hardly speak. Eventually, Mrs. Turner put his desk at the rear of the room to segregate his illness and germs, to some degree at least, from the other forty-four classmates. On one of the coldest days of the year, Mrs. Turner noticed Jimmy perspiring profusely. She felt his feverish brow, "Jimmy, when you get home today, you must tell your mother to take your temperature. And stay home tomorrow if the fever and cough persists."
Afternoon recess came in due time, welcomed as always by both teacher and students. The day was bitter cold, nineteen degrees Fahrenheit with a biting wind that played further havoc with the chill factor. Still, an energetic game of "Crack the whip" was played between boys and girls of the first few grades. Exercise helped to keep their bodies warm, their minds occupied. Jimmy was too sick to play but he did go outside to watch for a few minutes. The older male students too had been observing the younger ones at play. After only a few minutes, Jimmy decided to return to the warmth of the classroom. When he started to ascend the steps, a round of taunting by the older boys began. Don Fisk – Danny had learned the name of the seventh grader who had instigated the first day of school torment for the two new first grade boys – again led his gang in verbal banter: "Little Jimmy wants to go inside with Mama Turner"; "Little Jimmy doesn't like Georgia winters", "Little Jimmy acts like a girl", "Jim-Bo is a fraidy-cat". An older contemporary blocked each move that the young boy made up the steps. Danny glanced over and saw Jimmy's distress. Suddenly the game was no longer fun and he let himself be thrown from the line. He pulled his coat tight against the

winter cold while he watched Jimmy's unsuccessful attempts to gain entry to the building. Danny shivered and his heart ached as his mind commiserated with his conscience. He knew any attempt to help Jimmy would be futile. Heck, he was a first grader, even younger than Jimmy, what could he do? Still, he wished that he could have stood up for his friend. Thankfully, the bell ended the turmoil between conscience and intellect, and as well, between Jimmy and the older guys. All the students filed up the steps back to class.

Once inside, Jimmy laid his head on the desk and fell asleep. Mrs. Turner said nothing. In all likelihood, she was thankful that her sick charge was finally resting.

At home, Jimmy's temperature was confirmed as a dangerous one hundred six degrees. The doctor arrived late in the evening and gave the Frazier family the diagnosis that would prove fatal. Their only son had double pneumonia. Penicillin was unknown in rural western Georgia in 1941. Jimmy died thirty-six hours later, exactly one month after his tenth birthday.

Mr. Brown brought the news when he arrived home for supper. "Jimmy died this afternoon. I heard it at the Crossroads Store. I'll have to go over to the Frazier's after we eat, John and Sue will need friends with them. Danny, this is a part of life you've got to accept. I really don't know what to say to you. I'm having a hard time dealing with the fact that Jimmy is dead myself. He was a good kid. You two seemed to get on well despite your difference in ages."

Young Danny did not, at first, understand the consequences of death. To lose a friend so young had never crossed his mind. He knew old people died or "passed away." His parents had made him attend the funeral of a great uncle who died last year, a man in his eighties. His dad's mother died when Danny was less than a year old so he had never known Nana Eula. This was the first time death touched him personally. Trying to realize that he and Jimmy would never see each other again, never play pitch again, was beyond understanding. Perhaps one day he would comprehend the ways of the world.

During the next two days he began to realize his friend really was gone. Forever. Slowly, he came to realize that death was not like the movie serials where the hero miraculously came back for the next week's exciting segment. Jimmy was not coming back. Once that fact was accepted, personal guilt feelings flooded his thoughts. Along with the other classmates, he did nothing while his friend was mocked, shunned, and denied access to the comfort of a schoolroom warmed by a pot-bellied stove.

Finally, the day of the funeral service arrived. Danny heard the words, but the long and dispirited eulogy only deepened his somber mood. Absorbed in self-incrimination, he needed no memorial platitudes to confirm his friend was gone. He had tried to explain to his parents how the older students shared in the responsibility for Jimmy's sickness. The accusation went unheeded. Indeed, they argued, how could a twenty-minute recess kill a child? To Danny's chagrin, the boys he considered guilty of contributing to Jimmy's sickness were seated as a group on the fourth row right center. Finally, the funeral ritual inside the small church ended. In below freezing temperatures, a saddened assembly walked slowly to the country cemetery some hundred yards or so behind the church. Speaking in soft, hushed tones, the small groups of two, three, four, and five, strolled along the red clay pathway to the graveyard. In step between his parents, Danny concentrated every thought on Jimmy. On Sundays in this church, preachers had proclaimed the soul of a person to be as real as life itself. He wanted to feel, he wanted to sense this spiritual presence of his best buddy. As the small coffin was lowered into the ground, Danny peered intensely into the crisp air above, hoping desperately to see angels as they came to take Jimmy's soul to heaven. The burial ceremony took about fifteen minutes, but it seemed much longer to six-year-old Danny Brown. Jimmy's mother and father, along with Danny and his parents were the last to leave the hallowed ground that would hold forever the lifeless form of Jimmy Frazier. He had not felt a spirit presence. Nor had he seen the angels come for Jimmy. Was it because they came on the day he died, not on the day of burial? Perhaps when he was older, he could learn or be taught or find the meaning of life and death. On this day he could only hope that the preacher was right, that one day he would see Jimmy again so he could tell his friend how sorry he was he had not tried to help that fateful day at school.

Six-year old Danny Brown met *Death, the fourth horseman* from *Revelation 6:8* on those cold February days of 1941. It is doubtful that he had ever seen a caricature depicting the *Grim Reaper*, cloaked, dark and ominous, faceless, carrying a scythe. Still his young mind conjured a mental image of life's foe as sinister and formidable and relentless. The little boy could not have conceived of the lasting impact this first encounter with the dead and dying would have on his life. Memories of Jimmy Frazier, his death, his burial in the red dirt of Georgia, would return time and time again to haunt his inner thoughts over the span of a lifetime. Danny inwardly challenged himself to never forget his first and best friend.

*****

Chapter 3

IT HAPPENED AT THE MOVIES

Summer, 1944
Age: 8

In the middle of Danny's second year in school, the Browns
moved from rural Douglas County to Mableton, a small
community about twenty miles closer to Atlanta.
Most Saturday afternoons found young Danny at the
movies. Mableton had no theater but Austell, only three
miles west on Highway 78 was blessed with a silver screen.
The Saturday matinees saw the Ritz Theater come alive
with action-packed black and white Westerns. Roy Rogers,
Gene Autry, Hopalong Cassidy, Lash LaRue, Johnny Mack
Brown, and other lesser-known cowboy heroes rode their
horses and shot their six-shooters after bad guys. Eagerly
anticipated were the serials that always ended with the hero
or his heroine in dire straits. Miraculously saved in the
following week's installment, they would encounter yet
another dreadful situation as the new episode ended. In
those days before television, the cartoons, usually the only
feature in color, were always fun for both children and
parents alike. A fourth offering, Movietone News, had
made World War II a little more real to a nation protected
by an ocean on each coast. Twenty-five cents paid the
admission. Popcorn was a nickel. The first time Danny
became aware of inflation was the summer he was nine.
Movie prices increased to thirty-five cents and popcorn to a
dime. Happily, Cokes still cost just a nickel.

On that ordinary summer Saturday, the movie house was
filled. On the screen, crowded between two large boulders,
a bigger-than-life Lash LaRue was wielding his long whip
against a pair of evil bank robbers. Two high school teenage
boys arrived late and sauntered down the aisle, finally
finding side-by-side seats down front on the second row near
the center aisle. They were not local guys but Danny
recognized them as fairly regular visitors from Powder
Springs, a small milling community only a few miles away.

In those slower, simpler times, it was not unusual for young people from adjacent towns to spend Saturday afternoons at the Ritz, depending on the cinema offering. The more popular the cowboy figure, the larger the draw. Danny loved Johnny Mack Brown but had to admit that Roy Rogers and Dale Evans drew the larger crowds. Today Lash LaRue, comparatively much less popular than Roy, Gene, or Hopalong, had surprisingly filled almost every seat in the small theater.

Several minutes passed after the arrival of the two visiting teens. The action on the screen had subsided. Fighting had given way to personal drama. Now a hushed audience watched as the wounded star lay semi-conscious in the dust as a sidewinder rattlesnake S-curved its way toward the prostrate hero. Would Lash react in time to avert the fate that awaited him?

Everyone in the theater heard it: from somewhere down front near the aisle, the distinct and prominent sound of escaping intestinal gas. For a moment, just a moment, before the stunned audience could react in mirth, there was complete silence. During that oh-so-short interval, a little girl, perhaps 5 years old, seated on the third row left of center, stood and pointed at one of the latecomer teenagers sitting in front of her. She said simply but loudly into the quietness around her, "You-u-u POOTED." The crowded theater erupted in uncontrolled laughter. Kids seated nearby the indicated culprit jumped from their seats and moved quickly away, some holding their noses in disgust. The reel continued to run, so that many patrons, Danny included, missed the climatic moment when the movie hero recovered in time to avert the rattler's strike before decapitating the deadly reptile with a flick of his long black whip. When the lights came on at the end of the film, two seats on the second row were conspicuously empty.

*****

Chapter 4

THE FOUR ROSES BABY

March, 1946
Age: 9

Everyone, including young Danny, knew the situation was
dire. Pneumonia was winning the battle with his baby
brother, barely a month old. The infant's temperature was
one hundred six degrees F. Four ladies sat around the small
kitchen and talked in hushed tones. The youngest of the
four sitting nearest the doorway into the living room, was
their mother. Her eyes, red and teary, reflected the despair
felt by all in the small house. Danny wondered if she might
break down and scream at any moment. A woman next to
her in a chair under the window holding the frail newborn
was Danny's grandmother, his mom's mother, Grandma
Daniell. The older woman rocked back and forth in an old,
worn Boston rocker that had been brought into the kitchen
for that single purpose. The baby coughed again. Hoarse,
croupy, raw sounds cut the silence and tore at the hearts of
the adults gathered around the sick baby. When the
coughing seizure finally ended, he began whimpering as
only a totally dependent, critically ill baby can.
Danny could feel the tension in their home. He stared into
the kitchen from his Grandfather's bedroom where he, his
grandfather Melvin, and Lawrence Brown, his dad's
younger brother who occasionally lived with them, waited
and watched impatiently. His father was alone in the living
room, listening and watching through the open door.
Mrs. Wilma Brown was holding a black telephone and
handset in her hands. She had just hung up the receiver
after speaking with the doctor. The others had listened and
already knew the outcome of the call but Mrs. Brown
verbalized the conversation again. "The doctor says there's
no use to come. There is an outbreak of pneumonia in north
Georgia right now. Several people have died already. He
says he has too many sick in town to drive seven miles to see
my sick baby. He reminded me that he has been here three
times already in the past few days." Almost unnoticed,

while Mrs. Brown related the discussion with their physician, the baby's coughing and crying had ceased. Quietness again enveloped the setting. Gradually, everyone in the house realized the child was no longer making noises of any sort. Grandmother Daniell moved the baby to a new position in her lap and felt the little forehead. "His temperature is still so high." She moved the infant back to her shoulder and once more began rocking. The small bundle in her arms remained motionless and silent.

The ladies had seen pneumonia take its toll before. These were Georgia countrywomen who had lived through the Great Depression. They had given birth to their children at home. All four were well versed in the dangers of childhood sickness in rural areas, especially pneumonia. They knew the chances of survival for young Terry Brown were slim to non-existent. The third woman of the group, Mrs. Dailey was a dear friend and nearest neighbor of the Brown's. She had been leaning against the sink but now walked over and without asking, reached to hold the baby. While the neighbor cuddled the still and unmoving form, the grandmother put a small mirror to the baby's mouth. Any condensation on the silvery surface would indicate breath. Breath showed life. With any sliver of life, there was always hope.

No moisture appeared on the glass. Not a word was spoken but knowing looks from one to the other told the story. The baby had died. Mrs. Brown placed her face in her hands and began sobbing loudly.

Julian Brown had been quietly observing and listening. He was of the old school......death and dying, near death and near dying, was woman's territory. He had given his child over to their domain - until now. He appeared in the doorway and placed a loving hand upon his wife's shoulder. Mrs. Dailey still held the quiet and unmoving form in her arms.

The fourth woman, an octogenarian, had also been observing and listening closely. She was Salena McWhorter "Maw" Griffith, the child's paternal great-grandmother. She stood, took the mirror from the grandmother's hands, then walked over to Mrs. Dailey and the baby. She again placed the mirror beneath the little nostrils. After several seconds,

24

she gently rubbed the mirror with wrinkled, aged fingers, trying to feel moisture that perhaps the eye could not see. Finding none, she stood and spoke with matronly authority. Calling into the nearby bedroom she said: "Lawrence, bring me some of that liquor you have hidden away."

Lawrence Brown was surprised, momentarily flustered. Danny saw the puzzled reaction as total consternation registered on his face. But his uncle responded quickly: "Maw, you know I'm off the booze. I don't keep whiskey around anymore. Jute and Wilma have told me to keep it out of this house."

The older woman was not deterred. "Lawrence, _BRING_ me some liquor. And be quick about it."

The younger man averted the eyes of his older brother, looked down at his shoes, shrugged, and moved towards the bathroom. Danny twisted in his chair and could see his uncle reaching far into the recesses of the cabinet beneath the sink. Under old rags and miscellaneous toiletries, Lawrence Brown found the elongated glass bottle where he knew it would be. When the uncle turned back to the room he held in his hands a bottle of _Four Roses_ whiskey. He gave the nearly full bottle to Mrs. Dailey. Maw Griffith had already placed a large wash pan in the center of the table. The contents of the bottle were poured into the tin circular bowl. Two pairs of hands reached for the limp and lifeless body and quickly removed the gown, undershirt, and diaper. Putting as much of the baby's naked torso into the alcohol as possible, the matriarch of the Brown and Griffith families began hand-dipping whiskey over the remaining parts of his little body. Mrs. Dailey moved closer and rubbed the golden liquid on the baby's feet. A strong odor of raw whiskey filled the small room.

A minute, perhaps two, passed without verbal communication. Danny could identify the breathing of each person in the room. He had never witnessed such quiet intensity. He knew it was the face of people involved with dying and death. He saw his grandmother with head bowed, lips moving in prayer. Then she got up from her chair and retrieved the mirror. She leaned over the table and put the mirror back to the baby's mouth. All three women around the table saw a faintly fogged area being formed and exclaimed in unison: "We have breath." "He's alive!" "Look, there's vapor on the mirror!" The mother rushed to see the evidence, wanting to believe, perhaps still doubtful and unsure. She reached for the baby but her mother pulled her back. "Let Maw dry him first. Let's get his blanket warm and dry."

Julian Brown picked up the telephone. "I'm going to try an out-of-town doctor on the off chance that he might help us." He asked the operator for the listing of a doctor located in a small town a few miles farther west. Fortunately, the nurse that answered perceived the urgency of the situation and put the physician on the phone immediately. Dr. Evans could not come but he knew of a source for a relatively new drug that worked wonders against pneumonia. While scarce in rural areas, he told Mr. Brown he would call ahead to a specific drug store in Marietta and authorize a prescription for penicillin.[1] A nurse then gave directions to the pharmacy near northwestern Atlanta.

Danny rode with his dad to buy the medicine. Father and son rode in virtual silence, each with their own thoughts and memories. Mr. Brown, hopeful for yet another miracle, was anxious to procure the precious medicine and return. Danny, confused and bewildered at the events of the day knew it was not a time for questions. He could sense his dad needed no conversation. To pass the time, he relived the momentous occurrence over and over in his mind so that every detail was remembered in total clarity.

As the reader has surmised, the wonder-drug penicillin worked, the young boy survived. Death became life again through the everyday experience and knowledge of a worldly-wise woman born almost a century earlier.

At times following his little brother's miraculous recovery, Danny tried to organize his thoughts and feelings. His mind's eye remembered in detail the sight of the baby's lifeless body being bathed in pungent alcohol to save his life.

---

[1] Penicillin was discovered by Dr. Alexander Fleming in 1928/29 but was not manufactured until 1943.

The strange and curious episode had recalled in dramatic fashion the death of his friend, Jimmy Frazier who died of double pneumonia just three years ago. Pneumonia and double pneumonia, how he hated to say the words. He wondered what was "New" about the term _pneu-monia,_ or the illness itself. How could a bottle of liquor, which was so bad for his alcoholic uncle, be good enough to save the life of a dying baby? Danny knew this was a family experience that should never be forgotten. Perhaps some day he would write it all down for posterity.

As he completed his chores one April evening some weeks later, he looked up into a sky filled with bright and shinning stars. Stopping work and turning slowly in a complete circle, he gazed at the expanse of our universe. A black Georgia night embellished the radiance of the gleaming stars. Looking heavenward, he thought again of Jimmy Frazier. Was Jimmy up there? Was he an angel by now? Was he looking down as Danny peered skyward? Jimmy's death those few years ago was an abrupt introduction to the deadliness of pneumonia and the finality of death. Now a baby brother with an even worse case of pneumonia had been brought back from the dead by a bottle of liquor. A very young boy died, ushering in unbridled misery and grief for one family while a baby boy lived, providing unbounded joy for another. Perhaps life was just that way. Sometimes it didn't make sense; it could deal sadness or offer untold pleasure. Hopefully, most of the time, life would be orderly and good for Danny Brown. As he pondered those things, he was vaguely aware of an inner peace invading his being. Perhaps the stars overhead, so beautiful, so majestic, were precursors of good things to come. He sure hoped so.

*****

The Four-Roses baby grew up to favor our father Julian in physical likeness and perhaps more importantly, spiritual perception. A better epitaph could not be written.

Chapter 5

THE BOY AND THE BIRD

Summer, 1947
Age 10

The young boy walked across the field in the hot morning
sun. He appeared pensive, preoccupied. He was thinking of
starting fifth grade in a short three weeks. Soon, the fun and
sun of summer vacation would end. A couple of years from
now he would be concentrating on other challenges and
conquests, perhaps girls and the mystery of the opposite sex.
Today, for this moment in time, the paradoxical issues of
puberty were not yet central in his mind. His path had taken
him only a short distance across the open and empty lot. He
paused for a moment to pull an old red bandanna from his
jeans. On the right side rear pocket, *Clorox* bleach had been
used to eradicate color from the dark blue denim material,
forming his name in block letters, **D A N N Y**. As he wiped
dust and sweat from his face, the bird flew into his line of
vision, traversing a line from northeast to southwest, passing
directly in front of him. He stood completely still, his view
unobstructed, the bird's flight path only about fifty feet from
where he stood, approximately telephone-wire height above
him. The bird was beautiful. Not in an exotic faraway rain
forest manner like the *Quetzal* from South America he had
seen at the Atlanta Zoo, but almost as colorful. While this
bird's back was brownish, it certainly was not the nearly
nondescript Brown Thrasher, the state bird so often seen in
this red clay region of Georgia. He had occasionally seen
Southern Flickers before but not one as large nor in as close
proximity. Awed by the beauty and the array of vivid colors
around the bird's neck and wings, he realized that he had
never seen so colorful, so majestic a bird in open, rural
spaces. Innately, he perceived the graceful movement of
flight enhanced its beauty. Then, he forced those unwanted,
feminine-like thoughts of the moment from his mind.
Almost automatically, Danny stooped to pick up a medium
sized rock as the male consciousness within him reemerged.
His eyes never left the prey. He watched the Flicker as it

flew from right to left. Eyes glued to the bird, his right hand felt in the soil for just the right sized stone to fit his hand, one to go the distance required, big enough to do the job now before him.

The bird soared by, headed in the direction of a large oak tree on the southern edge of the property. Too late, the boy realized he had not yet selected ammunition for the throw. Against the backdrop of a perfect, cloudless blue sky, the Flicker spread wide its wings and glided the last few yards to the tree. Then the bird disappeared into one of the myriad of full branches comprising the oak's heavy green foliage. Soon it's calls, *wick wick wick wick, klee-yer, flick-a, flick-a* were audible over the open field.

Discouraged, Danny finally found a suitable rock -- a little too large and heavier than he would have preferred, but it would have done the job if he had located it while the bird was in sight and in range. As he looked at the picturesque oak that could have been the focal point of any *Currier and Ives* lithograph, he realized that he was glad the magnificent bird had lived. Then a second, self-conscious thought quickly entered his mind and flushed his face with embarrassment -- who was he to even fantasize that he might have hit the bird in flight? Yes, he could hit telephone poles with pebbles sixty feet six inches away in *pretend* pitcher-to-batter baseball scenarios. Those were a piece of cake, but a bird in flight? Who was he to think that such a throw was possible?

Rather than simply drop the stone or pitch it towards some imaginary object, he tossed the larger than golf-ball sized projectile into a high arc that brought it down into the upper third of the tree. He heard the rock as it crashed through the leaves and branches and saw it drop out the other side close beside the stately trunk.

Amazed, Danny first heard and then saw the second object fall lazily from the tree. The bottom branches were little more than head high off the ground and as the bird cleared that last obstacle, it fell as a dead weight the final few feet to earth. Its body did not flutter or make any movement at all. It simply fell straight down to land in the rich, dark dirt surrounding the oak. The unmoving feathery form lay silent and still only a few feet from the trunk of the tree in which it had sought sanctuary only moments before.

The ten-year old rushed to the bird and picked up the unmoving form. The body was still warm. There was no evidence of blood on the beautiful feathers, but life was non-existent. The rock had apparently hit the bird in the neck, breaking the fragile spinal column, turning life into death in the time required to blink an eye.

For the first time in his life that he could remember, Danny knew the mixed feelings of simultaneous joy and sorrow. One part of him felt a boundless energy unleashed, elated that his rock had struck the bird, sight unseen. Yet, concurrently, he was saddened by the reality of death to such a beautiful winged creature. The incongruity of success and loss at the same time triggered remembrance of another occasion in his life that had introduced the anguish of unanswerable issues. His best friend, Jimmy Frazier, had died of pneumonia just before Christmas of the year they were in first grade. He often thought of Jimmy and pondered the *Why* of death to one so young, so innocent. The death of the bird was different, yet vaguely similar. If asked to describe how the two events were connected, it's likely that he would have been unable to orally convey his feelings. He just knew both deaths were unjustified and defied logical explanation. On one hand, the bird's death paled in comparison to the loss of Jimmy. Still, the fact remained, the bird would not fly again just as Jimmy would never throw another baseball.

If he had been asked, Danny would have acknowledged his youth, his inexperience in the great scheme of life.
He might not have the answer to why the bird was sacrificed, yet he felt sufficiently mature to understand that what had just happened was extraordinary, remarkable, and unique. This kind of thing didn't happen every day to everybody. Years would pass before he understood words like *predestined, kismet, karma, joss.* He had no way of knowing that for most of his adult life he would question the meaning of this unusual occurrence. Still, even at this adolescent age, he conceded the unknown potential of the

event. Another question formed in his mind. Was it an omen or mere coincidence?

Head down, now more pensive than before, the bewildered boy started for home. He had to find a shovel to bury the bird. He walked slowly, kicking at clods of red dirt along the path. Had such a rare experience really happened to him? The motionless bird in his hand testified that indeed it had. His mood brightened a bit as his mind turned to another special incident in his brief years. It was a memory he cherished................. *The little boy was not yet eight years old, standing barely waist high next to his mother in the country store. She paid Mr. Barber, the storeowner, for the dozen eggs he had just counted out into a brown paper sack. After closing her purse, she reached for the Kraft colored sack now extended to her by the grocer. Looking up, he saw his mother grasp the throat of the sack and take the purchase from Mr. Barber. Then he saw the sack slip from his mother's hand and fall. Instinctively he reached out and caught the neck of the sack in mid-air. Mr. Barber checked the eggs and found none broken in the extraordinary exchange. Danny always remembered the astonishment of both his mother and the rotund grocer as they congratulated him on his swift reflexes. He savored recalling the particular event because he knew he had done something special.*

One last shovel full of dirt and the small grave was filled. Relieved to have the chore completed, Danny turned and walked towards the barn. The implement was returned to its proper hook in the tool room. Not surprising, his thoughtful mood persisted. Pausing in reverie, he leaned against the doorframe of the unpainted, nondescript structure. His mind replayed the circumstances surrounding the demise of the Flicker. He recalled the entire chain of events: the graceful flight, the loud and squeaky song notes emanating from within the dense branches, the arcing trajectory of the rock, the lifeless form falling from the tree. Older, he might have wondered about the odds against such a chance occurrence. Today, at ten going on eleven, he simply wondered.

He heard his mother calling for supper, "Danny"! He turned and headed up the path to the house aware of only one certainty - his grammar school buddies had never believed the egg story. For sure, they would not believe him

31

when he told them how with only a rock he had killed a bird he could not see.

*****

Luck? Yep. And for the record, I believe that I will win a lottery. You can quote me.

Chapter 6

THE BATBOY CONTEST

May 1951
Age: 15

Well, he didn't deserve to be the Atlanta batboy, anyway.
His mother had entered the contest for him and had even
written the poem's last line, *My least wish is their command.*

The saga had begun about two months earlier when Red
Dot Grocery Stores worked a deal with the Atlanta baseball
team to name the summer's batboy. Red Dot ran a contest
in all Atlanta and surrounding area stores. The boy who
finished their poem with the best last line would be the
winner. Danny Brown had been notified two days ago by
mail that his entry had won the coveted prize. Talk about
walking on air! Danny was on top of the world. Baseball
was his life, Atlanta was his team. And Country Brown,
same last name but no kin, was his favorite player. And this
might be Country's last year to play.
His dad had slept on the situation the first night. But
Sunday afternoon, after church and dinner, Julian Brown
asked Danny to go for a ride with him. His father always
liked to get in the car and drive for serious father/son talks.
Danny had assumed he would be challenged by his dad to
be courteous to all the players, to be careful getting to and
from the ballpark, and that he had to keep up his studies
until the school year ended. Or something along those lines.
But none of those topics were mentioned. To put it mildly,
Danny was blindsided. His father began by asking what
time at night the last bus left out of Atlanta for Mableton.
Danny had studied the bus schedules and knew them by
heart. He answered, "11 p.m., Daddy."
The youthful boy waited for the next question. Mr. Brown
. asked: "How far do you reckon it is from Ponce de Leon
Ball Park to the bus station." This one Danny did not know.
Julian Brown answered for him. "About two and half to
three miles, I'd guess. So in addition to Greyhound bus fare
to and from Atlanta, we'd have to come up with city bus

fare or possibly taxi money, to get you to and from the field." Danny was beginning to see where the discussion was leading.

His dad continued. "Danny, there are going to be tie games that run late. There will be rain delays. Remember you just told me the last bus departs Atlanta at 11. How do you plan to get home on those nights that run overtime?" Danny's face had become impassive while his heart was beating a mile a minute. He just looked at his dad but did not answer. Julian Brown's countenance seemed to droop as he began again. "Danny, we have only one car. I have to get up at five a.m. to get to work at Lockheed by six.

Your mother gets up earlier than I do to start her day's chores. If there were only two or three rain delays or tie games that made you miss the last bus, I guess we could manage. But you know there will be many nights you won't be able to get to the bus station on time for that last bus. I can't work the schedule I do and drive twenty miles each way in the middle of the night. And frankly, we just don't have the spare money for two taxi rides each way for seventy-seven times this summer."

Danny was surprised that his father knew that the team played one hundred fifty-four games, half of them at home. With double headers on a lot of Sundays, it wouldn't have been seventy-seven, but still his dad had made his point. Julian Brown continued justifying his thoughts. "A father hates to disappoint his children but you're going to have to let this batboy thing go. I know you will find this hard to believe but it hurts me to deny you this dream just as much as it does for you to give it up. To be honest, I guess if you personally had written the winning line to the poem, I might have talked myself into letting you accept it. Or, maybe to at least try it. Since you didn't, it seems to me it would be unfair to some other boy who rhymed it on his own. Regardless, the reality of the situation is that it's just too demanding on me and on family finances. I hope you'll try to understand. Oh, another thing, one of the reasons we're a little short on money these days is that we're putting all we can aside for your college next year and your sister three years later. I love you son, I hope you believe me."

Yes, the deflated boy's eyes misted heavily as his father turned the car around and headed back to Mableton. At least he had kept his real dignity – he had not begged nor offered an argument. Once home, the deep disappointment kept him wide awake most of the night.

Now Monday morning, he was on the bus. For some reason the three miles from Mableton to Austell High School seemed to be taking longer than usual. Sitting, looking, thinking, he realized that he was glad his letter about winning arrived on Saturday so that the whole gamut – joyful elation to total dejection - had all played out before he returned to school today. Danny never told his schoolmates about winning the stupid contest. It would have been too embarrassing to explain that being poor was why he wasn't permitted to accept the award that every boy his age coveted. And if he told them, he would have to confess that his mother actually won the contest for him.

It was a long time before he could forgive his dad. Yet, somehow, inwardly, he knew that the experience had been a lesson learned for a lifetime.

*Authors note: This was fourteen years before the **Braves** came to town in 1965. The Atlanta team at that time was called the **Crackers**, the AA level Southern Association's premier team. According to at least one source, the Crackers remain the winningest minor league team in baseball history. I'm sorry the entire poem could not be found.*

*****

Chapter 7

THE TEEN AND THE GUN

May, 1952
Age 16

......the vision

The lanky teenager leaned nonchalantly against a wooden
light pole and looked out over the endless, blue ocean. The
watery waves seemed to be pulsating as if the sea were alive.
Smiling, he turned his face up to sun, and spoke softly to the
hot breeze flowing in from the ocean. "I'm a high school
graduate on senior class trip. It's almost too good to be
true." He was speaking to no one in particular; he had
picked up the habit of talking to himself when alone. When
kidded about it, he responded simply, "I'm just thinking
aloud."

Recent events played in his mind. The high school class had
graduated just two days before. The year, 1952. Fifty-four
of the sixty-two graduates were there to enjoy three days of
sun and surf and a final taste of youthful companionship
before facing young adulthood and life's choices beyond.
He relished having the summer off, anticipating college to
come in the fall. For now, that experience was three months
away. Life was good. Eleven long years but high school
was over! Too bad the junior class behind them got caught
up in that new state law that required twelve years of
schooling! "Who needs an additional year of high school?
Well, that's their problem, not mine. As a matter of fact,
right now, I have no problems. Look at those great waves
breaking out there." He stood and watched several members
of the graduating class of Austell High as they swam in the
rolling crests twenty yards off the shoreline. The only
decision to be made right now was whether or not he had
time to re-enter the water and enjoy some of those high
breakers.

The sun would be setting in a few minutes, the beach far less populated than an hour previously. He decided it was a perfect opportunity to return to the hotel to shower and change and get back to the boardwalk for evening activity. Still mouthing words into the ocean breeze, "Who knows what the night lights of Daytona might bring?" Thoughts of young hard bodies with curves in all the right places filled his young, inexperienced but eager mind. Breaking into his quasi-carnal thoughts, he saw Marcia and Christy exit the shallow surf and slip wet, dripping feet into flip-flops. Marcia's two-piece royal blue swimsuit highlighted her pinkish-white skin now slightly burned from the Florida sun. She was smiling while towel drying her chestnut brown hair when she looked up to the boardwalk and saw him. She pointed him out to Christy. Both girls waved. Jet-black hair set in contrast to her fire engine red swimsuit, Christy then pointed a finger northwestward in the general direction of their lodging. Too far to yell, no possibility of being heard over the surf, she indicated via hand signals 'you' + 'us' signs. He nodded his head and signaled thumbs up, acceptance that he would wait for them. All the students had been asked to travel in groups when possible as a safety precaution - sort of a frontrunner of the *Buddy system* that would one day become popular in every activity from kindergarten day trips to swimming to hunting to standard military procedures. He wrapped the light blue towel around his neck and moved diagonally to intercept them. He met the still glistening duo atop the tired, wooden stairwell that ran up from the sandy-white beach to the concrete landing that was part of the Daytona Beach boardwalk. Three happy comrades started off at a leisurely pace to *The Sunset*, a modest hotel three blocks inland from the more expensive resorts promoting their scenic ocean views.

As they walked along, chatting, smiling, laughing and enjoying this once-only event in their young lives, they took little notice of crackerbox wooden houses that lined the narrow streets and sidewalks on both sides. Gone today to make room for commercial growth, these small homes were probably a maximum of eleven hundred square feet, with commensurately small yards nurturing little vegetation except dollar weeds and occasional patches of crabgrass. Every now and then a scraggly palm tree, the species without coconuts, was seen. Almost all the yards appeared to need care. Air conditioning was rare in 1952, even in more affluent towns and communities. As was the norm for this neighborhood and millions of others just like it in the south, virtually every home had screened windows and doors open to the outside. Almost all had small porches; some with wooden swings hanging by chains from porch rafters, some decorated with potted plants, most had old and weathered rocking chairs for relaxing in the cool evening breezes.

Only one porch was inhabited as the kids sauntered by. A couple, with their backs to the trio as they approached from downside, was swinging in a wooden two-seater swing. The male, wide and muscular across the shoulders, was sitting nearest the street. From the back, he appeared to be about eighteen or nineteen, possibly a little older. His left arm was draped around a girl companion. The couple leaned forward, heads bowed slightly and appeared in deep conversation. Both were in T-shirts and faded jeans - faded from wear and use, pre-stressed jeans were not yet in vogue in those years. Their appearance and demeanor did little to attract the attention of the three carefree walkers. As the trio passed, approximately five strides beyond the swinging duo, the boy in the swing called after them:
"Hey, you girls got nice tits. I'd sure like to f- - - either one or both of you."
The three friends stopped in mid-stride, surprised, disbelieving of the words hurled after them. It seemed incredulous to Danny Brown that a male under any circumstances, but particularly in the presence of a female friend, would make such an off color remark to total strangers. Regardless, the crude and vulgar statement had been issued. To simply walk away pretending nothing had been said was not possible. He turned to face the duo on the porch. Reluctantly, the two girls, one on either side, also pivoted to confront their vocal adversary.

He found himself in totally unfamiliar circumstances. Personal physical jeopardy by another person imagined or real, was a situation completely alien to any previous experience. Obviously, the potential for violence was imminent and he quickly evaluated himself in that context. 'This is for real, on a street in Florida'. He knew his limitations in size and strength, and was acutely aware that the young man in the swing was more mature, larger and more muscular than he. Danny had played football but had not bulked up nearly like the hulking menace in the swing. Knowing his weight to be one hundred thirty-eight pounds, he estimated the bully's at one seventy-five. But in 1952, a Georgia country boy took his beating before permitting strangers to insult, particularly in a sexually explicit manner, members of the fairer sex present in their company.

Danny admonished his protagonist: "You can't talk to these girls like that!"

"Wanna bet?" Came the reply by the older boy, his face now contorted with anger, his stocky body beginning to move forward as he stopped the rhythmic swinging in preparation to stand. His arm had dropped from the girl beside him and his left hand could be seen sliding under a cushion beneath him on the seat. As he stood erect, a revolver appeared in his left hand. The girl beside him also stood, then ran into the house. As she opened the screen door, entered, and disappeared from view, the young man brought the gun up to a perpendicular position, aimed directly at Danny standing between the two girls in the street. Someone, inside the house, screamed.

The .38 was pointed at his midsection, approximately 15 feet away, held in the hand of a person whose rationality was suspect. Quickly, Danny tried to size up his options. He saw them as threefold: confront, the least likely approach to be successful; discuss in a reasonable manner, hopefully the viable option; or run, for the moment an unacceptable alternative. He would later reluctantly admit to himself a fourth possibility was squeezing its way into his brain waves as he stood there waiting for the scene to develop. He could give in and "beg off". To his credit, he continued to realize that whatever conditions existed, he still had two young women beside him who, in the context of safety, remained

his responsibility. What were their choices - what were their thoughts? Total silence to this point confirmed their surprise and fear and complete disbelief at the turn of events.
Finally, almost in unison, they pleaded:
"Let us alone!" "Don't!" "We haven't done anything to you!" "Don't shoot him!"

Danny could see irrational anger creep into the older boy's face and he appeared to tighten his grip on the gun.
Danny's eyes were drawn to the open hole of darkness in the end of the barrel. The pistol seemed more ominous with each passing second. Doors opened along the street and he knew others were now watching the scene. Would anyone help? He felt again that he could not acquiesce to the armed bully. The prospect of certain death or at least serious injury by gunshot appeared probable. His mind screamed at him. 'You're going to die here on this ugly, ordinary sidewalk. Your blood will be in the sand and the weeds.' Another momentary thought: 'this is ridiculous. How did I get into this?' Yet he could not run from the confrontation. Scared and apprehensive, he contemplated the next exchange of comments. Perhaps there would be a chance to negotiate, to talk, to calm his aggressor. He noticed for the first time that it was dusk. Daylight was fading rapidly into evening shadows. But sufficient daylight remained to illuminate anything that happened here. At least there would be witnesses to attest that the three friends had not in any fashion provoked the aggressor.

Reluctantly, he reminded himself to 'Be brave', as he stood quietly, remaining motionless. Suddenly, he was aware of a strange vision, a holographic panorama of crystal clear clarity. Somehow the short distance between the boy-man with gun and himself elongated providing a few more feet of interval between them. Within that space appeared a three dimensional scene like a panoramic movie. There was no screen or backdrop, just scenes, or storyline events of a cinema-like illusion. The action was in 'fast forward', and to his amazement, were episodes of his life being shown sequentially, from his earliest memories to present! He could see all happenings in complete detail in a holographic, three-dimensional effect. At the same time, he was privy to the entire experience - he could see through the vision to the adversary standing on the other side in his soiled, beltless jeans and crumpled grey pullover shirt, holding a revolver leveled directly at him.

The review of his life may have taken only seconds but each occurrence shown was thorough and complete. Nothing was opaque or ill defined. Showing were scenes from his earliest memories as a young child up to and including the hot dog he had eaten on the beach moments ago. All major milestones and decisions of his life to date were, of course, shown, but other incidents, minor in nature, of no apparent consequence, were also incorporated into the total vision.

And there was a third phase to the memorable review. This aspect may have been the hardest to describe, the most difficult for the reader to comprehend. Yet it all happened as written here. In addition to the chronological events being reviewed movie-fashion, Danny was given the capacity to momentarily concentrate on a particular or special event and that occurrence would then become a still photograph. Not one scene of an event, but the entire happening would take on a framed picture-like image! Stranger yet, any still life scenes so selected remained in the vision so that soon he was looking at the gunman, at the movie-like apparition, and at a montage of event photographs from prior times in his young life.

Later, he would read in detail about persons who had gone through life-after-death experiences and would find that many agreed the most difficult aspect to explain was the vision imagery - that our language does not incorporate words or phrases that fully articulate supernatural appearances seen in extreme emergencies and especially in near-death encounters. In 1952, the ghost like, see-through holographic phenomenon experienced so vividly was mind boggling, completely beyond explanation to a second or third party. Delighted to find holographic figures and scenes at Disney World two decades later, he cycled through the featured attraction over and over, completely amazed at the similarity between the figures that came alive in Disney's

"Haunted Mansion" and the illusionary figures of his own vision years earlier. With the advent of IMAX theaters after another score of years had passed, Danny was again awed by the fact that he had been privy to just such a panoramic experience almost fifty years prior.

"PUT THAT GUN DOWN!" came the command from the doorway. A much more mature man, possibly an older brother or maybe the owner of the property, perhaps the father of the older youth, had emerged through the door with the previously mentioned young female and another older, plainer woman. "Get in here!" came the second admonishment from the speaker in the open door as the gun hand was slowly relaxed and then lowered.
Christy, pale and frowning, simultaneously spoke and moved to turn towards their original route, "Danny, Let's get out of here."
Marcia, a smile of relief cascading across her face: "Yes!"

The apparition, the unexplainable vision, had disappeared with the first words by the welcome intruders into the sequence of events. If not the actual intent of the aggressor, certainly in the mind of the teen, the thought of impending tragedy had been paramount. That promise, that contingency, had evidently triggered a psychological overload resulting in the unexplainable review of his life in holographic detail in two similar but varying forms. The review of a lifetime, even one as short as seventeen years, is necessarily filled with both positive and negative memories. Much of what he saw in the visions he did not enjoy - the bad was shown along with the good. He saw his first bicycle solo and a wonderful, memorable Christmas shared with strangers who had swerved into a ditch near their home one snowy, icy Christmas morning. But there was also his first little white lie, his last more deliberate lie any and all untruths in between. He had watched uncomfortably as he and a young girl cousin played *Doctor* the first time. The amazing experience would be played over and over in his mind, assessed, then reassessed. The thought that returned to haunt him so often was the mystery of the vision itself. Was it simply a predictable psychological response to intense fear? Or was there some deeper significance to the almost spiritual insight? No matter, he felt privileged to be a major participant in such a rare experience, to see images so real that other people could only read or hear about and perhaps imagine.

Sometime later, after the story of the near tragedy had been told and retold, after the other fifty three students had been warned to detour around that area between the hotel and beach, he found himself alone. The Daytona shoreline was bathed in full moonlight. Low tide now, little waves lapped incessantly at the luminous sand. Danny stopped and stared out once more at the vast ocean, now enveloped in blackness. Lightning silhouetted a dark storm on the horizon. He thought of the day's events that had colored his life since he last looked out over this vista of sand and sea. The memories were bittersweet. He had encountered extreme fear with a possibility of death, and while he felt he had generally passed the test, doubts clouded his mind. During those moments when the outcome was still uncertain, near panic had introduced feelings heretofore unknown, unwanted, never experienced previously. Somehow, Danny had stood his ground. But the temptation to plead for mercy or run had been options that were like neon signs in his brain, brands burning into his subconscious. Now that the crisis was past, some inner insecurity gave greater credence to thoughts of cowardice than heroism.
He had not told anyone of the supernatural vision so vivid in details of his life. His thoughts were almost a conversation with himself. 'I saw my life. I saw inside myself and it wasn't all good.' He would continue to share the amazing revelation with no one until his second marriage some twenty years later.

The solution came to mind as if by magic, or perhaps the young man's maturity grew in that moment. He knew what to do. He simply had to let it go and not dwell on it. It had been another learning experience, one of the crucial times in life that teachers and preachers and counselors talk about. There was no need to worry about what might have been. 'I

admit I was scared shitless but I guess just about anyone
would have been frightened in similar circumstances. I'm
just glad I didn't cry wolf and run or piss my pants.'
Stooping to remove tennis shoes and roll up denim cuffs, he
waded ankle high in the cool, refreshing water. It had been
a big day in his young life. Inexplicably, the memory of the
bird falling lifeless out of the tree came to mind. And then
he asked himself the question that every teen has asked of
themselves since young men formulated thoughts: 'Dang it,
I wonder what the future holds for me? The bird, now the
gun. Were these simply coincidences? Was today a test of
courage or morality? Will these unusual happenings be
important turning points in my life or just bumps in the
road?'
The distant storm continued to light up the evening sky but
turned southward, never coming ashore. Turning toward the
hotel, he smiled and realized that tonight it was good simply
to be alive. The future would come when it would come.

*****

*Lucky again? Yep. See, I told you – I will win the lottery one of
these days.*

Chapter 8

TRUTH AND CONSEQUENCES

September 29, 1952
Age: 17 and a day

Hands awoke him from deep sleep, gently tugging at his
shoulders. Through sleep-filled eyes he saw the luminescent
numbers of his alarm clock on the bedside locker: 3:30. The
faceless voice was ominously serious. "Mr. Brown, you will
appear before the Honor Council today at 2 p.m. to face a
charge of lying."
Danny had no trouble realizing this was not a dream. He
could now see there were two of them. While he couldn't
distinguish faces he knew the voice to be that of sophomore
Peter Mason. The other person, taller and holding a
flashlight, was probably Oscar Best. Peter and Oscar were
two of the four upper -classmen who made up the Honor
Council. Both were movers and shakers in the student body.
They had met and welcomed, even socialized a bit with the
freshmen as they arrived. While only sophomores in terms
of college years, sophomores were seniors at Emory-at-
Oxford. The little two-year school for two hundred boys
was the father and mother, the original home, of larger
Emory University in Atlanta.

 The four sophomores in question had spoken about the
time-honored Oxford Honor Code at chapel gatherings.
Now a little more alert with his eyes adjusting to the
shadows, he was sure it was Peter and Oscar standing beside
his bed.
"Mr. Brown, you were reported seen in Atlanta at the
Georgia Tech-Florida football game. You had signed out to
go to the local city of Covington. Atlanta is least 35 miles
from Covington. Signing out to one destination and going
. elsewhere, especially out of county, is considered lying. If
true, you have broken the Oxford Code you promised to
honor. You signed the Code just three weeks ago. If you
have forgotten, I'm afraid you may have a very short

memory. Report to Seney Hall at two this afternoon for a hearing on this charge."

Awake, unsure of a proper response after being accused of lying for violating the *Code*, Danny simply said, "O.K."

Minutes later, freshman Thomas James hurriedly entered the room. Wide-eyed, shaking his head in disbelief, Tom cursed the day he had ever agreed to attend Emory-at-Oxford Junior College. "I wanted to go to the University of Georgia, but my folks sent me here to dear ole EAO, a pissy little school with two hundred and five boys – no girls – located four miles from the metropolis of beautiful, downtown Covington, Georgia, in lovely, rural Newton County. And oh yes, they have stupid-ass rules like, 'You may leave the confines of Newton County only three times during the first quarter.' What bullcrap! I knew they were serious about cheating on tests, or of course, stealing, when we had to sign that Code in blood that they think was written by Jesus. But trying to beat the system out of an extra trip is Honor Code level lying? Christ! O.K., what are we going to do about the Honor Council?"

Danny lay back in his bunk and considered their predicament. Yes, they had gone to Atlanta to watch Georgia Tech beat the University of Florida in a great football matchup. Tech had won the game on a late field goal, 17-14. And, true enough, they had thought to circumvent the rules by signing out to Covington, the little city only four miles away in order to save one of their few and precious three times they could leave Newton County during the entire first quarter. In their young and inexperienced minds, the fact that in doing so they had lied and broken the Honor Code never entered into the equation. They were simply doing what boys do to get around dumb-ass rules. Besides, it had been Danny's birthday. They wanted to do something special, and with very little money between them, the free tickets Tom's family offered in Atlanta seemed to be calling their names.

Dispirited, the two young men discussed possible ways of extricating themselves from the situation they would face at 2 p.m. It was agreed that they would say they signed out to Covington, with original intentions of going into the small town but while walking and hitchhiking, decided to go on to Atlanta to see Tom's folks, especially since his dad had tickets to the big game between Tech and Florida. The next morning following breakfast, they rehearsed their story several times. Both assumed it would be an easy out – they would get their hands slapped and all would be forgiven.

At 1:55 p.m., the two college freshmen were standing on the steps of Seney Hall. As the bell in the tower struck twice, four sophomores exited the building. The boys were surprised to see the four upper classmen in coats and ties. That fact alone seemed foreboding in a way neither would have been able to describe. Peter Mason told the boys that Terry Rait and Jerry Strong would take Mr. James to the French classroom on first floor for questioning while he and Oscar Best talked to Mr. Brown in History on second floor. Danny sensed immediately they had been wrong in planning to continue the charade since they were to be talked to separately.

In the room behind closed doors, he recited the story that the two friends had agreed on. His premonition of failure immediately proved correct at Oscar Best's first comment followed by the $64 question. "That sounds feasible, Mr. Brown, but tell us exactly where on the road between here and Covington that you made this decision. Give us a landmark or a place of business - some concrete point where the two of you decided to hitch to Atlanta."

Danny was sure guilt was written all over his face. He realized their overlooking this most elemental of methods for discerning truth from fiction capitalized and underlined their immaturity. 'Stupid country boy done gone to town once too often,' he berated himself silently.

A myriad of discombobulated thoughts raced through his mind. What to say, how to say it? He felt contradicted - how could he know how or what Tom was doing or saying? Then he was struck with a single thought. 'Three strikes and you're out!' Danny had played baseball from the time he could say 'Ball' – it had always been his favorite sport. He halfway smiled as he realized it was completely normal for a baseball analogy to pop into his mind under stress. Still, he knew he had little time to ponder the metaphor. Peter and

Oscar were looking at him as though they could read his thoughts. He was faced with the fact that he and Tom had already told two lies – the first when they signed out to Covington knowing they were headed to Atlanta, and now in reciting the made-up story of how they changed their minds after leaving campus. He decided not to tell the third lie, to come clean. Disheartened, hoping somehow Tom was on the same track reaching a like decision, he admitted, "All right, we signed out to nearby Covington because we didn't want to use one of our three times to leave Newton County. We decided on Friday night we were going to the Georgia Tech game yesterday, Saturday. The tickets were sort of a happy birthday gift for me from Tom. Please tell Tom I'm telling you the truth about what happened."
Peter Mason: "You've made the right decision to tell the truth. But no, we won't tell Mr. James anything of the sort. He has to tell the truth of his own personal volition. We'll see how Thomas James handles this turn of events."
Oscar Best: "Mr. Brown, you have lied twice. Once the other members have finished talking to Mr. James, the four of us will meet and vote on your continued presence here at Oxford. Emory-at-Oxford prides itself on its Honor Code of no lying, no cheating, no stealing. You have broken that code. You have broken it twice in two days. I must warn you that you could be asked to leave campus and return home. Remain here in this room except to go to the bathroom across the hall until we return."

An hour passed. Then another long half-hour slowly ticked away on the big wall clock before the door opened to admit the four Council members. Peter Mason read from a white, lined pad, "Mr. Brown, you are hereby placed on probation and restriction for the remainder of the quarter. You may not leave campus at all until the Christmas break between Fall and Winter sessions. As such, your previously authorized two remaining trips outside Newton County are cancelled. Any other violation of the Honor Code will result in your being expelled from Oxford College. For your information, Dean Eason has been advised of and approved your punishment. Do you understand these conditions?"

And so Danny Brown, barely seventeen, just four months out of high school, was once more introduced to the paradox of ambivalent emotions. He recalled his feelings of elation and dejection over the lucky throw that killed the bird. Here and now, he could breathe a sigh of relief in not being sent packing back to Mom and Dad less than four weeks after leaving home for college. Facing them for lying was just unthinkable. At the same time he knew three months of campus restriction would seem interminable. He looked at the impassive faces of Peter Mason and Oscar Best. Danny knew he had watery eyes as he replied, "Yes, I understand. I am to remain on campus without leaving the grounds until Christmas break. What about Tom? Does he get the same deal?"

Oscar Best answered the query. "Mr. James has been expelled and is packing as we speak. His folks have been called to come and get him. They arrive this evening. He never recanted his lie. He told us you two decided to go to Atlanta as you stood hitchhiking in front of Dr. Evan's home, the associate dean's house, just past campus grounds. You are not to go to his room nor have any conversation with him before he leaves."

Dumbstruck, Danny tried to get his thoughts in order. Why would Tom make up some answer about where or when they made their decision to beat feet to Atlanta? Surely he would have known Danny had no way of knowing he had decided upon Dr. Evan's home as a reference point. Yes, it was a predominant landmark on the short road to Covington and he was the college registrar. Should he, Danny, have made the connection and told the third lie? Why didn't Tom just tell the truth like he had done? Tom was the best friend he had made in the short few weeks they had been at Oxford. Now Tom would be gone and Danny would be stuck on a campus barely the size of the high school he had graduated from just four months before. He stopped among the shadows of the tall oaks between Seney and Hagood Hall dormitory. He looked skyward and spoke aloud, as if petitioning an uncaring God: "It doesn't seem fair, not to me, much less to Tommy. It sure seems an overkill to kick him out." Walking slowly toward the dormitory, his mind and heart were once again conflicted with simultaneous dejection and happiness. As he thought of Tom driving back to Atlanta tonight with very disappointed parents, a wave of despair invaded his being because he knew, rightly or wrongly, he had contributed to Tom's expulsion. It had been Tom's idea and Tom's tickets, but it had been Danny's birthday they celebrated. And he had bought into the plan wholeheartedly. Yes, up the point of the third lie, he was as guilty as Tommy. And then when he thought of not having to face his own folks after being caught lying, he felt a rush of relief, perhaps even elation. Certainly, not a mountaintop jump-for-joy feeling - maybe just midway up a steep hill - since he still had ten or eleven weeks of probation and restriction. He didn't want to admit it but a thought was building in the back of his mind. Perhaps it was more destiny in his life. With the toughest math course he ever imagined under Tricky Dicky Dawson, plus Biology and European History this quarter, he could use the extra mandated time on campus. Would there be time for intramural football and basketball? Then more doubts surfaced. How would he ever do it? Could he stick it out and pass the courses? Maybe going off to a college which boasted one of the highest academic standards in the south, was not such a good idea - especially for a guy out of a country school with only eleven grades. Most of the other freshmen were at least a year older – a little more mature plus almost all had attended twelve-year schools. He remembered with some angst that he had been more than happy to graduate a year earlier than contemporaries. Now he realized that maybe he had rushed to a wrong conclusion. Sighing, he spoke to the silent oaks, "How the hell will I ever do it?" Then he realized his speaking aloud to God or the sky or inanimate objects or himself when perplexed was becoming a permanent part of his personality. "Oh well, I guess there's worse habits to worry about. Like I better worry about that five hundred word report on the Mid-East due next week." He turned and headed for the Library and study hall. There were books to be opened, especially history and that darned algebra.

*****

Chapter 9

A DATE WITH *MISS AMERICA* (Well, perhaps that's a stretch)

Spring Quarter, 1954
Age: 18

Posted on the bulletin board outside the Administrative Office:

NOTICE TO ALL STUDENTS:
A Dance Night at Wesleyan College

A trip to Wesleyan in Macon has been scheduled for Saturday, March 13th. A chartered bus will leave from Hagood Hall at 5:00 p.m. and return to Oxford following the dance. Departure time from Wesleyan is anticipated to be no later than 11:30 p.m.

25 students may attend. Cost will be $5.00 per student to pay for transportation.

Sophomores and Freshmen with "C" average and above may sign up for the trip. If more than 25 candidates want to attend, previous quarter grades will determine final approval for selected individuals.

Signed: Dr. E.A. Eason
           Dean

Danny Brown was one of the twenty-five lucky ones who made the cut and the list. Mr. Hudson, the Humanities professor was at the bus with last words of wisdom for the boys prior to departure. He covered the usual stuff: Emory-at-Oxford tradition, gentlemanly conduct, no alcoholic beverages on bus or at the dance, back on the bus no later than 11:25, etc., etc., was all reviewed in detail by Prof. Hudson. He then looked over the group before focusing in on Danny.

"You fellows look fine in your suits, sport coats and ties. I pronounce you ready to dance with lovely young Southern belles. Now, Mr. Brown, aren't you on Merit List from last quarter? I believe that was your first time to make the grades."

"Yes, sir." Danny responded, wondering where the interrogation was going.

Again Prof. Hudson turned and addressed the group of young travelers, "I am not going with you. Mr. Brown, who seems to have finally gotten his personal and academic act commensurate with the level of his sports interest and abilities, will be the EAO Representative for the trip. Danny, you are responsible for the behavior of this august group of debonair, young, dangerously virile and eager Oxford men, and for seeing this trip is a success in all respects. On return I'll need a verbal report of the outing, especially any out-of-the-ordinary events that might have occurred. Make sure you have twenty-five heads on the bus by 11:30. The driver has been told to depart the Wesleyan campus at that time. You'll need to coordinate a well-marked and convenient rendezvous pick-up spot. Do you have any questions?"

Danny answered, tentatively, almost sheepishly, "No, sir." Prof. Hudson waved to the driver: "O.K., it's a little over two hours to Wesleyan. Load up and be gone."

The sixty-four dollar question on the mind of twenty-five young men riding the southbound bus was, "Will *Miss America* be at the dance?" Miss Neva Jane Langley, the reigning *Miss America*, graced the campus of Wesleyan College for Women. EAO was home to several guys from Florida and they all knew that *Miss America* was from Lakeland. They surmised it could be their lousy luck to have her out on some muckedy-muck celebrity tour. No one seemed to know for sure if she would be at the dance.

Michael Allison sat with Dan and finally came out with it – another question several of the fellows wanted to know. "Danny, how in the devil did you suddenly become head honcho of this traveling road show? Especially since we all know you're a year younger than any of us. Heck, you're the same age as the freshmen even if you are going to graduate with us next month. You been brownnosin' ole Hudson or sumpin'?"

Danny had been asking himself the same thing ever since the professor had made the unexpected appointment. "Hey man – I was as surprised as anybody. It's hard to believe that I make the Merit List one time in two years and suddenly I'm responsible for the conduct of you jerks. You just remember I didn't ask for it. Never a dull moment at dear ole E.A.O."

Upon arrival at the Macon campus, the Wesleyan dance committee co-chairs met the bus. Thankfully – *God does work in mysterious ways!* - one co-chairlady being the heavenly Miss Langley. Danny exited the old privately leased tour bus and listened as the two young women briefed him on the particulars of Saturday Nite dance affairs at Wesleyan, including instructions as to where the bus would be directed to park. Danny stepped back on the bus and passed out the skinny to his waiting, anxious group.

Down the metal steps a second time, ahead of his entourage, he felt like royalty as the reigning *Miss America* escorted him to the dance auditorium. He noticed right away that she dressed like all the other co-eds. Tight skirt, loose blouse, penny loafers and white socks. And yes, she was definitely beautiful. And sophisticated. And perhaps best of all, very personable.

Miss Langley was the consummate hostess, too, and as such, danced often and talked with all the Oxfordites at one point or another. She probably tried to dance with as many of the visitors as possible, but the first dance, the last dance, and a couple slow melodies in the middle, found her paired with the young man from Austell, Georgia. Somehow she found time for one-on-one conversations with him over cokes and cookies. Most of the discussion was about EAO and Wesleyan courses, activities, and sports. In fact, the *Miss America* crown was never mentioned in their moments together.

At precisely 11:15 on his Timex, Danny began rounding up his band of EAO college guys and all 25 were loaded up and ready to go at 11:30.

The bus sped along the darkened highway after leaving Macon city limits. A few of the overhead console lights burned as the guys smoked and relived the evening. Danny was comfortable in his seat and just beginning to doze when Mike Allison spoke. "Well, Brown, you have hit the jackpot. For the rest of your life you can say you had a date with *Miss America*. You are one lucky sum'bitch. But you know what? I'll bet you're not the only one on this bus that somewhere in life they don't stretch the truth, and tell people they had a date with *Miss A*. at a dance in Macon."

Dan smiled. "Well, Mike, I tell you this. If I ever become a name-dropper and play the *'Guess who I know'* game, you can bet your sweet ass I won't be telling how many times I stepped on her feet. That woman can dance – made me feel like a hick novice."

Mike leaned his head back on the rest. "Brown, compared to any of those gals, we're all novices and hicks. They're probably back in the dorm right now laughing about those guys who go to the smallest college in the smallest rural town in Georgia. They had no idea where Oxford is. One girl confessed she thought we were going to be English and wondered why we came so far for a dance!" He closed his eyes for a few moments before adding, "But I do want to say one more thing. Thank the Lord for the differences between little boys and little girls, city, country or otherwise! I wish we had a few at EAO."

And guess what! The next year saw Emory-at-Oxford opened to girls. Class of 1955 had 201 boys and 5 girls.

Danny Brown graduated from Emory-at-Oxford, June 1954.

*****

"Mr. Brown, where did you attend college?"

"Why, Oxford, of course."

Chapter 10

"WE'RE GONNA FLY AIRPLANES"

Early April, 1955
Age 19

......nightshift

The Brown family had moved while Danny was away. He had grown up in Mableton, graduated from high school in Austell, before attending Little Emory. While he was at Oxford, his folks had purchased a brick home in Lithia Springs. The mileage between the home in Mableton and new one in Lithia was about seven miles along Highway 78, the Atlanta to Birmingham highway. Mableton had no traffic lights. Austell, about half way along the route had two or three, Lithia had one. As Dan left for work that afternoon, he grinned to himself as he evaluated the pros and cons of three small Georgia towns that shaped his family's existence. Heck, his birthplace, so rural it had no name, was only about twelve miles away. Definitely, he was a country boy.

The black Chevrolet, six years old but reliable, carried the two young friends along Highway 78 and then back roads and secondary highways from Lithia Springs to Doraville. Thirty-five to forty minutes later, they would be parking in a large, open lot at *B-O-P* Atlanta. Here, the automotive giant General Motors manufactured *Buicks, Oldsmobiles,* and *Pontiacs.* The plant had recently expanded into night shift production. Both buddies had landed jobs, compliments of Danny's uncle Lawrence who had worked there for several years. Danny, with two years college, had the better job. The GM interviewer had described the job in glowing terms, calling the position that of a *chemical analyzer.* Actually the job entailed watching over fourteen large vats of liquid, seven per side in an expansive room, staged in sequence that cleaned and prepared metal parts for proper paint adhesion. The process was called "bonding". Car bodies traveled through one line of vats; the other line carried fenders, hoods, trunks, and miscellaneous smaller metal pieces that would eventually be painted. All would be dipped and immersed in the first vat, exiting a final vat seven rinses later. The metal would have entered the vats dirty with grime and shinny from grinding after welding. After this cleaning and bonding sequence, the metal would appear more of a Navy deck gray, glistening in the overhead lights from a final cold rinse. The liquid in each vat had to be checked every half-hour for correct temperature and proper saturation readings. Liquid and or powder chemicals might have to be added or heat adjusted. Danny knew it was a reach to call him a "chemical analyzer". Still it was far better than being on the assembly line. His friend with whom he shared rides to work, Frank Terry, had only one year of college and wound up on the relentless, never ending line, painting his particular right hand fender on forty-four auto bodies per hour as the skeletal hulks moved along in a snake-like route.

At nineteen, both youths were extremely happy to have good paying jobs. The night work was confining in most aspects of their lives but had proven to be a blessing in disguise, at least in one very important tangent. While both boys lived at home with parents, they still found dating money hard to come by. Working five nights a week left only Saturday and Sunday nights available for extra-curricular activities. Savings realized from not dating on work nights had helped each boy purchase a modestly priced used car. Danny and Frank often discussed the pros and cons of their situation as opposed to the lifestyles of other young employees, particularly those married and not living with folks. Both boys made sure monthly payments were current. Yet after gasoline and auto maintenance upkeep, along with weekend expenses, their bank accounts were not increasing with regularity or frequency.

They had been on the road only a few minutes. Frank half-leaned against the passenger door, looked at Danny and said, "Dan'l my boy, we've got to do something with our lives. We've got to get out of this one horse, one red light town. We're lucky at our age to have jobs at General

Motors, but it's not what I want to do the rest of my life and I don't think you do either."

Danny responded unenthusiastically. "Yeah, but Frank, that's the whole reason I'm not back in college this year. I just don't know what I want to do in life. It's the old cliché, 'What do I want to do when I grow up?' At Emory-at-Oxford I found I'm not cut out to be a doctor, dentist, preacher or even salesman. I still wonder what I would be good at and what I'd be interested in doing for 40 years."

Frank was ready with his answer. Smiling, he said simply, "I think I have the solution. We get out of 'Dodge', we make an awfully good living, and we beat the draft. We're gonna fly airplanes!"

Danny was nonplused. "Frank, we don't have that kind of money. Flying lessons cost a lot of bucks."

Frank: "Not in the Air Force. We're gonna join the Air Force and let them pay us to learn to fly. Hey, look, there's a contrail way up there in the sky. How'd you like to be flying the plane making that big white tail of condensed water vapor?"

The remainder of the ride to Doraville was filled with dreams, wonder, questions that would need answers. Any doubts, indeed, if a lack of confidence existed at all, went unstated. Only a mile or two remained when an obnoxious odor permeated the air. Disgusted, Danny frowned at the passenger who was grinning ear to ear. Danny asked as he rolled down his window, "P-huew! damn, Frank. Did you fart?"

Happy with himself, Frank confessed readily. "Yep. You don't think an Air Force officer would shit in his pants, do you?"

The next day, happy and exuding self-confidence, the duo left home two hours earlier than normal. Smiles and high fives were in order when Frank picked up Danny in his old green Dodge. That morning Frank had found a poster in the local Post Office with the address of the nearest Air Force Recruiting office. Their future was waiting on them just twenty-five miles away in downtown Atlanta. Both boys were neatly attired in neatly pressed slacks and open-

necked short-sleeve shirts. Work clothes, jeans and
pullovers, lay in the back seat for changing into later.
Enthused and eager, two young men were about to take on
the world – and win!

Frank found a parking lot about two blocks from the Air
Force office address. Somewhere between the car park and
the Air Force recruiting office, the enormity of the step they
were contemplating hit them. Self-confidence deserted the
duo leaving in its wake apprehension and uncertainty.
Bravado, so animated and evident in the car only five
minutes ago was now nowhere to be seen or heard.
Swagger was replaced by timid, dragging footsteps. Less
than an hour earlier two motivated, determined young men
had left home in pursuit of success. Now they were just
country boys again, come to the big city of Atlanta. Alone,
each probably would never have made it to the recruiter's
office. Together, they trudged on and arrived at a door with
large black letters, "Air Force Recruiting".

Three enlisted petty officers smiled and moved to greet two
shy prospects. Sergeant Jerry Prescott, the officer in charge,
according to his nametag, shook their hands warmly. He
had dealt with apprehensive young men before. In short
order, he charmed Danny and Frank who were soon able to
feel comfortable and at ease. All three uniformed men
seemed genuinely happy to see them and interested in
helping them find a future in Air Force blue. They extolled
the challenge and satisfaction of flying high performance jet
aircraft. Military benefits were explained. Then the
sergeant talked about prestige and privilege enjoyed by Air
Force officers. The forms were ready to sign; the boys were
ready to ink their signatures. Pen in hand, Danny asked,
"When can we expect to report?"

Sergeant Prescott probably had hoped that question would
not surface. The smile faded as he glanced half-heartedly at
the other recruiters. His facial expression became more
serious, his demeanor slightly defensive and hesitant.
Matter-of-factly, he replied, "We have a nine month waiting
list. You won't be able to go to flight training until next
January."

The teen-ager laid the pen aside. "I'll have to think about it. A lot can happen in nine months. That's sort of a magic number in my way of thinking." Frank, too, was frustrated and refused to sign. The dejected *almost*-recruits left with leaflets and pamphlets in hand as three recruiting officers shook their heads in unconcealed disappointment.

Shortly, they were enroute to Doraville from the city, via busy and unfamiliar streets. Frank again drove, as it was his car. Danny poured over a map that would take them through Buckhead before cutting back to Doraville. When Frank eased to a stop at a red light, Danny looked out the passenger window and saw they were in front of a small satellite post office. To the right of the walkup was a small swinging billboard. Mounted on two poles, the center message board swung on two hasps attached to a horizontal bar across the top. The sign stood approximately seven or eight feet high, probably four feet across. Suddenly Danny sat up energized as he saw the large "**FLY NAVY**" letters emblazoned across the poster. Standing in front of a Navy jet fighter, a handsome officer in white uniform saluted anyone and everyone who would look at the billboard. Danny was ecstatic. "Frank, we forgot the Navy has airplanes, too! And look at those gold wings on that fancy dress white uniform!"
A broadening smile crossed the young driver's face. "Get the address. We'll go see them tomorrow! We may trade light blues for stark whites!"

In Atlanta once more the following day, the boys faced disappointment yet again. Whereas the Air Force would take high school graduates, the Navy required two years' college as a prerequisite for flight school. Danny qualified but Frank had only one year of college credits. The junior college graduate was determined to be loyal to his friend. "It was your idea. I can't go without you. It wouldn't be right."
Frank: "Yes, you can. Look at this way. Flight training is eighteen months. By that time I can have my second year of college and you can teach me to fly. Go on down to Pensacola and I'll come see you on weekends as soon as you

can have visitors. The only thing that bothers me about the
Navy instead of the Air Force is what does a guy do on
those long six and eight months at-sea cruises the Navy
recruiters warned us of? The Air Force guys didn't mention
any long tours away from home."
Danny laughed, "Refer to the Yellow Pages, I guess, and let
your fingers do the walking." Frank raised his eyebrows,
looked skyward, and said nothing.

*Frank Terry did not finish college; he did not visit Danny in
Pensacola. Still, in his own way, he did fulfill his dream of "We're
gonna fly airplanes". He eventually became a parts representative
for Lockheed Aircraft specializing in the
C-130 Hercules. He coordinated services for Air Force Material
Command for over twenty years with several assignments overseas.*

*****

The adventure is about to begin!

Chapter 11

REPEAT AFTER ME

Saturday, April 24, 1955
Age: 19

........you're in the Navy now

The man with gold stripes on his sleeves looked at the group
of young men assembled before him. "Stand and raise your
right arm. Repeat after me. 'I, *say your name*, do solemnly
swear or affirm, that I will support and defend the
Constitution of the United States against all enemies, foreign
and domestic; that I will bear true faith and allegiance to the
same; and that I will obey the orders of the President of the
United States and the orders of the offices appointed over
me, according to regulations and the Uniform Code of
Military Justice. So help me God'."
Young Daniell Brown dutifully repeated the words. He
knew that in some way, call it duty, responsibility, honor,
whatever, somehow the words carried an import far beyond
the words themselves.
The uniformed man who had administered the swearing-in
smiled and informed the men, "You're now officially in the
Navy. I want the six sailors, that's all of you except Daniell
Maurice Brown, to go with Lieutenant Giles. He will
arrange transportation for you fellows to Great Lakes where
your basic training will be held. Cadet Brown, your flight to
Pensacola has been delayed and is now scheduled for 1100
hours[1] tomorrow. You are free to enjoy Atlanta today or
even go back home to Lithia Springs, until that time. I do
need to know if you will spend the night at home or if I will
need to find you a bunk here on base."
The newest Naval Aviation Cadet replied immediately, "At
home, sir. My folks will have me here by 10:30. Is that
O.K.?"
The man in charge thought for a second before responding.
"1015 hours would be better. Meet LT Giles at Air

---

[1] 11 am

Operations – that's over at the tower." He turned and left the room.

Danny found the nearest pay phone. After dialing, he waited for pickup on the other end. Finally, after several rings, "Hello. This is Agnes Scott College. Where can I direct your call?"
With some delay, Danny was put through to a girl's dorm where he asked for Jeanette Coleman. Soon the young lady from middle Alabama was on the line. "Hello."
"Hey, Jeanette. The Navy didn't fly me to Pensacola today. I don't go until tomorrow morning. Let's do something tonight."
Her voice came back cheerful and excited. "Oh good, that'll be fun. I've heard about a great new film at the *Fox*. *Bridges of Toko-Ri* with William Holden and Grace Kelly. I think it's a Navy flying movie. Won't that be great for you to see a story about Navy fliers the night before you go off to be a pilot yourself?"

Well, maybe not so great. Many of you moviegoers know that the flick ends with characters portrayed by Bill Holden and Mickey Rooney (pilots), and Earl Holliman (helicopter crewmember) killed by North Korean Communist ground troops as the trio tries to escape on foot after crashing in enemy territory. Remember Danny had taken the oath only that morning! Korea was very much on the minds of all young men of draft age. The war had ended, that is firing had ceased, inconclusively in July 1953. Now, only nine months later, peace was still considered tentative. The movie hit home with a young, impressionable country boy.
But there was no turning back or changing mind. He had taken the oath, he was in the Navy now!

Perhaps, at least for a few hours, Danny Brown may have been a hero in the eyes of an Agnes Scott sophomore before he ever put on Navy blues or dress whites or saw a real Navy jet! Enough said, just don't let your imagination run too wild. Oh, a kiss or two might have been traded but remember, the '60's had not arrived yet!

It was in this film that Fredric March, as the Admiral commanding the Task Force, issues a great one-liner upon being told of deaths of *the two pilots and helicopter crewman mentioned above: **"Where do we get such men?"** This quote almost became the book's title.*

The next day, April 25, 1955, a very young hero-wanna-be was flown from the old Navy Atlanta airport to Pensacola Naval Air Station. Naval Aviation Cadet Brown[1] began Pre-Flight, three months of ground school and physical training, prior to actual flight lessons. Fifteen months of Basic and Advance Flight Training followed.

Daniell Brown was designated a Naval Aviator and commissioned an Ensign in the United States Navy (Ready Reserve) in October 1956.

*****

GO NAVY, young man, GO NAVY! (Oops, in this new Navy, I mean young people). Darn political correctness, anyway.

---

[1] The NavCad classification has been discontinued. At the time we shared equal rank with Naval Academy midshipmen.

Chapter 12

"MUSICA - MUSICA"

November, 1956 – January, 1958
Age: 21

Ensign Daniell M. Brown, one of the Navy's newest jet
pilots, felt screwed. Shiny gold wings pinned above the left
shirt pocket and gold bars on each collar declared he was a
United States Naval officer and pilot. But he was stuck in
limbo, going nowhere, stalled in a service squadron usually
manned by older officers, many who had been passed over
for promotion. By all normal accounts, he should be flying
new hot, fast jets by now. The hitch was by way of a left-
handed compliment in that he and his contemporaries had
beaten the Navy's anticipated graduation rate. According to
unofficial sources, late1956/early 1957 was the first time in
naval aviation history that the Training Command had
graduated more jet pilots than projected. Based on years of
experience, the Navy expected a certain percentage of
students to D.O.R.[1], others to fail academic requirements,
some to flunk flight checks. Sad but true, the expected norm
would also take into account a few students that would die
in either aircraft or auto accidents. The 1955/56 cadet and
officer recruits didn't quit or fail in numbers anticipated.
They had exceeded all expectations in a positive manner.
Only one or two had been killed. The Training Command
graduated a bumper crop of young, ready-to-take-on-the-
world Naval aviators. Consequently, fleet seats in
operational aircraft simply were not available for many of
the newly designated pilots. While this group of America's
"Cream of the crop" Naval Aviation cadets and aviation
officer candidates set new standards of excellence, the end
result was temporary chaos for fleet assignment officers and
disappointment for the newly commissioned 'Nuggets'.[2]
While Washington struggled to sort out the mess, upwards
of a hundred or more new officer-pilots were sent to air

---

[1] Drop on request
[2] New pilots are called 'Nuggets'

stations or service squadrons on both the east and west coasts.

Dan, along with several other 'Nuggets' waited their turn in the fleet in a squadron at Naval Air Station, Cecil Field, Florida, assigned to Fleet Aircraft Service Squadron NINE (FASRON NINE). FASRONs were support squadrons that furnished fleet units help in parts procurement and delivery, training, and administrative matters, etc. Ferrying repair personnel and parts to a military base nearest the ship or squadron in need was another responsibility of the FASRON pilots.

Dan was aware that he had it much better than most of his group. Luckily, he had been one of the first 'new guys' to arrive in Jacksonville, reporting as much as ten weeks before graduations *en masse* had materialized. Unaware at the time of the situation about to develop, the squadron had spent the time necessary to check young Ensign Brown out in four models of aircraft. While Dan was flying the F9F-8 *Cougar*, a jet, and three vintage propeller planes, virtually all newer aviators who reported after him spent their days on the ground.

The squadron had only two jets and those old clunkers spent more *down* time than *up* time.[1] Often parts had been removed and given ('cannibalized') to operational units. Day after day, week after week, the pool of pilots put on hold played acey-duecy in the ready room and read Navy regulations, military history books, or any magazine they could find.[2]

And Dan enjoyed another advantage over his contemporaries. Again, because he was among the first Nuggets arriving, he had been given a regular billet assignment. He was the squadron legal affairs officer which was more a counseling job for young sailors in debt than actual attorney-type duties. Processing report chits and scheduling Captain's Mast cases were among his

---

[1] Up = ready to fly; Down = not flight ready for any of many reasons
[2] Eventually all would be assigned to operational fleet squadrons.

responsibilities, but he didn't do much more along the lines of lawyer-oriented tasks.

An interested thing happened to him the first few weeks after reporting to the squadron. The young bachelor drove out to Jacksonville Beach to drum up some female action. Sitting in the *Salty Dog Bar,* he paid little attention when two shore patrol petty officers walked in. Shortly, they began checking identification cards for age. Ensign Brown handed his over and was immediately grabbed from behind by the second petty officer and told he was under arrest for impersonating an officer. With hardly another word, without giving Dan an opportunity to talk, the trio was off to Shore Patrol Headquarters. There, the Navy Chief in charge began writing his report and finally gave Dan time to talk. When Dan said that he was the FASRON NINE legal officer, the Chief laughed in his face, "Who do you think you're kidding? There's no way a wet behind the ears kid is a Naval officer - much less a legal beagle, and I bet you're not twenty-one either."

Dan looked at the Chief. "I guess I do look younger than my age," then smiling widely, he suggested the Chief call his commanding officer. Reluctantly, the Chief dialed Commander Harry Madrid's home number. The Chief explained the situation over the phone and abruptly handed the receiver to Dan. "Yes sir, it's me. I guess the Shore Patrol has never encountered an officer who is barely a month over being twenty-one. I'm sorry you were bothered at home, sir." He gave the phone back to the Chief whose downcast expression was evident as he finished his conversation with CDR Madrid. Soon, the bearded chief was apologizing to the youngest – and youngish looking - Naval officer he had ever seen. Dan was beaming as he left the little office, "Hey, Chief, no hard feelings. It'll be a great story to tell back at the squadron. I might embellish our adventure a little bit. You only chatted with me here in the office but I might tell it as *Officer jailed for being under age!* Or better yet, *FASRON NINE Legal Officer locked up for being under age.* I'll use one or the other, for sure – maybe both. Have a nice night."

As mentioned, FASRON NINE was *blessed* with an assortment of outdated aircraft with which to meet its varied commitments. The squadron had in its inventory a Douglas Aircraft Corporation AD-4N *Skyraider,* an older, earlier version of the more famous AD-5. The propeller driven AD's[1] were originally designed and built as a single piloted, single-seated attack aircraft but along the way a few planes had been modified to carry two or three additional persons as operators of electronic counter-measures equipment that could jam enemy radio frequencies. To make room for the extra personnel, the AD-4N was a beefier, pregnant version of the attack model. Stripped of its classified jamming gear, the FASRON NINE bird seemed a poor impersonation of a real *Skyraider.* It was, however, one of the four planes Ensign Brown was privileged to fly. On the occasion of this story, the young pilot was tasked to fly high priority repair parts to the naval base at Guantanamo Bay, Cuba. The *Skyraider* was configured with controls for only the pilot, but Lieutenant Junior Grade Kris McNally, another displaced Nugget begging for airtime, flew along for pay purposes and navigational experience.

The old, fat *Skyraider* performed flawlessly on the extended flight. First to Miami for refueling, and then a long over water leg to 'Gitmo', as the Cuban base was (and is) commonly called. The aircraft touched down on the airbase at Guantanamo about an hour before sunset. The two officers planned to spend the night in the BOQ before returning the next day. First, the all-important parts were handed over to GITMO Supply Department. Then Dan and Kris arranged for fuel to get the plane ready for an early AM departure.

As enlisted crewmen serviced the plane, Kris allowed, "Hey Dannie, we're on the opposite side of the island from Havana but surely there's a town nearby where we can taste the sights and sounds of local culture. Don't they make rum down here? And I have to find out if everything I've heard about Cuban women is true!"

---

[1] A' is for attack aircraft; 'F' for fighters. The AD was re-designated the A-1 in 1962.

One of the sailors helping fuel and oil the *Skyraider* heard LTJG McNalley's remarks. He offered: "Sorry, sirs, but a fellow named Castro has this island in an uproar. He's talking revolution big time. Lots of shooting going on up in the hills. New base regs just came out curtailing liberty outside base limits after dark. All transients, officers, enlisted, or civilian, are to stay on base after sunset. There is no more nighttime liberty in town unless you're attached to a Gitmo unit and live outside the base."

Finally, the aircraft was serviced, tied down and secured. A black staff car arrived to carry the two officers to the BOQ. Inside the car, conversation continued.

Kris: "Man-o-man, I can't believe we flew all day to land in Cuba just to be told we have to stay on base."

Dan: "Yep. The reason I was so happy to get picked for this flight was the chance to see a little of Cuba. All we're going to see is another BOQ, another Officer's Club, a cement runway and a helluva lotta water."

The enlisted driver interjected a possible solution. "Sirs, the fact is, those new orders are not being rigidly enforced right now. A lot of officers and enlisted still have families off base so there's a lot of coming and going through the gates. I think if you get on that bus up ahead, you can go right through security. It's the shuttle to Caimanera for Cuban employees here on base. You might try to sit in the back and stay down to keep the guard from seeing you in uniform. If you get outside O.K., make sure you catch the six a.m. bus back in the morning. There isn't another one until mid-day."

Both officers patted the driver on the back and thanked him. Soon the light gray bus stopped for passengers. Dan and Kris joined the line of Cuban nationals boarding. Except for the dingy color paint on the bus, their mode of transportation would have been recognized back home as an ordinary school bus. The aging Dodge vehicle was probably fifteen years old. The driver paid them no attention when they boarded along with the civilians. At the gate, the bus stopped, a Marine private gatekeeper stepped up into the boarding well, casually looked down the aisle, and waved the driver on through. Dan and Kris had conveniently picked seats on the last row behind two heavy-set Cuban men who easily screened them from view of the guard. The bus lumbered on its way. It made no stops on the eighteen to twenty mile trip to the small city of Caimanera. Outside, the night was moonless, the surroundings cloaked in pitch-blackness. Dan and Kris had fallen silent since leaving the gate. Left alone with their thoughts, they realized that perhaps their *escape* had occurred all too quickly. Jubilation and exhilaration had given way to anxiety. Maybe leaving the confines of Uncle Sam's security had been an error. They scanned the mountains for any sign of rebel forces. Every now and then a light could be seen far up a hillside. A campfire? A flashlight? A signal? A farmer's home? No matter, those lights they saw were too far away to be troublesome. Well, it was too late to worry about going back. Now they saw different lights – long streaks of light, some of them red. Sounds of far away gunfire could be heard over the rumble of the old bus. Everyone inside was looking or pointing up at the hills where the firing was occurring. Back and forth the fast lines of light shot through the black night. First, the tracers stopped, then after a few minutes all firing ceased. Darkness again enveloped the hills. Strangely, the Cubans on the bus were as quiet as the outside night. One overhead interior light about midway down the aisle burned dimly, casting muted light and shadows inside the cavity of the bus. The dull illumination added eerie shadows to the totally quiet and somber mood of the passengers. The two young officers, now apprehensive about being off base against orders, transients without any official documents, felt as if the atmosphere were charged with anticipation. Seeing and hearing weapons firing in the hills had been sobering. Castro and his crowd could be around the next curve or even seated among them as they rode along. Perhaps the bearded rebel was planning an attack on an American bus to make an international statement for his cause. Maybe the savvy leader had been waiting for just the right opportunity, two officers sneaking off base on a bus carrying Cuban nationals. What if an attack was set for this very night? Dan leaned over and whispered into Kris' ear, "Why is everyone so silent?" Kris shrugged his shoulders in a non-verbal response. Dan imagined their Cuban hearts were conflicted between loyalty to country and a job with the Americans.

Almost as if by design to answer Dan's unspoken question, a broad shouldered man seated several rows in front of them, stood up in the aisle. He turned sideways and looked around at the passengers. For a moment, he stared at the two Americans as though noticing them for the first time. Then he reached into the overhead storage space above his seat and pulled down a well-worn dark brown or black case. The long-nosed carry case resembled those in which Tommie-guns were concealed and carried in Prohibition Era movies. The tall Cuban unsnapped two catches and opened the ominous looking bag.

"Oh crap," Dan said to Kris. "The attack is going to come from within the bus. We've had it."

As the case came fully open, the Cuban lifted his face upwards and said loudly, "*MUSICA, MUSICA!*" Then he pulled a guitar from its nesting place inside the velveteen cavity as the bus erupted into revelry and clapping. He placed his right foot up on the seat and rested the instrument against his upper thigh. He flashed his fingers on the strings, and chords of music filled the bus. Again, joyous clapping from the passengers. Soon the riders were singing Cuban melodies as the bus bounced along the winding road. Even the driver began to sing and nod his head in time to the rhythmic sounds.

A relieved pair of young officers slapped each other's hands in a high five. Dan almost shouted, then said happily, "Man! For a minute there I thought it was horseshit and gunsmoke." Then he admitted, "I was so scared I thought the guy was speaking Spanish for *murder* or *kill them* or something like that. Isn't music wonderful? It's an international language in itself." Soon the dilapidated old bus arrived at destination. Two happy American bachelors departed the vehicle and stepped into the neon lights of the night. From inside the bus, gentle soft sounds of a Cuban folk chant, reminiscent of *Kum ba yah,* followed them as they walked away.

At seven thirty the next morning, Dan added power to the powerful AD engine as the aircraft began rolling down the long runway. Airborne into a beautiful clear sky, the island landmass fell behind. Nothing but blue water stretched before them. Enroute Miami, the large blades of the *Skyraider's* propeller purred along over a calm, almost flat sea. The mighty ocean at rest gave the pilot a sense of tranquility. He let his mind wander from the array of instruments guiding him on course to reflect on the previous evening. Their exposure to danger, real or imagined, had culminated in an exciting escapade. It would be a fun story to tell over and over. Several bottles of eighty cents-a-gallon *Bacardi*[1] now safely stashed in the empty electronic spaces below would sure help liven the telling! FAS-NINE was still the pits but he had visited a foreign country. Life wasn't all bad. Now if he could only get orders to the fleet flying jets, the world would be right.

*****

Yes, Bacardi – not Havana Club or other present day Cuban rums. See footnote below.

---

[1] *Bacardi* was made in Cuba until October, 1960

Chapter 13

GOODBYE JAX, HELLO NEWFOUNDLAND

March, 1958
Age: 22

"Check list complete," the copilot assured CDR Jack
Sullivan. CDR Sullivan had been commanding officer of
FASRON NINE for about a month. This was Dan's first
time to fly with the skipper and the first time in months that
he was in the right seat as copilot on a Sunday. Usually, he
rode left seat as aircraft commander on weekend runs
between NAS Cecil Field and Naval Station Mayport. The
other squadron pilots, most of them passed over has-beens,
liked to beg off on weekends and Dan was happy to oblige
as duty command transport pilot. Since he was the junior
aviator in town, whenever one of the other pilots flew, he
was copilot instead of aircraft commander. Sundays was his
day to shine as pilot in command while one of the several
Nuggets rode along in the right seat.

BOUNCE! And bounce again. Then once more before the
old C-45 was rolling down the runway on takeoff after the
touch and go landing. This was the fifth touch and go in a
row where the C.O. had pranged the front wheels into the
runway, resulting in BOUNCE several times before total
control was re-established. To the young copilot, the
problem was obvious: the plane was landing on the front
side of its two tires. The plane was going to bounce every
time.
Dan meant absolutely no disrespect or sarcasm when he
said to CDR Sullivan, "Skipper, would you like for me to
show you what you're doing wrong?" The left seat driver
shot his eyes at Dan and the younger man knew he had
made a serious tactical mistake.
The fiery darts in his eyes and the animosity in the C.O.'s
voice were unmistakable. "Yeah, Lieutenant[1]. Why don't

---

[1] Actually Lieutenant <u>Junior Grade</u>, but the "JG" is usually dropped
when addressing an individual personally.

you show me how to land an airplane I've flown for fifteen years?" He raised his hands off the controls wheel and opened his palms in a gesture showing relinquishment of control.

"I have the aircraft", Dan said aloud and he placed both hands on the yoke. Shortly, the tower cleared the C-45 downwind for another practice landing. Dan knew of no way to salvage the situation, so he simply called for the landing check list, made a smooth on-speed approach, and landed the plane on the backside of the wheels. "At about ten to twelve feet above the runway, all I do is bring the nose about two inches above the horizon – usually the trees at the end of the runway. I let the speed dissipate until we land on the backside of the tires," he told CDR Sullivan. Adding power, they took off for another go-round.

The C.O. took control of the plane for a final landing. His touchdown was better but again bounced a couple of times.

At 1000 hours the next day, a nervous and sleepy pilot was called to the Commanding Officer's suite. The C.O.' s face was dead serious. "Mr. Brown, I have just talked to BuPers[1] about you. You will have orders cut today. I told them I didn't need a smart-ass kid in my command telling me how to fly airplanes. They agreed. Let's see how you like your new duty station."

Having tossed and turned most of Sunday night due to anxiety over the day's *faux* pas, Dan was certainly not surprised. He asked simply, "Where am I going, sir?" Hoping against hope the Bureau would send him to fly jets in the fleet, he held his breath for the reply.

An *I gotcha* smile crossed CDR Sullivan's face.

"Newfoundland, staff duty. Maybe the cold weather up there will take some of the hot air out of you."

Five days later Dan was un-engaged to Ann and on a Navy C-117 transport plane to the southeastern-most outer edge of Canada. He had learned another lesson along the road of life. Rank not only has its privileges but also commensurate authority. But ironically, unseen angels who watch over

---

[1] Bureau of Naval Personnel

naive Navy pilots were busy at their post. His career was far from over. Upon reporting to EARLY WARNING WING ATLANTIC, he had official mail waiting from Washington advising him that a Navy selection board had selected him for regular Navy. Of course, his papers for the board had gone in several months previously with an outstanding endorsement by CDR Madrid. Dan felt vindicated. A board of senior officers had evaluated him and wanted him to remain in the Navy for at least twenty years. Simply stated, a regular officer was a permanent career officer as long as he made promotions; a reserve officer would have to be evaluated for retention at certain intervals.

It was beginning to seem like happy and sadness, good things and bad, all at the same time over the same incident, were always going to be Dan's lot. He considered a call to Jacksonville to tell the executive officer his news. He could ask the X.O. to "Tell CDR Sullivan all the hot air isn't gone." But he decided against it, a call would accomplish nothing positive. Besides, CDR Sullivan was going to get the last word anyway when he sent Dan's final fitness report to Washington. Calling back might actually be the worse thing he could do. No need to add fuel to the fire. What was done was done. He was in Argentia, Newfoundland. LTJG Brown was a staff puke instead of a hot-rod fleet jet pilot.

Gazing southward from an outside stairwell high on the ten-story BOQ, the highest building in all Newfoundland, he could see ice floes melting in Placentia Bay. He realized the sun was shinning for the first time since his arrival. Perhaps it was the sunny day that improved his disposition. To no one or anyone, he spoke into the crisp Canadian air, "But hey, they say the fishing up here is fantastic, a zillion streams nearby, and there's miles and miles of moose and elk to chase when flying. Dan, go and make the best of a shitty deal."

*****

Oh, but he wanted to make that call! Instead, he sold the ring and sent the hundred bucks he owed to Charlie Fisher.

Chapter 14

<u>CONCETTA ROSA MARIA FRANCONERO</u>

January, 1959
Age: 23

Yes, one wintry day Connie Francis came north to the icy
rock called Newfoundland to perform for Uncle Sam's
finest. She would sing for our boys in blue who were stuck
on the God-forsaken Naval Base at Argentia.

LTJG Dan Brown, Assistant Communications Officer for
the EARLY WARNING WING ATLANTIC staff, was
busy with outgoing encrypted messages when the Chief of
Staff walked into the Communications Center. Captain
George Grier, graying, a little pudgy, always positive and
cheery, asked Dan to join him as he toured the spaces.
"Yes, sir" was the automatic reply.
The jovial Captain appeared to have something on his mind.
"Dan, how old are you?"
Dan had no idea what was coming. "Twenty-three, sir."
The COS continued walking down the corridor with Dan in
step beside him. "Dan, we must have seven or eight
bachelors on staff. And I've got to pick one of you to escort
a famous young celebrity when she arrives here tomorrow –
maybe even take her to dinner at the club. I guess you've
heard we're going to have Connie Francis sing for the
enlisted men." The sentence was more a question than a
statement.
Dan's ears had perked up at the idea of escorting so popular
a female entertainer. "Yes sir, I guess the whole base is
talking about Connie Francis. She sure can belt out *Who's
sorry now.*"
The COS stopped in front of a paneled door. "Well, you're
the most senior of our single guys, you're not spoken for by
some gal back in the states, and I would think the age
difference – she's eighteen - might be just perfect for an
escort. At this point nothing is for sure. Her PR folks have
not requested an escort, officer or enlisted, but the Admiral
would like one on tap if and when needed. You got the

job......if you can call it a job," he added with a sly grin as he turned and entered his office.

That evening at the BOQ bar, Dan toasted his good fortune and even Captain Grier in absentia for his superb acumen and expertise in selecting young officers for escort duty. Finally, he bought a round of drinks for the bar crowd of over twenty guys. At twenty-five cents a drink, the extravagant gesture came to a whopping $6.75. As he settled the bill, he announced to the all male group, "Tomorrow evening, I will be having din-din with Miss Connie Francis. Eat your hearts out." He had just bet the bank that he would in fact be in the company of Connie Francis the following night. He had a feeling!

The following day was blustery and overcast with rain. The commercial plane delivering Ms. Francis due to land just after lunch arrived almost five hours late. Dan was advised that no escort would be needed before the performance but was to remain available for dinner with the artist at the Officer's Club afterwards if she was so inclined. Dressed in his winter best blue uniform, black shoes gleaming, perfect Windsor knot in his black tie, Dan reported to the Officer's Club immediately following her show. Once again he would be disappointed. Unknown by Navy brass in Argentia prior to this time, her mother was along for the trip as chaperone and had decreed that her daughter was too young to cavort with worldly-wise sailors. Mother and daughter entered together and dined alone.

Dan stood along the wall in the Club dining room and gazed expressionless at the young singer for several minutes, thinking about what might have been. 'Well, so much for gut feelings.' Then he turned and walked away – towards the open bar to buy another round of drinks, and to eat crow however it might be served: baked, fried, grilled, or stewed. Some of his buddies would want him to eat it raw.

*****

Chapter 15

THE MILE-HI CLUB

May, 1959
Age: 23

This chapter is inserted simply to tantalize the reader. The author has attempted to keep the contents of this written offering within certain moral parameters. To tell the secrets of initiation into the Mile High Club would violate that promise. That's really too bad, because it's a great tale of an old twin-engine C-45 *Beechcraft* like the one that caused our storyteller's exile to Newfoundland. Flying at five thousand feet above a panorama of pristine Canadian forests, trees laden by snow covered branches, grassy plateaus dotted with moose and elk, fresh streams of running water as clear as vodka, the setting was ideal. At that altitude, the sun could be seen sinking into the northernmost Appalachians of northern Maine and New Brunswick, Canada. Semi-darkness soon enveloped the small transport's cockpit. Once straight and level on course towards Gander, the pilot gave control over to the copilot. Then he un-hooked his safety harness, got out of the left seat and stepped back into the cabin. Pulling the cockpit curtain closed, he sat next to the only passenger, a Navy nurse. She leaned across the aisle and smooched his cheek. Let's not discuss the fact that she was fifteen years older than our pilot who shall remain unnamed.

The Mile High Club has no meetings, no dues, no plaques, not even certificates. It has only one requirement for membership. That criterion may be the most restrictive of any brotherhood, association, affiliation, fraternity, sorority, lodge, or league in existence today. What is that qualification? Well, like the saying goes, "If you have to ask the price, you can't afford it." If you don't know the prerequisite for becoming a Mile Higher, perhaps it's best for you to remain uninformed.

*****

Chapter 16

KEY WEST

July, 1960
Age: 24

.........*a man named 'Tennessee'*

*The story is told of a king who asked his wise men to reduce all the
world's knowledge into one sentence. After some time, they returned
with several volumes similar to the Encyclopedia Britannica. "No,
no," the king denounced the effort. "I said one sentence. Not a
library." The wise men worked feverishly for weeks and finally
summarized all information into just one, albeit rather thick, book.
"No, no", the king decreed. "I said one sentence. I want all
knowledge summed up in one sentence!" Retiring to their study, the
wise men needed only thirty minutes before returning to the king
with the following adage: "There is no free lunch."*
.....................................Anonymous

Perhaps the true story that follows embraces that simple philosophy.

"LT Brown, you're grounded. You have one of the worse
cases of mononucleosis I've ever attended." The young pilot
nervously toyed with collar devices shaped like railroad
tracks that denoted his new rank. Now he was a full
lieutenant, up a step from lieutenant junior grade. To
suggest that he was chagrined would be almost accurate.
Pissed would be more to the point. He lacked only two
flights to complete the rigorous Replacement Air Group
(RAG)[1] pilot training course for fighter interceptors. The
McDonnell F3H *Demon*[2] was an oversized, underpowered
fighter that demanded total and constant attention to detail.
This forerunner and father of the more famous F4 *Phantom*

---

[1] Intense, specialized training in a specific aircraft, usually over
several months
[2] Re-designated the F3B in 1962 by Secretary of Defense Robert
McNamara

was unforgiving in even minor lapses of forgotten procedures or tactics. Medical grounding had not been part of the course completion plan. Just getting kissing disease was embarrassing enough. His buddies would ride him unmercifully. More importantly, five to six weeks away from flying would be a giant step backward in mastering the *Demon*.

Facts are facts and must be reckoned with. Since time off from flying was mandated, he thought, at least he was in Key West, a haven synonymous with rest and recuperation. Hyped as the southernmost sun and surf paradise in the United States, the Keys were, in the vernacular, *laid back*. Key West locals, or *Conchs*, epitomized an attitude of "Let it wait until tomorrow" in all aspects of life, business or pleasure. It was a fun place - the "In" place - to be stationed for young hotrod - and hot-blooded - bachelor pilots on the east coast. And, he was quartered in one of the most beautiful, scenic hotels in the Keys. The Casa Marina, a converted castle (years later, the *Mariott Casa Marina* with rooms/suites going for $225-285 [and up] per night) was his home. For sixty dollars a month, Dan had an oversized room with ocean view, daily maid service, clean sheets every other day, and continental breakfast. Parked outside under luscious green hedges and flowering crepe myrtle was his pride and joy: last year's model *Cadillac* convertible, creamy white chassis, baby blue interior. The *Vespa* that he used for commuting to and from base was given its own special parking spot near the front door in full view of the night desk for security. Sometimes he showed up for dates on the scooter just to see the reaction of a young woman all primed - and dressed - for the Caddy. Life was good. Up to this grounding, 1960 had been a pretty good year. First, Admiral Joe Dunn had gotten him out of Newfoundland a year early and back into jets. He would be in the fleet soon. Kennedy had not yet been assassinated, Korea was fading fast from memory, the cold war was heating up which meant increased defense budgets and military spending. Vietnam was a country no one had heard of. If you stood in front of world famous *Sloppy Joe's and* yelled "VIETNAM!" passersby would probably think you were cursing in some foreign language. Yes, Martin Luther King had moved his headquarters from Montgomery to Atlanta. Civil rights issues with King at the forefront were getting lots of copy in the media. The late sixties would see that drama played out, but for now, it was a good time to be an unattached Navy pilot. It occurred to Dan that perhaps six weeks away from night fighter school might be a blessing in disguise. What was that girl's name from Miami that he met at the *Sun & Sand* last Saturday night? 'Oh hell, sierra hotel india tango[1]- I have mono. Kissing is out and how can you get past first base with a gal if you can't smooch her? Forget that mission for six weeks.'

As the motor scooter sped southward, eating up the few miles between *Boca Chica* air base and Key West proper, he thought about the changes in his lifestyle that would be forthcoming. 'Shoot, my daily, actually my nightly routine, is about to be blown.' LT Brown was famous in his own time among RAG contemporaries for circumventing the system that saw 90% of available female flesh working the joints as bar maids or waitresses until four a.m. every night except Sunday. Pilots cannot fly safely or professionally on two or three hours sleep, especially after drinking copious amounts of alcohol. Until our guy reported to interceptor training, bar maids and waitresses were weekend-only targets for the jet jockeys. Like others before him, he was at first frustrated. Ingenuity prevailed and a new concept in the art of "hunting without a gun" in the late night bars and cafes of Key West was fine-tuned.

After work, usually around four thirty or five in the late afternoon, it was off to the *Casa Marina*. Sleeping until midnight, perhaps as late as one a.m., he would rise and eat a light snack. Showered, shaved and on the go, he limited himself to two ounces of liquor on any given night of the workweek. Making the rounds of the overly abundant bars, more often than not, he was successful in finding feminine company for breakfast at *Charley's*. Or *Mike's Late Spot*. Or any of several other restaurants catering to the breakfast crowd. Then a walk on the beach, a stroll down the pier, or

---

[1] *S-h-i-t* spelled in military phonetic alphabet

other more private, intimate pursuits filled the hours and minutes (and he wondered where he was given *mono*?) until time to swing by the *Casa* and don khakis for seven-thirty muster at the squadron. Night flying, parties and special events occasionally interrupted the above schedule, but generally, it was the *modus operandi* for the innovative Georgia boy.

In a nutshell, the waitresses and barmaids were crucial to the dating game of Key West. Virtually no local girls over eighteen were on the island. All were away at school, had married young, or moved northward. There were a few nurses but most were older and married or engaged. All that remained for red-blooded young American flyboys to chase were bar maids, waitresses, or schoolteachers. And the competition was intense: civilians of all ages as well as thousands of sailors. LT Brown was happy with himself – he had faced the "enemy" of gals working late and won.

The schoolteachers were a story unto themselves. Key West was a relatively small city; consequently, the schools were manned with a minimum of unmarried teachers. Perhaps six or eight were available for the hundreds of single men comprising the male population of Key West and environs. Military officers and enlisted along with civilian government employees at two Naval bases, plus local fellows wanting to meet "Mrs. Right", or simply guys on the make, probably numbered around two thousand at any given time.

Dan grinned as he remembered three of the teachers that he and two friends, Ed King and Ray Joiner, dated sometimes. Cathy, Jill, and Janet were their given names but in casual conversation among themselves, the three men usually referred to the trio of girls as *"Dogface", "Horseface"*, and *"Scarface"*. Poor Cathy was the first to be awarded a pet nickname. She had a little round face with correspondingly small ears, eyes, nose, mouth, cheeks, almost like a Yorkie terrier. So much so, her nickname had been a natural. Consequently, hers had precipitated two more 'endearing' monikers for Jill and Janet. The quietest of the three, Jill, with her unusually long face was well suited for the equestrian naming. Janet had been cut accidentally by her brother as a young girl and had a two-inch scar on her right cheek. After years of growing and tightening of facial tissue, it wasn't ugly or defacing, it was simply there. Truth is, *Scarface* was probably the most congenial and fun of the three. A ten-dollar bet among the three friends was based on who would be the first to slip and call one (or more) of the girls by their special name rather than her given name. The Andrew Hamiliton ten-er was still unclaimed and Dan smiled again as he thought of their risky deception. The wind blew in his face and made him feel good. He would be O.K. *Scarface* had been a romantic project before this bout with mono but she would be there when he got well. All in all, life was good, heck, it was great. He'd just have to grin and bear it for the next few weeks.

Rest, rest, and more rest was prescribed as the cure for *mono*. The first morning after grounding, he slept in until eight thirty. Waking refreshed, he dressed for breakfast. Several pieces of toast with praline jelly, fresh orange juice and two cups of coffee reinforced a false feeling of wellness. "Heck, maybe the doctors were wrong. I feel great. I think I'll walk down to the ocean pool and check on that barracuda that likes to slip in through the hole in the mesh fence." Twenty minutes later he was exhausted and returned to his room for a morning nap. Waking, thinking to be revitalized, he ate a good lunch, followed by a brisk walk around the sprawling grounds. After just a few minutes, perhaps a half-hour, total enervation crept over his weakened body. Prior to falling asleep for a before-dinner siesta, he read the literature Dr. Zinn had given him on the effects of mononucleosis. Not surprisingly, his day fit the classic pattern of energy loss as outlined in the two-page brochure. As he fell asleep once again, he was thinking that perhaps it was going to take the full six weeks to be back in battery. The *Demon* would eat him alive if he were airborne in a missile shoot or practicing carrier landings right now. 'I wonder if it was *Scarface* that gave me this damn mono.............'. He slept soundly, awoke famished, then dressed for dinner.

And so the first week passed. An eight o'clock wakeup followed by breakfast. After devouring the morning Miami Herald, a quick swim in the fresh water pool preceded a nap. Sometimes he remained poolside in a hammock under a

Tiki hut, on most occasions he went back to his room.
Later, lunch, a walk, a few chapters of the latest best seller,
Advise and Consent, another dip in the pool, yet another nap.
Dinner with friends, no booze, not even wine or beer.
Afterwards perhaps a movie or other entertainment, then in
bed by ten thirty.

LT Ron Durning pressed him. "Danny Boy, surely you can
drink a beer. And if you can't, well, that will teach you to
know who you're swapping spit with!" Five beer glasses
with commensurate cheers were raised toward the comrade
drinking *Coke*. The six buddies gathered round the table
were pilots in the same RAG class. Seated on the patio at
Italian Gardens, the group had gathered one evening as Dan's
first week of grounding ended. Dan was still ahead of them
in number of syllabus hops completed but they would all be
finished and assigned fleet squadrons during the next six
weeks. "Hey guys, you'all will be graduated before I fly
again but I can take solace in the fact that all five of you are
still junior to me. Date of rank was set in stone when we
first got our wings so I'll always be ahead of you. Now as to
drinking beer, I guess one wouldn't kill me but it's like Mrs.
Gotrocks is quoted to a group of high-class lady friends in a
recent issue of a high-class skin magazine. I can't remember
how it goes exactly," he lied, "but listen up." Standing, he
continues. "Picture this. Several well to do, very socially
oriented ladies sitting around playing bridge. One of them
delivers a discourse on the wonderful attributes of
champagne." As he spoke, Dan began to imitate the
mannerisms of a haughty socialite. With affected voice, he
said, "I offer my compliments to our hostess for her excellent
selection of French champagne which so superbly
compliments the liver pâté. Champagne is truly nectar for
the gods. The delicate bouquet first encircles, then arouses
the olfactory senses. The taste buds are titillated by the
exquisite flavor imbued and inherent in the fruit of the vine.
The delicious liquid excites the palate. The mouth savors
the piquant, haunting aftertaste. The body warms to the
sparkling bubbly which in turn creates a yearning, a thirst for
the next sip. One's appetite is whetted by the aroma, the
taste, the velvety smoothness of the luscious drink. The very

act of lifting a toast in a Waterford hock filled with French Brut enhances the moment. Truly, French champagne is magnificent. Perhaps my point is best illustrated by Dom Perignon himself on the night champagne was invented when he said, '*I am drinking stars*'." Here Dan paused, injecting a moment of solemnity to his discourse. Then he screwed up his face as seriously as possible and added, "Now, conversely, beer looks and tastes exactly like horse piss and frankly, makes me fart."

After laughter had subsided, Paul Weston shook his head in mock amazement. "Dit dit dit, dit dit dit dit, dit, dahhhhhhh[1] - Brown, you're too much. How long does it take you to memorize those humorous ditties anyway?"

The second and subsequent weeks of grounding saw a new wrinkle introduced into LT Brown's daily routine. In fact, the change of pace was welcomed and soon became the highlight of his day. A very famous person was to make an unexpected entrance into the social life of *Casa Marina* residents, especially for those who availed themselves of Beach Club privileges. The club wasn't a true country club in the sense of formal membership, by-laws, meetings or minutes. It was simply an open bar and grill around the salt-water pool with a great ocean view. Beach chairs, umbrellas, and gin and tonics created an idyllic tropical setting. *Casa* guests and residents enjoyed free access while local *Conchs* paid a minimal monthly fee to enjoy the grounds, view, and amenities. Of course, everyone paid for food and drink orders.

Joe Poole was the Casa Marina's "Main man". Groundskeeper, maintenance man, occasional barkeep, and when the Beach Club met around the salt-water pool, he was bartender, short order cook, and lifeguard. He and Dan were becoming fast friends, simply from continued exposure to each other. Dan could not move around the hotel or grounds without running into Joe. Likewise, Joe seemed to always find the grounded pilot in his rounds of duties. "Say, Dan'l, try to amend your after-lunch sleep schedule and join

---

[1] Verbalized Morse code for 's-h-i-t'

us at the Beach Club today. I think you'll be interested in meeting one of our new members. We're there from one to three p.m. I open the bar for basic drinks and lemonade, I fix hamburgers or hotdogs on the grill, we relax and shoot the breeze around the sandy beach in front of the saltwater pool. I know you'd enjoy talking with our new guy. It's Tennessee Williams - ever heard of him?"

Dan was elated. "Oh yes. Two Pulitzer prizes, I believe. Hey, I'll try to be there." He knew he would go at least once. Who wouldn't want to meet the great Tennessee Williams of *Glass Menagerie, Cat on a hot tin roof,* and *Streetcar named desire* up close and personal?

Joe did the introductions all around. Dan shook the proffered hand of Tennessee Williams and felt good in telling the distinguished guest that he had seen *Sweet Bird of Youth* on Broadway just two months previously. "By the way, Mr. Williams, do you prefer 'Tennessee' or your real name 'Thomas', or even Tom?"

The writer smiled and raised an eyebrow. "Oh, I picked 'Tennessee' as my pen name, I'll stick with it. But I'm impressed. I expect you are the only person in the Keys who knows my birth name. And you've seen Geraldine Page in my play. Great. Joe tells me you're a flyboy."

Dan nodded. "Yes, sir. But for the next four to five weeks at least, I'm stuck here on the ground with mere mortals while I recover from mononucleosis. I must admit being able to go one-on-one with the winner of two Pulitzer Prizes makes my grounding a little less painful. I know *Cat* and *Streetcar* are great plays. I'm sorry I didn't get to see them. But I've seen both movies."

Mr. Williams beamed. "Well, I thought Hollywood did a better job on A *Streetcar named Desire* than they did on *Cat on a hot tin Roof.* I think both Brando and Newman did superb jobs. Enough about me for the time being. About this *mono* you have, step over here and let me feel your spleen. I want to see if I agree with your doctor's diagnosis. If you have *mono*, your spleen will be swollen like a balloon."

Dan Brown had never been called shy. On the other hand, no one (other than physicians) had ever asked to feel his spleen located so close to *Mr. Happy.* Fortunately, the young Naval officer had no prior knowledge of the famous writer's homosexuality. Still, more than a little ill at ease by the unabashed openness of the request, Dan glanced around to see if other Club members had heard their conversation. He was not surprised to see that five or six persons were waiting attentively for his response. A refusal would certainly affront the worldly writer. Dan timidly approached and opened his shirt. The older man pulled the right side of Dan's swimsuit down two or three inches and then slid his hand inside the waistband. He felt along the pilot's lower abdomen for only a few seconds. His touch went no lower than the spleen but the act itself hinted of shared intimacy. Removing his hand, he nodded his head and told Dan that indeed his spleen was swollen. "Like a watermelon, Son. Listen to that doctor about rest and relaxation. Don't overdo." Later, as he recalled the incident, Dan tried to imagine a movie scene with him standing at near-attention with a famous middle-aged man's hand and forearm down his swimsuit. Almost preposterous!

From that potentially auspicious beginning, a casual friendship developed between the three men: Joe Poole, bronzed by the sun, a street-educated maintenance worker; Dan Brown, a twenty-four year old Naval officer and aviator with strong rural Georgia roots; and Tennessee Williams, author and playwright, sophisticated, traveled, famous. The writer was an avid listener to any aviation stories that Dan would tell. Several times he interrupted Dan by reminding him, "Gee, I wish Tallu were here. You know my good friend Tallulah Bankhead loves Key West but she's working in Hollywood or somewhere right now. She would love your stories, especially the one about Cuba and the guitar player." Oddly, he seemed to relish hearing Dan's flying stories. Joe Poole's contribution to the three-way conversations dwelt primarily with his five ex-wives, alimony payments thereof, and dreams of making it big as a gigolo. Tennessee Williams captivated any audience by expounding on his travels and experiences. Sipping his gin

86

and tonic, the short, fattish, aging writer gave instant life to his stories. The three men often talked long into the afternoon as they relaxed in the Beach Club area. Dan had finished reading Allen Drury's novel, was now deep into *Hawaii* and would give his new friends a summary of the interesting events described in the lengthy Mitchner volume. Philosophy, religion, war, government, books, plays, movies, marriage/divorce ....topics that dominated any average conversation between friends were likewise discussed and dissected by the three newfound acquaintances.

Later, looking back, he was not surprised that the subject of homosexuality never raised its ugly head. True, they had rarely discussed women, and never women as sex objects. Following the spleen inspection incident, which was over within seconds and culminated without embarrassment, Dan had wondered if Tennessee might be, what was that new word, *Gay*? Other than that one time, Tennessee Williams had never given another hint as to his sexual orientation.

Dan reported to the doctor each week as ordered. Finally, in week five, Dr. Zinn seemed pleased as he studied the lab report. "O.K. Daniel, looks like another few days of inactivity and I'll let you return to work next Monday." Towards the end of that fifth week, the Beach Club scheduled an end-of-season cookout on Friday evening at sundown. Joe Poole made arrangements to buy fresh yellowtail snapper from the early morning fishing boats as they returned dockside. After cleaning by the *Casa* kitchen staff, he prepared the fish for grilling. Joe dashed the cleaned snapper with spices, then Dan helped him wrap the entire fish, head and fins, in foil. Next, Joe placed the silvery packets over dying embers. Ears of white corn still in the shucks had been laid carefully around the hot briquettes and steamed until done. Heaping bowls of salad fixings rounded out the simple but inviting fare. A local guitarist provided an additional splash of Key West color. Two female bartenders helped insure the success of the event as they joked and cavorted in skimpy *Playboy Bunny*-like outfits with powder-puff tails. A blazing Key West sunset of yellows and purples and reds against the contrasting blues of an open sky and a calm sea embellished an already enjoyable occasion. Virtually all *Casa* resident guests joined the usual Beach Club day group, including Tennessee Williams, for the festive event.

It was at this gathering that Tennessee Williams invited Joe and Dan to his home for dinner the following evening. Both men were elated with the invitation. Joe Poole hoped that maybe, just maybe, this would be a step in the right direction to meeting people that could help him get ahead in life. Dan Brown, young and impressionable, was smitten with the idea of having dinner at the home of so famous a personage as the writer, Tennessee Williams.

"Yes, fellows, I want you to be at my place around six thirty tomorrow night. Saturday is our night for conch fritters and Key lime pie. One of the lady guests here tonight told me about a new salad I want to try on you. She calls it 'Garbage Salad'. It got its name because you can put anything and everything in it. Basically, it's a green salad made ideally with three types of lettuce, slices of Vidalia onions - she said they had to be *Vidalia*, whatever or wherever that is - bell pepper, celery, cukes, shredded dried beef, ripe plum tomatoes, and topped with Planters peanuts instead of croutons. Any dressing can be used. Along with the conch, my roommate will prepare a delectable vegetable of some sort, maybe asparagus covered in Monterey Jack. It will be simple fare but delicious, I assure you. Dan, perhaps you can finish up your *Hawaii* briefings over drinks before dinner. See you then." The bearded author turned away with local friends. Joe Poole winked at Dan as though a remarkable event had just occurred. Dan nodded and acknowledged with a wide smile. After a while, he returned to his room exhilarated. 'A great way to end my time in purgatory. Tonight, great food, great entertainment, great conversation. Tomorrow night, an invite to dine with Key West's most famous citizen since Hemingway.'

The next evening the two men rendezvoused at the Casa bar to walk together to Williams' home. Joe Poole was wearing his casual best: off-white trousers with a red belt, white bucks, topped by a baby blue open necked Billy Eckstein shirt. Dan was dressed simply in a yellow golf shirt, Navy-blue slacks and loafers.

The two men walked the five or six blocks to the given address. It was a typical wooden Key West house with overgrown shrubbery engulfing the front and side yards. As they started up the sandy walkway, loud, hostile voices emanated from within the home. A heated argument was taking place inside. Then, unexpectedly, Tennessee Williams came storming out of the house, slamming the screen door behind him. He turned toward the newly arrived guests, his face bulging in anger. He placed both hands on his hips and stood there as if searching for words. For a moment, a long moment, an eerie stillness enveloped the three men. Finally, the exasperated host announced loudly to the two visitors and to anyone in hearing range, "I'VE BEEN MARRIED TO THAT BOY FOR TEN YEARS. THIS IS HOW HE TREATS ME. HE SAYS THAT HE'S NOT PREPARING DINNER FOR ME OR ANYBODY ELSE TONIGHT!" A slight pause, then "DAMNIT!" Regaining composure, in a quieter voice, he added, "I guess you fellows better leave now and let me try to straighten this mess out. I'll try to make it to Beach Club tomorrow." (He didn't).

As they walked away, both men looked at each other in astonished incredulity. The tightness of Joe's face signaled his visible disappointment. He was the first to speak. "What do you make of those apples, Mr. Jetjock?"

Dan, also disillusioned, looked at his friend. "So, now we know. Those rumors about our famous friend weren't rumors at all." Shrugging, he suddenly felt philosophical. "May I paraphrase ever so slightly a famous, succinct saying by an anonymous but very learned man?"

He looked back at the Williams' house. Peace and quiet prevailed along the sandy, unpaved street. Dan noted Joe's impatience as he opined, "There ain't no free supper!"

*****

Chapter 17

THE *"SHANG"* AND THE *"WASP"*

Date: December, 1960
Age: 25

The Landing Signal Officer looked at the three pilots before him. His tone and demeanor reflected something out of the ordinary. "O.K. guys, normally I would be leading you out to the carrier but there are only three *Demons* up and ready to go. So you'll fly out to the USS SHANGRI-LA, hull number 38, with your senior guy leading. Who is that?"
LT Dan Brown raised his hand. "Me."
LSO: "All right, LT Brown is flight leader. You're to take off in one hour, 4 o'clock. The *Shang* is somewhere off the coast between Jacksonville and Brunswick about 100 miles out. After Departure Control turns you lose, tune in the ship and head straight for it. They want to suspend flight ops by 5. Today, you'll just be taken aboard. Tomorrow you'll get ten day traps and if all goes well, six more landings at night. Then you will be completely qualified in the F3H. When you depart the *Shang*, report here to your squadron – you will have completed VF-101 RAG training. All three of you looked real good out there today in field practice and I know you'll do a good job at the ship. The ship's LSO is a friend of mine and he's ready for you. He'll wave you just like we've practiced these last few weeks."

Dan, along with Jim Powell and Buzz Settles, headed for Base Operations to file flight plans to CVA[1]-38, at-sea. At precisely 1600 hours[2], three *Demons* rolled down the runway at NAS Cecil Field, Florida. Once joined up, Dan turned port to a heading of 055 and tuned in channel 101 on the TACAN[3]. The needle immediately locked on, bearing 058, DME 84 miles. Climbing through FL 180[4], Jacksonville Air

---

[1] Designation for large, attack aircraft carriers
[2] 4 pm
[3] Tactical Air Navigation equip/DME=Distance measuring equip
[4] 18,000 feet

Traffic Control gave the flight permission to switch to the ship's frequency. Dan confirmed switching over, "Roger Jax, going 341.3." After dialing in the frequency, Dan listened for two sets of two clicks. He heard one, then the other and knew Jim and Buzz were up on frequency; each had clicked their mikes in turn.

Dan: "Big Man, this is Camelot 101, flight of three jets, climbing through FL 210 for 250. I have you 058 degrees at 75 miles."

Ship: "Roger 101, continue Big Man, I'm working on an approach time for you. Be advised our radar is inoperative right now and our TACAN and UHF communications have been spotty. This is a shakedown cruise for us – lots of work on equipment going on, so it's on and off at times. Getting you guys some landings was an unexpected added requirement. The weather is good, so if we lose communications, just keep coming present heading even if our TACAN goes out. Don't dump any gas until we get you an approach time."

101: "Roger that." At thirty-five miles the wake of the ship could be seen. Dan radioed: "Big Man, we have you in sight. We need to start down."

Ship: "Roger, 101. We just got the word. The Captain wants you on board ASAP. Your signal BUSTER[1]. Our radar still out so your IFR[2] flight plan is cancelled – go Visual flight rules for let down and landing. Switch to tower 323.6."

The three pilots switched over as Dan led them in a shallow dive planning to arrive at the ship at 1500 feet. "Big Man tower, Camelot 101, flight of 3, have you visual, descending through 15,000 feet. Are we cleared to dump fuel to landing weight?"

Ship: "Affirmative. What's your position?"

101: "Fifteen miles out, descending through 10,000 feet. We'll come along side the island at 1500 feet for break."

During the descent, Dan remembered the not-so-humorous stories about planes landing on wrong ships and so he

---

[1] Max power and speed, appropriate to situation
[2] Instrument flight rules

planned his descent to be directly over the ship at five thousand feet so he could look down at the carrier's deck for visual confirmation of hull number 38. Overhead, he found he could not see the vertical numbers on the ship's tall island structure so he zeroed in on the flight deck numerals. The sun was glinting so brightly on the first number it wasn't distinguishable but the second number was 8. 'Gotta be it' and he continued to let down, complimenting himself on remembering to check one of the cardinal rules of naval aviation: *Never land on the wrong carrier.*[1]

Leaving 5000 feet, communications with the ship was lost. Dan advised his flight: "OK guys, they warned us about the intermittent communications so we'll just keep it coming. Check maximum landing weight." Approaching from behind the carrier, the young first tour pilot leader made his mistake. Instead of looking left at the deck or the island (which would have had the ships numbers in large white painted numerals), he checked right to make sure Jim and Buzz were in tight formation. This leader wanted his group – his first group – to look sharp. Just forward of the ship he broke left for downwind, followed in twenty seconds intervals by 103 and 108.

The landing checklist absorbed his attention downwind. Abeam, Dan radioed: "101 abeam, gear down, hook down, 4.2[2]." Only after he had made the call did he look at the flight deck. Guys were playing volleyball!

A moment of complete confusion before 108 called: "This isn't the *Shang* – this boat's number is 18!"

Dan looked at the island where a large number 18 stared back at him. While vile expletives were being spewed into his oxygen mask, wave-off flares were shot into the air from someone manning the carrier's LSO platform.

Three *Demons* raised landing gear and flaps and added power to climb. Dan was still in the lead and turned to heading 058. It came as no surprise when climbing through

---

[1] It's tradition to paint errant aircraft with loud, obnoxious insults, designs, etc. The squadron skipper back on the home ship does not take kindly to such carelessness on part of the pilot concerned.

[2] Fuel state in thousands of pounds

5000 feet, communications with Big Man were reestablished (see note at end of chapter).

Ship: "101, what's your posit? You reported overhead, descending but no other reports. We have helicopters in the air looking for you. What happened?"

101: "Big Man, we followed TACAN channel 101 to another carrier. We are inbound heading northeast and should see your wake soon." Buzz in 108 interjected, "I see it ahead about 35-40 miles."

101: "Big Man, we believe we have you in sight. We dumped down to landing weight when we made our approaches to land on USS BOAT 18 so we won't have much extra gas on arrival. Is the deck ready?"

Ship: "101, the deck has been ready for 15 minutes. The Captain is not a happy man."

Dan responded almost inaudibly "Roger." And he was thinking, 'I'm not a happy camper either. My first time to lead a flight of jets in the fleet and I try to land in the middle of a volleyball game. Damn.'

The three jets trapped aboard. As the young aviators descended steel ladders towards the designated ready room, they heard the ship's loudspeaker system come alive. "This is the Captain speaking. We have enlightening news from LT Brown of VF-14. He tells us the USS Wasp is traversing the area."

Later info indicated the USS WASP was returning to home base Newport, Rhode Island, from the Caribbean. Only a finite number of TACAN channels are available to the military. The WASP was usually far enough north and the SHANGRILA normally down south so the same channel could be shared without interference. This co-usage was based on the theory the big ships would not operate in same waters at same time. What's that old saying? If something can go wrong, it will go wrong. And it did for our unlucky new flight leader. Communications was lost with CVA 38 descending through 5000 feet when the three aircraft went below line of sight parameters. Communications was reestablished climbing back up through 5000 feet attaining required parameters.

*****

Chapter 18

ONE MOVIE, ONE NIGHT

April, 1961
Age: 25

AT SEA! Magic words for LT Daniell Brown. After almost
five years of administrative assignments, he was finally in an
operational squadron aboard an aircraft carrier. Three
months earlier, FIGHTER SQUADRON FOURTEEN
(VF-14) deployed to the Mediterranean Sea aboard USS
FRANKLIN D. ROOSEVELT (CVA-42). The older, mid-
sized carrier departed Mayport Naval Station, Florida, and
relieved their Sixth Fleet predecessor, USS
INDEPENDENCE (CVA-62) two weeks later. Fully
operational, the ship carried about eighty planes and
approximately four thousand men. VF-14's contribution to
the ship's force consisted of twelve planes, eighteen pilots,
two aviation ground officers, two civilian representatives
(one each from McDonald Aircraft Corporation and Allison
Engine Company), and one hundred five enlisted personnel.
The squadron was fully trained and ready for war. There
were no armed hostilities requiring air support in the
summer of '61 but that was beside the point for the military
men involved. United States foreign policy dictated a show
of force around the world at all times. Should hostilities
break out, U.S. Naval power could usually be deployed to a
given theater quickly. Today, we still believe in and adhere
to that policy: a presence of air power can and does deter
wars.

The United States and Russia were in no way friends, each
watchful, cautious, and suspicious of the other. The *Cold
War* as we usually remember it was in its infancy. To some,
the first two years of the '60s gave that term a jumpstart and
before the decade ended, *Cold War* would come to exemplify
the deadly race for world dominance between the two super
powers.

The officers and men of VF-14, in their minds, were ready. The *Tophatters* as a unit, prior to deployment, had pulled a *coup* among East Coast fighter squadrons. In sports lingo that would become popular in later years, the squadron had accomplished a *double-double*. They had won both the coveted "E" for Battle Efficiency, Atlantic Fleet, and the Naval Aviation Safety Center's prestigious Safety Award, simultaneously and consecutively for fiscal years1958 and 1959. The *Tophatters* faced an opportunity to go for a *threepeat.*[1] Like their 1930's namesake who became famous for wearing tuxedo and top hat at the slightest hint of a party or gathering, today's *Tophatters* were not bashful about their squadron's past achievements. Adding fuel to their claims as the #1 fighter squadron in the Navy, VF-14 came armed with a recent letter from official Navy sources in Washington affirming that the *Tophatters* were indeed the oldest continuously active aviation squadron in the fleet. If fault could be found in this award-winning unit, perhaps an air of superiority among squadron pilots vexed other aviators serving aboard ROOSEVELT.

Three months before, on the last day of transit across the Atlantic, Commander Ken Newsome, the squadron's commanding officer, addressed an All Officers/All Chiefs Meeting. "Men, the Admiral wants all commanding officers to reiterate the importance of our mission in the Med. This simply stated is, we are a deterrent to Communist aggression. We are the frontline peacekeepers for any skirmish that breaks out on this side of the world regardless of who is fighting whom. In any crisis in Europe or the Mediterranean area, ROOSEVELT is the quick-reaction key. VF-14 is to protect the ship and its task force from harm in the air. Chiefs, your job to keep the planes up and flying and you must keep your men informed on all levels. You pilots know the game. We'll fly sortie after sortie where nothing happens. Then BINGO! An unidentified fighter or bomber will show up to challenge our resolve.

---

[1] And they did! VF-14 remains the only aviation squadron in Naval Aviation history to _simultaneously and consecutively_ win the Battle E and the Safety Award three years running (1959-60-61).

You have all proven you can fly and land the *Demon* under the most adverse situations. We've all fired our practice missiles. We rang up near perfect scores in the Operational Readiness Inspection with COMMANDER-IN-CHIEF, ATLANTIC FLEET. This squadron is a finely tuned machine. Every man in this unit knows we've won the Navy's two highest awards for the last two years running. And each and every man knows we're working for an unprecedented third "E" and at the same time, a third Safety Award. Washington-based historians have certified VF-14 to be the oldest Navy squadron. All that tradition is fine and good but not the most important thing we should be thinking about. We want to take that tradition a step further and prove to one and all that today's *Tophatters* are the best and safest squadron in naval history. First, let's prove it to the other squadrons and divisions on this ship. In doing so we'll again prove it to the Safety Center and COMNAVAIRLANT[1]. Protecting this ship and proving to be the best fighter squadron <u>ever</u> are our first priorities." CDR Newsome paused for a moment to look over his notes, then began again. "As both commissioned and non-commissioned officers, we are challenged with more than flying and fixing airplanes. We can't just fly planes better, we can't just repair planes quicker. How about those words, *duty, honor, integrity*? We must show proper judgment in all situations, whether the circumstances are good, bad, or indifferent. We must practice moderation when ashore, not only in consumption of adult beverages but also in lifestyle. Many commanding officers preach *responsibility*. I guess I go for slightly different wording. I like the word *maturity*. Maturity includes responsibility, but also encompasses intelligent decisions, and connotes perceptive judgment. Maturity carries over into our private lives, i.e., family values among married men. As for you single guys, we know you're going to be looking at the girls but we also expect you to treat them as ladies. Maturity means that we know when, where, and how much to drink. It dictates our conduct among foreign nationals. Remember, it's their country we're visiting. It's their women our young bucks

---

[1] COMMANDER, NAVAL AIR FORCES, ATLANTIC FLEET

will be chasing. I don't know of any awards given out for some of these moral categories, but maturity tallies up in my book. I'm counting on all you guys, officers and enlisted, to meet the challenges that will face us on this long seven-month deployment. Dismissed."

VF-14 was the only fighter squadron aboard ROOSEVELT. The big, lumbering McDonald F3H[1] *Demon* was not the pilot's weapon of choice. Single piloted, single engine, the aircraft's original design specifications called for a much more powerful engine to be installed but a factory fire had set that program back dramatically so that other engines had to be considered. A substitute power plant was found in the Allison J-71 turbo-jet but delivered far fewer pounds of thrust. The *Demon,* as such, was simply too slow for its mission in 1960. Saving grace was provided in the form of wonderful missiles slung beneath each wing. The *Sparrow,* a new first-generation air-to-air missile, salvaged the *Demon's* mission and potentially the Sixth Fleet's hind side while the more advanced dual engine, dual-seated F-4H *Phantom,* the Navy's workhorse-to-be for the next decade, completed development trials. While the F3H was sadly underpowered, the new *Sparrow* gave the McDonald-built airplane unique firepower capability: head-on attack. *Demons* could launch from the carrier, pick up its target and shoot the missile at an enemy plane ten to twelve miles away even while climbing out. With the F3H as the main line fighter, defense of the fleet was deemed to be adequate by Pentagon thinkers. Perhaps it was, at least minimally. Hindsight shows the *Demon* did fill the gap until the F4 was fleet-ready.

Three months into the cruise, life had settled into a routine. Fly the planes, fix the planes. "Chow hall" food three times a day, sometimes four if flying late, was predictable but

---

[1] Again, for clarification, the designation was changed to F3B by Defense Secretary Robert McNamara in 1962.

plentiful. Nightly movies in the ready room were sometimes shown three and four times before new ones could be swapped with other ships in the task force or bummed off passing tankers or supply ships. By this time, mid-point in the deployment, everyone on the ship had learned to sleep through the thunderous roar of jets taking off and landing on the deck above.

VF-14 had departed the states with few men and a lot of *boys*, some proficient at their tasks, but the majority largely inexperienced in shipboard operations. Many aviators as well as the men who worked on the planes were first-timers. During the past ninety days all had grown through metamorphosis into a worldly-wise cadre personifying the American fighting man. Or, had they? Well, maybe yes, maybe no. Because one movie, one night, wreaked havoc with the hardened John Wayne image so revered by hotshot fighter pilots and tour hardened sailors.

Night flying had been cancelled earlier due to deteriorating weather conditions. The C.O. called for a short AOM (All Officers Meeting) and then film reels were loaded for the evening flick. Seventeen of the eighteen pilots were in attendance for the showing. One, LTJG Peter Driscoll was still debriefing in Air Intelligence following the last hop of the day before night ops were scrubbed.

The movie began. Enthusiasm was high over the advent of a new film just received that afternoon from a supply ship. *ALL MINE TO GIVE,* starring Glynis Johns and Cameron Mitchell, was the story of a large Scottish family settling in America. Seven children and their parents tackled the Wisconsin wilderness, circa early 1900's. When both parents die, the oldest, a boy perhaps fourteen or fifteen, and next older, a girl, tried their best to keep the children together as a family unit. Eventually they were forced to face reality: it was wintertime and they were homeless without means of support. A plan to find a family who would take all seven orphans or even a family who would take the five younger kids met with the same predictable result. No one wanted five, six, or seven mouths to feed. Hungry, cold, disillusioned, the older siblings took the only avenue available to them. As the movie ends, the eldest boy is seen giving away a child at a time to various couples and families in the township and surrounding area. Finally, all the kids are given away. The boy, grown up by necessity and changed through the tragic sequence of events, also finds security with a rugged family needing help with their farm.

LT Dan Brown surreptitiously wiped a tear from his eyes with his sleeve and hoped the credits would roll for a few more minutes before the lights came up. He wanted no part of the verbal abuse that would follow for weeks if the other pilots and officers knew he shed tears over a mushy movie.

Movie credits were still on screen when overhead lights illuminated the room. LTJG Pete Driscoll entered from a rear passageway.

No one moved, all officers remained rooted to their chairs. Some continued to look directly ahead, others appeared to be studying notes, clipboards, anything that might be in their laps. Not a word was spoken for perhaps a minute, a long time under the circumstances. It was one of the quietest moments Dan had ever experienced. Finally, fairly composed, he felt sufficiently confident to glance around. An unexpected sight awaited his eyes. A room full of professional aviators fully trained in the art of war, ready to take on the Soviet empire, pilots eager to engage and fight deadly Russian MIGS[1], men experienced in leadership at management levels, *all* sat silent, eyes tearful and watery.

All except, of course, LTJG Driscoll who had entered late as the movie ended. The young pilot was known for a favorite saying which he offered anytime a situation did not meet his personal approval and concurrence. Unfortunately, that articulated thought involved regurgitation. The quasi-derogatory comment that he loved to use had on occasion

---

[1] Russian jet fighters

prompted CDR Newsome to point out to the young South Carolinian that sometimes he was dangerously close to crossing the line of disrespect. On this memorable evening, the cocksure young jet jockey had been spared the gut-wrenching movie. He was hardly prepared for the maudlin scene before him. His surprised gaze surveyed the room. Initially astonished, then disgusted to find tour-hardened seniors and war-ready contemporaries so moved by a simple movie, he blurted out: "Skipper, we gotta paint out the *Tophat* insignia on the planes. We should have wet, snotty handkerchiefs as new logo!" And then he added as every *Tophatter* could have predicted: *"Where do you go to puke?"*

*****

My roomie was one terrific guy. He died oh-so-young, at age 52, of cancer.

Chapter 19

THE AWARDS CEREMONY

May, 1961
Age: 25

"LT Brown, front and center."

The day had begun as most days aboard ship while
anchored offshore to a liberty port. After breakfast, Dan
Brown had dropped by the ready room to check messages
that might pertain to his area of responsibility, squadron
training. Few officers were in attendance at the normally
busy hour, perhaps not unusual in light of their port-of-call.
Cannes was a highpoint of any Mediterranean deployment.
The nightlife was superb, the food exquisite, the scenery
unforgettable, the prices affordable, not to factor in other
unmentionables that makes France so attractive to red-
blooded and virile sailors. Most officers and crew returned
well after midnight, many catching the last shuttlecraft at
0400.
On the blackboard, someone, presumably the squadron
Commanding Officer or Executive Officer, had written:
ALL OFFICERS MEETING TONIGHT AT 2000 hours.
AWARDS CEREMONY.

There was nothing out of the ordinary about an all officers
meeting at 8 p.m. Since the ship was getting underway in
the afternoon, all hands would be back aboard. The pilots
would be briefed on the next at-sea assignments: pertinent
information about the general area in which the ship would
be operating, divert fields available, anticipated weather,
rules of engagement. A myriad of other details would be
briefed and reviewed. The awards presentation was
something different and would be a diversion from the
ordinary.

After reading through the message traffic, Dan retired to his
room to work on enlisted evaluations. Several officers
would be going ashore for one last shopping trip but Dan

was satisfied to get his work done and then go out on the flight deck for a last look at the beautiful French city. The harbor, the boats, the street scenes, the artists and their canvases, all made for memorable viewing. The large ship had dropped anchor in the harbor five days earlier. Dan along with hundreds of other shipboard residents had gotten up early that morning to catch the first glimpse of land. Cannes was his first sight of the French Riviera. The beauty of the harbor, the boats at rest, the green hills behind, all enhanced by the morning haze, flooded his senses. It was a sight he wanted to always remember. Now on the day of departure, he took one last, long look at the colorful and charming expanse. The virginal expectation was gone but the scenery was still just as magnificent. Other ports of call would not be recalled quite so positively.

The officers assembled as directed. Each officer sat in assigned seating by rank. Number six in seniority; Dan was the first officer in the second row of seats. After a few brief announcements, CDR Ken Newsome enunciated the order above.
Dan, stunned, rose and stepped forward to the podium.

"LT Brown, turn and face the squadron officers while I read the citation as recorded in this award. Stand at parade rest." With no idea of what was about to happen, the surprised officer dutifully about-faced and relaxed his posture to assume the more comfortable stance.

"From: Commanding Officer, FIGHTER SQUADRON FOURTEEN (VF-14)

To: Lieutenant Daniell Maurice Brown, U.S. Navy

Subj: Life Saving Medal with embellishments

It is with great pleasure, pride, and honor I award you the VF-14 LIFE SAVING MEDAL. Inspired by Ensign Pulver in the famous movie, "Mr. Roberts," conceived by your roommate, LTJG Peter Driscoll, the award was commissioned, designed, and created late last night for this special ceremony. You are the initial and sole recipient of this prestigious if somewhat dubious award. To earn or qualify for this honor, you must have demonstrated bravery in the face of inescapable fear and your action or actions must have resulted in a life saved. In the late evening of July 14th, 1961, you so acted and indeed a human life was spared.

Saving a life is a worthy and tremendous accomplishment. In Chinese philosophy, once you have saved a person's life, you are subsequently responsible for their well being in this existence. That ancient abstract tradition is certainly germane in this case. It might be well to ascertain at this point that the life you saved was your own. It follows, in the Oriental tradition; you are now responsible for yourself.

The following facts are pertinent. On the night above you were seen in the company of a beautiful woman named "B.J." Calle at the '*Chez Francoise Bar*' in downtown Cannes, France. The bartender has confirmed that you purchased for her, and she consumed, four or five daiquiri cocktails. Simultaneously, you too, were imbibing a like number of intoxicants. You and Ms. Calle were observed in hushed and whispered conversation in a darkened booth. Soon the two of you were seen leaving the lounge area. Ostensibly, each of you appeared headed to the relevant restroom. First you, and then she disappeared and were unseen for about twenty minutes when you returned together from somewhere outside the establishment. Fortunately, the lady must have mentioned in that time that she was married and her husband would be joining her shortly. Almost immediately you departed for fleet landing where you caught the first liberty boat returning to USS FRANKLIN D. ROOSEVELT (CVA-42).

Following your hasty retreat, three of your fellow squadron officers present at *Chez Francoise* at the time, established that the gentleman in question is a champion middle-heavyweight boxer of some renown in this region. Other patrons of *Chez Francoise* offered information that Ms.

Calle's husband is the jealous type and has quite the temper. It seems he is quick with his fists when angered.

Considering this wealth of information, it appears that your clear thinking and quick action was the appropriate avenue for a man not versed in the pugilistic arts and weighing only one hundred fifty-six pounds. Shakespeare is quoted: "The better part of valor is discretion." Your acumen and tact in pursuing a timely departure give credence to that maxim. Others feel Tertullian may be more apropos in this instance. Roughly paraphrased, he opined, "He who runs away will live to see another day." Your presence here tonight proves truth in that old adage.

As we applaud your perceptive ingenuity, questions remain concerning the young woman involved. I am advised the lady's name is Ms. Michelle Maria Arnesto Calle. The ambiguity concerns the origin of her nickname, "B.J.". However, I have no reason to believe that you can cast any new insight into this seeming disparity. Perhaps the subject is best forgotten.

Again, LT Brown, you are to be congratulated on this achievement and award.

Signed: Kenneth L. Newsome, Commander, USN"

"Dan, I will now pin the award to your uniform. As you can see, the crest is a logo of the *Chez Francoise Club* with the initial "L" for life saving embossed in the center. A small, gold "V" for valor has been stamped on the lower right corner of the medal. Wear it in good health."

Applause and laughter filled the readyroom. Clapping squadron mates called out "Speech. 'B.J.' Speech! Speech! We want 'B.J.' Tell us about 'B.J.'"

CDR Newsome, evidently happy with the charade just pulled on his popular Training Officer, looked out over his happy campers. Over the roar and din, the skipper said simply, "Dismissed."

The ambushed recipient of the unexpected award was left standing alone in front of his contemporaries. Embarrassed to a degree known only to himself, he managed to smile sheepishly as he looked down at the obnoxious cardboard crest pinned on his chest.

Shaking his head, the "hero" of the moment declined to offer further information on the lady known as "B.J.".[1] Reiterating a line from his citation: "My lips are sealed. Truly, discretion is the better part of valor."

*****

Here, the author must take the 5th. See footnote.

---

[1] Decorum permits no discussion of Ms. Calle's nickname. Suffice it to say that she and Monica Lewinski might be soul sisters.

Chapter 20

AN EXPERIMENT IN INTERNATIONAL LIVING

June, 1961
Age: 25

Aboard USS FRANKLIN D. ROOSEVELT (CVA-42),
somewhere in Mediterranean Sea:

"Now hear this. Now hear this. Standby for CARDIV 6."
The Boatswain mate's voice boomed over the ship's
loudspeakers. A moment of silence followed as all hands on
the mammoth carrier waited for the Carrier Division
Commander to begin speaking.
"Good morning, men of ROOSEVELT. This is Admiral
Jackson. I want to talk to you about a program, an
opportunity that I strongly support and believe in. Our job
over here in the Med is peacekeeping – we practice war
games but our real mission is to keep the peace. I believe one
way of doing that is to get to know our neighbors better.
There is an organization, *Experiment in International Living,*
that promotes such a premise. It's usually for college
students to spend a quarter or semester as exchange students
in a foreign country while a student of that country swaps
out to his or her counterpart's native land. The young
people get to see first hand that others around the world just
want to live and let live. They get to see and enjoy different
sights, sounds, foods, language, traditions, clothes, etc. but
that smiles are contagious in whatever village, town, city, or
country a person might be. Now, I cannot spare any of you
as exchange college students but I have convinced the folks
at *Experiment in International Living* to try a pilot program for
2-weeks visits. All unmarried men, officers and enlisted may
apply for the program. All you pay is a $10.00 registration
fee plus the cost of transportation from Naples, Italy, to your
destination city. We'll be dropping anchor in Naples harbor
on June 2nd so we have about a month to clear all paperwork
for your visits. I hope you will want to participate. We will
accept ten enlisted and two officers. See LT Jerry Whitaker
in the library tonight after the evening meals. That is all."

The twelve selectees were flown into Capodichino Airport in Naples on June 1st. All ten sailors had picked destinations in Italy, ostensibly to take advantage of cheaper train fares. Ensign Tom Pollock of the ship's Navigation Division had chosen Paris for his two-week stay. His Air France plane would be taking off around noon.

Ten a.m. now, LT Dan Brown of FIGHTER SQUADRON FOURTEEN was on board *SAS*[1] Flight 212: destination Stockholm. The mid-sized passenger plane began to taxi and a new adventure was in the making.
The uneventful flight landed in Stockholm shortly after noon. Dan, in uniform, was easily picked out of the crowd and met by his host, Mr. Pierre Westerman. It became quickly evident that he spoke very little English; Dan spoke no Swedish, of course. Mr. Westerman, who soon became "Pierre", drove the duo to his club for lunch. They were in Sweden but the menu was Greek to Dan, so Pierre ordered for both. Over a delicious lunch in opulent surroundings, the two strangers communicated through the universal language of pointing and hand signals mixed with two, sometimes three fractured languages (Pierre also spoke French – wasn't much help to Dan who spoke as much French as Swedish!). The initial information sent by *Experiment* headquarters had briefed Dan that Pierre Westerman was about thirty-five, a music professor at the University of Stockholm. His wife, Bitte, 32, had participated in the exchange program a few years previously as a student at Penn State. She would be the primary interpreter. They had two children, a boy about five, and a daughter approximately three.

Bitte welcomed them at the door. Her English was rusty but adequate and she looked forward to two weeks of intense practice with their guest. From Bitte, Dan learned that Pierre's work encompassed much more than that of a music teacher. He had formed his own band, more like a combo, in which he did not play an instrument but managed and

---

[1] SAS = Scandinavian Airways System

booked the group into clubs and events. With the trio, he had just produced an exercise record for pregnant women, sort of an idea before it's time in Europe in 1971. Even so, while not breaking any sales charts, the 45-rpm record was available and selling in several music shops and some department stores. And Pierre had a third mission in life, his real dream of how to hit it big. He occasionally took trips to Lapland hoping to find a Swedish Elvis Presley. Dan's ears perked at the next bit of info. The band used two female singers. Bitte showed Dan pictures of both young women. Inger Soval and Anika Morse were equally beautiful, and according to Bitte, very talented. It seemed Anika had a steady guy but Inger was currently without a beau. She had just cut a double-sided record which she and Pierre hoped would bring volume sales. And Bitte added, Inger speaks some English whereas Anika did not. Plainly, that sealed the deal. Inger made the cut.

Over the course of thirteen days, Dan was adopted into the Westerman family. Meals were shared, sightseeing trips enjoyed, conversations over vodka and tonic interesting and scintillating. Time with Inger did not pan out as often as Dan wanted but they did manage a few dates. Her English sufficed nicely along with the few Swedish words Dan had quickly memorized.

Pierre Westerman was a most interesting and fascinating read. The illegitimate son of a Swedish woman and an Italian sailor, he had been adopted by a medium income, middle class family. In college he met a young girl whose father was the country's one and only Tetley Tea broker. Somehow, someway, two young people from different ends of the financial spectrum managed to fall in love and marry. Dan surmised that this was probably the reason for Pierre's dedication to working three jobs. Later in the week, Dan was invited for lunch at Bitte's family home – a very upscale home in very classy neighborhood. Pierre was not able to attend – he was working.

One evening over snapps, Pierre told Dan (through Bitte's interpreting) of the night he delivered their first child. They were invited to a big gala Christmas Party. Bitte was very pregnant but not experiencing labor pains. At the party, Pierre enjoyed several cocktails and then - Bitte began having the telltale intermittent contractions. Sobering quickly, he drove her to the hospital. The nurse, quite young and perhaps inexperienced or untrained in obstetrics, got them a room and called for the doctor. Almost immediately, Bitte's labors subsided and she wanted to sit up rather than lie down. There was only one chair in the room, so Pierre, a little giddy and unsteady anyway, happily traded places with her. She got the chair, he lay across the bed. Shortly, the doctor walked in. He took one look at Bitte sitting, Pierre lying on the bed, and sternly chided the nurse for calling him away from his rounds. Shortly after both the physician and the nurse left the room, Bitte's water broke. Pierre delivered his own baby boy before the situation could be straightened out with hospital staff. His words: "Talking seerius -I sober queeck!"

Towards the end of the second week, Pierre planned a family outing with Dan and Inger along, to visit his parents. Mr. and Mrs. Westerman lived about 2 hours away near a small village in the archipelago that lined the Swedish coasts. The numerous islands afforded an opportunity to see breathtaking, rustic, untamed natural beauty that Dan had seen previously only in National Geographic or Scandinavian travelogues.

The senior Westerman's had a smorgasbord buffet waiting. Meats and cheeses and veggies and breads along with milk and hot tea adorned a large rectangular table. A second table was laden with four or five scrumptious looking desserts. After introductions, the informal feast began. The young American realized this was the closest thing to an American meal he had seen since arrival and he really appreciated their serving food he was familiar with. Bitte had tried to cater their meals to dishes the young Southerner might enjoy, at the same time introducing him to Swedish cuisine. He had seen unfamiliar foods and dishes in restaurants that he would not have liked. Smoked salmon seemed to be a favorite in this part of the world but it was a food, like liver, that grew in his mouth. The guest of honor

selected a few of the delicious, yet familiar looking dishes
before him. This simple meal out here in the land of a
thousand islands would be just fine. Sitting, he prepared a
traditional sandwich of bologna, cheese, lettuce and tomato.
The first bite of bologna was strong but the cheese and
mayo-like spread covered most of the after-taste. He sipped
some hot tea after adding a sugar cube.

Soon Mr. Westerman senior joined the group at table and
sat across from Dan. In very broken English, he smiled and
spoke.
"Lootenaunt Broown, Ve are sirprize at ze meat on yer
plate. Ve heere Americans no eat harsemeat."

Horsemeat not withstanding, the two week stay in Sweden
would always be a top-ten memory for the young pilot. On
the guest's last day of his brief visit, Pierre broke a set of
1848 Sea Captain's pistols his father had given him and
presented one to Dan as a bond between two friends. Bitte's
gift was an impressionist painting she had rendered of the
Westerman family's waterfront property in the archipelago.
The gun and the painting still grace the walls of the Brown's
den. Dan promised himself that he would return one day.

*****

*And he did. In 1974, Dan and Becky Brown visited Bitte and
Pierre in Stockholm.*

Chapter 21

THE RIGHT STUFF

February 20, 1962
Age: 26

Two single-seat, single-engine jet aircraft awaited clearance
for takeoff on runway 27R at NAS Cecil Field, Florida:
leader LT Dan Brown in Tophatter 111, wingman LT Buzz
Settles in 108. To the casual observer, the flight of two
fighters appeared to be a routine training flight, one of many
departing the master jet base, scheduled to return home a
few hours later. The pilots manning the pair of F3H *Demons*
in question would have differed with that conventional view.
In their minds, this was not ordinary stuff – *they were on a
mission!*

That is not to say the morning had begun in other than a
normal manner. Pilots Brown and Settles arrived a few
minutes earlier than the rest of the squadron since they were
assigned first flight of the day. The two aviators suited up
and were briefing routes and navigational checkpoints for a
coastal surveillance hop when other squadron officers and
men began arriving for morning muster. The newcomers
interrupted the briefing underway in the ready room with
news of a late breaking bulletin heard over their auto radios
while driving to work.

The high profile announcement would alter in radical
fashion the day's course of events for Dan Brown and Buzz
Settles. Dan listened intently as more officers arrived and
confirmed previous reports off the national news wire. He
smiled at Buzz who was already grinning and nodding
agreement with his flight leader. They traded comments
while simultaneously reaching for maps of central Florida.
"Let's go!" "Do it!" Both pilots saw a rare opportunity that
should not be denied. Shortly, FIGHTER SQUADRON
FOURTEEN's Flight Schedule for February 20, 1962 was
modified. "Flight #1, Brown/Settles, navigation practice,
western Florida coastal" was scrubbed. The new write-in

change showed the same pilots but designated the flight "1A, new mission: practice intercepts". The modified scenario would call for one plane to be designated *friendly*, the other *bogey*, then to switch after an hour so that both pilots could practice radar acquisition of airborne targets, tracking and intercepts. The point of the change in mission was that air-to-air interceptor work would more conveniently lend itself to the real quest now on the minds of the two fliers involved. Perhaps the subtlety in changing the schedule was thinly veiled, but the squadron duty officer's signature made the sortie legal in all respects. Conforming to Naval Regulations was always important when dealing with news events of potential national import. Today's *biggie* was stuff that would make *world* headlines. Hopefully, the two pilots would get there in time to see it happen. That possibility appeared more likely when a late broadcast fixed a new time *zero* of 0905 local time. With luck, that should give them just enough window to make it.

The two jets lifted off the runway and climbed out into the sunny stillness of the morning. At 500 feet above terrain, 108 moved into close formation on the right wing of the leader. Dan simultaneously gave a head signal for 'left turn', moved his stick to port and continued climbing. They were proceeding to restricted area 2907 south of Jacksonville. Only approved flights were authorized inside the imaginary lines that defined the parameters of a large box-like operating area. Military aircraft could maneuver in combat scenarios without worry of conflicting with other civil or military air traffic. More to the point of this particular flight, it offered the most direct corridor to an area abeam Cape Canaveral.

NAS Cecil Tower called with instructions: "Tophatter 111, switch now to Navy Jax Approach on 267.8."
Dan keyed his mike and responded: "Roger tower. Triple Sticks[1] switching to Approach control." Dan tapped his helmet in the vicinity of his right ear and checked to see that Buzz in 108 had heard the transmission. LT Settles gave an

---

[1] Pilot vernacular for "111" – see the correlation to 'sticks'?)

affirming head nod and both pilots switched frequencies. Dan dialed the new settings and heard two quick clicks in his headset indicating that his wingman too was over on the new frequency.

"Navy Jax Approach, this is Tophat Triple Sticks, flight of two *Demons*, climbing VFR through four thousand, proceeding Romeo 2907 from NAS Cecil."

"O.K., 111, this is Navy Jax. Have you in radar contact. Climb to and maintain FL 300 upon entering Navy Jax Restricted Area 2907. You are cleared to operate in 2907 between Flight Levels 250 and 330 for the next two hours. I remind you to remain well clear of Cape Canaveral during this time. All aircraft are prohibited from operating within thirty miles of the Cape until further advised. Switch tactical frequency now."

Dan smiled into the oxygen mask molded against his cheeks. Thirty miles at thirty thousand feet would give a great birds-eye view of the goings on below. As he looked out over the nose of the *Demon*, he saw that visibility, while not 'CAVU[1] to the moon' was sufficiently good for their observing the show about to unfold.
"Roger Approach, Triple Sticks flight will remain well clear. Switching tactical."

On squadron frequency, Dan asked, "Buzz, I heard your clicks. Am I loud and clear?"
The expected reply came immediately. "Yep."
"O.K., let's go to the Cape's Mission Control frequency as briefed, but absolutely no talking. We'll do everything by visual signals. Switch – NOW." Both pilots switched their UHF radio receivers to the pre-briefed ultra-high frequency.

Shortly after tuning into mission control, the eavesdropping duo learned there had been yet another delay and launch was reset for 0920 Eastern. The two fighters leveled off at FL 300 and slowed to conserve fuel. Additional delays, if

---

[1] Aviation abbreviation for 'Clear And Visibility Unrestricted'

announced, could make sufficient gasoline an issue. The next several minutes were spent in mock training exercises as the two planes edged closer to the southern limits of Restricted 2907. Then came disappointing news. Another delay of twenty-five minutes duration was announced which made the new launch time 0945E. Both *Demon* pilots looked closely at their fuel gages and mentally computed remaining time on station before *Bingo*[1] was reached. Fuel flow was becoming a sweat factor.

At 0925E, the flight exited R-2907 and continued on a southeasterly course towards Cape Canaveral. Dan had noted during the abbreviated planning phase that Naval Air Station Sanford was right at thirty miles west of the Cape. Out in open air space, no longer enjoying the confines of a restricted area, the two fighters were operating under visual flight rules. They could see NAS Sanford directly ahead. Dan initiated a left-hand orbit a few miles west of Sanford's long runways. Looking out across eastern Florida, they could see two Air Force fighters, probably T-38 *Talons,* at approximately thirty-two or thirty-three thousand feet. Orbiting Canaveral as safety observers, the T-38 flight was there to insure unauthorized planes did not wander into the temporary prohibited area encompassing airspace above the Cape.

Dan slowed airspeed to 200 knots and signaled for LT Settles to join up in loose formation. Then he turned his nose towards the ocean with 108 abreast, wide on his starboard side. The Cape was due east, directly ahead 090 degrees, forty to fifty miles. Light morning haze hovered over the groundmass of the Cape, presenting a thin smoke-like screen that momentarily caused concern as to visibility. Flying toward the ocean, looking directly into the morning sun could also have presented a visibility problem but for the moment high, thin clouds blanketed the big orange ball. Soon, Florida's white sandy coastline began to break out of the smoky haze allaying any fears that reduced visibility would preclude the eavesdroppers being afforded a good view. Shortly, Dan was able to pick out the Canaveral

---

[1] Code word for minimum fuel required to return safely to field of choice

peninsula. From approximately thirty-five miles, he saw the
Space Center complex roughly fifteen degrees right of
course. Maneuvering smoothly and purposefully, he
worked to keep the target area between the nose and right
wingtip of the plane. An angular aspect was much better
than head-on since line-of-sight would not be impeded by
the nose of the *Demon*. There was no mistaking the launch
pad in use. A mammoth superstructure resembling a giant
erector set pointed skyward. Standing next to the web array
of red steel framing, tall and upright, was the nine story
high, silo-like rocket. Even from a lofty perch at thirty miles,
thirty thousand feet, the *Demon Driver* was able to discern the
astronaut's space vehicle sitting atop its liquid oxygen
payload. The spacecraft was small and dark and miniscule
compared to the elongated, shinny cylinder that housed fuel
for its massive rocket engine. His first impression would be a
lasting one: 'so that's the Mercury space ship. Hell, it's
shaped like a Hershey kiss and from here looks about the
same size and color. Actually, the whole thing looks like a
big silver bullet.'
Already encroaching on the thirty-mile limit, the *Demons*
made a lazy, left-hand circle to return and maintain proper
distancing outside the protected area mandated by higher
authority (and guarded by the pair of *Talons*). Midway
through the turn, Dan noted the time: 0940E. He knew his
positioning was perfect for a side-on view in five minutes.
Excitement escalated as zero launch time neared.

Above all the excitement on the ground, high in the sky, the
two Navy jets waited and looked, maneuvering constantly
for a direct view of the launch pad. Another agonizing
delay was relayed to the T-38 pilots (and heard by *Tophatter*
flight) – Bermuda's tracking station was having radio
difficulties. Indecision was becoming a major player in the
game. Dan did not want to make another four-minute circle
which might catch their birds turned the wrong way for
observing the launch. He maneuvered thirty degrees left,
then came right back to original heading. He realized it was
tough on Buzz but knew his wingie would know the cause
for the erratic heading changes. By now they were directly
over Sanford still heading 090. In just moments they would

be again cheating on the thirty-mile limit. The time was 9:47 Eastern Daylight Savings Time and he was just about to initiate another orbit when Mission Control gave the OK to "light the candle". Then it happened. An unforgettable scene unfolded on the ground below. A rapidly expanding ball of fire seemed to engulf the entire launch pad. Bigger and brighter than Dan expected, the base of the rocket appeared to have exploded. For a long moment it was all fire and smoke and no discernable movement of the rocket. Then he saw the slumbering giant begin to awaken. Seen from 30,000 feet, the Atlas-D rocket initially looked to be ascending in slow motion. Dan would have guessed that he was looking down at the missile for an interminably long minute. He read later that it had taken only 13 seconds for the missile to reach transonic speed, just a few seconds longer to go supersonic, ultimately reaching a speed of 17,500 miles per hour. It had seemed much longer. His gaze remained frozen and locked on the spacecraft as it climbed on an easterly track. For a fleeting moment he was looking out his canopy straight-ahead and level at the space vehicle as it zoomed through 30,000 feet. Then, incredulously, he realized that he was not just looking up, he had to *crane* his neck *upwards* as he tried to follow the rocket's path. The stark contrast between the agonizingly slow liftoff and climb to thirty thousand feet as opposed to the acceleration above that level was mindboggling. Thankfully, the upward and seaward trajectory was beautifully defined and clearly visible by a plume of exhaust smoke from the fuel boosters. Modern technology was powering a new Buck Rogers into outer space. Dan could only wonder about the thoughts and feelings of the astronaut on his way to one hundred miles above the earth.[1]

Someone, perhaps a T-38 pilot, thrilled and energized, cheered over the airwaves, "Up, up and away!" Buzz Settles was excited, too, and broke the flight's self-imposed radio silence. He yelled into his transmitter, "WOW! Look at it go!"

---

[1] Actually, the space ship would orbit the earth three times and attain an apogee of one hundred sixty-two thousand feet.

Dan fought back the urge to participate in unauthorized "Attaboy" transmissions, but he, too, was as genuinely affected by the frenzied success of the moment. His heart was racing and he knew his breathing was too rapid. Only after the space shot disappeared into the eastern skies did his composure return somewhere near normal. Jubilant, he tried to take mental stock of the entire range of emotions he had felt during and after the launch. Awe, yes! Elation, yes! Wonder, yes! There was little doubt that the enormity, the immensity, the impact of this special space flight would be huge. He had just seen a controlled fireball send a rocket on its way to the heavens, to orbit the earth, one hundred miles up. Pride? Damn right! 'John Glenn may be a Marine but he is also a Naval Aviator, and so am I!'

Via hand signals, Dan motioned for 108 to join up and return to squadron common. "Buzz, Dan. Think about it, what we just saw is an American *happening*, a historical event we will never forget. John Glenn in *Friendship 7*, the first American to orbit the earth. And we were here to see it, up close and personal with a bird's eye view. Don't you know the Air Force pukes are eating their hearts out? First, Navy Commander Alan Sheppard was the first American into space, and now a Marine is first to orbit the earth! And do I remember some Air Farce toady named Grisson with a flight in between these two? And did he lose his spaceship? What's that old saying out of Pensacola? *Navy pilots are the cream of the crop.* No argument here, let's go home."

The two fighter interceptors turned north, the Cape disappearing to the rear. Minutes later the jets descended into NAS Cecil where landings were accomplished without event. As he taxied his jet toward the flight line, memories of the experience continued to flood his mind. Yes, there would be other launches at the Cape, lots of them, there was even talk of moon landings at some point in the future. But there would never be another American *first* to orbit-the-earth. John Glenn in *Friendship 7* had won his spot in space history. So be it. But unknown and unheralded, Dan Brown and Buzz Settles would forever share the moment with him. While aviators everywhere would be cheering John Glenn in spirit, Dan and Buzz had aced them all. 'Ahhhh, but we were there on scene, overhead, with the best seats in the house.' Helmeted linesmen gave visual directions for parking the big noisy jet, followed by hand signals for securing the engine. While waiting for the turbine to wind down, Dan looked skyward as his thoughts turned to the lonely pilot, now called astronaut, orbiting the earth. Over the noise surrounding the planes, he yelled out the open cockpit, "We're of the same breed, Col. Glenn, *Naval aviators*. We've got ....*the right stuff*."

Author's note: with apologies to writer Tom Wolfe for plagiarizing his famous title.

*****

Anyway you cut it, this was a giant coup.

Chapter 22

THE PAUSE THAT REFRESHES - No. 1

June, 1963
Age: 28

LT Dan Brown, instrument ground school instructor, had lectured well over two hours. The constantly changing and intricate rules of instrument flying in the mid-sixties were a nightmare for all jet pilots. Review upon review, coupled with practical examples underlined by real life scenarios, easily took more time than the scheduled two hours. Finally, after extending the period an additional forty minutes, Dan reached a good stopping point. "O.K., let's take a fifteen minute break. We'll review the lost communications procedures again when we come back."

Twenty-four aviators walked briskly to the men's head. Large amounts of coffee, coke, and water had been consumed during the morning sessions. Bladders were near capacity. A ten-foot long community urinal was accommodating seven or eight pilots while four stalls were being used in a like manner. The remainder of the group was queued behind the lucky first arrivers. Conversation was generally quiet to non-existent.
A sadly used cliché today but an old standby in 1963: "Coca Cola, hell, this is the pause that refreshes". Truth is truth, 1963 or 2005.

LTJG Judd Jackson was the first officer to finish urinating. He zipped up his blue trousers, buttoned the double-breasted uniform coat and headed to the nearest lavatory. As LTJG Jackson was soaping his hands, LCDR Turk Mixon ceased voiding and walked over near the door while zipping the fly to his khakis. LCDR Mixon was an older pilot, a "Mustang"[1] passed over for commander and command

---

[1] Mustang' is slang for a commissioned officer who worked his way up through the enlisted ranks.

several times, patiently putting in his last two or three years before mandatory retirement. Mustached, outspoken, Turk Mixon was known for his down-to-earth, occasionally crass, humor.

LCDR Mixon faced the young pilot, observing the junior officer washing his hands. The entire contingent of officers, most still busily engaged in the purpose intended, easily overheard the exchange of conversation between the two men.

Mixon to Jackson: "Say, son, didn't someone tell me you're a ring knocker, a graduate of Annapolis?"

Jackson responded politely, "Yes sir, United States Naval Academy, class of 1961, sir."

The older officer hesitantly shook his head, an air of conflict in his voice: "Well, didn't they teach you not to piss on your hands?"

Unsmiling, the crusty old pilot turned his back to the startled junior aviator and walked out of the restroom.

Spontaneously, to a man, every pilot followed suit upon completion of business. Zipping up, none stopped to wash their hands, all playing Turk Mixon's game to the hilt.

They exited the john quickly and quietly. As each walked past the red-faced young officer, some shook their heads, others rolled their eyes, all in apparent disdain of such uncivilized behavior by one of the Navy's finest new crop of graduate officers.

*****

The camaraderie of men is a noble thing to be enjoyed.
The author, 1990

Chapter 23

BIRTHDAY AT THE *"BUCCANEER"*

September, 1964
Age: 29

The small gathering of six had grown animated and lively.
A *Happy Hour-like* atmosphere prevailed. Abundant alcohol
fueled spirited conversation, fun and laughter followed in
lockstep. Three wives clustered in the living room; three
men manned a corner of the kitchen hovering around a
makeshift bar on a small card table. The oldest of the three,
and the tallest, was talking with both hands extended, palms
outward, one hand closely behind the other. Any pilot
observing the scene would immediately know that some
aspect of flying and flight was the topic of conversation.
Perhaps oddly, a white cake on the counter behind them
might have precipitated the hands-in-motion aerial
demonstration by the taller man. In the adjacent living
room, the hostess, with martini in hand, was making her
point that local shopping sucked in the small town of
Brunswick, Georgia.

The theme décor of the cake offered credence of the subject
so captivating to the husbands. It was decorated with a
small plastic, yellow biplane of yesteryear skywriting a
message across the creamy surface. The cake decorator had
done a superb job of using colored frosting to represent
emitted smoke a real plane might expel for writing a
message in the sky. The grayish 'smoke' frosting snaked
around and made relatively large numerals, **29**. Beneath the
29 were edible cherry red block letters that spelled out,
"Happy Birthday, Dan".

"Twenty-nine. Can you believe in one year I'll reach the
ancient age of thirty?" Dan Brown asked his wife over
breakfast the previous day. Later that same day, he twice
more bemoaned the topic of age on the eve of his birthday.
Eleanor began to realize it was more than just another
birthday for her husband. To her gung-ho hubby, it really

was a milestone of sorts, the final year of *twenties*. Originally today's dinner was to have been a low-key family-only celebration but Dan's repeated references to the significance of the day played on her mind. "What the hell", she finally decided on a change in plans – and besides, she did like small, intimate parties! She invited special friends over for cocktails and finger food. John Hanover and Ted Fontana were both somewhat older, by at least six or seven years, than Dan. But they were always fun and it might be good to have *over-thirty* guys around for this particular evening. The Browns, John and Susie Hanover and Ted and Mary Fontana had become great friends over the past twelve months. The three Naval officers had reported to Naval Air Station, Glynco, Georgia, within a week of each other during summertime of the previous year. And of course, all three men were pilots. Dan flew jets; John and Tom flew the four-engine propeller-driven behemoth, the C-121[1] *Super Constellation*, usually dubbed the *Connie*. While John and Tim filled pilot billets at this particular setting that is Naval Air Station, Glynco, aviation and flying were secondary to their administrative duties. When flying, they drove the big converted transport while other non-pilot officers taught radar and navigation procedures to new student operators at consoles specifically installed aboard the big bird for such training. Dan's job was quite different. He trained other pilots. As the station's Jet Training Officer, his job was flying, flying, flying. In the J.T.O. billet, he wore four hats. First, Instrument refresher flights and check rides in the two-seated T-1A[2] *Seastar*. Numbers two and three hats were training previously qualified jet pilots recently assigned to various on-base units in the F1E[3] *Fury* or the North American T-39 *Sabreliner*. Lastly, he was tasked on occasion to transition propeller or helicopter qualified aviators to jet aircraft, again using the *Seastar*. Dan wore the railroad tracks of a lieutenant and was junior in rank to Lieutenant Commanders Hanover and Fontana.

---

[1] Originally, the "WV ('Willie Victor') before Secretary of Defense McNamara's order to change designations (in 1962)
[2] Called the T2V before 1962
[3] Called the Fj4 before 1962

Predictably, the different venues of flying led to spirited discussions as to the better aviator: jet pilot versus prop pilot. Tonight, Dan was again being out-argued two to one. The fact that it was his birthday, his house, and his booze didn't cut any ice with John or Tim. In fact, the celebratory occasion probably gave them added incentive to debunk the ego of their friend, the jet driver. Several drinks into the conversation, Dan winked at his wife and threw up his hands and arms in mock surrender. He said, "Honey, never invite these two guys at the same time. They're ganging up on this pore little ole jet jock. They drink our liquor and eat our *"horse's ovaries"* but give me no respect, not even on my birthday. But wait, I just remembered, they're both so much older than I am! That may be the reason the Navy won't let them fly anything faster than an old four-engine meat wagon. I'm still a young stud in my twenties. Hey, they must be thirty-five or thirty-six by now! Old as dirt!" Good-natured insults continued to fly as the men moved once more to the den while the three women shifted their gossip klatch to the kitchen.

The impromptu party lengthened and then was extended again. Around 8 p.m., Dan returned to the kitchen and announced: "Hey, *Happy Hour* has become *Hungry Hour*. El, call our baby-sitter and see if she's available and let's go into town for dinner." Shortly a teenager appeared to watch the three children.
Mary appeared in the doorway between living room and den, and broke into the three-way conversation. "O.K., the baby sitter is here. Enough flying - low and slow or high and fast, no more airplanes. Let's talk din-din. Where are we going? It's almost 8:30. Dan, you have first dibs on picking somewhere to go."

Dan allowed as how the birthday boy had no particular place in mind. "My taste buds are open for suggestion," he offered.
John: "I've heard about a great fish place up past Darien called the *Buccaneer.* It's twenty-five to thirty miles up there

but let's give them a call and see if we can get a reservation for 9:30, maybe 9:45."

Eleanor made the call. A few minutes later she yelled for quiet, "We have to make a decision. They have a big group from Savannah arriving at 9:15. We have to be there before they're seated or there will be a long delay. It's 8:25 straight up. Can we make it?"

"Yes!" Three male voices cried in unison. Within five minutes, Dan had deposited his drink in the sink and was backing the Buick station wagon down the drive. Six happy people, five with plastic cups filled with joy juice were on their way to the station gate. Hanover had called a friend for specific directions out of Darien. "All right, straight up to Darien, then it's right on 99 for about fifteen miles. At that point, the turn off 99 isn't marked very well, but it's supposed to be easy to find a sign advertising a Baptist Church. The real problem is that after we take the right turn, the next sign we have to find is just a little twelve or fourteen-inch arrow sign up in a tree that says *Buccaneer*. My buddy says if we miss the sign, we're S.O.L.[1] in finding the restaurant." Twilight had fallen over South Georgia by the time the station wagon had been waved through the gate and turned north onto U.S. 17.

Despite a posted speed limit of 55, Dan eased the powerful vehicle out to 70 in comfortable light traffic until entering the city limits of Darien. The Route 99 marker was easy to find under a large oak tree in the center of the small Georgia town. The green dial of the dashboard clock read 8:47 as Dan made the ninety-degree right turn and resumed a more than moderate speed. They would be pushing their reservation time frame, fifteen miles to go to the next checkpoint and then two or three miles to the restaurant. Dan again inched speed towards 70. Darkness now enveloped the unlighted secondary road. John, from the back seat, mentioned an appreciation for the fact that traffic was sparse. Dan smiled to himself in the dark, presuming the comment was a gentle, non-verbal reminder to the driver that 70 was fast enough on a dark, winding, narrow road

---

[1] Common slang for *shit outa luck,* a popular phrase in the sixties.

unknown to the driver, especially after said driver had consumed several (defined as more than three) drinks back at Armstrong Avenue. Eleanor and Susie began counting off the miles. At 9 o'clock straight up, Dan saw the Baptist Church sign. "O.K., take the next right," John directed from the back seat.

Dan maneuvered the yellow ranch wagon onto the secondary paved road. Eleanor expressed alarm as she watched minutes tick off the dashboard clock, "We're going to be late."

Dan had to agree and at the same time knew he had to slow down. "Gosh Almighty, I thought 99 was dark. This back road is pitch black with all the live oaks hanging a canopy over the road. This is a perfect spot for Ichabod Crane to meet the headless horseman out of that book. We're never going to see a twelve inch sign up in a tree tonight." He noted the speedometer decelerating from 75, still exceeding 60. He was surprised that at least one of the women hadn't griped about the speed on this dark and winding and narrow route.

"We're past two miles. Did anyone see the sign?" John asked.

Five sets of eyes were looking left and up in the trees while Dan's attention focused on the road in front of him. He had eased off the accelerator and was leaning forward over the steering column, staring intently into the stillness of the night ill defined by auto headlamps. Suddenly, an unbelievable sight appeared directly ahead. Astonished, Dan yelled "Oh HELL!" as his mind tried to comprehend the totally unexpected hazard in their path! The paved road was ending and he could see water rapidly approaching head on! They were only yards away now. This time he yelled, "HOLD ON" as his right foot felt for and found the brake! He applied maximum ever-increasing pressure to the anti-skid system, fighting the inclination to stand on the pedal. The big vehicle began responding immediately. The unexpected momentum created by rapid deceleration inextricably and forcefully threw all five passengers forward.[1] Eleanor was able to deflect some of the blow against the console with her hands and purse. While flailing for a handhold, she turned her head and saw the water. "Noooooo!" she screamed. Tim had not yet identified the problem but gritted his teeth while his hands and arms deadened the impact against the dash and windshield. The back seat occupants grabbed handfuls of the front seat backs amidst squeals of surprise and confusion. Mary, in the middle, fell forward and wound up on the floorboard. She uttered a muffled "Ohhhhhhh" as she hung onto Susie's legs with one arm and pushed against the passenger seat with her left hand. Dan became aware of screeching rubber against pavement, then felt the overtaxed tires losing traction and the car seemed to have a mind of its own, wanting to veer left and onto the dirt shoulder. Fighting the steering wheel, somehow, he was able to maintain linear control. The car was slowing, the heavy mass losing the battle with brake power, but still moving toward the black wetness at a scary rate. As calamity neared, Dan saw the pavement continuing, sloping, descending into the water! The stupid back road ended as a boat ramp!

Still slowing, the big wagon continued to move forward over the hump and down the incline of the ramp. Finally, the vehicle came to a halt five or six feet from the water. Six stunned people sat for a moment in silence as they regained composure and realized how lucky they were to be high and dry. "We almost went swimming," Eleanor sighed weakly. John added with a weak smile, "Thankfully, it's low tide." Mary was finally able to extricate herself from the floor and regain her seat. Dan finally breathed easier when all five passengers reported they were shaken up but uninjured. After a few moments, he shifted into reverse and began backing up the ramp.

Tim was the first to heap praise on their driver. "Danny Boy, I don't know how you did it, pal. I'm telling you, I didn't know whether to crap or go blind. There are no warning signs. Nothing to tell you what's ahead! And you must have been doing 60-65 when you saw the water. How

---

[1] My memory sees no red-blooded Americans buckling up in those pre-Vietnam, pre-Ralph Nader years. Were belts installed then?

you got this big piece of iron and metal stopped in time is beyond me."

As his heart rate returned to normal, Dan saw an opportunity to needle his pilot buddies. He smiled widely and held his head high as he spoke over his shoulder, "Just routine everyday jet pilot reaction time. I've told you before, jet drivers think faster and react faster than prop pushers. We routinely fly at speeds up to 500 miles an hour and sometimes exceed the speed of sound. Have you four-bladed fan guys ever seen 250?"

Neither *Connie* pilot responded.

Dan grinned. "What, no argument? I guess you old guys are beginning to believe. This is a *happy birthday!*"

He turned the car around and headed in the opposite direction along the same route they had come. Checking, the entire group confirmed that no warning sign was posted on either side of the road advising of the upcoming boat ramp.

This time he drove much more slowly and they did find the miniscule sign high up in a pine tree, virtually hidden by limbs and needles. They turned off onto a sandy path-like road and found the rustic building that housed the *Buccaneer*. Thankfully, the tour group was also late; the party of six was seated and served shortly.

*****

The Buccaneer is still there – renovated and with big signs giving directions. Great Fisherman Platters!

Chapter 24

<u>HEMORRHOID</u>

January, 1965
Age: 29

The discomfort had finally sent him to sickbay. Somewhere in his travels over the last few days an alien germ was ingested which wreaked havoc with his digestive system. Everything was working properly again but there was one lingering side effect from the previous disorder: an aching, puffy, enlarged hemorrhoid. He had reported to the medical facility.

"O.K., guy, drop your trou and stick your rear end up in the air. You know the drill," CDR Tom Brooks, flight surgeon, U.S. Navy Medical Corps, smiled as he watched Dan loosen, then lower his khaki work pants.

"Sure, sure. Let's just get on with it," the unhappy patient responded. He was glad that CDR Brooks was the only other person in the closed cubicle. Dan assumed that in general, men were not as squeamish as women about their "*privates* lives" but still, the idea of his naked ass jutting upward in midair did nothing for his self esteem. Fortunately, Tom Brooks was his next-door neighbor. Good friends, they jogged together, they socialized together. In fact, they flew together when Tom needed time in the air for pay purposes as a flight surgeon.

The metal table was cold to his face as he assumed the compromising position. The doctor took one look at the engorged bulbous swelling and moved to retrieve a scalpel. "Dan, it's real simple. All I'm going to do is lance the protruding tissue, there will be some minor bleeding. I'll apply a salve and you go back to work. It is a big one. I expect it's quite uncomfortable now but in a minute you'll never know it was there. All right, spread your cheeks for me and it'll be over in a second."

With no option but to comply, Dan reached for his bottom with both hands, and applied outward pressure to each buttock. He tried to think of something, anything to take his mind off the present indignation. "Tom, get it over with." "Dan, wait a minute, I got an idea. In a training session last week, I learned that my new Physician's Assistant has never seen a thrombose hemorrhoid. I want to show this perfect specimen to Petty Officer Sears. I'll be right back." Moving to the doorway, CDR Brooks called into the adjoining treatment area. "Petty Officer Sears, come in here for a moment. I want you to see this." Too late, Dan realized his fear of additional exposure was about to occur despite his intense desire for privacy. His face still glued to the tabletop, he managed to mouth, "Dammit, Tom, you could have showed him somebody else's butt another day." Almost immediately, his peripheral vision picked up a pair of white tennis-like shoes topped by a knee length skirt. Dan moved his head to observe the newcomer as she passed alongside the table. He was astonished to see a young woman about twenty-two, slender, blonde, perfect 36's up top, dressed in immaculate Navy Nurse whites, so beautiful she could have been an entrant in a beauty contest. He was treated to a view of her perfect hips and legs just inches away from his face. He turned his head, looked over to the doctor and saw the jovial, devilish smile of a prankster. The good doctor was evidently enjoying the scene that he had precipitated. While the young woman was occupied, the doctor smiled even wider, then with an exaggerated gesture, pointed to the immobile pilot, drew a vertical exclamation point in air, followed by a tightened fist as pulling a drawstring. Dan understood his friend had just given him the universal "Gotcha" sign. Dr. Brooks quickly and quietly exited the room as Dan suppressed a curse. Meanwhile, without greeting or comment, Petty Officer Sears had walked around to Dan's backside. From his face down-rear up stance, he could no longer see her face but he could mentally visualize her examining the inflamed center of his discomfort. He felt his face burning from both anger and embarrassment as she touched the area with gloved fingers. His thoughts were unprintable.

The young medical attendant spoke. "I have seen these in textbooks but this is my first opportunity to look at a real thrombose rosette. Did Dr. Brooks say whether this is normal sized or enlarged?"

Finally regaining his composure, but completely pissed-off at his friendly flight surgeon, Dan answered, "He said it was a big one."

As the young woman continued to visually inspect the disfigured anal ring, Dan realized he was in a no-win position. Actually, he had already lost. Tom Brooks would be telling this story at his expense for the next week. In a moment of inspiration, he realized his only recourse was to have the last word today.

"Petty Officer Sears, I do have one concern. CDR Brooks said he would have to lance the extending tissue. 'Lance' means to 'cut', right?"

Finally turning her attention to the forward end of the table, the young woman looked at the patient as she answered, "Of course."

Straight-faced, he asked, "Well, do you think it will leave a scar?"

*****

Tom Brooks was a fine friend and neighbor. He left the Navy after a few years to enter private practice. He died of a heart attack at age 47. Kentucky lost a great doctor; his family lost a wonderful husband and father. I lost another close friend.

went unquestioned. A *Top Ten* list of the decade's highlights might include the following chaotic, sometimes grim events: racial upheaval across the South, President Kennedy's assassination, Vietnam with its associated fallout of draft card and flag burning, draft dodgers fleeing to Canada, the space race to the moon. Preparation for the war, or *non-war,* would dominate the time and energy of all hands aboard the huge military vessel undergoing modification and updating at Hunter's Point Naval Shipyard. When finally deployed, family responsibilities would be necessarily forfeited to wives; the men of CORAL SEA became fathers and husbands by allotment check. Girlfriends learned to wait. Letters enjoyed coveted status.

Undergoing modernization, the CORAL SEA was dry docked at Hunter's Point for several months after the Browns relocated to the San Francisco/Alameda area. Once out of the yard and fully operational following training and *Shakedown* [1]cruises, a schedule of sorts for the carrier would become routine: seven months deployment to WESTPAC including two weeks transit time over, six months operating 'on the line',[2] occasional in-port time for rest and recuperation[3], two additional weeks to return to dockside, Naval Air Station, Alameda. Once back under the Golden Gate Bridge, the ship would be stateside for the next five months but neither the ship nor the men of CVA 43 would necessarily be home. A total all-out effort had to be expended getting ready for the next upcoming WESTPAC[4] assignment. Five months would pass quickly.

Homecoming after the long and arduous deployment usually meant an abbreviated leave period (usually two weeks max) for officers and men of the ship who would be staying on board for "next time". Many of the forty-five hundred men who just completed the WESTPAC tour would be

---

[1] Inspections to ascertain readiness
[2] On station in the Gulf of Tonkin, supporting Seventh Fleet actions against North Vietnamese aggression into South Vietnam
[3] Usually referred to as 'R&R'
[4] Western Pacific Theater of operations

132

Chapter 25

I LEFT MY HEART IN SAN FRANCISCO

May, 1965
Age: 29

The Commanding Officer, Naval Air Station, Glynco,
Georgia, Captain Gene Evertt, beckoned LT Brown to his
office.

Once announced, Dan stood at attention. He felt somewhat
out of place in his flight suit here in the admin palace of staff
types wearing scrambled eggs on their caps and lots of
stripes on their sleeves. The Captain held a single piece of
paper in his hand. "Dan, at ease. Well, we just got your
orders for next assignment. Where had you hoped to go?"
Dan replied without hesitation. "Skipper, I've told
Washington I wanted a fighter squadron. I've had good safe
tours: Jacksonville/Newfoundland/VF-14/Glynco, all
regular peacetime assignments. But now we've got a war
going on and I'd like to go and get some ribbons before it's
over. All the experts are saying it'll end in just a few
months. Unfortunately, the Lieutenant's Desk at BuPers
told me I was probably going to sea as ship's company. So I
asked for a boat out of Mayport or Norfolk. What did I
get?"
The C.O. looked down at the message sheet in his hand
again. "Well, I'm afraid you've been skunked. The BuPers
God is sending you to the USS CORAL SEA (CVA-43)
stationed at Hunter's Point in San Francisco." The Captain
came around his desk to shake Dan's hand. "Dan, we'll
miss you and we wish you smooth sailing. And I want to
tell you again that I'm sorry we were just not able to let you
take those orders to Graduate School at Monterey last year.
I think you realize by the amount of flight time you've
logged this past year that losing you was not feasible.
Anyway, Good luck in your career."

It should be no secret to the reader that the '60's saw unusual
times in America. Previously accepted standards no longer

transferred to new assignments. Conversely, replacements would be waiting to take their places.

Two weeks of fun over, training began in earnest for the new upcoming extended commitment. At-sea exercises and accompanying work-ups filled much of the *at-home* time. Being stateside for a ship or a squadron did not necessarily mean the fellows were home cutting grass and watching their kid's soccer games. Sea duty mandated that each man realize as quickly as possible that *they were now* temporary husbands and fathers and lovers. Their number one assignment was to prepare for war - physically, mentally, professionally, and psychologically. The best way to get ready was to practice <u>*at sea*</u>. New crewmembers would learn lessons already ingrained into the veterans who had been there before. The fact that Vietnam was an increasingly unpopular 'conflict" was only a side issue of little consequence. It goes without saying that the men looked forward to any amount of time the ship was moored dockside at NAS Alameda. On reporting for duty, Dan found the *City by the Bay* fun, entertaining, always interesting. He was glad for an opportunity to see how the *left coast* lived, to experience first hand the difference in lifestyles. Yet, at the same time, he found California's culture confusing. He encountered an attitude towards life that he never knew or dreamed existed. The city and surrounding environs were and remain so today, fascinating, beautiful, almost beyond words. But for Dan Brown in 1965, anti-culture nooks like Haight-Ashbury and North Beach were heretofore found only in books or movies. Now, those places were real, as real as life itself.

A year after his reporting on board, the ship sailed under the Golden Gate on its way to Hawaii and points west: Philippines for replenishing stores and to the Gulf of Tonkin, off the coast of North Vietnam. Dan, now thirty years old and selected for promotion to Lieutenant Commander, was assigned to the Air Operations Department. He was only one of many aboard CORAL SEA enroute a combat zone for the first time. Vietnam, the unpopular *conflict* awaited them.

*****

Chapter 26

FLIGHT TO CUBI POINT

Date: September, 1966
Age: 31

......*Precious Cargo*

Newly pinned with gold leaves, LCDR Dan Brown watched
the launch of nearly thirty airplanes from a catwalk position
near the Tower, high above the flight deck. The all-out air
strike[1] orbited the ship once, then turned west and headed
into North Vietnam. Oh, how he had wanted to launch off
on his first combat mission. But no, Navy types sitting on
their butts in Washington had decided that he should serve a
tour as ship's company before another operational tour.
"You got too much flight time at Glynco," his detailer had
said. "You've had three great years flying five different
kinds of planes – now it's time you learned about ships and
the real Navy." So here he was in the combat zone, but
there would be no operational combat flying. The closest he
would come to being shot at would be when he piloted the
ship's little cargo plane, the twin-engine C-1A *Tracker*,
commonly called the *COD*[2] into an airfield in South
Vietnam. At Da-nang and Hue, the enemy sometimes shot
small arms fire at landing planes. Two weeks earlier the
COD had returned to the ship with a small bullet hole in one
of the landing flaps after a flight to Da-nang. Dan had not
been on that flight but he was getting his share of flight time.
Better yet, occasionally he was tasked to carry mail all the
way into Naval Air Station, Cubi Point, in the Philippines.
Usually, after the four-hour flight, that meant a night on dry
land and steak and drinks and slot machines at the Officer's
Club.

---

[1] Called an "Alfa" strike – a major bombing raid with many aircraft,
including not only tactical bombers but fighters, tankers, jammers,
communications relay platforms, and others
[2] Stands for 'Carrier On Deck' delivery

In the Command Center, all on-duty officers and enlisted men plus numerous other ship and squadron personnel, listened to radio transmissions from the attacking and participating aircraft. Suddenly, the call everyone dreaded: "Mayday, mayday. Mustang control, Comet 501. I've been hit. Returning to ship."

Combat Information Center (CIC) watch officer: "Roger 501, say extent of your emergency and say position."

501: "Going feet wet, 40 miles out. I've taken a round through my left leg. Blood is spurting everywhere."

CIC: "Cleared direct Mustang – descend at your discretion. Say your status."

501: "Gages normal except for blood everywhere. The bullet came up through the belly" (of the aircraft).

CIC: "The Air Boss and LSO want you on their frequency. Switch to Mustang tower."

All over the USS CORAL SEA, crewmembers responded to the announcement that a damaged A4 *Skyhawk* of VA-22 was to be brought aboard. The bombing strike on a power plant south of Hanoi had progressed as planned until LTJG Jarrod Hall in Comet 501 reported hit by enemy fire. The immediate question was could the pilot handle the injury and land the plane back aboard the floating mother ship? The flight surgeon and three medical corpsman arrived on deck with appropriate equipment. A UH-2 *Seasprite* helicopter, called "Angel" lifted into the air and took plane guard position along the starboard side of the massive carrier.

Hall, voice weak and labored: "Tower, 501, 10 miles west descending through angels five and I don't think I'll be able to trap aboard. I'm getting ...weaker ...and my vision is blurred. Besides .....the instrument panel is all covered with blood. I wiped the airspeed gage ......but now it's all smeared over."

"501, this is Mustang tower. Do you think you could divert to Hue or Da-nang with a wingman?"

Hall, haltingly: "Negative. Too far. Pain .....increasing and ....blacked out once already." Heavy breathing was heard over the airwaves before the injured pilot finally released the mike button on the throttle.

A hurried call to the VA-22 ready room ensued. CDR Flip Nestor, the squadron C.O. was himself on the air strike still in progress and not available. The Air Officer, only a few months removed from commanding an operational squadron, acted on cue without reservation. "O.K. 501, this is the Air Boss. I want you to let down and fly along side the ship at 1500 to 2000 feet and eject. Let the automatic features of your seat and chute do the work. C'mon home, Jay. Angel is ready to pluck you out of the water and the doc is on deck waiting for you."

Shortly, through light, scattered clouds, the *Skyhawk* could be seen letting down from the west. The hot four o'clock afternoon sun glinted off the gray steel fuselage and wings like a shinny Christmas ornament. Ten seconds after passing by the carrier up the starboard side, the pilot ejected and was seen floating lazily downward in his parachute. The plane flew on for a mile or two before diving into the sea well away from the scene. Once in the water, the Angel driver hovered and dropped a line with an orange oval collar to pick the pilot up. When there appeared to be no movement in the water, the helo crewman jumped into the ocean, swam over and worked frantically to loosen the injured pilot's harness before the chute filled with water and dragged one or both men into the deep. Somehow, the crewman single-handedly secured LTJG Hall to the recovery collar. Both men were pulled to safety by hoist and within minutes, the helo was on deck. But like the old-not-so-funny line, "the operation was a success but the patient died" – all the foregoing was to no avail. LTJG Hall was pronounced dead on arrival – he had simply bled to death from the artery wound in his leg.

"Dan, you're on tap for the next C-1A run to Cubi Point. Your copilot will be Jake Brown from Air Department. You're scheduled for a 0800 launch. You know what your load will be, right?" CDR Lemon's face was serious and unreadable.

Dan didn't understand the significance of the question. "No sir, it's usually outgoing mail and/or somebody being transferred with early orders. Whaddaya got? A sailor or

two from Supply Department going in to scrounge parts?
What's different about this cargo?"

CDR Lemon replied impassively, "You'll have a body bag
in the aisle. You're taking Jarrod Hall's body to the beach
to be flown back to states on commercial air. And there will
be a VA-22 escort officer along. I can't remember ever
having to fly one of own off the ship. Usually when we lose
a pilot, it's a problem for the state department to wrangle out
with the North Vietnamese. Now don't let this spook you.
You just fly the airplane and let Medical people here and
there worry about the cargo."

The 'Brown Boys', as they were facetiously dubbed, manned
aircraft at 0730 the following morning. As they ran through
the preflight checklist, they heard the escort officer, LT Russ
Harwell along with two other passengers, take seats in the
cabin. Dan and Jake were still busy with checks and
procedures when the body came aboard but were keenly
aware of the important load being manipulated into the tight
linear space between the seats. The *Tracker* was not
designed as a med-evac craft so the body would have to lie
free and unbelted on the deck between rows of seats.
Medical Personnel along with two aircrewmen carefully and
reverently placed the elongated bag in the aisle. The single
aircrew petty officer assigned the flight sat in the back seat
near the toilet, behind the zippered bag. Mustang 022
catapulted off the starboard cat at 0803.

Normally, the 4 plus hours flight was filled with chatter
between the pilots, crew, and passengers. Discussions on
any and all topics helped pass the time. Of course, on any
flight the two pilots stayed busy with necessary radio
broadcasts as well as challenge and response in-flight
checks. It was not unusual for passengers to stick their
heads in the cockpit and shoot the breeze for a time if flight
conditions permitted. In the back among passengers, the
officers always anticipated drinks and lumpia at the O'Club
while the enlisted couldn't wait to down a cold *San Miguel*
and catch a jeepney[1] into Olangapo City. Those were

---

[1] Glorified, decorated jeeps used as taxis. The beginning of *Officer and a Gentleman* shows jeepneys in Olongapo.

discussion staples under normal circumstances. This flight
was different. The only words spoken between Yankee
Station[1] in the Tonkin Gulf and arrival at NAS, Cubi Point,
consisted of minimal radio position reports by the copilot
and the required checklist items between pilot and copilot.
The 4 hour 15 minute flight seemed much longer than usual.
It was a time for Dan to look out at the beautiful light blue
sky above, and at the deeper, darker blue water below, and
reflect on life. Surrounded by the beauty of sky and ocean, it
was hard to realize the body of a lifeless buddy was lying in
the aisle. The total quietness hung heavy – the twin engines
seem to pay homage to the fallen hero by humming more
evenly and quieter in perfect sync. Jarrod Hall had been a
neat guy with an infectious smile, a fun guy to be around.
He didn't fit the hot jet pilot stereotypical image, but had
been a good, steady stick in the air. Dan looked back again
at the body bag. The 25-year-old Naval aviator, hidden in
his black cocoon, would be lying headfirst. The mental
image of the form inside was unsettling. At Cubi Point, Dan
landed and taxied to the parking ramp. An ambulance
vehicle and medical personnel took over the precious cargo.
Dan extricated himself from the cramped left seat, exited the
craft, and the flight was over.

But was it? Probably not within the minds of the six men
who were there. Surely the flight was indelibly etched into
memory cells of a lifetime for those who accompanied the
black bag from catshot to touchdown. Dan knew that Jay
Hall was now part and parcel of his own makeup and
personality. Just like Jimmy Frazier from first grade.
Thoughts of them would return again and again over a
lifetime. Except now, he knew the identity of the unseen
rider of the pale horse who visited Yankee Station day
before yesterday. *Death* was no longer a stranger.

---

[1]An area designated as 'on station' in the Gulf of Tonkin, just off the
coast of North Vietnam.

Chapter 27

<u>HONG KONG, the first time</u>

October, 1966
Age: 31

"The ship's in!"
USS CORAL SEA (CVA-43) anchored outside Hong Kong
harbor just before daybreak. Finally, around 0900, officers
and sailors not on duty plus any others among the crew who
could conjure up justifiable reasons for being ashore, rushed
for the liberty boats as soon as the waterborne shuttles were
called away. *Port duty section*[1] claimed first rights to enjoy the
sights and sounds and tastes and smells of the city whose
name, *hong kong*, simply means 'fragrant harbor'.

Hong Kong was everything and more, far more, than Dan
Brown could have imagined growing up back home in
Georgia. An English metropolis built on Chinese soil, this
city of inestimable economic impact promised fascinating
and intriguing experiences. Tasting Oriental culture with an
English accent was a totally new adventure for the young
Southern gentleman. Hong Kong was one of the ports of
call for CORAL SEA after extended days at sea *on the line* in
the Gulf of Tonkin. The aging carrier would be once again
launching and recovering aircraft in just ten days hence.

Several "Admins" - shared community suites paid for by
squadron or ship's company officers, were booked in the
Conrad Hilton. Most of the admins were standard hotel
suites that would be used only by those participating in the
cost of room and amenities. Beds in two bedrooms were

---

[1] All enlisted men and many officers are assigned to duty sections,
usually port and starboard. On any given day of a week, one duty
section will be required to stay aboard ship while the other is given
liberty. The duty section is there for emergencies, i.e., fires, as well as
routine duties such as preparation of meals, handling of liberty boat
traffic, etc. The following day, duty/liberty assignments are reversed.

assigned officers by name by date to insure fair utilization. The sitting rooms had been converted to open bars and were available twenty-four hours a day to any and all participating (paying) officers and their guests. On the final day, costs would be divvied up. A pro-rata amount covering the cost of the suite, booze, setups, and *hors d'oeuvres* for six days would be charged the officers involved. A few well-heeled officers, usually those more senior, would forego the admin arrangement and stay in private or semi-private rooms, returning to ship as necessary.

Added to exotic intrigue of Hong Kong was shopping in Kowloon. The mainland, Victoria, touted marquee or name stores found to be expensive to very expensive. Kowloon, across the harbor, a name known world wide as a shopping *Mecca*, called to the men of CORAL SEA. As far as Dan could figure, anything and everything was for sale there. Tailor-made clothing, women's wigs, and electronics seemed to outnumber by far all other retail offerings but virtually any commodity or item desired could be found in Hong Kong's *other* city.

To get to the hustle and bustle and bargains of Kowloon, one had to take a Star Ferry from Victoria. These large, almost gargantuan auto-passenger ferries ran continuously in both directions. A one-way trip took only a few minutes. Dan spent the first day ashore getting to know Victoria and lazing around the admin. The next day he visited Kowloon. At the top of his *to do* list was finding the tailor recommended by officers who had visited Hong Kong previously. After some initial difficulty, the shop was located. Material selection and measurements for a sport coat and a new suit were completed in short order. For a while, he walked the busy streets, window shopping and enjoying the sights. Around 1700 hours[1] he was on the ferry back to Hong Kong proper to rendezvous with his buddy, LCDR Will Baker, at the *Hilton*.

The ferry pulled alongside its pier in a mild harbor squall precipitating higher than normal wind and sea conditions.

---

[1] 5 pm

Docking in the rain and waves, the big ferry's deck rocked back and forth, in turn causing the massive hull to rub up and down against oversized rubber bumpers attached to the deck's pilings. The big black cushions were fashioned from large tires, the type used on farm tractors and heavy industrial equipment. Waves washed haphazardly over the ship's deck after splashing against the pier. Low tide further complicated an orderly exit of the ship. A lower water level required departing passengers to step up to the dock from the boat. For some, the step, which was about two feet at high tide, was even more precarious when the deck bottomed out at its lowest point. Getting off the large triple deck ferry slowed measurably as passengers fought the rolling action of the waves, the up and down movement of the boat, and the unanticipated high step to dock level. Star Ferry employees working dockside reached to assist passengers as they attempted the giant step upward to pier level.

As Dan's time in line approached the exit ramp, he noticed the woman ahead of him. She was wearing a tight skirt and mid-length heels. He guessed correctly she was going to have trouble negotiating the tricky step to the landing. He saw her reach for a helping hand. As she stepped forward and upward, the boat rocked down, her fingers slipped from the attendant's grasp, and she fell backwards. He caught her upright, kept her from falling, and gave a steadying hand as she readied once more to exit the ferry. This time with extra effort, she made the hurdle to safety. Dan followed next and they walked along the exit route together.

Once outside the concourse, she took the initiative and introduced herself. "Thanks. I'm Nanette Proctor. I'm sure glad you caught me back there. I don't think I would have been injured, but I would have certainly been embarrassed. You're an American?"

Dan was caught mildly off guard. Her English accent was similar, yet different from that spoken in Hong Kong. He answered, "Yes, I'm Dan Brown, a flier off USS CORAL SEA. We're anchored off shore for a port visit of five more days. You've probably seen a lot of U.S. Navy sailors and

officers today. We sail for the Tonkin Gulf on Friday. Your accent is a little different – you're not a local, I'd bet."
She smiled. "I'm Australian, on an around-the-world cruise. You could say we're both sailors."

Nanette Proctor was an attractive woman. Her jet-black hair was striking against a sky blue blouse. A brightly colored scarf tied loose in a big Windsor knot emphasized her expensive outfit. She continued talking and told him the around the world voyage was a gift from her husband. They lived in Perth where Mr. Proctor dealt in semi-precious gems. Shortly, too soon, Dan thought, they reached a main intersection where busy streets ran in three directions to various heartbeats of the city.
They waited for the red traffic light to turn green. Dan pointed left. "I go that way to the *Hilton*, about ten blocks away on Queensway."
Nanette nodded straight ahead. "I take the cross street at the next intersection to my hotel. All of us from the cruise ship are staying at the *Mandarin Oriental*." She offered her hand and said softly, "Thanks again."
The handshake over, Dan's light flashed a green 'GO'.
"O.K., guess this is goodbye. Glad to have met you and happy you didn't fall back there."
She smiled again. "Me, too. Goodbye." And she was gone.

Two nights later, the two officers bemoaned the fact the in-port period was almost *finito*. They finished their drinks, then Will Baker suggested, "Hey, we have only two more nights in H.K. Tonight let's eat at *The Mandarin Grill* over on Connaught Road. I hear the steaks are as good as Kansas City stockyards offer."
Dan had no better suggestion. "O.K., we've tried authentic Chink food which I thought was disappointing. I'd rather have it Americanized a little more like what we get in San Francisco's China Town. You're right, we had shrimp and fish last night at the *Floating Restaurant*, so it's time for a little red meat. Let's do it. But I doubt the T-bones will match up with K.C."

142

Predictably, the *maitre de* advised of a thirty to forty minute wait. Will discussed the delay with the Eurasian waiter. "One more drink cried the drunk. We'll be in the bar. Find us when the name *Baker* pops up - we're starving. There are five *American pesos* in it for you to get us a table in less than twenty minutes."

They found Todd Tyler, Assistant Air Operations Officer from CORAL SEA, sitting alone in a booth. Dan and Will liked the Texan, both having served with him in prior squadrons. Joining him and sitting, drinks came amid small talk of the forthcoming at-sea period. After a while a sole woman came in and sat facing Dan and Will across the aisle and down two booths. She watched them closely while absent-mindedly playing with the cherry in a Manhattan cocktail. Will noticed her first and said, "Boy, catch the blonde two doors down. She is something else. Too bad we're all married."

"We can always look," Dan countered and moved his gaze toward the booth in question. As his eyes met those of the woman described, she waved a hand ever so slightly and grinned.

Will questioned his pal. "Do you know her? She's sure acting like you two are old friends. Either that or she's a high priced hooker."

Dan stared at the woman. "No, I've never seen her." Even as his words were being uttered, the woman motioned with her forefinger, beckoning him to come over to her table. And then she smiled wider than ever.

Dan shrugged and moved to get up. "You know, there's something familiar about her. I guess I'll see where our paths have crossed. I'll bet she's not hooking but I've been wrong before." Sliding from the booth, he tried hard to remember where he might have met a beautiful blonde, perhaps a sales lady in one of the many shops he entered. The blonde hair simply did not compute in his memory bank, but that smile.........suddenly he knew who she was and how and where they had met. Returning her smile, he moved quickly to lean against the end of her table. "Well, it's Mrs. Nanette Proctor. My Aussie friend, that is quite a wig! Or is it? For all I know, maybe the jet black hair was not the real thing." The contrast between Nanette's coal black hair seen at the Ferry and the new Marilyn Monroe look could not have been more pronounced. He would not have recognized her if they simply passed in the street. Then Dan remembered she had said she was booked at the *Mandarin Oriental* and *The Mandarin Grill* was one of three restaurants in the hotel. So they were in her hotel. As he eased into the overstuffed seat opposite Nanette, he marveled at the coincidence of seeing her again. In a city of over five million people, two persons met accidentally in a crowded passenger terminal. Against astronomical odds, a second chance meeting occurred within forty-eight hours. What were the odds? Go figure!

"No, this is the wig, the black hair is mine. I thought this might be fun. I think the look on your face just now was worth the cost."

At Dan's invitation, Nanette joined the three naval officers for dinner. Delicious steaks, complimented by carafes of house wine, energized lively conversation from all quarters. Stories, jokes, laugher seemed to feed a frenzy for more stories, jokes, and laughter. Dan thought it must be the Aussie in her because Nanette told as many good or risqué stories as did the three tipsy aviators. To the men's credit, the demarcation line of impropriety remained intact. Risqué jokes with mild expletives flowed hot and heavy but three married men facing extended periods at sea tossed no sexual innuendoes at their beautiful and interesting, also married, female companion.

The spontaneous warm and friendly times lasted long into the evening. Finally, dessert dishes, coffee cups and ashtrays askew, the new friends called it a night. Before leaving the table, Nanette gave each of the three men a small gift: solitary green and blue opals from her husband's collection. Walking together, the foursome fell oddly quiet as they exited the restaurant. In the lobby, last good-byes and handshakes were offered all around. Sadly and abruptly, the group dissolved as the three men exited into the lighted night. Todd caught a taxi to fleet landing for a shuttle to the ship, Dan and Will walked north towards the Hilton to sleep at the admin. Nanette took the elevator up to her suite.

It had been a special evening. Exhilarated, Dan felt it could be the platonic high point of his thirty-one years. The simple fact of finding and seeing Nanette a second time against overwhelming odds and under the comical circumstances of a blonde wig on a very brunette lady gave him a warm and fuzzy feeling inside. Well, maybe the booze contributed to that special perception. Will, too, seemed to be taking introspective evaluation of the evening's spontaneity. The two men walked in silence back to the high-rise hotel. Dan tried to recall the poem about ships that pass in the night. He'd look it up in the CORAL SEA library tomorrow. He realized Eleanor might not appreciate nor condone his total enjoyment of the evening. She would allow that men going off to war were permitted some latitude in the pursuit of harmless fun when and where they could find it. But the pure pleasure he had received from Nanette's company would probably exceed that limitation in the mind of a wife back home. His mind and conscience wrestled over these thoughts. Ultimately, rationalization prevailed. 'It was an unplanned, innocent encounter. Still, I guess this is one experience I won't write home about. There's no need to rock the marital boat.'

Ships that pass in the night, and speak
    each other in passing,
Only a signal shown and a distant voice
    in the darkness;
So on the ocean of life we pass and
    speak one another,
Only a look and a voice; then darkness
    again and a silence.
            The Theologian's Tale. Elizabeth IV, Longfellow

*****

Chapter 28

THE PAUSE THAT REFRESHES - No. 2

December, 1966   *Yokosuka, the first time*
Age: 31

"Nippon. Hirohito. Tojo. Hara-kiri. Geisha girls. 'Hotzi'
baths and girls that give you a massage by walking on your
back. It's our first day in Japan and here we sit drinking
warm beer on a crowded sidewalk. There must be
something better to do with our time," LCDR Dan Brown
lamented to his good friend and fellow pilot, LCDR Will
Baker. Dan continued, "We've seen the shops. We checked
out the strip clubs for late nite activities. C'mon, let's take
that tour the public affairs folks recommended. There's still
over two hours before we rendezvous with the guys at the
club." His tall companion shrugged, drained his *Kirin* beer
and nodded lackadaisical approval. The two naval officers
walked six or seven blocks back to the naval base entrance.
Inside the gate, a red and blue tour bus belched black smoke
as it sat idling, awaiting scheduled departure. Counting out
their yen, the duo of American pilots first paid, then found
seats among a diverse passenger mix of mostly American
servicemen and women, and a few Japanese tourists. Soon
the bus pulled out to make the rounds of interesting sights
that define the large, industrial Japanese port city.

Nearly four hours later, dusk was giving way to darkness.
The bus finally jolted to a stop. Dan stepped from the loud
and smelly vehicle into the bright lights illuminating Naval
Station Yokosuka entrance. The planned two-hour
excursion had lengthened decidedly as a result of an
accident and resultant traffic tie-ups. A moderately
interesting two-hour ride, an avenue to kill time before
happy hour, had deteriorated into total boredom as autos,
taxis, buses, scooters and bicycles honked and inched along
to destinations. Dan complained to Will: "Thank
goodness, we're back to base.....over four hours without a
restroom stop. I'm starting to feel those three beers I had

before the tour began. I'm going in the Duty Office and find the head."[1]

Will grabbed his friend by the arm, "No, you're not, pal. There's the bus for the "O" Club just turning the corner. Hold it till you get to the top of the hill. Let's make this bus or it's another half-hour wait for the next one."

Reluctantly, Dan had to agree. They flagged down and boarded the bus. A few stops later, perhaps a period of twelve to fifteen minutes, the two officers stepped down from the bus in front of the Officer's Club.

NAVY WIVES CLUB GALA, large red letters on a white canvas banner, greeted visitors at the front entrance. The new arrivals could hear the Beach Boys belting out "Surfer Girl" emanating from inside. Will surmised, "Gaiety reigns! Wish we could have gotten here earlier." Rolling his eyes skyward, he added sarcastically, "Wonder why we're so late? Whose idea was that stupid 'tour-de-tour' anyway?"

Dan retorted, defending his suggestion for the tour ride, "We would have gotten here with time to kill if the tour bus had kept schedule. Forget it, Will. It's a done deal. Let's get inside, I really need to talk to the man about a dog."

They entered a foyer reminiscent of an earlier era. Teak, mahogany, walnut, brass, and nautical antiques gave the entrance a rich, inviting look. Dan immediately saw the "MEN" sign pointing down a long hallway to the right. "See you at the bar in a few minutes. I can't believe you don't have to take a whiz after all this time and all that beer."

"An iron bladder", ole buddy." Will smiled and moved away.

Dan hurried to the indicated door and moved quickly inside. Later, he would remember that subconsciously he had noticed a twin door immediately adjacent that opened into the ladies' lounge. A long white ceramic trough hung on the wall opposite four stalls and a double lavatory. The half-cylinder shaped latrine dated the club's facilities to World War II times. He walked to the urinal and unzipped.

---

[1] Navy's word for restroom or toilet

Immediately, he could hear them coming down the hall. A twelve or fourteen inch wire mesh screen ran horizontally atop the corridor wall extending to the ceiling. The open-air screen was probably built initially to help with circulation from overhead fans before air conditioning was installed. For whatever reasons the mesh originally served, the screens had never been replaced. Conversations in the hall were easily audible inside adjacent rooms. Dan made out three feminine voices, the owners of which evidently were having a grand time. Their light hearted and jovial dialogue was punctuated often with laughter. Dan could imagine their animated gestures as they made their way between the main dining room, the site of the Wives Club party, and the bar located just down the corridor past the restrooms.

His pent-up flow had just begun when he heard one of the female voices announce: "I've got to run in the ladies' room. See you at the bar in a jiff."

The door to the men's room opened. Facing the wall away from the door, he instinctively turned his head to the left to see who entered. A young woman was looking back over her shoulder talking to her companions as she burst into the room. Now already two or three steps inside, she turned to find a man in the act of urinating. Her face froze; her body became rigid as stone. She was hypnotized in astonishment, perhaps awe mingled with fear added to her embarrassment. About twenty-five or six, tall for a woman, light brown hair, she wore a loose fitting classic yellow blouse over a navy mini-skirt. Like a figure in a wax museum, she now seemed incapable of movement. Even in her confused state, Dan could see by the tailored clothes, the cut and style of her hair – not one out of place – a gold coin pendant, and the total sophistication of her appearance, that she was one of the beautiful people.

He had never seen a person so mesmerized. Her face was a study in complete disbelief. She stared at the stream of urine being released into the urinal.

The need of his bladder was not to be denied, he could not shut off the flow that had just started. Dan tried to utter an apology. "I'm sorry, I can't stop, I waited too long to go."

His voice seemed weighted, the words had not come easily.
Both the watched and the watcher were attempting to regain
composure.

Finally, his urgency diminished to the point he could stop
and reach for a paper towel to cover himself. That
movement appeared to break the spell as the woman stepped
backward and now looked into his eyes. Her cheeks flushed
red, then paled again as she stammered, "I'm sorry. I'm
sorry. I'm sorry." Her eyes never left his as she backed out
the door. He could hear footsteps rushing down the hall to
the safety and comfort of friends. He finally finished his pee
and zipped up.

Relaxed and comfortable again, he washed his hands and
straightened his tie. Before looking for Will, he explored the
club's dining and bar areas wanting another glimpse of the
beautiful lady in the yellow blouse. He didn't find her.
The ship remained in Yokosuka two more days and nights.
Dan returned each evening to the Officer's Club hoping for a
chance to see and meet the beautiful young woman who had
mistakenly stumbled into his private moment. She did not
show up. On the third day following the highly unusual
encounter, the USS CORAL SEA departed Yokosuka for
fleet exercises in the China Sea. Aboard the aircraft carrier,
Dan realized he would never see the young woman again.

In telling of the incident later, some would tease and joke
that the mysterious woman knew exactly what she was
doing, that she was a voyeur. They said she was probably
living out her fantasy, she may have liked what she saw.
One acquaintance suggested that perhaps she had pulled the
same stunt before, that the suspense of possibly being
recognized was like a narcotic's buzz. Dan knew better.
The men's and ladies' toilet facilities were located side by
side and she had simply picked the first door instead of the
second while preoccupied with her companion's chatter.
Her friends had not even noticed the mistake. He wondered
if she ever told anyone of her unusual social blunder. Not
that it made one speck of difference, but he would have liked
to know her name and her circumstances for being at the

club that evening. Perhaps they could have had drinks together and laughed over their shared experience.

Two more ships passed in the night. No names, no introductions. Again, a line from Longfellow's famous poem:

> *Only a look and a voice; then darkness again and a silence.*

*****

When you gotta go, well, you know.........

Chapter 29

THE PARTY'S OVER

Spring, 1967
Age: 31

CORAL SEA was back from the war. Coming home to
Eleanor and the kids was great on one hand but on the
other, the mood in California, perhaps in all America, was
disquieting, even disturbing. During the return voyage, the
ship's commanding officer had warned his crew not to
expect a hero's welcome. He stopped just short of
recommending always going ashore in civilian clothes.
America, at least the news media, was turning against U.S.
involvement in Southeast Asia.

But he was home and ready for some quality family time
and *R&R*. It seemed California was even more liberal than
when the ship left eight months ago. A new culture shock
awaited the men of CVA-43. The just issued President's
Commission on Obscenity and Pornography had changed
the map of big-city morality. Pretty much accepted today in
most cities of size, nudity and pornography were shockers in
1967. That is, at least for southern folks transplanted across
country to the great state of Ronald Reagan.

The large group had finally been seated at a long table
hastily arranged by adding a table to a table to a table. Eight
CORAL SEA officers and corresponding wives found
themselves in one of the more famous topless bars of North
Beach. *Bob's Bar,* well known not only in the *city by the bay*,
but renowned up and down the west coast, was one of the
first to take advantage of the recently liberalized outlook on
morality. The Presidential Commission on Pornography
had recommended, among other findings, that individual
communities be permitted to set their own standards of
nudity. Within hours following adoption and legalization,
Bob's was open, waitresses and lady bartenders *sans* attire
above the waist.

The party had begun earlier at NAS Alameda. Terry and Sally Barrs celebrated a wedding anniversary and invited Dan and Eleanor Brown, along with other close friends, to dinner and cocktails at the Officer's Club. There, as usual, additional acquaintances occasioned by, and to close out the evening revelry, *Bob's* had been voted the bar of choice.

It was not a unanimous selection. Jim and Janet Burgess had to be coerced into going along with the group. Jim was fairly easily persuaded but Janet was more difficult to convince. Finally, she acquiesced and attended under duress. In her own words, "It's not that I think I'm better than anyone else, it's just that I don't care one damn thing about having a drink in a place famous simply because of bared boobs."

A blue and white nametag pinned to her scanty apron confirmed that *Trina* was their waitress. At twenty-five or six, the young woman was fairly attractive and pleasant. Like all working females at *Bob's,* she was indeed topless. The fact that her breasts were exposed for any and all to gaze upon appeared not to matter to her in the least. Her breasts were of average cup size, probably 34 B's, just beginning to sag slightly, decorated with large, chocolate brown areola. The men, even the women at the table, looked, but tried not to stare.

Not unexpectedly, several of the partygoers were already tipsy from the on-base dinner gathering prior to arriving at *Bob's.* Drinks all-around were ordered. On stage, the featured star performed her sexy and spirited dance. Near capacity, the excited crowd roared loud and enthusiastic approval. The sixteen recently arrived customers talked while watching the show. Generally, they seemed to be enjoying themselves except for one notable exception already mentioned. Mrs. Janet Burgess remained moody, complaining loud and often. The men around the table were admiring the overly large, taunt and pointy breasts of "Barbara Bared", the quasi-naked performer on the runway. "Silicone," Dan overheard Janet say to no one in particular. He wondered if there was a hint of jealousy in her tone. He checked out her bosom and decided she was probably envious since hers were definitely bite-size. 'No pun intended', he grinned to himself.

Janet Burgess continued deriding the scantily attired dancer. "Cleavage by injection. Disgusting. What's the difference in that and foam falsies or even balloons? I can't believe I let myself be talked into coming to this joint. It's apparent that in just a few more sexy moves around that fake firemen's pole she will be more than topless."

Under hot spotlights that illuminated every move of the exotic dancer, room temperature inched upward. Waitresses and bartenders alike perspired profusely. Tell-tell sweaty wetness could be seen glistening on large and small bosoms as the women worked the room. Men removed coats and lowered ties to half-mast. Ladies shed any sweaters still on after entering and checking coats. Janet Burgess remained surly and unsmiling.

"Jim, what are we doing here? It's hot, look at the sweat beads on your forehead. Forget the drinks, pay our share of the bill and let's get out of here. This is ridiculous."

The others, particularly Terry and Sally, tried to keep the evening's reverie alive until drinks arrived. Terry asked George Elliot to tell his latest joke. Before George could respond, Jerry Starnes began offering a verbal play-by-play description of the performance on stage, paying particular attention to the size, development, and other eye-filling attributes of the star's forty-four inch bust line. Jim Burgess, seated next to Alice Starnes on his right, hunched forward to hear the entertaining monologue over the noisy din. In doing so he missed the event that would send him packing home in about thirty seconds. For others at the table, the event would make or break the evening, depending on the individual's point of view. Janet Burgess seated on her husband's left, leaned over to her left to retrieve her purse from the floor. Ostensibly, she wanted the purse in her lap to be ready to leave at a moment's notice. While Janet leaned well to her left side, waitress Trina arrived with a heavily laden tray of drinks and moved close to the table on Janet's right between her chair and Jim's. Bending, Trina began placing drinks on the table. Sweat droplets were dripping profusely down her bare chest as she worked quickly to please the demanding crowd. As the waitress reached to deposit a third glass, Janet located her purse and straightened to a normal sitting position.

Dan, sitting opposite Janet, had an unobstructed view of the encounter. The left breast of the hardworking waitress was at the correct height and extended outward at the exact angle to directly contact Janet's right ear as she sat upright in her seat. To ascertain what was touching her ear, Janet instinctively jerked her head around to the right. That move put a nipple directly against her lips. Blushing, the waitress was in a no-win situation, she still had a tray of drinks to manipulate. Trina simply held her ground and said, "I'm sorry" in a quiet voice. But the psychological damage of having an exposed mammary in her face, almost in her mouth, was *fait accompli* as far as the unhappy officer's wife was concerned. Completely nonplused, Janet, for a few seconds, seemed at a loss for any course of action. Her face blank, her eyes conveying total disbelief, she hastily looked for reaction around the table. It was as though she needed a champion, a spoken show of positive support to reinforce her bankrupt spirit. Most of the people around the table had no idea what had happened, so offered no such consolation. Those few women who saw the incident had no idea what to say under uncomfortable circumstances. Dan may have been the only male to observe the *titillating* scene. A little devilish voice inside moved him to ask, "Janet, are you having fun yet?"

Janet glowered at him, then ignoring the waitress, without acknowledging her husband or any other member of the party, indeed, without conceding the incident ever occurred, she stood and began walking briskly for the exit.
Her husband, still unaware of the real problem, got up to follow. Jim called questioning after his wife, "Honey, something wrong?"

Janet never looked back.

*****

Some people just have no sense of humor.

Chapter 30

<u>YOKOSUKA, the second time</u>

September, 1967
Age: 32

Think 'James Bond, shaken-not stirred'

In early August, CORAL SEA had once again departed
California for another WESTPAC tour. Now, late
September, the unsung heroes were *on line*, and launching
strikes against the enemy. Forty-four days of continuous
operations before an in-port break. Yokosuka, Japan, would
again the first *R&R* stop.

Dan Brown had duty the first day in port, so by day two, he
was antsy to be ashore. He had decided to treat himself to a
Japanese bath. Unfortunately, his usual pard for new and,
hopefully enjoyable, events had been stuck with a late report
his boss wanted. "Well, ole pal, you didn't wait up for me
yesterday so today, it's my time. I'm gonna find me a *hotzi*
bath. And I'm not interested in those Jap *sento*[1] communal
baths – I want the one where the gal ends up walking on
your back. If I'm going to go, I want to go the whole route."
Will Baker gave him an all-knowing smile. "All the way –
the whole banana? Eleanor will emasculate you – how you
like the big word I learned studying my *Better Language*
paperback?"

Dan was shaking his head. "No, no – I don't mean all the
way to getting laid. I mean I want the entire Nip bath
experience: hot water, hotter water, rub downs, and then if
she can convince me she's an expert, and depending on her
waist size and weight - I'll let her walk on my back. I don't
want some hundred and fifty pound mama using my one
and only back for a treadmill. Sorry you're stuck here on
the boat." He winked at Will and stepped down to the
motor launch that would take several officers ashore.

---

[1] The communal baths where all bathers are nude. Remember the
William Holden/Grace Kelly scene in *Bridges at Toko-Ri?*

Outside the gate, he walked towards the garish lights beckoning any and all sailors. Numerous taxis drove by honking for pickups and Dan waved one alongside.

"Ere goo?" the smiling Japanese driver asked.

"You mean 'Where to?' I want a good Hotzi bath– HOTZI. HOTZI", Dan replied using the colloquial word for the local baths.

"Ahhhh, hottzee, yesss." The driver pulled ahead and was off. Winding through the streets for about ten minutes, he eventually took a route up a long hill to a less dense part of the city. There the driver stopped in front of a decently maintained whitish stone building. Dan pulled out his wallet to give the driver the ten dollars agreed on back at the taxi stand. Then he asked, "You sure this is good *hotzi*, right? OK?"

The driver smiled big and wide and nodded affirmatively. Dan saw that he only had twenties in his wallet. He realized his mistake right away in not stopping at the cambio for yen. The driver would not have a U.S. ten to give him in change and would fudge on the exchange rate in yen. He handed a twenty over; the driver gave back a handful of yen.

Counting his yen, a feminine voice called to him from the porch of the house. He turned to climb the steps up to the front door as the driver hurriedly got in his old Chevrolet to leave.

An older woman, at least fifty he guessed, awaited Dan but Japanese women of middle age were sometimes hard to figure. His first impression was that she looked hard and used. An inkling hit him that maybe this wasn't a first rate bathhouse. While asking the geisha dressed woman about *hotzi* girls, he started to put the uncounted yen into his wallet. That's when he saw that two real yen notes covered pieces of newspaper. The taxi driver had ripped him off for almost the entire ten dollars. Pissed at himself now for being so naive, he looked around at the surroundings in a more critical way. Down a hall that probably led to the hot bath rooms, he saw a naked girl and a naked man – a fellow from the ship that he knew – come out of a side room. They were both laughing and she was holding him by his erect manhood. Now he knew the taxi driver had not only beaten him out of ten bucks but delivered him to a house of prostitution. Shaking his head at the Mama'san, he backed away and turned for the door.

The house set at the entry to a deep cul-de-sac. After maneuvering to turn the fifteen-year old Chevy around in the small space available, the taxi was just getting back to the original drop off point. Seeing this, the angry Naval officer rushed down the steps into the road. Never expecting to see the American pilot again, the driver braked to a stop, more in surprise than an offer of taxi service. Just as Dan stepped around the side and onto the running board, black smoke billowed from the tailpipe as the unhappy driver floored the gas pedal.

Instinctively, without thought of consequence, Dan reached through the rear window and wrapped his arm around the post separating the front and rear doors. The taxi was now accelerating and the driver wanted no part of the angry 'Melican'[1] hanging off the side. He swerved dangerously close to a truck parked on the opposite side of the street trying to wipe out his unwanted passenger. Dan barely ducked away from the truck's rear view mirror.

Next, the road opened some and the driver began to zigzag trying to dislodge the angry man hanging on to the side of his car. Pedestrians and passersby gaped at the sight of an American hanging on the side of a racing taxi and the driver evidently trying to get rid of him. Dan felt the rush of air on his face and clothing as the taxi hurled down the hill they had ascended just minutes before.

The driver saw a chance for a ninety-degree turn to the right down a side street and took it at a speed that had the old heap leaning so far over two tires almost came off the pavement. Dan was holding on for his life and looked down to see his legs completely parallel with the ground. He didn't know how fast they were going, just FAST. But he was able to hang on and when the car straightened out, he felt his feet back on the running board. Images of an old Sean Connery movie ran through his head and he smiled to himself when he realized how the situation was both

---

[1] Often the Japanese who learned English on the streets can't get out the 'A' in American.

exhilarating and ridiculous at the same time. *Brown's the name. Rum and coke, no lime.* He knew it must look strange to people on the street, but hey, this was a port of call for ships around the world. Maybe this kind of thing was routine in Yokosuka. He felt confident that the driver was not going to be able to throw him off. The driver had not yet figured that out however, and continued to try and remove the human appendage from his taxi. He tried sharp turns, hard braking, another right turn, even an extreme left turn with centrifugal force pushing Dan up against the car doors, but to no avail. The determined officer held on.

After a few more zigzags and close encounters with oncoming vehicles, the driver gave up, slowed to normal speed and turned down the original street where Dan had engaged him. When the auto came to a stop, the driver opened his door quickly and handed over the original twenty-dollar bill. He seemed pale and nervous. Perhaps suddenly rational and now fearful that he might have actually thrown his passenger off? Dan could feel his own pulse racing excitedly. Proud of his athletic ability to hang on throughout the wildly menacing ride, yet realizing what a stupid thing it was, he glared at his counterpart but said nothing as he pocketed the money. Feeling an "I win" moment, he reached in his pocket and gave the fistful of yen and newspaper money back to a nonplussed driver.

Adrenalin and excitement waning, he walked towards Fleet Landing. The entire sequence of events had been another story to tell the guys but not to write home about. 'The mother of my children would never let me hear the end of it. Oh well, surely there's a beer in my immediate future before catching a boat back to the ship. Maybe Will will know of a real *hotzi* place that we can go to. O.K. Scarlett, tomorrow is another day.'

*****

And they did – just the baths, wives, just the baths (and the feet).

Chapter 31

MRS. DAVID O. SELZNICK

October, 1967
Age: 32

The flight had been a routine parts and personnel run from the ship operating in the Tonkin Gulf to Cubi Point, remain overnight, and return to CORAL SEA early the next morning. Airborne at 0600, the C-1A with the Brown Boys, Dan and Jake, pilot and copilot, was about ninety minutes away from completing the assigned mission.

During the humdrum boredom of several four plus hour flights, this being one, Dan and Jake found time to discuss anything from fruit to nuts – any topic to fight off the tedium of weariness. Often, it was about the fair sex, sometimes wives. Today, Jake was sharing the fact that his wife had breast implants. "And you know what that damn roommate of mine asked?"

Dan looked at his copilot and shook his head.

Jake: "He wanted to know if they still taste the same after a boob job."

Dan looked straight ahead for a full minute before an impish response. Still not looking at his friend and clenching his teeth to keep from grinning or laughing, "Well, do they?" The bicep muscle in his right arm hurt for the rest of the flight after Jake's fist hit it square on. Then they both chuckled when Jake finally muttered, "Yes. But like *Lucky Strikes*, so firm – so fully packed."

Unexpectedly, the radio crackled. "Mustang 022, this is Mustang control. Over."

The copilot responded. "Mustang, this is Mustang 022. Go ahead."

Both pilots listened attentively. "022, you have new orders. Divert to Da-nang Air Base and pick up high priority cargo. Air Force representatives will brief you on your VIP passenger. Do you copy?"

Jake spoke into his mike. "Affirmative, Mustang. 022 changing course for Da-nang. Do you have a new recovery time for us?"

A short delay and then the voice over the radio continued: "Negative 022. Land Da-nang, refuel while awaiting passenger. Proceed Mustang as soon as she is aboard. We will give you landing instructions on arrival Mustang."

On route, Dan wondered, "And who do you reckon 'She' will be?"

Jake: "I saw *The Graduate* just before we left the states, so I vote for Katherine Ross. She is so hot in a girl-next-door sort of way."

Dan recognized her as soon as she exited the Quonset hut used by the Air Force as an Operations Building. In the flesh was Mrs. David O. Selznick, or better known to her fans, Jennifer Jones. He was enthralled to know that she would be his passenger out to the big boat. She had starred in some of his favorite films, among them *Duel in the Sun, The Man in the Gray Flannel Suit,* and one of his all-time favorites, *Love is a Many Splendored Thing.* As he watched her walk across the improvised tarmac, he remembered she had won an Academy Award for Best Actress but could not have named the film for all the tea in China. Nor was he aware she had been nominated for four others. Once back on the ship, he would research her bio and find that *The Song of Bernadette* won her the Oscar as a twenty-four year old newcomer to Hollywood. He was pleased to learn that one of her other nominations was for her role in *Splendored Thing.*

She was on a USO hand-shaking tour, one of several screen stars to show their patriotic zeal for the sailors, marines, and soldiers caught up in an unpopular war. Jake started the engines while Dan unstrapped and welcomed their guest. He assisted her up the steps and then helped strap on the safety harness. Once she appeared comfortable, he returned to the cockpit. Soon the twin-engine *COD* was taxiing to the runway.

Once airborne, Dan asked Jake to offer his seat to their guest. Permitting VIPs to experience flight from the pilot's perspective was usually well received. And besides, Dan wanted to chat with the famous star, one-on-one. He knew that once he landed the C-1A on CORAL SEA, he'd be lucky to lay eyes on her again – the Admiral and his staff plus the Captain and his guys would hog her time.

Ms. Jones moved into the copilot's seat and buckled in. It didn't take long to get to know her. He felt their conversation was that of two old friends who haven't seen each other in a long while. She seemed genuinely interested in the plane, his role in flying, the many instruments on the panel, as well as his thoughts on the Vietnam conflict. She asked about landing on a ship at sea. "Would it be uncomfortable?" "Was it dangerous?" "How many times have you landed on a carrier?" He was pleased to tell her that he was approaching three hundred traps, Navy lingo for carrier landings. She allowed as "How that helped ease her apprehension." Ms. Jones confided that at first she had declined to accept the trip to a ship at sea because of the dangerous landing. USO officials had assured her it would be safe. Then Bob Hope told her the Navy only sent good pilots for visiting dignitaries.
Dan: "My ego tells me that I think they sent the very best." Ms. Jones didn't seem surprised at his confidence level. "May I call your wife for you when I get back to California?" she offered. "I can tell her about seeing you handsome and healthy. Give me you phone number and address and I promise to either call or write." (She did both).

The flight to CORAL SEA was just a little over an hour. Thirty minutes out, with Ms. Jones still riding copilot, the radio speaker came alive with a call from the ship. "022, we have a crash on the flight deck. Conserve fuel and anticipate at least one hour delay in landing."
Jennifer Jones uttered a whimper. When Dan looked to see the cause, he could readily see her pained frown. She was evidently chagrined. "Dammit", she said, "I knew I should have gone to the ladies room before we took off. I'm about to pee my panties."

With Jake back in the right seat, Dan picked up the microphone. With Ms. Jones safely tucked away in the back where she could not hear cockpit conversation, he called the ship and asked for a discrete frequency. "Listen, Ms. Jones has had a little airsickness. As soon as I touchdown, have an escort get her to the nearest head that can be sealed off for her private use. And tell the tower that I need to be the first plane to land. Let's give Jennifer Jones the royal treatment." Turning to Jake, he said, "Did you know that movie stars have to tinkle just like mere mortals?"

Back on board ship in the library, delving into her life, he was surprised to find that she wasn't yet fifty. With all her films and nominations, plus of course, *Oscar*, he had guessed her age had to be around sixty. Then he read that David Selznick had died in the summer of 1965. He wondered if Selznick's death had anything to do with her decision to visit the troops. Of course, he could not fathom that she would return from her USO tour to WESTPAC, call his wife Eleanor and tell her what a great pilot her husband was – and shortly afterwards, check into a Malibu hotel and take an overdose of sleeping pills.[1]

The men of CORAL SEA gave Ms. Jones a warm and appreciative welcome!

*****

Thank you, Jennifer Jones, for caring.

---

[1] She was found on beach and revived – Thank goodness!

Chapter 32

DEAD MAN WALKING - AND TALKING

December, 1967
Age: 32

LCDR Dan Brown relaxed when the Duval County-Jacksonville road marker came into view. As the late model Chevy wagon carried him nearer and nearer to Jacksonville, he was thinking about seeing his college roommate again. He had last seen Michael and family about three years earlier. Dan had never been big on corresponding with old friends via mail. This had proven particularly true for his two Vietnam tours to date. Writing letters about birthdays, port visits, and overseas shopping while watching pilot friends fly and die in combat conditions was an incongruity he didn't like. Family responsibility was one thing, penning a note to individuals outside that circle was another. He knew he would be returning to the Tonkin Gulf within the year and probably wouldn't change his philosophy. The thought of a long distance telephone call never entered his mind unless a bona fide emergency existed. On the other hand, he was very loyal about visiting friends whenever an opportunity arose. He had once driven two hundred miles out of the way on a 1965 vacation to spend a few minutes with an old friend from flight training. He glanced in the rearview mirror and straightened the Windsor knot of his regulation black tie. Out of habit, he checked to make sure both shirt pockets were buttoned. In doing so, he touched the gold wings pinned above the left pocket. Without conscious effort, he ran his fingers over the outline of the metallic emblem that meant so much to him.

He was being sent to Jacksonville for seven or eight days to attend Jet Instrument Refresher Training at NAS Cecil Field. He had completed his two-year tour aboard USS CORAL SEA. Detached at sea, he flew home from the Philippines on an Air Force transport via Guam and Hawaii. He delayed in California just long enough for the Navy to pack up his wife and family and their household goods. They left the Alameda-Oakland-San Francisco area enroute to the large jet base in Sanford, Florida. There, a neat three-bedroom '50's dwelling tucked away near an orange grove was found and rented. Moderately affordable, the lemon green house was built in the bomb-scare era. There was a large 20 x 30 cement block atom bomb shelter in their back yard. It was somewhat of a conversation starter although there were several others to be found in the Sanford community.

Dan would be training in the sleek, supersonic RA-5C *Vigilante.* While checking out in the airplane systems and flight procedures, he would also be training in photographic reconnaissance and electronic intelligence. Before he could climb into the cockpit of the big fast bird, annual instrument refresher training was required. For fleet pilots on the east coast, Cecil Field, Jacksonville, was where this special training happened.

He crossed the long bridge over the St. Johns into Green Cove Springs. Remaining on U.S. 17 through Orange Park, he began to recognize scenes and old haunts from his tour in the area some ten years before. There was the Orange Park Kennel Club where Michael and Jennie had introduced him to greyhound racing. A half frown, then a grin framed his facial features as he remembered they had also introduced him to losing over a hundred dollars that night. Eleanor had not been happy with her husband or his friends from years past.

Continuing north on Roosevelt Boulevard, he began watching for Ortega Boulevard which would take him to the Allison's door. As always, he had not called Michael purposely, wanting to surprise him. He hoped Mike and Jennie and the kids would be home. If not, he'd go on to Cecil, get a room in the BOQ and call Mike later. If the Allison's were not home now at four o'clock in the afternoon, they would surely return by early evening. He expected that four children, all girls, kept them close to home on school nights. Hopefully, they could get together for cocktails and dinner. He found the brick Colonial easily. He saw two cars in the drive, indicating the family was probably at home. Dan parked and exited the car, stretching his legs and torso as he straightened up. Standing erect, the officer adjusted his uniform and then walked briskly to the back door. He always used the rear entry to Michael's home. In rural Georgia when he was growing up, only company came to the front door. He didn't consider himself company at the Allison residence.

Michael answered the door. Seeing Dan, his face whitened into a blank stare and he involuntarily stepped back from the entryway, as in genuine disbelief. For a split second Dan thought Michael's countenance was one of non-recognition. Dan was dumbfounded, totally surprised at his friend's reaction at seeing him. Recovering after the momentary shock, still somewhat confused, Michael blurted out the words that explained the unusual reception. "Brown, you're dead! We heard you were shot down!" Only a few seconds had passed but for both men this unexpected encounter may have seemed longer. Now they smiled broadly and reached to shake hands. Perhaps a manly hug was exchanged between two guys whose friendship went back to freshman days in college.

"Buddy, we heard you bought the farm.....that you flew some bombing mission into North Vietnam and a SAM got your plane. We heard that story two, maybe three months ago. Man, it's good to see you. How did you get out of that airplane and back to your ship?"

Dan broke from the grip of his closest civilian friend. "Hey, I don't know what you're talking about. This ole flyboy has never been smoked. I'm just here wanting a rum and coke or a glass of wine, and some friendly chit-chat. I just got into town. I haven't even been to the base yet."

Michael called up the stairwell to his wife. "Jennie, come down and see who's back from the war. Alive. You won't believe it."

Jennie Allison descended the stairs. Quizzically, she called, "Who in the world is here?" As she entered the room her puzzled expression changed to bewilderment, then to a broad smile. Delighted to see Dan standing in their living room, she rushed to greet him. "Welcome home, old friend", she simultaneously hugged him and offered her cheek for the customary kiss. They released as she reiterated her husband's statements about their complete surprise at seeing him. "This is so spooky. We were just talking about you the other night at the Club. Michael said he couldn't believe you were dead, that you'd probably come back and haunt us."

"Hey, you're looking at me. I'm haunting you for a glass of wine. It's really me. Walking and talking. Flying and swapping lies. Yep, it's me. Daniell Maurice Brown, Class of '54, Emory-at-Oxford. Naval Aviator personified."

There was a lot of catching up to do that evening. After a late meal, Dan was finally beginning to feel mellow. "Drinks before dinner, white wine with dinner, and now heavy wine after dinner. We've talked so much, I feel like I'm telling it all.....even the part about the goat.[1] It's great to be here, *back from the dead,* I might add." They moved to the den and continued to reminisce and swap stories. Other than Dan's safe return, the whys and wherefores of the conflict in Southeast Asia were not mentioned.

Slouched comfortably, he half-sat, partly reclined on the brightly colored sofa near the picture window. When he moved an open letter on the end table to put down his glass, Jennie said: "Oh, let me have that before it gets lost. It's an invitation to a debutante party. That reminds me, remember some of those parties you attended with us when you were a brand-new Navy Ensign, a handsome young pilot, single and eligible?"

Michael added, "And so virtuous."

Dan nodded, "Oh yes, the old debutante stag line. But do you know, I have a story that I'll bet Mr. Michael here has never told you. Do you remember Elizabeth McDonald's *debut* party at the Tolland's home?" Jennie nodded that sure, she recalled the occasion.

Michael frowned, "No, no, whatever he says I didn't do it."

Dan continued. "Yes, you did, Pal. Jennie, you probably don't remember what the three of us did after that party. I'll remind you. We went to 7-11 and bought a coke and a ginger ale. Then we drove out to the Yacht Club docks and sat there till well after midnight drinking our bourbon and coke and CC and ginger. Remember? That was before I flew to Cuba and discovered rum and coke."

---

[1] An old joke not worth telling here

Jennie nodded affirmatively. "Yes, now I do. I had forgotten but that's exactly what we did. I can't imagine that I ever liked such obnoxiously sweet drinks. Today, I stick with either wine or bourbon." As if underlining her remarks, a half filled wine glass found its way to her lips as she sipped the nearly clear liquid.

Dan continued. "Do you have any idea where the booze that we mixed in those drinks came from? It happened like this. About two minutes before the party ended, Michael came to me and said, 'Brown, you got any money?' I told him I had two dollars. He confessed he had only a buck and change. He said it was too early to go home and we should go somewhere to sit and talk and 'Drank.' Since we didn't have enough money, we would need a source for liquor. He told me to look over at the bar where the bartender was beginning to clean up. As the help turned away to tidy the area and empty trash, Michael walked to the bar and filled a fresh glass three-fourths full with straight bourbon. He handed it to me and said, 'Put this in your inside coat pocket.' Then he did the same thing with a nearly full glass of Canadian Club. But he was real thoughtful. He reminded me twice on the way to the door to be careful about how I moved my arms and shoulders as I said goodnight to Mr. Towland. We walked down the steps very carefully. That's my best debutante story - even better than the one you've told fifteen times to every woman I know. 'I fixed Danny up with a beautiful girl but when we got to the party, she met an old boy friend and dumped him!' By the way, do the Towland's still live in that same house on the corner of Ortega and Yacht Club? I hope someday to see Mr. and Mrs. Tolland and tell them this story. As I remember, they were a fun pair."

Michael, in mock chagrin, chimed in, "Hell, Brown, while we're at it, we'll just tell Mrs. Elizabeth Howard McDonald Durkin about it, too. Ah heck, who cares, that was ten or eleven years ago. Go ahead, tell everybody that Allison's a thief – he stole liquor when he was twenty-two!"

Their quiet time was interrupted with a call from a young voice upstairs. "Mommy. Daddy. Come here!"

Michael and Jennie left the room for a few minutes to check on children. Sitting alone, Dan pondered circumstances that could be the source of misinformation on his supposed death or missing in action status. 'Why would the story be out that I was shot down?' Then he remembered.

Michael returned to the den. "Jennie will be back as soon as she reads Lizzie a bedtime story."
Dan: "Michael, this 'He was dead but now alive' story is going to be a great one to tell for years. But I'm still amazed that you saw me and said, 'Brown, you're dead!' It seems to me you would have said, 'Brown! You're alive'."
Michael shrugged, "I dunno, it's just what came out."

Jennie Allison called from the hallway. "I'm back. I hope you didn't tell any stories without me."
As Jennie reassumed her seat in the large red wingback chair near the fireplace, Dan shared his theory with the hosts. "I think I know how the misinformation of my demise got started. Here's what probably happened. There's usually two carriers on station in the Tonkin Gulf. I was on CORAL SEA, our sister ship was the CONSTELLATION. There was an attack pilot on Connie named Donald Browne, B-R-O-W-N-E, who was shot down - and killed as far as we know - over Vinh about three and a half months ago. I'll bet the similar name Donald Browne with an 'e' compared to Dan Brown without the 'e' is the key. The word had to come from the base[1] from people who were privy to the list of wounded and missing. They tell someone that LT Don Browne was smoked and the word gets around it was yours truly who took the SAM. Oh, another thing, LT Browne was assigned to an A7 squadron which meant he would have been on a bombing run like you heard. I'm sure that's how the incident was misinterpreted here in River City. However it began, it's a happy ending right out of a Disney script. Well, happy for me, not so happy for Donald Browne. I hope he's POW[2] and not dead. Who knows for sure?" Perhaps pensive over the real fate of LT Browne, he

---

[1] NAS Cecil Field (now closed by BRAC)
[2] Prisoner of War

appeared to study the glass of *Grand Marnier* in his hands. Then, extending the glass, he offered a heartfelt toast. "Anyway, anyhow, here's to us. The Allisons and the Browns."

Three glasses were raised in silent unison.

*****

Friendship is a lifetime thing.

Chapter 33

CASSADAGA

May, 1968
Age: 32

Central Florida, "B.D.", that is, *before Disney*, was about as close to heaven on earth as any spot on our planet. Orlando, dotted with lakes and more lakes, was quietly beautiful. Altamonte Springs, Castleberry, Longwood, Lake Mary, and Sanford lie north along Interstate 4. All the cities mentioned are generously endowed with orange trees and exceptional scenery. Northward-flowing St. Johns River adds immensely to the beauty of the region. Before the invasion of Disney, *restful* and *serene* were oft-used adjectives for Florida lifestyles in the vicinity of Orlando and Lake Apopka. *Disney World, Universal Studios,* and *Sea World* initiated massive changes that introduced Orlando to a new *World,* one of mass tourism and unbridled commercial expanse.

Dan and Eleanor Brown and children were privileged to live in Sanford for several months during 1967-68 during the B.D. peaceful times. Here Dan would trade in his fighter pilot credentials for new aviation experiences in photographic imagery and reconnaissance. He would be training in the RA-5C *Vigilante.*

As one leaves Sanford, driving north past Deltona toward Deland, an exit marker on I-4 might catch the eye. The Department of Transportation sign announcing LAKE HELEN also has in smaller lettering, CASSADAGA.[1]

Four o'clock finally came and ground school, much hated by all aviators, was over for the day. Arriving home, Dan knew something special was in the air. Eleanor's countenance could only be described as the proverbial, "smiling ear to ear".

---

[1] Today (2005) 'Cassadaga' is on a much larger sign

Dan had to ask. "O.K., what's the big deal? I know something is up."

Eleanor announced to her family she had an appointment in Cassadaga the following day. "I will be seeing a medium there. The Cassadaga mediums have quite a following. As I understand it, the seers in that quiet little town are not just palm readers or horoscope gurus or anything like that. They are somehow religious in their own way. You must be present with them, perhaps even holding hands or touching in some way, for them to give you a reading. I called for an appointment today but used a false name and didn't even tell them where I live. I'm going to drive up with Teresa Baker who is borrowing her cleaning lady's car. And I'm going to leave my wedding ring at home. I'm planning to wear very casual clothes so that I'll be just another Florida tourist looking for a reading. There will be no way the medium will be able to know I'm from a Navy base married to a Navy pilot."

"And what is the cost of this little foray into the world of hocus-pocus?" Dan inquired.

Eleanor answered curtly: "Somewhere between twenty and thirty-five dollars, depending on the length of the sitting. And Dan, it's not something to ridicule. You know how intrigued I am in horoscopes, the zodiac and such things. Consider the expense as my recreation for the month. Actually, it's a pretty cheap way to satisfy my curiosity."

Her husband gave in without a fight. "Go for it but I still don't see........................"

Eleanor cut him short. "Dan, mediums can tell you both the past and the future. We still don't have orders and you're supposed to graduate in less than four months. I want to know where you're going, where my family is going. We don't know if you'll be sent to a squadron deploying in the Mediterranean or if you'll go straight to Vietnam. After the medium tells me all the general information he has for me, and I'm sure he's for real, I'm going to ask specifically about your next assignment."

Dan was home the following afternoon when Eleanor returned from her mysterious appointment. She was glowing.

"Hey, fix me a martini and pour yourself a double rum. I have so much to tell you. You're not going to believe how much the medium told me."

The dutiful husband returned with drinks and awaited Eleanor's soliloquy.

Her exuberance was readily apparent. She began.

"Remember, we were afraid a car with a base sticker would give us away, so Teresa's maid loaned us her six-year old Plymouth with no markings. We had to wait about twenty minutes while Mr. Sears, that's his name, finished whatever he was doing. I think he was writing in a journal, or something. Anyway, he finally came out and sat with me while Teresa met with Mrs. Sears in another room. She's also a medium."

Eleanor sipped her drink and nibbled at an olive. "OK, I sat across a desk from him. He's around fifty. Not young, but not as old as I expected. He held both my hands and closed his eyes. He asked me to think about my family. He was quiet for seven or eight minutes, then he said. 'I see your husband is a flier. Oh, tell him not to worry about going to Vietnam when he finishes training, he will be going the other way instead. He won't go to Vietnam for at least another year. I see you with three children, all happy and healthy.' His eyes blinked several times as though a splinter or a tear impaired his eyes. Then he added, 'Well, the boy did have some vision problems but he is better now. You lived somewhere out west before moving here, California I think. Now, when you concentrate on your two girls, I see another shadow behind you, someone from the spirit world. I see your husband more clearly and he's in a dark blue uniform - I see this spirit form in a light blue uniform from another service. Oh, he has a message for you. He says to tell you he is proud of you for taking such good care of the children. I think I understand now, he must be the girl's father. The other man, the husband in dark blue, is the father of your son. That's all I see for now; contentment in the spirit world, no unusual sadness in this one.' That's about it, what he told me, but was he right or was he right?"

Husband and wife sat staring at each other. The seer had hit several homeruns with no errors. Only one prediction was yet to be determined – Dan's next set of orders. Yes, she was a service wife and, of course, her husband was a pilot. They had lived "Out west", in San Francisco, California, for the past two years before reporting to replacement air group training at Sanford. And their four-year-old son had undergone eye surgery for myopia, which seemed to be 100% better. Eleanor was an Air Force widow with two young girls before marrying Dan. Her first husband was also a flier and had been killed off the coast of England some years earlier. Holt Woddall had ejected over the North Sea in the dead of winter. Survival time would have been only six or seven minutes in the icy water. In military wintertime dress, his Air Force uniform would be a lighter color than Navy blues.

Dan took a deep breath. "That's pretty amazing stuff. I wonder why the television crews aren't camped out there day in and day out."

CHAPTER EPILOGUE. Some months later, Naval Air Station, Sanford, Florida, closed. All planes, equipment, officers and men were moved to Naval Air Station, Albany, Georgia.
Dan Brown completed RA-5C training in November 1968.

Two days after completion of carrier qualifications, orders from Bureau of Personnel, Navy Department, Washington, D.C., arrived ordering Lieutenant Commander Daniell M. Brown to Reconnaissance Attack Squadron TWELVE (RVAH-12) operating from USS FORRESTAL (CVA-59), deployed to the Mediterranean Sea. Dan would gain a year's experience in the high performance reconnaissance jet before joining Seventh Fleet forces operating in the South China Sea in opposition to communist aggression in Vietnam. The Cassadaga medium had been correct on all fronts!

Today, an estimated 50,000 visitors a year are drawn to Cassadaga for it many psychics, mediums, and spiritual healers. The small hamlet is truly a 'Metaphysical Mecca'.

*****

Chapter 34

THE FOOT LOVER

September, 1968
Age: 33

RA5C *Vigilante* training was finally complete – except for proof of the pudding. The last step, you could call it a *final test*, was carrier landings qualification. Pilots had to demonstrate proficiency by successfully landing the demanding airplane aboard ship sixteen times. Called 'traps', ten were to be accomplished in daylight, six at night. Dan Brown and several other pilots flew *Vigies* to Naval Air Station, Alameda, California. USS ENTERPRISE (CVAN-65) would be conducting carrier ops for the next few days. For Dan, going to San Francisco was old home week as he was only a year away from living there while attached to CORAL SEA. As luck would have it, his brother had been transferred to California and was working in San Jose, about thirty miles south. He had recently acquired a second automobile. Dan borrowed the car for the ensuing week and became tour guide for as many would fit in the '64 Ford *Fairlane* when free time was available.

The pilots, crews and planes arrived NAS Alameda and were anxious to begin carrier quals but for whatever reason, the ship was delayed in getting underway. Stuck ashore without a definite plan of action, flight crews had time to kill until the big carrier was actually at sea. Dan picked up the Ford, returned to base, and loaded up his passengers for a sight seeing tour. Crossing the Bay Bridge, the five pilots were greeted to the scenic beauty of San Francisco, many seeing the *City by the bay* for the first time. In the heart of the city he got their attention with a speedy descent down the steep and daring Filbert Street. Then over two blocks to Lombard for a slow and calming drive down the famous winding street so loved by tourists. A big folk music fan, Dan made it a point to drive to Broadway Avenue and find *the hungry i* made famous by the Kingston Trio.

Crossing the Golden Gate Bridge northward toward
Sausilito, photographs of the rustic red span were dutifully
snapped. Shortly, Dan parked and pointed out Alcatraz to
his charges although haze diminished the usually   ·
picturesque view. Several boats dotted the water between
the bridge and the island. Again, busy cameras snapped
picture after picture of anything that moved with the old
prison in the background.
After crossing the bridge and touring Sausilito, Dan and
group backtracked and turned south toward Golden Gate
Park.
The enormous expanse, usually filled to capacity with
humanity on Saturdays, Sundays, and holidays, had
relatively few visitors. Weekdays, fortunately, saw not so
many tourists, which permitted the visitors from NAS
Albany, Georgia, to take in the true beauty of the park. At
one small pond a flock of ten or twelve Canadian geese
zoomed in for a wet landing. The group exited their vehicle
and walked the manicured grounds for several minutes.
Exiting the park Oceanside, the visitors were impressed by
leaning, windswept Juniper trees lining the park's perimeter.
At a nearby street corner, a young man in bellbottom
trousers and faded gray shirt was selling newly printed issues
of *The Bay Life Communicato*r. Dan pulled alongside and
purchased one of the twenty-five cent papers. He handed
the paper over his shoulder to the back seat. "Here, guys,
this is a Hippie underground newspaper. Somebody read a
few topics. Which reminds me. Let's turn around and go
back by way of Haight-Ashbury. I want you genteel folk to
see the new generation up close and personal - the Hippies
of the Sixties. You won't believe your eyes."
As they drove eastward through the park, CDR Tony
Grimes, a good ole Southern boy from a little no-name town
in South Georgia, perused the paper purchased only a few
minutes before. Shaking his head, he said in his heavy
southern accent: "Hey, Danny, why are all these want ads
in code? What do these weird abbreviations mean?"
Dan smiled, knowing some fun was about to begin. "Tony,
pick one and read what you can and read the letters and
numbers that you don't understand to me letter by letter,
number by number. Let's see if we can't figure it out."

CDR Grimes read aloud. "WM, 35, WANTS FEM 18-22 TO SHARE RM/RENT. I get that line except for the WM. Somebody wants a female age 18 to 22 to share the room rent."

Dan grinned again and replied, "*W.M.* means white male. Read on."

Tony Grimes continued. "6-1, LOVE ORAL, BIG STICK, F-R, G-R-K, GAMES. 641-7706. NO FATTIES, WHITES ONLY." He glanced up at the others. "I think I'm getting it. He is six feet one, he loves oral sex, he's well endowed or at least brags that he is. I'm not sure about F-R, G-R-K, or what kinds of games he wants to play. After listing his phone number, he says he doesn't want any fat girls and only Caucasian women should respond."

Dan: "You're doing pretty good for a novice, but c'mon, Tony. You should know *F-R* is French, *G-R-K* is Greek. He likes French and Greek sex. Surely I don't have to tell you the difference? *Games* can mean anything. Maybe he likes to dress up like a cowboy or a policeman. He might like to tie girls up. He may want to be handcuffed to the bed himself. We'll never know. Unless, of course, you want to call and ask him?"

CDR Grimes gave Dan the "you must be crazy as hell" look and said nothing.

As Dan drove, his awed friend continued to scan the personals. "Hey, here's one I can't believe. Listen to this weirdo. 'GIRLS, I LOVE YOUR FEET. I KISS THEM, I SUCK THEM, I SMELL THEM, I WORSHIP THEM. CALL 367-8854 FOR A FOOT MASSAGE BY TONGUE. I WILL CARESS YOUR FEET WITH WARM SALIVA. WAITING FOR YOUR CALL'."

From the front seat, Dan confirmed the original premise, "I told you this place is a little different; wonderful and unusual at the same time."

Ten to fifteen minutes later, the sedan approached the intersection of Haight and Ashbury Streets just east of Golden Gate Park. Dan slowed so that the newcomers could take in the sights and sounds of "the groovy Peace and Love generation." Blankets of all colors and sizes lined up as ground kiosks on both sides of the street. Handmade jewelry seemed to be the number one offering. Corner vendors with real kiosk stands were selling soft drinks, kites, even old *Playboy* magazines. A tall skinny fellow was enthusiastically hawking yo-yos. Strangely, at least to the Southerners, no hot dog stands were to be seen. Used clothing items hung from makeshift racks for bargain basement prices. Many of the men were shirtless and it seemed that everyone, men and women were in well-worn, faded bluejeans. Children who could walk were constrained by shoulder harnesses with leashes held by parents. Many babies were in backpacks. The scene was alien to the occupants of the *Fairlane* but appeared to be totally normal and in context within the hippie community.

As their car neared the next intersection, LT Barry Moore pointed out a young woman walking on the opposite sidewalk. She was just a few yards away, coming west as they traveled east. Her hair was askew, uncombed, long and matted. She was wearing a faded granny gown, a print of non-descript pink and blue daisies. She looked straight ahead, face unsmiling, and she held a rolled up newspaper in one hand. She wore no shoes, her feet caked with dust and grime and filth from the streets. Alone, unhurried, she carried no purse; one could only wonder where she might be going, if she had money for her next meal.
From the back seat, Tony Grimes grabbed Dan's shoulder and called out excitedly, "Danny Boy, stop the car! Hand me that underground newspaper and give me a dime. I have to call the foot sucker for that gal. We'll cure his ass!"

*****

Different strokes for different folks!

Chapter 35

"FLYING IS NOT DANGEROUS - CRASHING IS DANGEROUS"

Author Unknown

20 January 1969
Age: 33

Two more aviation sayings appropriate to this topic:

> *Flying is the second greatest thrill known to man...landing is the first.*
> *...any landing you walk away from is a good landing -* an adage long purported by fliers, military and civilian.
Authors unknown

Time: mid-afternoon, aboard USS FORRESTAL (CVA-59). Position: Latitude 36:35 north, Longitude 19:00 east, approximately 300 miles west of the Island of Crete in the Mediterranean Sea.

Dan Brown looked at his instruments, braced the back of his helmet against the headrest of the ejection-equipped seat, and saluted, the Navy way of saying "I'm ready to fly." The ship's catapult officer, LCDR Charlie Fuller, became the focus of the pilot's attention. On deck, the *Cat* officer looked one last time at the twin-engine plane tugging at, actually struggling against its hold-down apparatus. The roar of two afterburners creating 18,000 pounds thrust to an uninitiated observer would simply have been obnoxiously loud. To LT Fuller, attired in yellow flight deck gear and protective ear covering, the engines sounded normal and in sync. Both flame patterns shooting out of the twin tailpipes also appeared symmetrical, he could see no gasoline or oil or hydraulic leaks. Deliberately, he reached down and touched the FORRESTAL flight deck with his left index finger. At a control panel in a protected walkway along side the flight deck, in direct sight of the Cat Officer, an enlisted man interpreted that signal as "OK to launch". He pushed a red button on the gray box before him. Instantaneously, many thousands pounds of steam fired the huge plane down the catapult track. 2.1 seconds later the eighty thousand-pound *Vigilante* was airborne at 180 knots, speed and altitude increasing dramatically.

The tandem team of pilot LCDR Brown and his reconnaissance attack navigator[1], LT Tommy Thome in the back seat, had been assigned a *seek and find* mission. Russian trawlers were known to be operating in the area. *Speartip 604* was to checkout a reported sighting near the Niso Islands just off the coast of Greece. If confirmed, the reconnaissance aircraft equipped with five different cameras was to take photographs. In addition, a passive electronics counter measures receiver on board the aircraft would be making a tape of any electronic emissions transmitted by the clever Russians. Air intelligence wanted pictures from all aspects of the modified fishing vessel, now converted to a sophisticated Soviet spy ship.

The sighting proved correct. Two hundred twenty miles northeast of the carrier task group, *Speartip 604* found the trawler wallowing in light seas. The pilot dove the plane steeply from thirty-five thousand feet, decreasing altitude rapidly at a speed of just under six hundred knots, the speed of sound. Using all five cameras mounted on the *Vigilante*, the crew snapped numerous photos of the trawler's silhouette from port and starboard sides, as well as numerous fore and aft shots. Finally at 800 feet altitude Thome snapped a picture from directly above looking down the stack. A first for him, Dan saw two women among several men working on deck as they flew by at lower than the internationally prescribed altitude of one thousand feet. One of the women and several of the men waved at the American jet. Dan knew the *Air Intel* guys would be working late into the night identifying every antenna and mast, confirming *yes or no* that updated radar or jamming equipment had been added to the "Enemy's" cloak and dagger arsenal.

In the "Cold War", this was standard reconnaissance procedure. All sighting reports were checked out as soon as

---

[1] Usually referred to simply as RAN

possible, airborne photos taken, then scoured over by intelligence types to see if any new surveillance equipment had increased the trawler's capability to spy on American or NATO forces.

From the back seat, LT Thome, over the "hot" interphone which permitted the two cockpits to talk to each other without having to push microphone buttons or switches, pronounced the mission complete. "Cameras functioned as advertised. Danny my boy, these pics will be so good we may get an academy award! Idea - we're only fifteen miles from the island of Scorpios. We got plenty of gas and a little extra time. Why don't we swing by and say hello to Jackie and Ari?"

Dan: "My map says the island has been declared a restricted area." Leveling the plane at fifteen hundred feet, he turned the plane northeast again toward the Grecian archipelago. "But I guess we could always get lost in that bay just ahead. To get out, we'd have to egress over an island sitting just left of my nose." Four minutes later, the famous island resort of the Greek tycoon was one-half mile straight ahead. "So that's the Onassis' little vacation place. Velly nice. I bet they serve pistachio nuts and everything! Tommy, make sure the cameras are on."

The navigator again flicked five camera switches upward and *on* as the fleet jet approached landfall. They crossed the middle of the island heading 248 degrees. Tommy was elated. "Good idea, Dan-o. The intelligence crew can have a little fun after they work the trawler film. I wonder if the rich and famous are home?"

The fly-by was disappointing. Dan saw no people, no activity of any nature. The island appeared deserted. There were no yachts moored at the docks, nor ships of any size anchored nearby. The buildings on the compound were drab and anything but spectacular. "Oh well," Dan sighed, "We tried. At least there was no one home to report our flyover. So long, Ari. Goodbye, Jackie. We gone."

"Hey, Danny Boy, let me, as the New Yorker's say, *ast* you a question," Tom Thome said over the intercom. "Have

180

you ever tried to imagine that rich, overweight Greek
making love to our boy Jack Kennedy's Jacqueline?"
Dan smiled in his oxygen mask but didn't bother to answer.
He pushed both throttles forward; the aircraft responded
immediately and began climbing. At around thirty thousand
feet, Dan leveled the sleek jet and let speed increase to four
hundred fifty knots, or .76 mach. With nothing but blue
choppy water beneath them, LT Thome had turned off all
cameras, loosed his oxygen mask, relaxed in his harness a
bit, and began singing. It was a routine well known to the
front seat driver. When Tommy Thome was bored in the
rear seat, he either hummed or sang. The only visibility out
the rear cockpit was through the camera lens pointed
directly beneath the plane or one very small side window
where the navigator could see out at a ninety-degree angle.
The man in the back seat never saw what was ahead in the
air or on the ground except on his green radarscope. Today,
as Tom often did, he was making up his own words to a
song. Singing in marching cadence, he crooned, *"Now, I
don't know but I been told, Eskimo nookie is mighty cold. One two
three four, one two, three four."*
Dan: "Tom, you should have been a Marine sergeant.
They would love to have you in Pensacola calling cadence
for cadet recruits learning to march. Now if someone could
teach you to sing!"
In response, came different words, different tune. *"Country
boy, take me home, to my carrierrrr... where I belong. USS
FORRESTAL, Ocean Mama, take me home, country boy."*
Dan grinned wide as he commented to the back seat, "John
Denver, Tom Thome is not."

The two-hour flight was nearing conclusion. Dan eased
throttles back and began descent towards the postage stamp
sized ship forty miles ahead, almost thirty thousand feet
below. At 20,000 feet, fifteen miles out, the postage stamp
had grown in size to that of a loaf of bread. Steaming
northeast away from the late afternoon sun, the elongated
straightaway wake behind the ship indicated that recovery of
aircraft was already in progress. Tall whitecaps as far as the
eye could see meant the ship's deck would be wallowing a
bit side to side, perhaps some fore and aft. Today, this

translated into eight to ten feet of deck movement up and down at the point of impact as the planes touched down on landing.

The back-seater called the ship. "Blue Bell, *Speartip 604*, ten miles out, have you in sight. Request landing."

"*Speartip 604*, this is Blue Bell tower. Your signal Charlie. The deck is open and ready. We're waiting on you. All eighty feet and all four wires are yours. Altimeter 30.12. Over."

"Roger, on the way. See you in two minutes."

The swept-wing, two-engine jet approached the ship from behind at four hundred knots. Called *In the break* under visual flight rules, the jet flew ahead of the ship on the same course as the carrier for less than half a mile. Then, Dan banked the sleek craft into a forty degree turn, rolling out to again parallel the ship's course, now in the opposite direction, about one quarter mile distant. The RA-5C was *downwind* at one hundred eighty knots, six hundred feet altitude. Pilot and navigator completed landing checkoff, verbalizing through challenge and reply confirmation of each item on the list. Anyone on the flight deck looking skyward saw three wheels descend at the end of shinny silver struts from the underbelly of the airplane. Flaps were lowered and the plane assumed a slight nose-up attitude as it slowed for landing. The large A-frame hook was lowered and hung four feet beneath the tail of the *Vigie*. At a point exactly opposite the fantail, called *Abeam,* navigator Thome depressed his mike button and stated standardized information for the tower and landing signal officer: "604, 3 down and locked, 5.2, hook down."

Dan banked the *Vig* left to make the one hundred-eighty degree turn to ship's heading. Simultaneously, he decreased power slightly to begin a gentle descent. With ninety degrees turn to go he wanted to be around three hundred feet and on speed, approximately one hundred sixty knots (about 175 mph). Just past the ninety position, he picked up the yellow ball that gave visual depiction of his altitude. He was starting out slightly high.

"604, this is Paddles. Keep it coming. Work it down out of that high start." Dan could ascertain the voice of LT Jack Jones, the air group's landing signal officer. The LSO came on again. "604, now you're a little fast and flat. Work that nose up without going high again."

Dan again eased throttle and adjusted the nose position ever so slightly. Satisfied with attitude and altitude, he inched the throttle forward to stop further deceleration.

LSO: "Brownie, you're on speed, on altitude. Check your lineup. Lineup!"

While maneuvering to correct lineup to be in the center of the runway lines painted on the landing area, Dan let the ball go slightly low. Now he was working nose and power and stick simultaneously to get the aircraft on speed, on altitude, and lined up straight down the deck. His efforts culminated in all three aspects coming together in unison at a point twenty-five yards from the fantail. Over the radio, he heard the LSO mutter in his ears, "OK, land it."

The seventy-six foot long jet crossed the fantail about twenty-five feet above the deck. The big plane touched down in the landing area just forward of the #2 arresting wire.

A muffled explosion, a dull B-O-O-M beneath the right wing signaled that the landing was not normal in any context. The plane's right side collapsed and the starboard wing contacted, then slid along the deck. Pieces of metal and fiery sparks arc-ed outward from the right wheel well. Deck crewmen scattered to avoid flying debris. Dan knew immediately the situation was dire, something, he didn't know what, had gone awfully wrong. In his headset he heard Tom Thome mutter and ask, "Oh, crap! Are we going in (the water)?" Something on the right side was digging into the deck while the left side of the plane continued to roll normally. With the starboard side dragging and the left side rolling on its good wheel, the plane turned almost ninety degrees to the right. Sliding sideways, the tail of the plane was now pointing outward toward the sea while the right wing was pointing behind at the fantail. Fortunately, forward momentum left over from the one hundred seventy five mile per hour landing speed propelled the canted plane down the deck or it might have headed for the island tower, now directly ahead of the plane's nose. Sliding down the deck left wing first, right wing hanging down and dragging, the flight crew was simply along for the ride. Urgency dictated their only option. Eject! Both men reached for ejection handles when suddenly the plane was halted as if grabbed by an invisible hand. Crash alarms sounded, crews came running with fire extinguishers. Plane captains jumped on the lower wing to help the pilot and crewman deplane as rapidly as possible since fire was a definite possibility in any crash on deck. As hurried hands reached in to assist his departure from the cockpit, Dan looked out the left side of the now open canopy. Since the plane was canted downward on the right side due to the dragging starboard wing, looking left presented only a view of ocean expanse....he could not see metal decking at all. Once out of the aircraft, he made it a point to ascertain how much deck was left for the plane to use before it would have tumbled off the end sideways into the water. He found only a few feet, perhaps eight or ten, remaining until the deck rounded off into nothing, and beyond that, water. Virtually all available flight deck had been used before the plane was jerked to a stop, averting disaster.

Looking aft, the pilot saw telltale evidence of what had caused his first and only aircraft accident. And what saved him. On touchdown, the right main landing gear strut collapsed which in turn broke off at the right wheel. Only two or three feet of vertical strut remained attached to the *Vig* airframe. That stump, shortened by loss of the wheel, had dragged along the flight deck and fortunately engaged the last arresting cable, bringing the big jet to a stop before it could slide overboard, plunging into the rolling sea. In all probability, had the plane slid off the deck left wing first, the ejection sequence would not have met parachute-opening parameters.

Dan looked at Tommy Thome. His back seat rider solemnly returned his gaze. The two men knew Lady Luck, or fate, or somebody, had just dealt them a very good hand. Making their way through handshakes and congratulations and exclamations of unbelief at their good fortune, the two happy aviators headed for the squadron ready room. It was Tommy who brought up the old saying so dear to aviator's hearts. He kiddingly quipped, "Hey, man, we're walking away. It was indeed a very good landing! Was I scared? Hell yes! But it was still a great landing."

Dan Brown smiled only halfheartedly. Yes, they were safe now. And the Admiral would love the pictures of the Ruskie trawler. The thirty-three year old aviator was mature enough to realize that he was once again experiencing that old puzzling feeling: concurrent exuberance - at being alive - and dejection, over having an accident on his record. The crash had occurred so suddenly there had been no time for feelings to enter the scene. Elated to be safe and unhurt, still he could taste bitterness in the pit his stomach. His dream of an accident-free career was laying severely wounded back there on the flight deck. Having served on several accident boards, he knew from previous first-hand knowledge that members for a team to investigate this accident were already being considered, even recruited. The next few hours, heck, the next few days were not going to be fun.

Sleep came hard that night. Debriefing the accident took hours before the commanding officer, CDR Robert 'Chip' Carson, finally called it quits around 2300[1] hours. Exhausted, Dan returned to his stateroom and lay down immediately. Sleep, for whatever reason, remained elusive. He had recounted the details of the accident over and over to the powers that be, but here in the quiet of his stateroom, he relived the ill-fated carrier landing again. Then, it hit him. He had not experienced the holographic vision that was so key to the gun incident in Daytona Beach those many years ago. He did not see his life pass in review as the *Vig* slid sideways down the deck in those last moments when it seemed he was about to die. Perhaps it wasn't so strange after all. In Daytona, he had had time to think. The landing accident was over in seconds and after the strut broke off, he was simply along for the ride. His only option was to eject, but then he got lucky. The #4 wire came along and grabbed them.

---

[1] 11 pm

185

Always the "Why"? Here he was again, same place, same time, same results. He was O.K., he would live to fly and make love again. But Jimmy, Tommy, Woody, where were they? He closed his eyes as he recalled each special friend who lived now only in memories. Ten-year old Jimmy Frazier had been the first to introduce Dan to the finality of death. Dan remembered himself as a naïve first grade boy that expected to see Jimmy's soul or ghost or spirit or whatever rise from the casket on its way to heaven as the box was lowered into the ground. Tommy Dixon's Catholic funeral, formal and lengthy, was next on the memory agenda. Tommy's fatal mistake in rendezvousing too fast on a slower lead aircraft and tow target was like a dagger in his heart each time he thought of it. "Tommy, dammit, when I see older blue and white Pontiacs, I expect to find you behind the wheel, still twenty-two years old." Perhaps Woody Miller's accident was the one that hurt the most. He cringed as his mind played back the events that terrible day. Dan was leading a flight of four *Vigilantes* orbiting overhead USS ENTERPRISE while Woody made the first practice approach and landing on the ship. The crews overhead watched in disbelief and horror as the arresting gear cable snapped when Woody's *Vig* touched down. After engaging the cable, the plane didn't have sufficient speed to fly again and dribbled off the end of the flight deck into the choppy green sea. Both Woody and his back seater died. For a moment Dan saw two very similar images playback in his mind. Except for 604 sliding sideways down the deck because of the broken strut instead of a severed arresting cable, today's accident could have been a re-play of Woody's disaster. He wondered which of his friends or acquaintances would be the next to die in an accident or get smoked in that war so faraway from home. He knew, and the Navy knew, there would be a next one. These are the vexing thoughts that haunt the inner mind on sleepless nights and goad men to cross-examine God. *Are you listening? Will it be me? That was a close one today – too close. Look Lord, if it's my time, take me, just don't give me to the gooks. If not me, who will it be? Who, of his most familiar friends and acquaintances, would be next?*[1] His last thought as rest finally arrived, 'Where were the fourth horseman and his gray horse today? Always questions, never answers.' He slept fitfully, dreaming of horses in an open field of green grass. He couldn't make out the indistinguishable faces of the riders.

The accident board found that the mishap was due to material failure, exonerating the pilot from any responsibility in the crash. A hairline fracture of the starboard landing gear strut was identified as the culprit. The crack had probably been there for a good while, creeping minutely in length with each successive carrier landing. Finally, the plane endured one 'trap' too many.

604 was a "Hangar Queen" for the duration of the deployment, which wasn't all bad. The plane became a spare parts locker for Maintenance Department. Often, 604 would be "cannibalized" for vital components needed to keep the remaining Vigilantes onboard FORRRESTAL up and flying.

Note to our Young men – and now in the new Navy, women, too. Catapult launches and arrested landings aboard carriers near speeds of two hundred miles per hour are thrills you can't buy, not even at Disney World or Six Flags. **FLY NAVY!**

*****

---

[1] One of his best friends, Lieutenant Commander Buzz Settles, flying off USS ENTERPRISE, would be killed within a few weeks when his Vigilante was catapulted into the water. Another close friend and his favorite skipper, Les Lincoln, would die in an aircraft accident prior to RVAH-12 deploying to WESTPAC and Vietnam 'Conflict'.

WARNING: THE NEXT STORY CONTAINS ADULT LANGUAGE AND CONTENT. *Author's note: Ladies, particularly, may not like or relate to this story. But I feel its inclusion is important insofar as it portrays men – your husbands, lovers, sons, brothers, perhaps your fathers – about to face war for the first time. What do they think, what do they talk about those final hours before the first real taste of battle?*

Chapter 36

"SCARES ME – AND I'M FEARLESS"

May 28/29, 1970
Age: 35

Boldness is a mask for fear, however great.   Lucan

Fear is sharp sighted, and can see things under ground, and much more in the skies.   Cervantes

Courage is not the absence of fear but the ability to carry on with dignity in spite of it.   Unknown

Perhaps more current philosophy on the subject of fear is appropriate:

Courage is being scared to death - and saddling up anyway.
                John Wayne

Men are afraid to admit that they're afraid. Why? If you're not afraid, there's no reason to be brave. And bravery is what you do in spite of fear.   Joe Torre, Yankees

.......Will I measure up?

Finally, fifteen years since those gold wings flew onto his chest, he would see combat. Dan Brown was still assigned to RVAH-12 but now the *Speartips* were headed the other way – west. No more Mediterranean Sea *fun & sun* cruises.

Now time on the ocean would be called 'deployments', the very change of wording connoting business – the business for which they had been trained. The squadron had come home on FORRESTAL in April of '69. A North Atlantic NATO[1] exercise awaited them for October, then they began preparations for Vietnam, Yankee Station, and Gulf of Tonkin. For this tour the squadron was aboard USS AMERICA (CVA-66), Dan was now squadron Operations Officer.

All but one of the reconnaissance pilots, six of seven assigned, assembled in the commanding officer's cramped stateroom. To a man, the compatible group was imbibing liquid refreshment of an unauthorized nature. The *BYOB* party not only ignored but violated a typed official notice framed on the back of the entry door. The same notice was posted in every stateroom. The mimeographed sheet included excerpts from naval regulations prohibiting consumption of alcohol aboard United States military ships. On aircraft carriers, usually only the flight surgeon or medical officer had authorized access to spirits. As doctors, they could prescribe miniatures of cognac under certain stressful circumstances. The perfect example for permissible issue of alcohol aboard ship is the need to settle a pilot's nerves after he has had a tough time landing his aircraft back aboard for any of several legitimate reasons. Flying tons of steel to a controlled crash in eighty feet of deck space on a moonless night with no horizon and a pitching deck can unnerve the steadiest pilot, even a 'Maverick'[2] clone. In those cases, the magic of cognac given by the Medical Officer can work wonders.

The preceding scenario would be atypical for peacetime operations because if the violation were known, higher authority very likely would raise eyebrows. Wartime interpretation of those regs is more lenient. The 'by-the-book' no-booze standards are usually relaxed in a hostile environment for those members routinely engaging the

---

[1] North Atlantic Treaty Organization
[2] Tom Cruise in *Top Gun*

enemy directly. Each commanding officer is tasked with keeping an eye on his officers to make sure alcohol does not become a problem either for the individual or the unit. On this occasion, the *Speartip* pilots were simply getting a one-night's head start. AMERICA was on schedule and would be 'on line' day after tomorrow. Many of the hundred-plus aviators aboard had 'been there, done that', and wore the 'Vietnam' belt buckle to prove it. The photo pilots of RECON-12 had no such advantage. None of the *Speartips*, including the commanding officer, had ever experienced combat.

Makeshift *hors d'eurves* of summer sausage wheels and cheddar cheese in spray cans along with various canned nuts appeared, it seemed, from nowhere. A clock on the desk read 0015[1] but the party had begun much earlier. LCDR Brown arrived late and was only now pouring his second Bacardi and Coke. A general slurring of speech and a lot of discordant chitchat indicated his peers were incrementally ahead of him in drinks consumed. At least three different animated conversations were in full swing. Country music blared from a tape recorder in the far corner of the room. Finally the last pilot made an appearance. Administrative department head LCDR Tom Gordon arrived as Dan loaded his second drink. Likable and loquacious, the admin officer entered and apologized for being late. "Sorry. It's been like a three-shit morning. I just got the message we were getting together. Anyway, all seven of us now present and accounted for. Dang it, Skipper. Don't you have any other music to play? Surely you've got a tape of *We Five* or *Jefferson Airplane*. That Conway Twitty stuff reminds me of the time I hitchhiked to California just out of college. In every diner we stopped, we played 'How-bad' songs on the jukebox. You ask, what's a 'How bad' song? They're songs nobody knows by unknown artists, always country, real country. Man, they were awful. You should have seen the folks in those little cafes wrinkle their noses and frown at us. O.K., here's Gracie Slick and *Jefferson Airplane*. Now we'll hear some good sounds." Soon, *Crown of Creation* replaced

---

[1] 12:15 am

190

twanging ballads. LCDR Gordon moved to the desk to
pour vodka over ice into a styrofoam cup.
Dan inquired: "Tom, what's a three-crap evening? That's a
new one on me."
Tom Gordon gulped down about a third of his drink.
Raising his eyebrows, displaying a façade of disbelief that
Dan would ask such a naive question, he explained:
"C'mon, Dan, it's just another way of saying you're having
a bad day. Haven't you ever gone to the bathroom #2,
thought you had finished, wiped your butt, stood up and
suddenly knew that you weren't finished with your jobbie?
So you do it all again, then wipe, flush, stand up – and, uh
oh, here we go again. Three times. Well, that's a three-shit
morning - or evening or whenever. Now in my case, I was
using the parallel, metaphor if you will, to describe the
hellish gauntlet I have been subjected to for the last few
hours. First the Air Group Commander called a meeting to
discuss delinquent muster reports. Then the ship's X.O.
called a meeting of all administrative officers because muster
reports just aren't getting to his office in a timely manner. I
wouldn't have been surprised if the Admiral himself wanted
to talk about muster reports. Well, it turns out the glitch is
not Air Wing related at all, it's another ship's company
prob. Wartime paperwork, Lord, give me a break......and
another drinkie-poo."

Executive officer CDR Tex Martin finished pouring a fresh
bourbon and water, then indicated for the group to hold it
down while he addressed the two relative newcomers.
"Hey, Dan. Hey Tom, we've just been shooting the breeze
about this and that and everything in general. Now that
you're here, what's on your minds? What gems of wisdom
would the operations and admin officers like to pass on to
this captive audience?"

Dan sipped on his darkened cola drink before commenting.
"X.O., I'm not sure this fine group of aviator flesh is in any
shape to remember anything I say. But here goes. As Ops
O., I've said it all before in ready room briefings. We've
watched the films, we've read the books, we've studied the
mistakes of predecessors, we've practiced for this as long as

we've worn gold wings. I think we're ready for day after tomorrow. To hell with Ho Chi Minh. One thing still amazes me......thankfully, it's on the 'Plus' side of the ledger. We see so many World War II movies where the planes are over Germany for great lengths of time. I think I remember a B-17 bombing mission to Hamburg where they were over enemy territory for four hours each way. In that sense, we're fortunate. I've looked at the missions being flown by CONSTELLATION, the ship we're relieving, and they're 'Feet dry' over enemy territory only eight to eleven minutes on average. Their longest mission so far has been a road run from north to south that lasted eighteen minutes. According to reports from *Vigilante* pilots on *Connie*, the initial photo runs are a piece of cake. To get the pictures of targets to be hit the following day or night, we have the advantage of surprise. They don't know where we're headed, if or when we might feint towards a decoy target, etc. Now the downside is the BDA, the bomb damage assessment runs. They're real killers. After the bombers have done their thing, the Admiral wants to see if they hit the target. So sometimes the very afternoon of the same day or the next day at the latest, we have to go in and take pictures again to confirm what our bomber buddies claim they destroyed. This time the enemy knows we're coming so they give everybody in the area, all the civilians, even women and children, guns and tell them to shoot straight up when they hear us coming. They don't have to actually hit us - one piece of lead ingested at 30,000 RPM will play hell with jet engines and we'd be talking parachutes. Anyway, back to your original question about what I think. I think we're ready. We've certainly talked it to death. Hopefully, training and planning will prepare us for the unexpected."

Tom Gordon found a corner of the bed and leaned against a corner post. He drained his white cup before responding to the exec's original question. "Dan and I have the same philosophy. Yes, I think we're ready to win some air medals. Hell's fire, isn't that why McNamara wanted us in this *'conflict'* anyway, to put some bric-brac on the chests of future admirals and generals? While I've got the floor, I might add one other thing. As the only one of this prestigious group that gets his ass up every Sunday morning and goes to the forecastle for church services, you might be interested in knowing I've interceded with the Almighty on our behalf. *Lord, please no Hanoi Hilton for any of us.* I assume you guys know the meaning of the word 'prayer', but my petition to God is explicit: 'Dear Jesus, if it's my time to go, let it be quick. Make it a bullet or a missile. Not fire, not drowning, definitely not as POW fodder. That's been my prayer for me ever since I learned I was joining the *Speartips* on their way to 'Nam'. I've petitioned the Lord to keep you fellows totally safe. You can thank me in October when we've flown the last mission and this bucket is homeward bound."

LT Gerald Watson, the youngest aviator of the group, was obviously well acquainted with the Chivas Regal bottle he was holding. "Wha'd you mean, Tom? I'm religious. I know 'bout prayin'. I'm a bona-fide bead carrying Catholick, you know, even iffen I doan get up for church on Sundays. What are you ennyway? Are you one of those Baptists from down south that can't stand us fish-eaters?"

Tom winked at Dan, which meant some fun would ensue. "Gerry, I'm from the Deep South but I'm not Baptist. I'm a Methodist if it makes any difference, which it doesn't. No, we don't disparage Catholics. Heck, we're only a divorce and a prayer group away from being Pope devotees and Friday fish eaters."
LT Watson blinked his eyes, "Huh?"
Tom Gordon smiled knowingly. "Elementary, my dear G. Watson. King Henry split from the Pope because he wanted to divorce Catherine of Aragon and marry Anne Boleyn. So he established the Church of England, which was basically like the Roman Catholic Church except divorce was allowed. The new Church of England was called the 'Anglican' Church. John Wesley, an Anglican priest until the day he died, founded the Methodist Church after he experienced the Holy Spirit at a Moravian prayer meeting in London. That's why we teach our members not to berate Catholics - except for an English king's divorce and a prayer

meeting at #12 Aldersgate Street, we'd still be Catholics ourselves."

Imbibing, but far from inebriated, CDR Rich Martin, the commanding officer, waved his drink in an attempt to gain the men's attention. "Enuf, enuf, you two. Thank you for the history lesson, Tommy, but we're not here to hold Sunday school." (A fleeting thought passed through Dan's mind – 'Maybe we should be'.) CDR Martin stood to address his pilots. Five heads turned toward him, perhaps more in traditional courtesy for his rank than genuine interest in what he might say. Untested in war himself, he had yet to gain the respect of his juniors. He had assumed command of the *Speartips* only a few weeks before deployment when their much-loved skipper, Les Lincoln, had been killed on a routine training flight over South Georgia.

The sixth junior member of the group, maintenance officer LCDR Joe Stokes, sat with his head between his knees, impervious to any conversation around him. The C.O. continued. "This isn't a prayer group and it's definitely not a wake. And I don't want us to get into the politics of this war either. None of us have faced guns before and I thought it would be a good idea to get together and loosen up. I think we're doing a pretty good job of that. On a serious note, now's the last opportunity for getting any concerns off your chest. I specifically ignored the navigators tonight just in case any or either of us had doubts to discuss. If you don't want to talk about whatever might be bothering you in front of others, see me first thing tomorrow for a private talk. I just don't want anyone taking on their first combat mission with personal problems on his mind. For the record, I agree with Ops O., we're ready to see some action. Enough said on that subject."

Joe Stokes finally raised his head. Smashed, zonked, soused, zapped, in other words, plain drunk, the paunchy man of thirty-five held a jigger glass for someone to fill. Joe was famous among his acquaintances for his love of the infamous 'Flaming hooker'. This not-so-popular drink was at least an ounce of straight bourbon lighted afire and consumed in one gulp before the glass became too hot to touch the lips and tongue. By all accounts, Joe had imbibed one too many fiery 'hookers'. No one responded to his gestures for more booze. Eventually, shot glass resting on his knee, he began speaking to no one in particular. Amazingly, considering his inebriated state, his words were almost distinct: "You bastards. Screw you and the horses you rode in on. Why don't all of you choose up sides and smell armpits? Better yet, let's talk about Mar'lyn? Poor Mar'lyn. Died, killed in a car when she was just 35. I loved Mar'lyn Monroe. I'd sniff a mile of her stuff just to see where it come from. Man, she was so fine, the Feds should have arrested Joe DiMaggio for violating the Food and Drug Act. She had the kind of legs that ran all the way up to her ass.........oh, crap, I'm going to puke." Dan happened to be sitting on the floor near the drunken officer. He sat with his legs wrapped around the only trashcan, using it as a receptacle for boiled peanut hulls. Hurriedly, he handed the metal container to the sick pilot. "Here, hurl in this for Pete's sake." The inebriated officer regurgitated into the can while six persons made every effort to get out of the way of possible splatters. X.O. Martin and Gerry Watson, the fortunate two nearest the door, hastily exited into the passageway. When the vomiting finally ceased, Joe Stokes stretched out and lay prostrate on the metal deck. Now mumbling, his words slurred and ran together. "Ifeellikeasackofcrushedassholesrunover byaMacktruck." He rose up on an elbow only once, adding, "Puckeringinth'noondaysun." Almost immediately, he lay back and was soon snoring loudly.

Tom Gordon could not pass up the opportunity to get in a last dig. "Yeah, Joe, you say you feel like an asshole, well, you smell like one, too. Skipper, we've got to clean this mess up or you're never going to be able to sleep in here tonight. This odor would gag a maggot."

. Trashcan dumped, contents flushed, Dan returned to wash the face of the sleeping drunk. "O.K., Sleeping Beauty, I'd just as soon you didn't wake up. Where you spend the night is between you and the Skipper." Tex Martin found a can of spray deodorant and alleviated the noxious odor fouling the confined space of a small shipboard stateroom. The distasteful fiasco had sobered the others into a need for 'one more drink'. What probably would not be the last round was poured as Gracie Slick sang out *Somebody to Love* on the Akai tape deck.

The flight schedules officer, LTJG Harry Goodwin, bachelor *extraordaire* by his own admission, had been relatively quiet to this point. Now he added his bit. "Hey fellas, new subject. I read an article in a magazine last week that was a lot of fun. It was fiction, a short story, but the point made was this. Think how wonderful the world would be if all the ugly people stayed home. We fair-haired folk wouldn't have to wait in line at restaurants, sporting events, or grocery store checkout counters. Picture it. Everywhere you go there are ugly people. Some are really ugly. Boy, I'd be happy if I never had to look at another 'ug-o'. All the good lookin' people could go anywhere, anytime, but them nasties would have to stay inside. Now, think about it. Have you ever seen a truly ugly naval aviator? Never. Not one. And while I'm not fenced in yet, let me tell you - you married guys are matched up with some of the most beautiful women in the world. I'm telling you, I love the idea of hiding away pigs. When we get back to the states, let's promote the idea. What do you say? I think we should make it a Reconnaissance Attack Squadron TWELVE *cause celeb*, a *Speartip* crusade." Raising his voice along with his glass, he said, "Our motto: Ban the uglies of the world." Good-hearted kinship led the others to concur. "Hey, right on." "Hear, hear!" "Cheers!" CDR Martin could only shake his head and smile as he thought, "Yes, they are getting loose." Seeing Joe Stokes' empty shot glass on the floor, he kicked it under the desk - just in case Joe rose from the dead.
Harry Goodwin proposed a second toast. Five plastic glasses and a styrofoam cup were lifted in salute. "Here's to the country's next great movement. If Eskimos can sell ice water, then certainly a bunch of war heroes can sell *Ban the Uglies*!"

LT Walt Rizzo, Assistance Maintenance, a non-aviator, arrived, crowding into the already cramped space. While he did not fly, he was 'one of them'. He and his men kept the planes in the air, sometimes working around the clock to "Up" an aircraft for flight. He pulled a pack of O.C.B. leaves and a bag of loose tobacco from his hip pocket. Raised on the streets of New York, Walt was known for his outhouse humor. As he began to roll a cigarette, he casually asked the X.O. a question. "Exec, do you know why you should always have one cigarette paper in your wallet?" CDR Martin bit - hook, line, and sinker. "No, Walt. But knowing you, I'm sure you're going to tell me why."

Most of the group had heard the spiel before. The room became quiet as LT Rizzo held forth. "Well, X.O., it's like this. There may come a time when your bowels just have to move and there is no paper around. Not even a Sears catalog or as you Southerners like to add, nor a corncob. But if you have just one cigarette paper, you're OK, not a problem. How, you ask, can you wipe your ass with just one inch and a half by three-inch piece of paper? Here's the secret. First, you tear a little round hole in the middle of the paper just big enough for your index finger. Now save the little round piece you tore out. It's very important later. Stick your social finger through the hole and then use your finger and wipe your behind real good. Then you squash the paper around your finger very tight and slide the paper down your finger, cleaning it as you go. Bingo, the paper is off and your finger is clean, relatively speaking, of course. You throw away the crumpled paper. But remember the little round tear-out? Now you make a tight roll of it so that it looks sort of like a short matchstick. Gotta be tight. You take that and clean your fingernail. Man, works every time. Here, put one of these in your wallet for that embarrassing time in your life. Hey, I make my wife carry one all the time."

Reluctantly, unsmiling, CDR Martin reached for the paper. Wide smiles around the room told him he had been had.

It was getting to be a long night. Subdued conversations indicated that perhaps the last drink had been poured. Tom Gordon sided up to Tex Martin and said softly, "X.O., I did want you to know I may have a problem with Chief Stallings. He told me this afternoon that he thinks his girl back home who is almost his fiancée might be having an affair with another chief. He's our best avionics man – I'd hate for him to get screwed up mentally."

By this time, after several highballs, that is, more than five, Tex Martin was in no mood to talk serious squadron personnel business. He responded offhandedly, "Tell him it's all right. She won't wear it out and hell, she might learn something new." He then mildly chastised LCDR Gordon, "Tom, just kidding. See me in the morning after I've slept off Mr. Jack Daniels." Tom Gordon nodded, "Call me, X.O., when you're ready. I do want to try and help the guy. He's our key supervisor in Avionics and we don't want him going off the deep end."

Gerry Watson had been leaning against the partially closed door. He opened it just enough to stick his posterior out into the passageway. A loud, unmistakable sound, one not seen, heard, nor discussed in finer social circles, could be clearly distinguished. He smiled sheepishly, "Sorry but I hadda cut cheese. It musta been sumpin' I ate."

Frowning, CDR Rich Martin waved a *Stars & Stripes* newspaper back and forth and reached again for the spray deodorant to help dissipate the obnoxious smell creeping back into the room.

Gerry Watson continued. "Which reminds me to tell you this. You know the best place to pass gas if you're out in public? Go into a department store to the cosmetics department. Man, *Chanel* and stuff in all those fancy bottles will mask even a bad onion fart."

CDR Martin waved his arms and without ceremony dismissed his group. "That's it. On that sour note, and I do mean sour, LT Watson, it's off to your rooms you go. You want to talk about cosmetics and perfume, Gerry? O.K., it's as Polly Bergen, perfume spokes-lady personified, says, '*The Party's Over*'. A couple of you carry LCDR Stokes to his sack. X.O., you too, Dan, stick around for a few minutes."

Four more than slightly inebriated pilots and a bearded maintenance type departed with Gerry Watson and Harry Goodwin struggling to keep Joe Stokes upright. Dan heard Gerry saying, "Guys, I'm going to my bunk and will myself to dream about Dolly Parton's boobs. I'll probably wake myself up because there won't be any skin left to cover my eyes! I wish Dolly had been my mother so I could have nursed on those juggs. O.K., forget the carnal innuendoes for a moment. Wouldn't it be fun to look at those apples? Wouldn't you just like to see them?" And they passed out of earshot.

After the others were gone, CDR Martin confided in his senior officers. "O.K., I think we made some money tonight. It was good for just 'us girls' to get together and let our hair down. Verbalizing nonsense and bullshit is a good outlet for the tension that has to be building up inside all of us. Hey, I've never been shot at either. I know exactly what all my pilots are going through. I just wanted to tell both of you that I think you've done a great job getting the squadron ready. I didn't sense fear of any degree in those guys. I didn't hear one word about targets or SAMs[1] or MIGs.[2] The only times the war was mentioned was when you, Tex, asked Dan and Tom for their opinions on our readiness to do business. Oh, we've all talked a little about us all being novices but again, no indication of stress or worry tonight. Now, go to bed yourselves. Tomorrow will be a busy day planning for those first-day missions on Friday."

Dan returned to his stateroom and sat on the lower bunk, contemplating 'his immortality'. Whether U.S. involvement in Vietnam was popular or unpopular with Americans at home, that question would be neither a concern nor an option thirty-six hours from now. Day after tomorrow they would zoom along at 500 knots taking photographs of enemy targets and return to land on AMERICA. Bomber pilots would use their pictures to plan the destruction of tactical sites. Smiling, he reflected on the shared

---

[1] Surface to air missile
[2] Russian built jet aircraft used by North Vietnam

camaraderie of the late evening and early morning. He tried to recall verbatim some of the uninhibited conversations. All seven pilots, individually and corporately, had successfully masked any anxiety about facing the unknown realities of war. Each retained an inherent air of invincibility. He stood and looked at his image in the mirror and spoke to himself: 'I know the others have the same doubts as I do, even the Skipper. In our heads, we think it will always be the other guy. In our hearts, we know it could be us. And we all say, 'God, if there is a God. Please, not me. And if it has to be me, make it quick. The bottom line, the key word, is quick. Just like Tom Gordon has been praying.' He lay back down and turned off the reading light above his pillow. Total darkness enveloped him.

But sleep would not come. He couldn't shake the C.O.'s asinine remark about the pilots exhibiting no signs of fear. 'What the hell did he expect? Did he think seven Navy pilots were going to sit around telling each other how scared they are? Certainly it was good for us to relax and unwind tonight but it went exactly as I would have predicted. We discussed every topic under the sun, mostly women and booze, sex and girls, jokes and nookie. Well, with a little religion and history thrown in by our resident historian. Not a word about SAMs or POWs. Bogus bravado personified? Or the real thing? Shaking his head, he flicked the reading light back on and sat up once again.

He spoke aloud to the dull illumination around him. "Dan, save the crap. Stop beating around the bush and cut to the quick. No pilot wants to die but it's always in the back of our minds, peacetime or wartime. I think the bigger worry in facing combat for the first time is the one never spoken aloud. Go ahead and say it. '*What if I don't measure up? What if I can't hack it? What if I panic the first time I see enemy fire? Can I do the job that guys before me have already done'?*"

He had finally put words to the vexing juxtaposition: sixteen years of proving he was not afraid to die but agonizing over doubts that he might not be up to the challenges that came with the morrow. "Is this the first

horror of war? I'm sure the jarheads[1]and grunts[2] on the
ground must have these same feelings the night before their
initial taste of live fire. Well, Danny Boy, soon enough, like
thirty-six hours, and you'll know. Just remember guys just
like you have come through it – you can too. Now turn out
the damn light and check the inside of those eyelids. You've
got to get to sleep."

*Not a very charming picture for Mom or wife back home, is it?
Well, truth is truth and not always pretty. But look inside the
inane, wandering dialogues above for the deeper truths. I think
there you find successfully veiled inner fears and doubts tucked
behind the façade of a masculine bull session. Back in respective
bunks, each pilot, at some point, would, like me, wrestle with the
same question as their day of reckoning drew nearer and nearer.
'Will I measure up?'*

*I plead guilty of dallying with author's license to some degree in this
narrative. The officers portrayed in the story are not actual, real
individuals but represent mosaics of several friends and
acquaintances I observed first hand in booze klatches the night
before battle. Because of my two previous tours as ship's company, I
was able to listen in on two of these occasions as an onlooker before
the final one with me as a participant. These were men whose
inherent strengths, weaknesses, and unique personalities combined
to mold and exude requisite bravery to face the unknown that
accompanies that first taste of real war where men shoot at men.*

*And the modern generation should remember this was a time before
females became part of our combat force. I hesitate to even conceive
of a similar scenario where women would be included in these
conversations. As I will offer later in the book, there are some things
about getting older that aren't bad. Now don't get the wrong idea.
I love the fairer sex –I love looking at them, I love the smell of their
perfume. Hell, I even love talking to them. I just don't think these
lovely specimens of the female form should be put in combat*

---

[1] Slang for United States Marines ground troops
[2] Slang for United States Infantry ground troops

situations wherein their femininity could be exploited, capitalized upon sexually as well as denigrated for not having requisite strength in a given crisis situation. I'm glad I won't be there for scenes I don't even want to imagine.

I was told by the AI's (Air Intel types) on AMERICA that RVAH-12 (in 1970) was the first reconnaissance squadron to serve a full tour in the Vietnam Conflict without losing a pilot or plane. As Operations Officer, I take great pride in that accomplishment. Admittedly, we were not allowed to fly north of a line about thirty miles south of Vinh whereas many of our predecessors took it on the chin in and around Hanoi. They faced SAMs and fire from heavy guns. For the most part, we faced threats of SAMs and heavy gunfire. In 1970, our biggest worry was small arms fire. It was wonderful not to lose planes or pilots but sometimes kudos don't tell the whole story.

*****

American military guys (and gals!) think about it, worry about it, and then go out and measure up.

Chapter 37

A PHOTOGRAPH FOR A PRESIDENT

May 30, 1970
Age: 35

...Did you get the picture?

A pilot never forgets his first combat mission. Our favorite
aviator's was memorable in more ways than one.

Aboard USS AMERICA (CVA-66) (call sign, *Big Boy*).
The ship's first day in the Gulf of Tonkin; initial launches of
war birds - the beginning of a long seven months "on the
line."

It was to be CDR Martin's flight, simple protocol for the
unit's commanding officer. Taxiing to the catapult for
launch, the C.O.'s plane, *Speartip 601*, began bleeding
hydraulic fluid dictating that deck crews "down" the
aircraft.[1] The standby crew, manned and ready in *603*,
LCDR Brown and LTJG James, were launched as backup.
Their mission, a *road recce*[2] to photograph the main highway
that runs from Hanoi to Da-nang beginning at a junction
just south of Vinh to a midway point near the village of Hue.
American flight crews dubbed this main supply road near
the beach *Route 1A*, after the well-known and scenic
California highway.
Approaching the shoreline, an F4 *Phantom* escort, call sign
Black Belt 206, joined loosely off the photo bird's right wing.
Shortly the section of aircraft went "Feet Dry". As the
planes crossed from sea to land, seven cameras were
activated ON. First, Dan feinted north towards Vinh, then
headed due west for a minute before turning back south to

---

[1] Aviator-*speak* for a plane developing maintenance problems while
getting ready to launch. The plane is *'downed'* for maintenance and
repair while a standby plane and crew is sent as backup to make sure
the mission is completed.
[2] Reconnaissance flight of a highway or road for several miles

follow the snake-like highway as planned. The vista of North Vietnam was beautiful – and totally peaceful. Multi-colored patched fields and paddies, all in numerous hues of green, met the eye in all directions. An alien from outer space arriving at that time and enjoying the scenic landscape would never guess a war was going on.

Running south, away from North Vietnam towards Hue and Da-nang, the two aircraft sped along at 2500 feet above the narrow, curving highway. About halfway through the planned recce route, Dan spotted a convoy of over a hundred trucks and vehicles moving south. At 500 knots, all cameras clicking, the *Vigilante* and *Phantom* arrived undetected depriving the enemy of time to stop, disembark troops, and hide or offer resistance. Dan, in the lead plane with a head's on view, saw no soldier shoulder a weapon much less get off shots. Indeed, there simply was not time for them to react as they were caught flatfooted from behind by two screaming jets at nearly the speed of sound.

At a point directly over the long line of trucks, jeeps and armored vehicles[1], a loud explosion jolted the left engine, quickly followed by intense shaking that jarred and rocked the *Vig* airframe. Dan jerked both engines out of afterburner and called over the air, "Mayday, Mayday, *Speartip 603*, we've taken a hit, turning for water and climbing. Port engine decelerating rapidly." After closely checking his own instruments, another call: "*Black Belt*, come up and check the damage. I hope I can hold around 300 knots." He watched the F4 in rearview mirrors as the escort came up from behind, dropped ten feet below *603* and slid side-to-side. Climbing through fifty-five hundred feet, the planes went "Feet Wet" back over the safety of water. After twice checking for damage, the *Phantom* pilot reported, "I can't see a thing, no fire, no smoke, no oil, no hydraulic fluid or gasoline. I'm not sure you've been hit. The gooks might have gotten got off a few rounds so you may have ingested a bullet through the intake of the engine." Dan's breathing

---

[1] I can't remember the exact number but I'm sure there were over a hundred, perhaps upwards of two hundred

was slowly returning to normal. He had an engine problem of some sort but the good news was there was no fire to complicate matters. He had plenty of fuel, there would be time to evaluate options. If the plane were on fire, he and *Numnuts[1]* would be swimming by now.

Dan checked the starboard engine. It was A-OK so he knew he had power to keep flying – to somewhere. He eased the throttle forward on the left side. At about thirty-eight percent RPM (revolutions per minute), loud banging noises started up again, the aircraft shuttered violently as the engine began stalling.

Dan: "O.K., *Big Boy,* I guess I've eaten either a bullet or a blade.[2] Request instructions. Do I go to Da-nang Air Force Base?" normally a moot question with only one engine operating properly. Standard operating procedures for a sick *Vigie* with one bad engine was to take it to the nearest appropriate military facility. Even in the excitement of the moment, Dan was already mentally savoring a cold beer at the shack that served as an Officer's Club at Da-nang.

Instead, "*603*, Wait one for the RVAH-12 C.O." In about five minutes CDR Martin came on the air. "Dan, it's our first day on the line. I'd like to have all my planes on board. The Admiral agrees. I know the book calls for divert with a single engine but you say you've got nearly 40% power left on the bad engine. I want you to bring it back aboard ship. I think you can do it with one good engine and a little help out of the other as backup if you need it. Come on home." Semi-pleased thoughts flooded the pilot's mind. 'It was nice to have seniors respect your flying ability - or was it?' Over the air, Dan replied matter-of-factly, "Yes, sir. *603* and *206* level at six thousand feet. My nav instruments show you 350 degrees, seventy-two miles. Request straight-in approach."

---

[1] A pet name for LTJG James, the back-seater
[2] Pilot speak for a foreign object ingested by an engine; blade would be from the engine compressor

Shortly, the Landing Signal Officer came on the air. "All Right, Danny Boy, *Paddles* here. You're starting out in good position. Don't let it go low and don't get slow. I'm going to work you a couple knots faster than normal. Keep it coming – check lineup, you're drifting right. You got a ball?"

Dan made the minute left correction and noted with satisfaction that his airspeed was inching down to where it should be, maybe 165 knots. And that he had the bright orange ball exactly in the center of the green threshold lights of the Fresnel Lens.[1] He responded, "Yep, Roger, ball. 6.2. Gear down, hook down."

Finally on speed, Dan found the big plane responding sluggishly, wallowing in the groove much more than normal. He wondered how much the left engine, purring at idle, was contributing – if any - to the lift required to land 40,000+ pounds of *Vigilante*? He breathed over the intercom to the RAN, "If the port engine is in fact helping, then landing this big mother aboard ship with only one turning by itself would be hell. It feels like we're within three knots of stalling. Heck we might be."

More verbal help from the Landing Signal Officer, deft handling of a wounded, underpowered, high-performance aircraft by an experienced pilot, and *603* arrested safely. Dan had successfully nursed the lame duck back aboard AMERICA. Before plane captains could get the aircraft tied down, an Air Intelligence Officer was on a ladder with his face in the cockpit asking the pilot: "Did you get pictures of the convoy?" Dan nodded affirmatively. As quickly, the AI was off the ladder and below helping recover the film. Dan slowly shook his head in wonder at how quickly reality returns in wartime. A few minutes before, the film was not

---

[1] A visual landing aid that tells the pilot if he is high or low on the glide slope. An orange (or red) ball moves up and down a vertical light panel located between fixed green horizontal 'threshold' lights. Ball above the green 'line', the aircraft is high; ball below the green lights, the plane is LOW. The Lens apparatus does not help with lineup.

even a feather of consideration – getting the multimillion-dollar plane back aboard safely was everyone's major concern. Now suddenly, the pictures were paramount again, as indeed, they would always be. He mused, "*Did you get the picture?* Must be a great lead for something, somewhere, sometime."

Inspection of the engine showed that a compressor blade had broken off and gone through the engine, wreaking havoc while the turbine was spinning at 30,000 revolutions per minute. The reluctant hero took a lot of good-natured kidding for reporting that his plane had been hit by anti-aircraft fire. Dan smiled, taking their comments in stride, noticing with pleasure a new respect in their eyes for their Ops Officer's flying ability. All ribbing turned to kudos when Air Intelligence reported that the convoy photographs were being sent to President Nixon, the first ever-combat pics forwarded to an American president via satellite.

*****

Where do we get such men?

Chapter 38

THE WAR ON "MONKEY MOUNTAIN"

July, 1970
Age: 35

The engines of the small propeller transport purred evenly.
Looking out the port side window, passenger Dan Brown
could see only water. It was late afternoon; they would be
landing in about an hour. The Air Force base at Da-nang
was dead ahead, around a hundred miles. He eagerly
awaited the thin, white shoreline of Vietnam that would
soon appear in his southward view. Now midway through a
third tour to this troubled part of the world, he continued to
be enthralled by the serenity, the beauty, the contradictory
peacefulness of the Vietnam countryside. He always looked
forward to seeing the lush and verdant patchwork fields that
dotted the countryside. Finally, the plane was over land. In
the daylight remaining, as seen from the air, tranquility
reigned below. Little fishing boats, some more on the order
of outrigger canoes, nonchalantly ignored the aircraft
overhead as they rowed homeward with the day's catch.

The C-1A cargo plane landed and Air Force counterparts
met the contingent of officers from USS AMERICA.
Colonel Tom Matson appeared to be the ranking host
representative and advised them "The reconnaissance
meeting is set for 0800 hours tomorrow morning." He told
them that overnight quarters had been arranged and then
added, "Why don't we all have a beer before finding what
the chow hall has to offer?" The small gaggle of pilots and
photo interp officers made their way to a small wooden
shack. Over the door was a hand painted sign, *Da-nang
Officer's Club.* Shortly, American-brand beers appeared as if
by magic. Dan's preferred drink was rum but for the
moment, he caressed the super-cold Budweiser bottle as if
the proverbial genie were inside.
Dusk was giving way to darkness as Dan walked to the
doorway to peer outside. Northeast of the air base, Monkey
Mountain dominated that quadrant and loomed dark and

ominous in the remaining twilight. Perhaps as high as eight hundred to a thousand feet, the mountain was probably four or five miles beyond the paved runway. The pilot was reminded of Bali in the movie *South Pacific.* As he peered at the silent, silhouetted hill, a series of red streaks raced north to south across the darkened landmass. Immediately, south-north tracers answered the initial volley. Within moments, the sounds of live ammunition being discharged in the distance wafted in the air as the darkened mountain came alive with erratic crimson lines.

Unacquainted with small arms fire at ground level, Dan called Col. Matson over and asked, "Is there an exercise going on over there tonight?" The colonel smiled knowingly. "No, that's the real thing. It's our guys against the Cong. It goes on virtually every night. The tracers will die down soon, then you'll only hear the shots. You get used to it."

The beer in Dan's hand was cool but his hands suddenly felt sweaty and hot. The scene unfolding in the distance was like watching a "B" movie or reading bad fiction. There was a word that perfectly fit such inconsistent behavior but at the moment he couldn't articulate that description. What was the word he was looking for? Incompatible? No. Incredulous? No, even though the criss-crossed, red streaked scene before him reeked of incredulity. Then he remembered. He continued to stare at the imposing mountain and uttered aloud *"Incongruous".* The world was not in harmony. The world – this war - was not right.

Dan felt his perception of war was skewed. He had faced ground-to-air fire but this, this was different. Zooming through the air at five hundred knots taking pictures was a breeze even though the enemy below was shooting at his young ass. He knew that his photographs were used to plan and conduct bombing runs – missions that would rain havoc, death and destruction on the enemy. But during the flights to get the pix he never thought about that part of the equation – that he was contributing to the death of others. Probably the bomber pilots didn't think about it either. His thoughts, theirs too undoubtedly, centered on the fact that "Those gooks are trying to kill me." OK, so a guy tries to

forget the end result or rationalize his way out of the
responsibility of killing or maiming – but dammit, that's how
it's done. One on one, men against men, planes against gun
or missile sites and vice versa. *Mano a mano.*
Here, men were shooting at men while he watched, listened,
and chatted up friends while calmly drinking a beer. It
seemed that his conception of right and wrong had
somehow been violated. It was possible, and likely, that
human beings were dying under the hail of tracers and
muted gunfire. This panorama in dusk and shadows, with
Happy Hour onlookers, should not be happening. But it was
real, very real. He continued to stare at the mountain while
his heart screamed '**FOUL**'! In that moment, looking out at
Monkey Mountain, he grasped the futility of trying to
understand the human bent of men killing men. Turning
away, he could not finish his beer.

*Author's note, Summer, 2005. I still don't get it – the meaning of
war. Now we get to watch it on TV while we munch popcorn and
drink Cokes. As I look at tonight's news, Jews and Palestinians are
killing each other and liberated Iraqis are ambushing our boys. I
remember it so well, I can still see in my mind's eye, the 'rocket's red
glare' (actually rifle fire) on Monkey Mountain.*

*****

War is hell.   Gen. William Tecumseh Sherman (1810-1891)

Chapter 39

IT WAS A VERY GOOD YEAR

October, 1970
Age: 35

......a fine romance

It was not a good year for him in many respects. Vietnam
was still on and remained a festering sore in the spirit of
most Americans. The peace talks in Paris were stalemated
again. Dan Brown felt sick in his soul for himself personally
and the country he had served fifteen years. Two weeks
earlier he had returned from a third deployment to the
Tonkin Gulf, this time as a jet reconnaissance pilot aboard
USS AMERICA. Nine long months at sea had bitten a big
chunk out of his life. Now it was time for a break from the
rigors of an unwanted, undeclared war. He should have
been happy to be home, to be back. But the fire inside, the
zest for life he had always known and exhibited, was
missing. His personal life was in shambles, his military life
was being denigrated from every corner of public life.
Taking advantage of rest and recuperation leave offered all
returning military personnel, he decided to spend some
leisure time at his mother's home in north Georgia just
outside Atlanta. Fatigue from the long combat tour was
overshadowed by disappointment stemming from a recent
divorce. His moods led to elongated periods of pensive
debate within his inner being. If you had asked, he would
have told you it was simply a time for hibernation, perhaps
perfect timing for introspection into *himself.* He needed to
evaluate his performance as a failed husband, and he wanted
to examine his feelings about a war gone bad. His failure to
be selected for full commander undoubtedly contributed
heavily to his moodiness. It still galled him that he didn't
even have to go to Vietnam that third time. He had
volunteered and extended to go with Les Lincoln. And the
results would have made Les more than happy. The
first *Vigilante* squadron not to lose a plane or pilot. A single-
engine landing aboard AMERICA. The first actual combat

picture ever sent to a sitting president by satellite. All squadron readiness inspections passed with flying colors. Rich Martin just "didn't get it." Les would have come through. Martin didn't.

And he was beginning to know loneliness first-hand.

It was an early winter that year which afforded long hours of sitting and watching a fire crackle and pop and burn in the open fireplace. Dense overcast clouds, the remnant of a passing front, lent a gray dimness to the normally open and sun splashed den. The ever-changing flames, the constantly varying red hues in the embers, the shadows cast by the flickering blaze, the smell of burning Black Jack oak, all were in tune with his somber mood. Even the sky cooperated. A steady rain began falling again. A torturous exercise in self-psychoanalysis continued for forty-eight hours.

His mother put an end to this quiet reverie. "Well, have you gotten an ample serving of self pity along with self-incrimination over Eleanor's leaving you? You know, when you came home in the past, you always hurried around seeing as many of your old friends as possible. This time, you have visited no one, you have called no one. If you don't feel like facing your old friends, then perhaps I can find you some new ones. There are two young unmarried women who teach with me. Each one is a beautiful person in her own way. Donna teaches one of our first grades, Becky is the school librarian. I'd love for you to come to school and meet them. And I think I have the perfect subterfuge for you to be at school to have an opportunity to get acquainted. I know you remember Mrs. Copeland, your seventh grade teacher. Well, she is still there, still teaching seventh grade, and has been asking about you. She'd like for you to come and tell her class about Vietnam. You know, in a general way, about the country, the terrain, the people, the climate, the money they use. I know you can make it interesting for them on their level. You don't have to and probably shouldn't, go into the war and politics bit. You could bring donuts for our coffee break, meet Donna and Becky, and then go with Mrs. Copeland to class. But young man, let me make two things clear. These girls share an apartment together so I don't want you trying to see both of them at the same time. Or one of them now and one of them later. You may only date one with my blessing. And, you have to look me in the eye and tell me you will be a 'Good boy' because those two young ladies are very good friends of mine. I don't want Donna or Becky to suffer any grief over love affairs, and I capitalize and underline the word 'affairs'. You know what I mean!"

Dan knew what she meant. He agreed to her conditions, if for no other reason than to make her happy. He certainly had no interest in new or long term female relationships just now. But perhaps it was time to get the war and the divorce out of his head. He did want to see the new Underground Atlanta that every one was talking about. State-of-the art design, convenient parking, great restaurants, shopping. Oddities, too. One of the theme shops was operated and popularized by Lester Maddox, ex-governor of Georgia. He could be seen nightly selling novelty items the media had made trademarks of his administration: straw hats and ax handles. Yes, he did want to get downtown to see Atlanta underground. Perhaps this was the way to get a personal guided tour.

"It will be good to see Mrs. Copeland. I liked her a lot. I can't believe she's still there. I'm thirty-five years old now. How old was I then? Twelve or thirteen?" She really had been his all-time favorite teacher at Mableton Grammar. With her tutelage he had won (actually co-winner) the Cobb County mathematics competition that particular year. As he had told the story many times, "that honor and twenty-five cents will usually get me a small cup of coffee." But still it was a good memory and he had liked and respected Mrs. Copeland. "Sure, I'll tell her kids some interesting stuff. I know they will love hearing about the zillions of motorbikes and bicycles on the streets of Saigon. And the rainy season. And the monkey meat on sticks they sell in the street for shish kabob. Maybe I'll leave out the part about the five dollar prostitutes." His mother made a face at his weak attempt at humor.

The following day, attired in dress blue uniform, he visited the grammar school of his youth. Arriving around ten o'clock, he brought three-dozen donuts for teachers to enjoy on a rare morning break. It happened to be the one-day of the school calendar that students were given immunizations. Over coffee and glazed pastry in the facility cafeteria, he first met Donna. She wore a neatly tailored aqua pants suit that enhanced her natural beauty. A few minutes later, Becky arrived wearing a simple green frock reminiscent of a Girl Scout uniform. Both women were quite attractive, in their late twenties. Donna was personable, a statuesque beauty as tall as he. Becky was five feet two - cute, quiet to the point of being reserved. Initially, he had no idea which young woman he would ask to help him discover the joys of Atlanta nightlife, if either. Donna looked to be the fun his mother thought he needed; Becky seemed to be more in tune with his present psyche.

Mrs. Copeland came in and they talked over his impromptu briefing on Vietnam. Yes, he would keep it general, he would not get into politically oriented discussions. "I brought some Vietnamese currency and coins I thought your class might like to see. Also a Vietnamese doll....the kind the Cong used for miniature bombs that would blow off a hand. And a picture of my airplane. I have some photos of enemy targets that I took with the aircraft cameras." He passed over a stack of glossy 8 X 10's all marked "Confidential". "Don't worry, these have now been declassified. They were confidential when they were taken but it's OK for me to show them now. I like to pass these photos around because whoever sees them thinks they're getting to see something really secret and special. I know the boys will like them. Especially the ones of crashed planes - I have a good one of a Russian MIG-17."

The graying teacher agreed. She added, "Oh, I meant to get a map from the library but I ran out of time and didn't get over there to select one for you. I'm sure Becky will walk you over to her library and show you what's available. We reconvene my class in twenty-five minutes. Will you have time to get a map? I think you'd better have one because half my kids won't even know where Vietnam is! Your class almost twenty years ago would have known but the kids today don't care." Dan looked at Becky who nodded her accord to the suggestion. He agreed to be back for class at the set time.

The short walk to the other wing of the school was pleasant while conversation was pristine and formal. Becky pointed out his mother's third grade classroom adjacent to the media center. She told Dan, "Donna and I often have lunch with Mrs. Brown and Mrs. Copeland. Do you know that Mrs. Copeland never misses an opportunity to let people know she had you as a student? Or that you are the only Mableton student to ever win the County math competition?"

"Co-winner," Dan corrected. "Did you know they still played marbles at County Field Day in those years? I had entered the marbles match earlier that morning. The games were into the semi-finals and I was still in the running with a good chance to win when the math event was called away. Mrs. Copeland marched out and made me leave the marbles tournament. I'm sure given a choice I would rather have been County Marbles Champ than the co-champion of solving math problems. I've always wondered why, if I was so good at numbers then, why did I make D's in math and algebra at Emory-at-Oxford?"

"Could I guess extracurricular activities may have been involved?" Becky offered behind a knowing grin.

Once inside the library, Dan was pleasantly surprised at the noticeable change in Becky's personality. In Dan's vernacular, "It was as if someone turned on her friendly switch." Previously, he would have described her as quiet, private, possibly introverted. Here, surrounded by books and shelves and art drawn by children, her individuality emerged like the proverbial butterfly from its cocoon. She exuded the confidence of a young career woman in charge of her world. She knew immediately which topographical chart would best enhance his project. He warmed to her presence. To this point they had engaged in polite conversation. Now they talked.

She was from Alabama. She had attended "the" University during the same four years as a famous pantyhose salesman, Joe Willie Namath, and she was there for the famous George Wallace "Stand in the doorway" speech. She loved reading and Alabama football, she liked tennis. She admitted to being a clotheshorse as much as a schoolteacher's salary permitted. She thought she might like to learn to sail. Becky had come to Mableton four and a half years earlier, her second school assignment since college. Mrs. Brown's friendship was one of the many rewards she enjoyed at the school. She confided to Dan that she knew a lot about him from long conversations with his mother. She knew he had lived in California prior to his reassignment to Sanford, Florida; he had served three tours in Southeast Asia as a Navy pilot. Mrs. Brown had reluctantly told her friends of his divorce only a few days previously.

As Becky talked of Mableton school, he sensed her genuine interest and concern for her work with children. And he noticed for the first time that her smile was captivating. Dan felt the air magnetically charged. 'Pretty good figure, too, for one so slight,' he thought. So fate....the need for a map......had played an ace in helping him determine which young woman to ask for a date. He would ask Becky to guide him through Underground Atlanta. Dinner at a restaurant of choice would be her reward for spending time with a man nearly ten years older than she. Surely one of the many celebrated eating establishments inside the Underground would be perfect for continuing their stimulating dialogue. He asked to see her the following evening as he rolled up the map in preparation of leaving for the lecture. She accepted.

The night was cool, the city lights bright and beautiful, Underground Atlanta scintillating. Becky had neglected to tell him that she too had not been to the Underground. No matter, the area off Peachtree Street was easy to find. Parking was readily available, and to become familiar with the active and noisy area, all you had to do was stroll along and take in the sights and sounds. Their long give-and-take conversations continued over surf and turf and candlelight at *Monte's*. Superb Maine lobster highlighted the late dinner. Later, Dan would consider his first date in nine years a success. On the way home to his mother's after dropping Becky at her door, he was astonished to realize that only forty eight hours before he had been sitting in front of a fireplace, staring blankly into the flames. "O.K., I <u>was</u> feeling sorry for myself. Thank goodness for mothers."

On the fifth date, he asked if he could kiss her goodnight. The awkward kiss that followed did not move heaven or earth for either participant. Neither the man nor the woman closed their eyes for that first attempt at innocent intimacy. Both wanted total sensory perception for the moment, probably for reasons neither could explain. Doctors of the mind might have hypothesized that he was frightened of the second time around; she was terrified of the feelings stirring within her mind, her heart, and her body for an older, divorced man, a war veteran who had seen the world from many vantage points.
The next evening, snow began to carpet Atlanta. Virtually all connector routes were deadlocked for a few hours. The news bulletin flashing across the television screen advised that their plans for a folk music concert at Chastain Park had been cancelled.
He stood up and switched off the tube, turned and looked over at her on the sofa. She was dressed neatly in a monogrammed turtleneck and blue slacks, her bold black hair glistened in the lamplight. He asked, "What would you like to do?"

She looked directly into his eyes, took his hand in hers, and said, "I want to put an Andy Williams album on the stereo, I want to dim the lights, I want to dance, and I want you to kiss me.......with your eyes closed."
As the sounds of *Bridge over troubled water* emanated from two bookshelf speakers, the earth moved, at least shuddered, for two persons embraced in a kiss, two people beginning to fall in love.

Dan was now stationed at Naval Air Station, Jacksonville, living in a nice two-room suite in the BOQ. NAS Jax is three hundred and sixty four miles from the old Highview Apartments in west Atlanta. He was thankful for the low price of gasoline at the time of their budding relationship. 29.9 cents a gallon for high test kept the price of traveling via *Camaro* reasonable. Despite three speeding tickets, the national speed limit of 70 miles per hour also helped their cause (while it is 70 again today, readers must remember that the limit was dropped to 55 mph in the mid-seventies and remained 55 for several years). The elapsed time to Atlanta was just over five hours. Officially, he was authorized to leave the base on Friday afternoons around four o'clock. By working overtime during the week or reporting early on Friday mornings, he usually managed to be away by the time the little hand was on three. Playing a good tennis game as the Executive Officer's doubles partner at lunch undoubtedly helped his strategy. By eight thirty on Friday evening he would be arriving at his mom's home. Forty-five minutes later, showered and shaved, he would be pulling into the entrance drive to Becky's apartment complex, ready to do what people do when falling in love. Movies. Plays. Restaurants. Walks. Braves' games. Antique bottle collecting. Long drives. Museums. Picnics. Later, even family reunions on both sides.

Friday nights, Saturdays, and Sundays until around five o'clock became a ritual of romance sandwiched between travel to and from Jacksonville for the next several months. Weekends remained their only time for each other during the ensuing summer since she had signed on for graduate courses at Emory University. Over the fourteen months following the initial coffee klatch, he found himself in the capital city of Georgia visiting Highview Apartments on forty-nine of the fifty-seven available calendar weekends. Five were unaccounted for due to command duty rotated among all officers. Once, Becky and Donna drove to Jacksonville for sailing and double dating. Becky flew down a second weekend for the Navy Ball after his mother had confirmed proper sleeping arrangements. Becky would stay in his comfortable second story suite, he would take a sterile guest room on the first floor.

The one Friday-Sunday span they did not see each other (other than the five noted previously) during those months is worth mentioning. One week in late March, Becky finally yelled "Time out". She had to go home to let her family know that things between them were getting serious. No, he could not go with her.

She received her engagement ring on Labor Day. He smiled as he slipped the round circle topped by a solitaire Tiffany setting onto her finger. "Most rings are measured by carats," he began. "This almost one carat comes measured in four *caveats*: two warnings and two confessions. Warning #one: The Navy expects me to have inspection ready, spit shined shoes 100% of the time. In my other life anytime I got out the shoeshine kit, there was suddenly numerous pairs of women's shoes lined up alongside mine to polish and buff. In my mind I can still see those damn shoes waiting to be worked on so I have taken a vow never to shine shoes, men's or women's. At least when I'm home. Now I might have to aboard ship. In Jacksonville, I get mine done professionally. Secondly, also in my previous life, whenever I was not at sea, I had to cut grass and cut grass and cut grass. In this new life, I do not plan to own a shoeshine kit or a lawnmower. So an add-on to the marriage vows must include, 'I don't shine shoes and I don't cut grass'."[1] She listened quietly and offered no resistance to the somewhat unusual demands. Continuing, "Then, there are two other things you should know about me. I hate to admit it but I snore awful if I roll over on my back while sleeping. You'll have to jab me with an elbow so that I'll turn on my side."
She finally felt compelled to ask. "And what is the other horrible personal thing you feel compelled to confess?"
Up to this point he had been smiling widely. Now the smile disappeared. He looked right into her eyes and said matter-of-factly: "I love onions but they don't love me."

---

[1] And he didn't for twenty-five years! But things change, and years later, retirement brought a shoeshine kit and a lawnmower.

She simply reached out to pull him closer. Their kiss was tender, loving, right.

On Sunday, December 19th, 1971, at four o'clock in the late afternoon, in Anniston, Alabama, a little over a hundred people gathered in the Methodist Church to see a radiant, happy bride walk down the long aisle to the altar where a Naval officer in full mess dress blue uniform (waist length *tuxedo* coat, bowtie, and cummerbund) stood erect and waiting. Miss Rebecca Farrow Knight became Mrs. Daniell M. Brown under a tall and full, beautiful and fragrant Northern Spruce, perfectly shaped, resplendent with numerous shiny, golden Chrismons.

1971 had been a much better year.

CHAPTER EPILOGUE. Longtime Navy friends had given Dan and Becky the use of their Gulf Shores beach house as a wedding gift. They were in bed, lights dimmed. For a while they lay quietly, each thinking personal and private thoughts. Both stared out the large picture window at a sky dotted with twinkling stars. Whitecaps decorated the soft, lapping waves of the Gulf. White sand on the shoreline sparkled in muted, golden moonlight. His bride of three days was cradled in his right arm; the warmth of their bodies gave added comfort to the chilly December night. Fire in the Swedish stove was reduced to smoldering ashes. The room had cooled to a snuggling and sleeping temperature. Morning light would signal an end to the abbreviated honeymoon. Christmas was a beautiful time of year for a wedding but with the season came holiday celebrations and mandatory family gatherings not to be missed. The couple had promised to return to Becky's home for a traditional Christmas Eve feast.

Becky was breathing steadily now, sleeping peacefully. Dan continued to lie awake, his mind re-running the events since Sunday night. Walks on the beach, candlelight dinners, long, telling conversations, lovemaking. The honeymoon would end tomorrow morning but the adventure would begin at that same precise moment. There would be years for long walks, hopefully many on other beaches, there would be candlelight dinners galore, and a zillion intimacies to be shared, physically, mentally, spiritually; all still to come.

Relaxed physically and emotionally, he tilted his head downward and kissed the top of his wife's head. Moonlight spilling across the tufted comforter permitted him to see Becky's beautiful face in muted detail. His eyes explored every feature of her face and he realized how much he enjoyed simply looking at her. Turning on his side, his thoughts assumed a new tangent. He was thinking of the drastic changes in his life in the past fifteen months. 'Ever-changing avenues, opened doors, second chances, is that what life's about? I'm here, warm and cozy, lying next to a beautiful, sexy woman and so many of my friends are still on a carrier off the coast of Hanoi. And what of the guys that didn't get a second shot at the gold ring?' Again, his mind replayed memories and events surrounding the deaths of Tommy, Woody, Buzz, and his favorite skipper, Les Lincoln. And he remembered Jimmy who died so young. 'Is it dumb luck? Is it some predestined divine plan? Or just the way the cookie crumbles? I don't know the answer, that's for sure.' Finally, he slept.

*****

A secret of life: a 10-year younger working wife!

Chapter 40

THE HITCHHIKER

July, 1971
Age: 35

The '67 red *Camaro* had just left I-10 and turned north on
I-75 toward Georgia. The weekend run to Atlanta from
Jacksonville to see his favorite librarian had begun a little
over an hour ago.
A favorite mix of tunes from the tape player was keeping
him company. The *Kingston Trio* was about to hang *Tom
Dooley* but not unexpected, Dan Brown could feel the
familiar heaviness working its way into his eyelids. The
interstate highways between Jacksonville and Atlanta are
long, flat boring stretches of concrete going up the map to
Georgia, down the map to Florida. The always-
monotonous drive usually made him drowsy and today was
no different. The centerlines reminded Dan of a hypnotist
swinging a gold watch back and forth, back and forth except
now the watch was going fore and aft. His sleepiness
increased to a point that he considered pulling off at the next
rest stop. A run-over meeting had caused him to leave
Jacksonville later than expected. He didn't want to stop for
a rest area nap or he would be late-late. Dinner was already
beginning to look like a ten o'clock happening because of the
delayed get-away.

He began hoping to see a hitchhiker. As a boy he had
routinely "thumbed" his way to and from college and home
numerous times. He enjoyed meeting people who would
stop and give rides to strangers. His roommate and life long
friend, Mike Allison, had hitchhiked with a friend from
Atlanta to California and back to Florida. This was 15 years
later. In that relatively short interim, hitchhikers had
become *persona non grata*. Television, radio, newspapers,
periodicals, all carried police and AAA Auto Club warnings
against stopping to offer rides to strangers. Dan weighed the
pros and cons of well-meaning public service messages, and
opted to "Selectively" offer rides when sleepiness began

overtaking his body. As he would tell friends, "In the vernacular, I'd rather be done in by a hitch-er, than go to sleep and wipe out a car load of kids."

Soon a male form near an off-ramp appeared in the distance. Dan slowed the *Camaro* to look at the person standing along the highway. He was young, clean blue shirt, grey dress pants, no hat, neat except for his windblown hair. His only baggage was a small black duffel. Dan decided to take a chance.

As he slowed the car to a stop, the young man ran to catch up and open the front door on his side. The drawstring bag was dispatched to the back seat and the two men were on their way north to Georgia.

The driver greeted the young fellow, "Hi. Where you going? What's your name?"

The young man flashed a toothy smile, "Jeremy Tolkes. I'm on my way to Macon. Will you be going that far?"

Dan shook his head. "I'll have to let you off at the I-475 cutoff. I'm heading for Atlanta and I was late before I left Jacksonville. Sorry I can't swing by Macon proper for you."

His passenger shrugged off the inconvenience. "No problem. This will help a lot. I'll still be in time for my revival meeting."

Dan asked, "Church revival?"

Jeremy Tolkes nodded, as he asked in turn, "Yeah. I'm preaching there tonight. You a Christian?"

Dan replied, "I'm a Methodist. I guess some Baptists would question whether we're real Christians or not. What's your affiliation?"

Half smiling, Jeremy Tolkes turned and looked at Dan before he answered. "Pentecostal. But folks usually call us 'Holy rollers'."

Dan made no effort to suppress surprise. "I don't think I've ever met a minister so young. What are you, nineteen, maybe twenty? How did you come to be ordained at such a youthful age?"

Jeremy Tolkes nodded again. "Well, I haven't actually graduated from a college with a preaching degree. I'm twenty years old. About two years ago, I got the call to get up at a tent meeting and tell my story....how I was stealing to buy drugs. But then a friend introduced me to Jesus and I was saved. I've just been telling my story ever since. At first, I was only witnessing but after awhile I began preaching, too. You get paid for preaching, you don't get nothing for witnessing." The youthful rider proceeded to tell Dan that his preaching territory covered an area from middle Georgia to North Florida.

Evidently at ease with a brother Christian behind the wheel, the young man continued to elaborate on his calling by the Lord to preach. From his knapsack he produced a Bible. Holding it forth, flipping the dog-eared pages, he continued. "Yes, sir, me and ole King James are friends. I read this here book everyday and you know what, I learn something new just about every day. Did you know Noah was six hundred years old? Did you know Goliath was nearly ten feet tall? I wish we had more information on Jesus as a young man between twenty and thirty. But the Bible has advice for any situation in life you come face-to-face with or any problem you run into. There ain't nothin' it don't have answers for. Yep, me and Jesus and the Bible, we work for the Almighty. Praise the Lord."
Dan wanted to correct the young minister's English but overcame the urge to do so.

They traveled a few miles in silence before Dan spoke again. "You know, Jeremy, I have heard a lot of sermons about giving to the church. You're a pastor, what's your feeling on tithes? You know, the government takes more than twenty percent before I ever see my paycheck. Should I tithe money I don't even get? What do Pentecostals say about how a good Christian should tithe his income?"
The young man turned his head and looked at Dan from behind a quizzical, almost frowning face. He asked, "What's a tithe?"

Years later, Dan would be diagnosed with sleep apnea and an associated disease, idiopathic-hypersomnia, and told he probably had the diseases for years. And he's still not sure of God's definition of tithe.

*****

224

Chapter 41

THINKING FAST

August, 1971
Age: 35

Young Robert Daniell Brown was visiting his dad in
Jacksonville for the summer. Bobby would be returning to
Memphis and his mom the following morning. Dan and
Bobby were at the Allison's for one last cookout before
summer vacation ended. Five children ranging in age from
two to eleven played noisily in the den. On hands and
knees, the youngsters were rolling two or three tennis balls
back and forth across the room to each other. The three
adults, seated in the adjacent living room, chatted over wine.
A doorbell's chime brought the next-door neighbor's little
girl over to play. As the seven-year old child entered, so did
Frosty, the family dog. The young newcomer and the pet
eagerly joined the playful action in the middle of the floor.

Dan and Mike and Jennie Allison continued to talk over the
din of excited participation by six kids and their
spontaneous, makeshift game. Finally, one of the balls
careened into a far corner of the room. The young lady
guest who had just arrived, jumped up, and went over to
retrieve the elusive toy. As she bent over, the unmistakable
sound of loud, escaping flatulence punctuated all
conversation as well as all other room clatter and noises.

Immediate silence, unbroken stillness. Each child seemed
frozen in place, each adult trying to think of something,
anything appropriate to lessen certain embarrassment for the
young female visitor. Eight-year-old Bobby finally broke the
ice, chastising the family canine: "Frosty! You nasty dog,
get out of here!"

*****

Chapter 42

NAKED IN KINGSTON

June, 1972
Age: 36

The Browns' were enjoying the sights and sounds of
Kingston. Jamaica by cruise ship was Dan's choice for a
super getaway. This was more than a summer vacation; it
was the promised finale to their abbreviated Christmas
honeymoon and they were celebrating a new Master's
Degree for Becky. Three Mediterranean tours, numerous
Caribbean training exercises, a North Sea deployment and
three Western Pacific *rides*, all on aircraft carriers had
ingrained in him a love for the sea. He wanted to share that
feeling for the ocean with his bride. Dan thought this, a
Caribbean cruise, the perfect way for her to experience open
water in a romantic setting.
Various half-day tours of the city were offered by the cruise
ship's activity office. Montego Bay would be the next port
of call and promised a more exciting agenda for the money.
Still, the relatively newlywed travelers wanted to experience
Kingston to some degree so they opted for a budget
excursion by taxi. A two-hour taxi ride would at least
acquaint them with a few of the city's more scenic tourist
spots. They requested an English speaking driver, but fluent
or no, the fellow they had drawn almost never offered
comments. Dan and Becky continuously referred to their
tourist guidebook for information about the various routes
and places the big Packard was taking them.
After leaving Devon House, a home built by George Stiebel
in 1881, one of the Caribbean's first black millionaires, they
proceeded to *Royal Botanic Gardens.* As the car slowed for
the entrance, Becky pointed out a traffic sign: "Caution -
Sleeping Policeman Ahead". She asked aloud, hoping the
driver would help, "Have you any idea what it means? I
can't imagine a policeman on duty and asleep." Again, the
driver remained mute and before Dan could answer that he
didn't have the slightest idea, the taxi slowed for a speed
bump in the road.

"Well, now we know what a 'Sleeping Cop' is. A concrete hump in the road. Really, the nomenclature couldn't be more appropriate. We should use that back home." They had the driver stop so they could take photos in front of the unusual marker.

Around eleven a.m., the taxi driver began working back towards the docks via Old Hope Road. Along the way, he broke his self-imposed code of silence and pointed out *National Heroe's Park*. Then he headed the car for downtown, turning onto King Street. Dan commented about how unusual it seemed that both auto and pedestrian traffic was nearly non-existent for that hour of a weekday morning. The driver again chose not to respond. The Browns could only surmise that lunchtime in Kingston must have kinship with lunches in southern Europe.

Dan was first to see the man on the sidewalk. He noticed him initially because he was the first person they had seen on the street for several blocks. Facing traffic as he walked north while the car traveled south, the man was large, strikingly tall and muscular. He was not in any manner heavyset or flabby. Dan thought him evidently a Haitian from his features. He carried a small red radio in his right hand. And he was completely naked except for rubber flip-flop shoes.

Dan reached for his Nikon. Becky too had seen the unusual sight, and grabbed his hand. "No!" she said. "No pictures!" She lowered her voice, "The driver is Haitian. You'll either embarrass him or insult him, there's no telling what might happen. Be quiet and don't make a scene." By that time the automobile had passed the nude walker and remained on course for the port. The driver, as always, seemed not to notice anything out of the ordinary.

Back aboard the *Sunward*, Dan tried to tell others of their strange sighting. Most listeners among the passengers laughed off the story, assuring Dan he must be mistaken, that the man probably had on a black bikini swimsuit. Dan let their skepticism roll off his back even though Becky too, had seen the naked stroller.

That evening the Browns signed up for dinner ashore with a Jamaican family, part of the *Sunward's* people-to-people program. There, Dan's eyesight was exonerated.

He told his hosts of the strange sight they had seen and was elated when both members of the Jamaican family confirmed the rather ribald sighting. Radio news bulletins had carried the story all afternoon. It seemed a naked Jamaican man was having fun at the expense of the Kingston police. He would be seen in one section of Kingston, then reported again in a different location of the city, blocks away, the two reports only minutes apart. It appeared more than one person was involved. As far as the Jamaican hosts knew, the unidentified man or men remained free and at large.

Sunward sailed for Montego Bay the following morning. Over breakfast, tablemates asked Dan if he had heard anything further on "his" naked black stroller.

Dan was happy to tell them the news learned the night before. As he ended the update, he added a new twist to the already semi-risqué story. Later, he would say, "The devil made me do it." He shook his head in an all-knowing fashion and said, "Frankly, I wish I had never seen the guy. Ladies, excuse my French, but everything we fellows have ever heard about black males is true. I have seen the proof. It, and I do mean 'it', was enough to give this white boy an inferiority complex!"

Becky's cheeks colored. Her husband had done it again – pushed the decorum envelope in mixed company. He may have heard the word *degenerate* softly escape her pouting lips while her laughing, flashing eyes told him otherwise.

*****

Chapter 43

THE NAVY WAY

July, 1973
Age: 38

July 23rd, 1973 was a Monday. At four o'clock in the
afternoon, Dan and Becky Brown signed a mortgage for
their first home. They would be moving from a two-
bedroom apartment into a three-bedroom ranch in an older,
established section of Jacksonville. Prior to the real estate
closing, Dan had called the Bureau of Personnel in
Washington, D.C., to confirm his status. He didn't want to
sign a twenty or twenty-five year mortgage and then get
caught unawares with orders to Timbuktu.

The voice on the other end of the phone spoke.
"Commander Brown, are you happy in Jacksonville?"
Dan: "Yes, sir."
The voice: "Is your commanding officer happy with your
performance?"
Dan: "I can get you a letter that says I walk on water if you
need it."
The voice: "O.K., you're happy, your C.O. is happy, BuPers
is happy. You can plan on staying in Jax until you retire.
Frankly, we don't have funds to move anybody, anywhere."
Dan: "Yes, sir. Thank you, sir."
One hour later, the Browns were happy owners of their first
home.

On Friday morning of that same week, BuPers order
78649321 was wired to Jacksonville, reassigning Lieutenant
Commander Daniell M. Brown to FLEET TACTICAL
SUPPORT SQUADRON TWENTY FOUR (VR-24),
Naples, Italy for a three-year tour of duty. The Navy had
worked in typical bureaucratic fashion. In defense of the
detailer in Washington, his information on Monday was
basically correct: no money available for moves. But on
Wednesday, Congress voted funds to facilitate change of
duty orders for the needs of the Navy to be met. One of

those needs was occurring in Naples, Italy. A computer in Washington, D.C., spit out LCDR Brown's name as the pilot most qualified for the new billet. The card also carried a footnote: *LCDR Brown's duty preference cards for past fifteen years in his service record indicate that he "Desires overseas European shore duty."* For eighteen years he had hoped to have an assignment overseas in Europe. Now, the exact same week a mortgage is signed for a first home ever, up pops the devil!

Luckily, the present occupants of 4205 Salerno Road South wanted to continue renting from the new owners. Arrangements to that end were agreed upon and completed.

After vacationing in Atlanta and Alabama, Dan completed a two-week refresher training session in the T-39 *Sabreliner*[1], at LaGuardia airport. One day later, he and his wide-eyed bride, not quite believing this was really happening to her, winged their way to Naples, Italy. New experiences, new sights, new sounds, new tastes, new friends awaited them.

Note. In spite of how the move came about, it was a fantastic three years in Italy with opportunities to visit so many interesting and intriguing places, including several other countries.

*****

Elephants have retired. Now it's computers that never forget.

---

[1] Original time in type was at NAS Glynco, Ga (1962-65)

Chapter 44

A BAVARIAN HERO

Thanksgiving, 1973
Age: 38

They arrived in Naples in late September. A brand new
Opel four-door compact and household goods came by
ocean freighter a month later. By November 1st, Dan and
Becky were happily ensconced in the Italian seaside
community of Pinetamare. "Pine trees by the sea", located
eighteen miles north of Naples, was comprised of both
single-family homes and high-rise condominiums. A few
other Americans were already in residence when the new
couple moved in. The picturesque yet modern village
promised to become an Italian summer resort with several
apartments designated as base housing for American
enlisted personnel serving the various Army-Air Force-Navy
units in the area as well as NATO assignments.

Upon reporting to VR-24, Dan was greeted with the news of
another Navy SNAFU[1] - the airplanes purchased for and
assigned the squadron for implementing a fast reaction
transport program, the new aircraft that he was to pilot,
were missing in action. Three CT-39G *Sabreliners*, executive
jets capable of carrying three crew and six passengers, had
not yet arrived. The sleek new planes that would become
the elite transport vehicles of Commander, Fleet Air
Mediterranean, were still being manufactured in St. Louis.
It was another classic example of the military adage, "Hurry
up and wait". Dan, of course, was assigned administrative
tasks to perform until the new jets arrived. The plus side of
the equation was that the unexpected time at home gave the
couple ample opportunity to explore Naples and
surrounding environs.

Around the middle of November, Dan was called into the
office of the Commanding Officer.

---

[1] Situation normal, all [fouled] up

"Dan, what are your plans for the Thanksgiving four-day holiday?"

"I don't think we have anything special in mind, sir. Probably hang around Naples, play some tennis, eat at home. Maybe go to the club."

"Dan, I have reservations in Garmisch at the *Von Steuben Hotel*. I know you haven't been here long enough to know much about Garmisch but it's an Armed Forces Europe Rest and Recreation Center in Germany. Garmisch is about forty miles north of Innsbruck, Austria. It's a great place to go for an *R&R* holiday. I'd like for you to take our reservations. My wife has just advised me that one of our daughters will be arriving here in Naples on Friday following Turkey Day so we cannot go to Germany. Please go if you can."

Naturally, the reservations were accepted. A long weekend in beautiful Bavaria, compliments of the Commanding Officer - who wouldn't have taken such a sweet deal. Of all Europe, besides London, the snow-capped mountains of Bavaria topped the Brown's want to see list.

Two days before Thanksgiving, Dan purchased tire chains to fit the Opel in anticipation of their trip north to Germany requiring passage over and through the Alps. Raised in the south, he had little experience driving in snow conditions. Yes, there had been lots of snow in Newfoundland but that was years ago and there he had rarely driven, usually riding on base buses. He had no idea how to attach chains to tires. Opening the instructions that came with the purchase, he found the words printed in Italian and German but not in English. He decided to ask a neighbor for help.

The neighbor, Jack Sloan, chided him. "Dan, I've lived here for 5 years. We always go to northern Italy/southern Germany around this time. You will not need chains at Thanksgiving. Trust me. It doesn't snow hard enough for chains until just before Christmas. Go enjoy yourselves. I'll show you how to use the chains when you really need them."

By leaving very early in the dark hours of Thursday morning and driving almost twelve hours, they arrived in Garmisch

232

around 2 p.m. As far as United States personnel were concerned, it was Thanksgiving Day. In Germany, it was simply Thursday. As Dan parked the car, intermittent snowflakes began to fall. He and Becky were excited to see snow and walked several blocks around the town square with small flakes sticking to their clothes and stocking caps. The two first-time visitors immediately fell in love with the locale. Garmisch was not only interesting but also fun, the farms and countryside were as picturesque as advertised. Schnitzel, too many varieties to count, was a newfound food treat. Stopping for hot tea became special moments. King Ludwig's Neuschwanstein Castle was a highpoint as was Oberramagau. Snow continued to fall off and on throughout the weekend blanketing the region with virgin whiteness. All too soon, Saturday evening arrived. They would be leaving early the next morning.

After dining in the *Von Steuben* restaurant, Dan approached the desk clerk to ask about the forecast. He was assured that while light to medium snow was predicted, the German road crews were excellent and would be out very early. They always had the road to Innsbruck open by six o'clock.

Awake at five, the Opel packed and coffee in hand, Dan checked out with the desk clerk. There he learned the white stuff had fallen steadily during the night. Assured once more of the German road crew's excellent track record, two inexperienced tourists from the United States by way of Italy, drove away towards Innsbruck under lightly falling snow. The city streets were no problem as heavy equipment crews were out in force as promised. As they drove farther into the countryside, it became readily apparent that the rural crews had not yet arrived on this stretch of highway. Still, the road was negotiable at 30-35 miles per hour so Dan made the decision to keep going. Surely they would meet the scraper crews soon and have smoother going thereafter. Seven or eight miles out of Garmisch, the car unexpectedly entered a dip in the road where the snow was deeper than the car's wheels. The little Opel came to a stop, wheels spinning with no effect. Becky looked at her husband, her eyes questioning their next move.

Dan cursed Jack Sloan *and his mother*, and then looked around. Unbelievably, for just a moment it appeared that two angels stood there right by the car. He had not seen anyone or anything on the side of the road as they approached the unseen snowy hazard. Actually, at second look, it was two men dressed in heavy work clothes. As Dan realized who they might be, the men turned their attention to the automobile that now appeared stuck in the snow. Dan exited and walked over to talk to them. Through sign language he ascertained they were part of the clean-up crew and were waiting for the road scraper from Innsbruck to arrive for them to go to work. Dan returned to the car and retrieved a tire chain and the instructions. He envisioned they were not out of trouble when one workman shook his head and passed the instruction sheet to his partner. The second man acted like he was reading every word. Dan's heart sank when he saw the instruction sheet was upside down – there was no way the guy was reading either German or Italian. Finally, the fellow shook his head apologetically and handed the now crumpled and damp sheet back. It seemed the Opel and the Browns and the two workmen were stuck there until help arrived.

But the two workmen were resourceful and practical chaps, something Dan had not expected or counted on. They spoke words in German to each other and then motioned for Becky to drive. The three men would push.

And sure enough! After a few feet of manual push-power, the tires caught hold and the Opel was on its way again.

It was still snowing steadily and they hoped to see heavy equipment clearing the road at any moment. For a few long, slow miles it appeared the worst was behind them even though no road crews appeared. But the adventure was not over. After a few miles they came to the last mountain incline before topping out and heading downhill to Innsbruck. Dan slowed as he saw several cars in the ditches on either side of the road at the base of the hill. Dan stopped and again spoke sign language with German and Italian drivers and occupants of the stalled vehicles. Several of the onlookers pointed to the Armed Forces Italy auto tag identifying Dan and Becky as Americans. After animated

discussions, the consensus was that there was nothing to do until the road crew arrived. No doubt, expletives in all three languages represented were expended into the frosty air.
A half hour passed. Dan looked at his watch and reminded Becky that he had an early morning flight the next day and there was still a long way to go. Suddenly he remembered how the men back at the first snowdrift had managed to push them through the problem and get them going.
"Honey, take the wheel again and when I pound on the trunk, ease the accelerator to the floor and hold it there regardless of any slipping or sliding this way or that. Don't take your foot off the gas until you get going properly or you see we will wind up in a ditch like these other poor folks. Got it?"
He took off his coat and put on his gloves. Behind the car, he tapped the trunk and began to push. At first he was only aware of the wheels spinning wildly, the car going nowhere. Then it began to move forward but quickly skewed sideways to the left. Becky got it straight again but almost immediately it started sliding right. It was cocked with the tail end slipping around to the left, but was making forward progress. He pushed harder on the right side trunk and was vaguely aware of yelling and clapping behind him. Surprised by the noise, he was in no position to look backwards to see what the fuss was about. He just kept pushing and finally felt the tires take hold and suddenly the Opel straightened out and was climbing the hill. Becky continued several yards up the road before stopping when she was sure they were in good shape. Dan turned and looked to see the Italians and Germans waving and screaming, "Yay! Americano! Buono! Americano! Bene! You win. Car go up. Go." Dan was huffing and nearly winded but the exciting sight down the hill was invigorating. He bowed and then saluted his admirers. At the car, he took the wheel for the long drive home to Pinetamare.

While buckling in he looked over at his beaming bride. "Did you hear those people cheering for me? I'm their hero!"
She was feeling his exuberance. "Honey, you're always my hero."

Now he gave her his best devilish, cocky eye roll: "I don't know about German heroes or Italian heroes, but Navy heroes from the South need a lot of sex."

She heard it coming and was ready for him. "Well, Mr. Navy Super Hero, during this four-day out-of-town weekend in the snowy, romantic Alps, you got enough loving for *Batman, Captain Midnight,* and *Tarzan,* all rolled into one." Furrowed brow, eyes twinkling, she elbowed him in his left side, which is easy to do in an Opel, and added, "No, better yet, the way you're always reaching for me and my body, maybe my hero is *Spider Man!"*

*****

Golly, this really is a hero storybook!

Chapter 45

"SEE THE PYRAMIDS ALONG THE NILE"

September, 1974
Age: 39

Following the Yom Kippur war in 1973 between Israel and various united Arab countries, American military aircraft were prohibited from operating in Egyptian airspace or landing on Egyptian soil. This was in retaliation for U.S. involvement on the side of Israel. In fact, only one United States civilian carrier, - Trans World Airlines - was permitted to carry passengers in and out of Egypt. TWA was authorized one flight per week. The following story chronicles events surrounding the first military plane to be ordered into Cairo almost a year after the Yom Kippur war ended.

The flight had gone smooth as silk to this point. Naples to Athens, a two-hour milk run, was, as always, routine. During the second hour, his VIP passenger, Admiral Rance Smith, had napped for a good twenty minutes. On course, at Flight Level 370, cruising at about six miles a minute, plenty of fuel, weather clear to the moon, the small sleek jet was soon in Greek airspace. Right on the two-hour mark, he was easing the plane onto the runway at Athenai Airport.

The landing, refueling and re-filing flight plan at Athens proceeded as briefed. The ho-hum flight may have lured the crew into forgetting a cardinal tenet from the All Pilot's Bible[1]: *flying is hours of boredom interspersed with moments of stark terror.* And so far they were in the hours mode. Other than going to Cairo as the first U.S. military aircraft to land in nearly a year, nothing out of the ordinary was in the wind or even slightly anticipated. With diplomatic clearance from

---

[1] A verbalized tradition of aviator's sayings. For example: "Four engines are better than two, two are better than one". "Murphy's Law: If a part can be installed wrong, someone will install it that way." From previous stories, "Any landing you walk away from is a good one." And "Never run out of gas." And many others.

Egypt coordinated through the state department, all appeared copasetic.

Departing Athens International, the T-39 climbed out on a generally southerly heading to flight level 370. In due course, Juliet Mike 1-2-3, with a crew of three plus four high profile passengers, was about 60 miles north of El Daba, a navigational fix on the coastline of Africa approximately 150 miles east-northeast of Cairo. Previously, Athenai Control had instructed the small jetliner to contact Cairo Control on 115.7 MHz as soon as radio contact could be achieved. Pre-flight information forewarned that radio reception would be lost for a period as the aircraft traversed over open water at distances beyond that which radio frequencies could extend. They had been in the "Dead zone" for several minutes after reaching the extremis of Athens's radio range and not yet close enough to Egypt to pick up Cairo Control.

"O.K., Jack," Dan said to his copilot. "Let's see if we can raise them now that we're only a little over 70 miles out of El Daba. The shoreline is beginning to break out of the haze." The north shore of Egypt was just beginning to be visible through a blue veil over the landmass. Out over the water, visibility was unlimited.

"Roger." The copilot depressed the mike button and spoke into the little black mouthpiece. "Cairo Control, this is Juliet Mike 1-2-3, Fl 370. Over."

A raspy voice over loud and erratic static answered in labored English. "JULETTE MECK 1-2-TREE, THIS IS KY-RO CONTROL. WHY YOU CALL?"

Copilot Gridley: "Control, J M 1-2-3 is on diplomatic clearance 0869257 to Cairo Airport. I have VIPs aboard who will be meeting with your president. Over."

Controller: "1-2-TREE, STANDBY. I HAVE NO KNOW OF SUCH CLEER. CONFIRM YOU AMERICAN FLIT."

Copilot Gridley: "Affirmative, Control. United States aircraft, flight originated out of Napoli, Italia. Over."

"JULITTE MECK 1-2 TREE. OONITED STATES AEERCRAFT NO ALLOW IN EGYPT." The controller used a persuasive, forceful voice inflection, "DO NO

CROSS SHORELINE. YOU NO VEOLATE EGYPTIAN AEERSPACE. OVER."

The wary pilot flicked a switch on the communications panel, which permitted the passenger compartment to hear all radio transmissions. Using the intercom that allowed talk in the airplane without transmitting out over the airwaves, he said. "Admiral, I think you'd better be privy to all radio conversations. We're being told by Cairo Control that they have no advance notice of our flight." He looked over his right shoulder through the open door to the passenger area and could see the Admiral shoot him a thumbs-up in agreement.

The radio receiver came alive again. Excitement was evident in the controller's voice, "JULETTE MECK 1-2-TREE, ARE YOU MELITEERY?"

Dan was beginning to feel antsy about the developing situation and took over the radio exchange. He answered in a matter-of-fact tone. Speaking very slowly, "Control, this is 1-2-3. That's affirmative; we're a United States Navy aircraft, a T-39 *Sabreliner* with high-level representatives who are to meet with Mr. Sadat. I repeat our diplomatic clearance number is 0869257."

The Egyptian voice came back – was it less agitated? Perhaps he too was attempting to remain cool. "JULETTE MECK 1-2-TREE, WHAT ARMS-A-MENT CARRY YOU?"

Dan told him the details quickly, masking a growing annoyance. "Control, we are an executive jet transport with a total of seven persons on board. We carry no armament; the passengers carry no small weapons. Have you confirmed my diplomatic clearance to Cairo? Tell your superiors that my VIP will discuss cleanup of the Suez Canal at your president's request."

Control: "NEGATEEVE CLEER, 1-2-TREE. MY SUPEERIORS ORDER YOU RETURN TO GREECE OR DEEVERT TO CRETE." He continued, more emphatically: "DO NOT CROSS OVER LAND TO EGYPT. WE ARE, HOW SAY YOU, SCRAPPLING (scrambling) FIGHT PLANES. WE POOTING FORR

JEET FEGHT-TERS IN EER (air) AT THIS TIME TO
INTERGET (intercept) YOU."

Dan felt the same creeping sensation at the back of his neck
that had been there in on that first mission in Vietnam; a bit
of fear, maybe, but more to the point, apprehension over
events beyond his control. He knew he must be absolutely
precise in any and all radio transmissions. He spoke to his
copilot, wanting to keep the younger man 'in the loop' as
much as possible for experience. "Jack, you're new to flying
over here across the pond. This is a good lesson for you.
Always remember when talking to a foreigner, you're never
sure exactly how much of your language they know or
understand. In this case, we're screwed if anything does go
wrong. Only the Egyptians will have radio transmission
tapes - tapes that could be altered or purposefully lost if
needed to save someone's ass. Nobody else can hear us out
here. Our only justification will be we did have diplomatic
clearance." The copilot tightened his lips and nodded in
agreement. Looking again into the cabin, Dan saw the
Admiral speak to his aide who pulled out a pen and opened
his briefcase for a notepad. "Good", Dan thought as he
realized they might need a record of events if this
misunderstanding wasn't cleared up soon.
Dan tried dropping the Egyptian President's name again.
"Control, this is 1-2-3. I suggest you have your superior put
in a call directly to Mr. Sadat's aides. We are on diplomatic
clearance 0869257 from Athenai to Cairo."
Control came right back, at first rationally, then excitedly:
"1-2-TREE, ALL FORR JEET FEGHT-TERS TAXI
NOW WETH INSTRUCTIONS TO SHOOT DOWN
YOU IF YOU CROSS OVER SHORE INTO EGYPTIAN
LAND. YOU MUST TURN A-ROUND AND GO
BACK ATHENI. WE HAVE NO CLEER FOR YOU."
The pilot turned again and looked at the senior officer
present. Over the intercom, Dan stated, "Sir, we are now
passing over El Daba. They evidently have no radar out this
far and don't know we are already *feet dry* and into their
airspace. What are your instructions?"
The answer came back quickly. "We have to keep going.
There is a big state affair dinner tonight and I'm guest of

honor. I've got to believe this mess will get straightened out."

"Yes sir," Dan replied. "For information, sir if they do launch jets, we will be intercepted about 8 minutes after they're airborne."

The pilot looked through the opening between cockpit and cabin at his VIP passengers. The admiral's stoic countenance was telling. Dan had flown the admiral to over fifty destinations in Europe and knew this was his leadership face. Some of his staff liked to say that "Two-star Rance Smith may not be a great military strategist, but he is a consummate leader. He remains calm and collected; he always sets the example for his officers." Admiral Smith nodded his head in acknowledgment of the information Dan had offered on the Egyptian jets. All conversation in the cabin had ceased. Solemn, concerned faces stared toward the cockpit area while all ears were tuned to the radio speakers overhead. It occurred to Dan that in the last ten minutes, regardless of the brave face Admiral Smith was wearing, the stress level in the cockpit – and he imagined in the cabin as well - had gone to hell. The definition out of the *aviator's bible of flying* had come home to roost again. Hours of boredom vanished while terror invited itself to the party. Whether or not those four jets became airborne, an uninvited guest named *Fear* was already feasting at the *hors d'oeuvres* table. He wondered if Jack Gridley would be any help if things worsened. Dan looked at his copilot and saw that the younger man's face was devoid of color. Jack turned to his pilot and muttered, "Dan, if they launch those jets, we won't know whether to shit or go blind! No way can we out maneuver them – right?"

Before Dan could reply, the radio receivers began picking up new foreign voices. Then the controller's familiar voice answered in Arabic. Dan knew instinctively that the first voices were those of pilots in taxiing jets. Probably, the controller was giving vectors to the fighters, magnetic headings that the interceptors were to turn to after takeoff. Knowing Egyptian Air Force jets lacked head-on missile capability which our fighters carried routinely, Dan expected he would see their fighters, if they did in fact launch, when they passed abeam 4 or 5 miles on one side or the other, positioning for a turn-in to fall behind them for a *Sidewinder* shoot........the *Sidewinder* was a heat-seeking missile which would track straight up and into one of their engines. When fired from directly astern the target, it was deadly accurate and totally reliable. The only drawback to the *Sidewinder* was that it had to be launched from behind the target. Dan was counting on that shortfall if the situation continued to go south. He would be running full bore for the airport and public eyes as witnesses.

Still at flight level 370, the small Navy jet had reached a point seventy nautical miles due west of Cairo. Dan knew the predicament had just become two-pronged and that it was decision time. On one hand was the diplomatic clearance problem. On the other, he needed to start getting down from altitude. It appeared Egyptian clearance might not be forthcoming. Trying to divorce thoughts of how that status might conclude, Dan concentrated on delivering his VIP as scheduled. He had to begin his descent shortly, or they'd wind up high over Cairo, requiring a steep descending spiral to the landing pattern. That would not cause a problem as far as the aircraft or safety was concerned, but it would delay their landing time. In the VIP transport game, early or late arrivals simply were not tolerated short of an emergency or unforeseen inclement weather. VIPs were accorded all possible means at the pilot's disposal to be on time within plus or minus 5 minutes of expected arrival time. Dan knew that an American two-star would not want to apologize to President Sadat for being late even though it was apparently an Egyptian screw-up that was responsible for the present quandary.

In hopeful anticipation that diplomatic clearance would come through any second, Dan throttled back, nosed over, and left altitude. He would try his damnedest to make his landing time in the event they got lucky and received arrival permission. Normally, aircraft leave altitude only when instructed to do so by the controller. Since that possibility was out of the question at the moment, the T-39 pilot made a command decision that made sense on two fronts. First, it was 'CAVU - clear and visibility unlimited', in VFR (visual flight rules conditions), so safety would not be compromised (if they had been flying in clouds or having to descend through clouds, quite the contrary would have been true). Secondly, on a practical note, Dan thought, if push came to shove and he had to play real war games with jet fighters, he needed to be lower and faster. If those assholes did send the jets after them, he would need all the airspeed the *Sabreliner* could muster and the heavier air of lower altitudes to turn and dive. The outcome of an air battle would never be in doubt – after all he was driving a transport aircraft and carried no weapons and would be going against jet fighters with all the advantages. In a face-off, he would be dead meat. Still, he could try to make it to the airport, crash landing wheels-up on the runway if he had to. He had made up his mind they would not go like a sitting duck. Tightening his shoulder harness and taking a deep breath, he mused almost aloud, "Worse case scenario, we get shot down. O.K., then we'll make a big burn spot right on Cairo airport in front of all those dignitaries. Screw 'em if they can't take a joke!"

Descending rapidly through twenty-nine thousand feet, he saw his airspeed was a notch over four hundred knots. He could see the city of Cairo dead ahead but as yet had not made out the runway. *Hope* had joined *fear* at the goodies table. Dan spoke into the intercom: "Admiral, if they keep those fighters on the ground just two, maybe three more minutes, we'll have a chance to get to the field before the game is played out." Glancing backward, Dan saw the two-star officer once more communicate with a thumbs up. Again, the exasperated voice of the controller came over the air in his barely adequate English: "1-2-TREE, YU MUS' REE-TURN TO GREECE OR DEE-VERT TO SOUDA BAY (Crete). THE FORR JEETS ARE ON RUNWAY FOR TAKE-OFF. THE JEETS AAR HEAVY ARM-ED AND AAR CLEERED TO FAR (fire) ON YOU......." A new voice in calm and perfect English on a better and clearer transmitter interrupted and overrode the first controller. "Juliet Mike 1-2-3, I have you descending through FL 250. Do you have the pyramids in sight?"

Dan responded happily: "Affirmative. Dead ahead about 20 miles."

The new controller came back. "Roger, 1-2-3. You are cleared for two circuits around the pyramids before landing. Welcome to Cairo! President Sadat's car just came through the front gate of the airport. He is expecting Admiral Smith." The original controller was silent now, if indeed, his equipment was still up and on frequency.

In any event, Dan probably would not have heard him over the din of hoorays and high fives taking place in the cabin behind him.

Banking hard right to zero-in on the ancient landmarks, Dan began singing a line from an old Jo Stafford song from the fifties, "See the Pyramids along the Nile". Soon his copilot and crewman joined him, both off-key but who cared! And they were not surprised when four voices behind them chimed in, repeating the beginning words of *You Belong to Me*, "See the Pyramids along the Nile, See the Pyramids along the Nile…"

The sightseeing circuits over the world famous pyramids were cut short so that the desired landing time could be achieved. Mr. Sadat's long, black limousine was waiting at the terminal and whisked Admiral Smith away as soon as he de-planed. (NOTE: The Suez Canal was cleared with U.S. and U.N. involvement. Anwar el-Sadat was assassinated October 6, 1981.)

*****

Chapter 46

"I WANT YOU TO HAVE MY BABY"

Early October, 1975
Age: 40

......fate?   ......or fateful coincidence?

She knocked twice as a courtesy, then entered his office
without waiting to be beckoned. Yeoman striker Rebecca
Andrea Cone, typing clerk, stopped two feet in front of his
desk in an erect inspection type stance. Dressed in the work
uniform of the day, her blue denim shirt and slacks fit a little
too loosely. The officer behind the desk noticed that she was
'not quite as neat and tailored as images portrayed in
recruiting posters.' He called her his "Secretary" although
the operating Navy had no such enlisted classification.
Navy clerical work was done by *yeomen.* Her office, just
around the corner, was a shared cubicle with two other
enlisted women, all assigned duties in the administrative or
personnel field. She had been in the squadron less than a
month, assigned to his office for only two weeks.
Demurely, as if unsure of herself, she asked in a soft voice,
"Mr. Brown[1], may I talk to you?"
Khaki clad, loosened black tie, Dan sat behind a well-used
and scarred military issue desk. A hand carved mahogany
nameplate lay casually awry on top of the gray metal work
surface. Abandoned by some unknown predecessor, the
Helvetica block letters proclaimed his present job
assignment, "Safety Officer". Several stacks of papers in
various stages of completion lay before him. She probably
recognized some of the paperwork as an aircraft accident
investigation she had typed, others as reports due quarterly
on all enlisted personnel. He nodded affirmatively and
motioned for the young woman to sit.

---

[1] By Naval tradition, a lieutenant commander may be properly
addressed as *Commander* on occasion, and all officers below rank of
Commander may be called *Mr.*

Of average height, weight and looks, the young woman before him could have been the girl-next-door from any small-town, USA. She began hesitantly. "I'm sorry but my desk is so close to the corner near your open door I couldn't help but overhear your telephone conversation with Dr. Matthews a few minutes ago. I know that you've talked to him two or three times in the past few days. I've heard you say that you and your wife want a baby and she's having trouble getting pregnant. You sounded sort of mad or agitated today so I guess he didn't give you good news." Her boss frowned: "Yes, Yeoman, that's true. I guess I should have made sure the door was closed. I didn't realize you could overhear my conversations quite so clearly in the next room. I hope you won't say anything about it just yet to anyone in the squadron. Becky is very private about this kind of thing and she would be embarrassed to think people were talking about her not being able to have a baby." The young girl took in a deep breath and looked him directly in the eye. "Mr. Brown, I want you to have my baby. I don't know your wife but I feel like I do a little because of you, and because my name is Becky, too. I've only known you for two weeks but I really enjoy working for you, better than anyone I've known in the Navy. I really would like for you and Mrs. Brown to have my baby. If you want it."

She could see the confusion, even consternation in his face and quickly added. "Oh, I'm already pregnant. I didn't mean *that*."

Dan was astonished, surprised, shocked would not be an overstatement. As is so often the case in life, ambivalent feelings invaded his senses. He recognized the tribute accorded him by a subordinate suggesting a proposal of so personal a nature. Simultaneously, he felt inadequate in some manner, he wasn't sure he deserved to be considered for such an unparalleled honor. The gift of a life. He sat back, still stunned at the unexpected, unorthodox offer. *Flabbergasted* might be a more appropriate description of his reaction. Recovering some semblance of official composure, he asked: "Miss Cone, Becky, do you mind if I ask, who is the father?"

She did not hesitate to answer. "Oh, it's my husband. But he's back in San Diego and he has filed for divorce. When he went to a lawyer to start proceedings, I asked for a transfer and that's how I got here to Naples. I didn't know I was pregnant until last week. Johnny don't care nothing about me. He slapped me around the last night we were together, really hurt my arm and gave me a black eye. I know when I write him I'm having a baby he'll claim it's not his. But it is. I've met a marine here on base but I have not slept with him yet. And I didn't mess around in San Diego. I was married, you know."

Dan looked at the young girl across his desk and saw that her confession had prompted tears. He wanted to console her but repressed an urge to offer a shoulder. In a quiet and, he hoped, comforting voice, he explained. "Yoeman, I am speechless. Honored. Mystified, I guess. I'm certainly complimented to be considered as a stand-in parent for your child. I'll talk to my Becky tonight and give you an answer tomorrow. Tell you what.....you go on to an early lunch and take some extra time before getting back to that report you're typing for me. I'll see you back here around 1300 hours"[1].

Later, as they discussed the ramifications of accepting Rebecca Cone's generous, unparalleled gift, he remarked to his wife, "In this new era of women's liberation, who knows what will come out of the mouths of babes." Qualifying the statement, he added, "*Babes* as in young, innocent children, even an eighteen or nineteen year old girl alone overseas - not *babes* as in sex-oozing *Playboy* goddesses of feminine wares." After long discussions into the night, an answer was agreed upon. He would tell Yoeman Cone, in Navy jargon, "Affirmative". Dan introduced his Becky to the young mother-to-be later that week. The two women made plans for Becky Brown to begin taking part in the prenatal program: shared visits to the obstetrician, dietary planning, etc. Dan made an appointment with the COMMANDER, FLEET AIR MEDITERRANEAN Legal office to start the adoption process. As the child would have dual citizenship,

---

[1] 1:00 pm

the Italian authorities would also be involved. The legal
department would handle the necessary details.

Becky Brown wrote long, happy letters advising both Knight
and Brown families of their plans. Shortly, return letters
began arriving from Anniston, Alabama and Lithia Springs,
Georgia questioning the couple's decision to adopt the child
of an acquaintance. In 1975 the adoption process in the
United States was an exercise in secrecy. Short years
afterwards confidentiality requirements would be lessened,
even reversed in many states and adopted children would
know the identity of their real birth parents. But in 1975, the
old ways still existed and were the norm. In separate
communiqués Grandparents Knight and Dan's mother
conveyed their misgivings. Their argument was that the
Cone woman held a trump card, knowing who had her
baby. With that knowledge and Navy records, she could
find them and elect to show up at any time. Even at some
late date, she might want to become a part of the baby's life.
She would have access and opportunity to disrupt the lives
of Dan and Becky, as well as the child's. Both letters ended,
in effect, "Don't discount our concerns. Stranger things
have happened before in adoption cases. She could even
join the local P.T.A."

The couple was offered a reprieve from the apprehension
and anxieties generated by the worrisome letters from home.
An unexpected opportunity for a Thanksgiving holiday in
London presented itself and was eagerly accepted. Dan flew
U.S. Navy air while Becky rode the wings of *Alitalia*.
London was as fun as anticipated but the weather
deteriorated and turned terrible. The first day was rainy and
chilly but the visitors enjoyed the sights and sounds
immensely. Hearing English spoken again was a treat in
itself. The second cloudy and cold day saw more
sightseeing, Christmas shopping, lunch at *Harrod's* and a
romantic dining adventure at the *Red Pot* that lasted long
into the evening. The third day began as the others, overcast
with drizzle, but in the late afternoon, the rain stopped
ominously. Soon one of London's famous fogs rolled in
from the English Channel. By six o'clock the fog had

enveloped the city to the extent businesses were shutting down. When traffic came to a standstill, the couple decided to take sanctuary in their hotel room. Not surprisingly, neither was discouraged about the weather or the inconvenience caused. Fog this dense was new to them, previously an experience they had only heard of or read about. Now they were seeing it firsthand for themselves. Walking from the underground station was almost like being cast in a black and white "B" remake of *Jack the Ripper*. Glove hand in glove hand, two married lovers strolled from Lancaster Gate Station to their room in *Columbia House*, an American military hotel, providing accommodations for *R&R* personnel.

There was no TV in the hotel room. Becky sat on the edge of the bed looking out the window into dark nothingness. Her husband relaxed, almost lounging, in the overstuffed chair, tie removed, shoes askew. The room became overly warm. Soon, Becky sat reading a magazine in her slip. Standing to remove a sweater, he said amorously, "Me Tarzan, you Jane. We have fun now......seriously, put on that new teddy you think I don't know you smuggled into the suitcase and model it for me."
Coyly, she asked, "Are we going to play *Spider Man* now?" The gleam in his eyes brightened. "The weather forecast is for a lot more of this soup – I may need to be *Superman* this time."
No further discourse or details are needed to explain physical attraction or innermost secrets between husband and wife. They lay in tight embrace, whispering reassurances of their love for each other. Their intimacy did not summon thunder, lightning, or explosions so vividly portrayed in paperback romances. Rather, it was an ardent, loving, giving, taking time of tender sensual sharing. Afterwards, at some indefinable point during that long foggy night, the miracle of conception, the beginning of a new life, occurred within the woman's body.

Dan had not used all his annual leave. Thanksgiving had whetted their appetite for more England, so they decided to return to London for Christmas and New Year's. It was there on Christmas Eve morning that Becky found out she was pregnant. What a Christmas gift!!! The beaming husband was overjoyed and immediately placed two overseas phone calls back to Alabama and Georgia. Her parents and his mother were elated at the news. The holidays were especially happy, joyous ones. The question of what to do about the other baby lay dormant while festive activities filled the last six days of the year.

Back in Italy, in enlisted women's quarters on base, Yoeman Rebecca Cone faced the New Year unaware of changing circumstances, which could and would radically affect the future of her unborn child.

They had returned from England on January 2nd, two days ago. Now, they were leaning on the railing of their balcony, looking out at a gray, angry, turbulent sea. The continuously undulating waves seemed to mirror the inner turmoil both were feeling.

Dan was briefing his wife. "I guess the meeting went as well as it could. I called her into my office and told her that you would be having a baby about four or five months after she delivered. I didn't mention that our folks are giving us unmitigated grief about adopting. Of course, she asked right off the bat, did we still want her baby? I said that we are exploring the possibility of having two kids at once, that basically they would be twins. I admitted that the thought was exciting but frightening at the same time. I assured her that she didn't have to worry, that we would be here for her and the baby regardless of circumstances. I'm not sure that helped much but I hope that she knew I meant it."

Becky sat in one of the straight-backed chairs around the small kitchen table. Her pensive husband took a seat opposite her. He laid a ruled tablet on the table. Pulling a Government Issue pen from his shirt pocket, he drew a vertical line down the center of the page. "O.K., on one side we jot down the pros, on the other the cons. The only problem with solving a matter in this way is that you have to give different weights to the various entries. That's the hard part. One side of the paper may have the most reasons numerically but in fact be the weaker case. But anyway, let's try. What's the first reason for going ahead and keeping her baby?"

Becky: "I think it's because we said we would. If we don't, we leave that poor girl out on a limb. I wouldn't be happy with myself."

Dan: "I wish we could write the first reason is 'We want her baby.' But you're right. Now that you're going to have our little Dana or little Dano, that's not the number one factor. But we will adopt and have quasi-twins before we cut Becky Cone adrift to go it alone. O.K., that's the first 'Yes'. I think the primary 'Con' reason is the issue of having two babies at once but one of them always a few months ahead in development."

The discussion had been underway for several minutes. Reasons for and against the adoption had been written on the yellow legal sized paper.

Dan was in the process of writing yet another reason for declining when the phone rang.

He answered simply, "Hello, Brown."

A familiar voice on the other end began, "Dan, this is Charlie Jordan at the squadron. Hey, we just heard the news about Becky's condition. Kudos, ole buddy."

Dan smiled as he accepted congratulations from a fellow officer and pilot. Charlie and Sarah Jordan had been in the squadron about a year. Charlie would probably be taking over as senior checkpilot in the T-39 when Dan retired in six months.

The voice on the line continued. "But I called for another reason. We sort of have the opposite kind of news. Sarah went to the obstetrician today and was told she can't have any more children. We really wanted one more, boy or girl, doesn't matter. Dan, now that your Becky is with child, we were wondering if you'all might want to back out of your deal with Yoeman Cone. If so, we'd appreciate it if you would recommend us as prospective parents for the baby. Look, we would treat that baby like he or she was ours. And we'll be just as good to Becky Cone as you two have been. Please consider us."

Fate? Divine intervention? I'll let the readers draw their own conclusion. The facts bear out that Dan and Becky Brown departed Italy just over five months later. Dan would retire from the United States Navy on June 30, 1976. The adoption process for Mark Jerome Jordan would not be finalized until May 1977. Although Charlie and Sarah Jordan took the baby home from the hospital almost a year earlier, the adoption procedure was far from a done deal. The paternal father's reticence to sign custody papers combined with Italian red- tape and bureaucracy delayed the formal adoption signing for nearly a year after Dan and Becky had gone home.

*****

Do you believe in miracles? I do.

Chapter 47

THE DINING-OUT

Late October, 1975
Age: 40

The *Italia* room in the Officer's Club, AF SOUTH, Bagnoli, Naples, was impeccable, the decor lavish and resplendent in every detail. A desired festive ambiance had been more than simply achieved. Subdued lighting from eight ornate chandeliers hanging overhead bathed tables below in soft illumination. Centerpiece arrangements featured tall candelabra, shimmering like bright stars. Tables were covered with dazzling white Army-Navy cloths and perfectly set with fine china. NATO (North Atlantic Treaty Organization) crests embossed in twenty-four karat gold adorned the expensive plates, cups, and saucers. Each place setting was finished with two Waterford wineglasses, gleaming silverware, and lush linen napkins. Fourteen national flags of countries comprising NATO embellished the international flavor of the room. The flags, vibrant and majestic, stood erect like wooden sentries along the front wall. A panorama of color, the flags added a dramatic backdrop to an already impressive and opulent setting. Parallel to and in front of the flags was a long, imposing table on a slightly raised platform. In the center of the table, just forward of the center place setting, a tabletop lectern with microphone awaited the first speaker. This was, of course, honorary seating for dignitaries and spouses. Guest seating was at tables placed end-to-end along three rows perpendicular to the head table. If one could look down from above, the tables would appear to form a large E laying on its side with the long vertical leg of the E at the top with three lesser lines hanging on.
The front table was set for thirty places. The center seats were reserved for the evening's speaker and his wife. On his left would be the *president* of ceremonies and wife. Fourteen NATO representatives and their wives or female guests would be divided evenly on either side of the four central figures. The flag of each nation was located directly behind

the assigned chair of that country's dignitary. Our Stars and Stripes stood in the virtual center since the United States representative was guest of honor, senior officer present, and the evening's orator.

Dan Brown, twenty-one years a Naval officer and pilot, had never participated in, nor attended a party as grand as this. Unless the reader has personally experienced an impressive ceremony on this scale, it will be difficult to imagine a social function of this magnitude. It's dubious that the reader, without hands-on knowledge, can appropriately comprehend or fully appreciate the visual pageantry, the culinary anticipation, the heightened atmosphere filled with festive camaraderie. All this and more awaited the attendees.

The occasion for the jubilant activities was a FLEET TACTICAL SUPPORT SQUADRON TWENTY-FOUR (VR-24) *Dining-out.* In an adjacent room, a forty-five minute cocktail party preceded the affair and was presently underway. Squadron executive officer CDR Hugh Howard was holding forth among a group of captive junior officers and their wives or dates. CDR Howard delighted in explaining the nuances of *dining-in* versus *dining-out* to the uninitiated. "A *dining- out* includes nonmilitary women. Conversely, a *dining-in* permits attendance by only military men or women. The term *dining-in* derives from a Viking tradition of celebrating great battles and feats of heroes by formal ceremony. The tradition eventually spread to monasteries and universities. When the military mess was established, our Army and Navy leaders predictably adopted the occasion. Somewhere along the way, wives demanded to be included so the *dining-out* was inaugurated. Basically, it is the equivalent of a civilian black tie reception. There will be numerous toasts. Each head of state of the fourteen member nations of NATO will be so honored. Think about it, before one of us can offer a toast to anything or anybody; we will have raised our glasses fourteen times already. Admittedly, the toasting sometimes becomes the highpoint of the evening. At a *dining-in,* energetic and enthusiastic officers sometimes forget we are gentlemen by act of Congress. Excessive toasting has been known to precipitate rowdy and boisterous behavior by our military's elite and finest officer corps. That will not be the case tonight as we have our better halves and dates on hand to make sure we conduct ourselves as gentlemen should. By the way, toasts are usually made with port wine."

Stopping a moment to sip his cocktail, the executive officer continued. "Admiral Smith will be the senior officer present tonight and will offer remarks but our commanding officer is the president of the evening's agenda. He's in charge of the whole banana - the MC so to speak- he says when to eat, when to toast when to adjourn. The only other *dining-out* appointment is 'Mr. Vice'. Mr. Vice is usually a junior officer but not necessarily the most junior officer in the unit. Mr. Vice is the workhorse that helps develop and coordinate the details of the occasion. Tonight, LTJG Higgins is our Mr. Vice. The most junior officer, Ensign Akins, is on duty at the airfield. All other officers are required to be in attendance unless medically excused. So, now, you know the basics of a *dining-out*."

Promptly at 1940 hours[1], the bar closed. Great oak doors into the dining room swung open and officers and guests began filing inside to find their assigned seats. Each of the fifty-three officers and their guests were seated based on the officer's rank and seniority. Those designated or invited to sit at the head table would enter last after being announced. Dan as squadron operations officer, number three in the all-important seniority pecking order, found his and Becky's places opposite Commander and Mrs. Howard. Once place cards were located, ladies were permitted to sit until the distinguished guests were presented.

Ding-ding. Ding-ding. Ding-ding. The chiming of six bells over the loudspeaker system meant the honorees were beginning to enter. A clear and distinct voice enunciated: "COMMANDER, FLEET AIR MEDITERRANEAN, ARRIVING" and was a signal for everyone to stand. All eyes were on Rear Admiral and Mrs. Rance Elliot Smith as the area's number one couple entered through massive

---

[1] 7:40 pm

carved doors and walked along the red carpet runner that wound its way to the center table. As mentioned, Admiral Smith was the ranking officer present, the guest of honor and distinguished speaker.

Ding-ding. Ding-ding. Four bells rang next over the loud speaker followed by "TRANSPORT SQUADRON TWENTY-FOUR, ARRIVING." Captain and Mrs. Thomas Ryan Hilton entered and made their way to the dais where he would direct ceremonies. Mrs. Hilton would be seated to the right of Admiral Smith; Mrs. Smith to the left of Captain Hilton.

Ding-ding. The traditional two bells rang for honorees lower than a Navy Captain, Air Force, or Army "Bird" colonels. "LIEUTENANT COLONEL GUIDO GAROFALO, AF SOUTH OPERATIONS OFFICER, REPRESENTING ITALY, ARRIVING." Colonel Garofalo, operations officer for Southern Forces, Italy, entered with his petite wife, Maria. They approached the head table where Mrs. Garofalo would sit to the left of Captain Hilton, Colonel Garofalo next to her.

Bells, announcements, and dignitaries followed as appropriate until finally, the fourteenth nation, the fifteenth couple, was presented. **Ding-ding**. "LIEUTENANT PIERRE D'ORNAY, ASSISTANT AF SOUTH SUPPLY OFFICER, REPRESENTING PORTUGAL, ARRIVING."

The large doors closed. Officers and guests were seated. Stewards began filling wine goblets.

Dan looked at Becky, then to CDR Howard. "X.O., it appears that this gig is a big deal. I've been in the Navy a long time but this is my first *dining-out*."
The executive officer nodded and agreed. "It sure is, Dan, it sure is. And it's only my second *dining-out*. I've also participated in a couple *dining-ins*."
Conversation around the group was animated. LCDR Dick Watson, the unit's safety officer, sitting adjacent to Dan and

Becky, was known for his sometimes risqué, often provocative comments. "Dan, listen to this. I read in the Stars and Stripes that women have control of most all the money in the world."

Dan smiled and answered. "Yes, I saw that. 87% to be exact, as I remember."

Dick Watson held up a finger to make a point. "Yeah, but here's what the article didn't say. Do you realize that in addition to 87% of the money, they have <u>all the nookie!</u> 100%! Think about it - even ugly women have one of those little *kitties* that all normal guys want to pet. Hell, fat broads who haven't even seen it for five to ten years, they've got feline equipment, too. Who was that famous *kitty* that started a war, what was her name? Joan of Troy, or something like that."

Dan started to correct his friend and tell him the lady's name in question was *Helen,* but LCDR Jake Kincaid broke into the conversation. "Along the same line, let me interject a saying that my first mother-in-law loved to tell. Using your feline analogy, it would go something like this. 'Big woman, big kitty. Little woman, *all* kitty'!"

By then every officer within hearing was laughing uproariously at the sexist remarks. Picked up and passed on to other officers, the entire room (less the front table) was soon aware of Lieutenant Commanders Watson's and Kincaid's comedic perceptive on the status of women's wealth and *their other unique physical attributes.* Most of the women followed suit in apparent mirth, at least subdued chuckling or polite grinning at the humor of the moment. Rarely were such comments challenged as harassment in the military of 1975. This was true due to several factors. First and foremost in this instance, all present of both genders were enjoying the merriment of a very special outing, the vast majority who were pleasantly warmed by one or several aforementioned cocktails. Secondly, the loquacious officer was well liked and had a reputation for basically innocent jokes even when colored with mild expletives. Then too, perhaps the not so pleasant memories of a recent unpopular war allowed their men a little more leeway.

FLEET TACTICAL SUPPORT SQUADRON
TWENTY-FOUR DINING-OUT
October 21, 1975
The Italia Room

Antipasto

Sliced plum tomatoes with mozzarella fresca
Mateus Rose

Primi Piatti

Vichyssoise caldo
Orvieto Classico

Pasta Alla Panna e Parmigiano Cream
Pinot Grigio delle Venezie

Secondi Piatti

Pesce
Sauteed Scandinavian flounder
with steamed asparagus in cream
Soave Bolla

Carne
Steamboat Round Roast Beef
with Roast Potatoes
Morellino di Scansano della Quercia

Dolci e Caffé

Gelato Melba (peach ice cream over melon)
Assorted pasticceria
Vin Santo del Fornello

Coffee and tea

258

Dan and Becky discussed the menu offerings with Commander and Mrs. Howard.

Dan pointed to the gold embossing inside the elegant menu. "Man, gold *fluer de leis* or whatever you call these curly-cue gizzies. This is first class. Now let's see about my Italian. *Piatti* would be plate, so we have first and second *plate* courses after the *antipasto* and before dessert."

The vino selections caught CDR Howard's eye. "Look at the wines! *Mateus, Classic Orvieto, Pino Grigio, Soave Bolla,* even *Morellino di Scansano.* All good wines, especially the *Morellino.* Great selections! Whew, and then we get to the port for toasts. I don't know if our kiddie corps will be up to this. We may have to worry about our young guys driving home." He added, "Especially the bachelors."

Becky, too, was astonished. "Have you looked at the entrees? There is no way I can eat this much! But won't I sample everything!"

Mrs. Howard agreed. "And did you notice the *vichyssoise* is hot? I don't think I've ever seen that."

Dan: "Who picked these selections? X.O., are you the guilty gourmet?"

CDR Howard: "Nope. I wish I were. These are excellent choices."

When wine had been poured for everyone, Captain Hilton raised a glass to his lips. All in attendance were then free to do likewise. Shortly, the massive doors opened again and a four-wheeled cart, covered in white linen, laden with an enormous serving dish, appeared. The impressive silver server gleamed in the muted light of chandeliers overhead. Perhaps most striking was the dazzling, starry images reflected to and fro when flickering candlelight touched the enormous silver platter as the cart passed candelabra adorning table after table. A Philippine steward, in white cook's attire wearing a traditional stovepipe cap, pushed the imposing yet mobile apparatus. Following behind, marching in step, a color guard carried an American flag and a VR-24 squadron insignia banner. Three paces behind the color guard, a fife and drum corps duet marched, playing the traditional "Roast Beef of Olde England".

All present, officers and ladies stood; men at military attention.

The procession paraded slowly, making a complete tour around the room, then returning to the head table. The route took several minutes, long enough for the fifes and drummers to play the English ditty two or three times. Stopping, the steward removed the cover of the serving dish. Inside a perfectly browned steamboat roast exuded steamy wisps of aromatic essence. Admiral Smith approached the cart and picked up silver slicing utensils. Holding the roast steady with the fork, he cut off just a bit of the roast near the crown. As all watched in rapt deference, the Admiral chewed and then swallowed the bite of meat. Nodding approvingly, he smiled and turned to the filled room. He said simply the words that embodied the occasion. "I pronounce this beef fit to eat."

All guests, including honorees and wives at the front table, cheered and clapped.

Almost immediately, stewards appeared carrying small plates of antipasto. Small, sweet oblong tomatoes sliced in wheels lying over fresh mozzarella were attractive and delicious. Both the ripe Plum tomato and Southern Italy's local cheese are treats not to be missed when in the Naples area. Homegrown Plum tomatoes have evolved into a delicacy anywhere. Neapolitan mozzarella is special because of the freshness of the local milk from which the cheese is made. Buffala, a domesticated animal akin to oxen and the water buffalo, is the source of milk. Garnished with basil and hint of olive oil, this dish proved an excellent beginning to a delightful meal.

Next came warm potato soup, perhaps not as well known as the more favored cold variety. The cool October evening gave credence to this not so ordinary selection. The soup proved to be popular with the VR-24 group, many wives making mental note to remember that Vichyssoise can be served hot.

Several minutes were planned between the second and third courses. A seven-course dinner is not to be rushed, but savored. The dishes, individually and corporately, are an experience, not simply sustenance.

260

The third serving was the fish course. Sautéed in olive oil and spices, the richly browned flounder fillets could have been a main course under other circumstances. Tender and tasty, not overly done as so often happens with the unique flat-bodied fish, the third course was once again well received by the patrons. *Soave Bolla*, a local favorite of white wine lovers, complimented the appetizing *pesce.*

Eventually, the main course was served. Having seen the roast previously, the diners had eagerly anticipated this moment. Chefs carved the beef in the kitchen and piled generous portions on plates now being offered. Small beds of white asparagus added contrast to the large meat serving. The Howard's smiled widely as they saw the bright red cuts of beef before them. They had hoped for rare beef and were not disappointed. Becky was relieved to see an almost medium slice on her plate. Dan was not so lucky. His serving was *very much* in the *very rare* category. He politely refused the dark red offering. He told the young waiter: "I don't mind waiting until you serve in the order you've been instructed as long as you remember to come back. I prefer medium, but I'll take burned over this bloody rare slice. Bring me an outside piece if you have to."

Dan watched as everyone devoured their meals. The empty plate before him went unnoticed except for Becky who offered him bites of her portion. Waiters disappeared into the kitchen; the main course was well underway. Exasperated, Dan rose and addressed the front table. "Sir, Lieutenant Commander Brown, request permission to speak, sir."
Captain Hilton, slightly surprised at the early, unusual request announced, "Gentlemen, let's hear what your Operations Officer has to say. Permission granted, Dan."

Dan knew his request would be a verbal bombshell akin to the ludicrous and said simply, respectfully, "Sir, request my dinner be served, sir."
Captain Hilton was incredulous. "You haven't received the main course, Dan?"

Dan: "Negative, sir."
Captain Hilton's tone left no room for interpretation.
"Stewards, find CDR Brown a plate and serve his meal.
And advise me how this inconvenience could occur."

For a long moment the room was quiet, graveyard quiet.
Squadron members seemed mesmerized by the
announcement that their number three officer had received
no main course meal while they had feasted. But, 'Surprise
does not ingenuity defeat'. Within seconds, Dan was
deluged with plates. Dinnerware arrived from port and
starboard. All soiled, some empty and stained, others with
fatty gristle and vegetable remnants remaining. Soon the
area in front of him was stacked with china. Then came the
water and wine goblets filled with uneaten pieces of fatty
beef and cold rolls and asparagus ends. Stem after stem
arrived, so many that CDR Howard and LCDR Watson
helped arrange the glasses into a large semi-circle around the
plates. Intense laughter and joviality filled the room as the
junior officers reveled in putting a great one over on their
"Ops O".

A sheepishly grinning steward came forward from the
kitchen with a fresh cut of medium-well, browned roast.
Other waiters rushed to help clean up the plethora of dishes
and glasses at Dan's table.
Dessert and coffee was delayed................while Dan ate his
meal under the scrutiny of contemporaries. For the first
time in his life, at least that he could remember at the time,
Dan Brown was totally speechless.

*****

*Well, maybe Becky Cone and "I want you to have my baby"
was the first time.*

Chapter 48

HEATHCLIFF

April, 1976
Age: 40

They had been married two years. Living in Italy was a
once-in-a-lifetime experience even though Dan was gone
much of the time. Flying T-39's and VIPs around Europe
was gratifying and educational for him but had proven to be
a time consuming assignment. In addition to VR-24 flights,
he was Adm. Smith's personal pilot. He was on call day
and night, twenty-four hours a day.
Becky felt a dog would be good company for her while Dan
was flying. Soon, Heathcliff of Devonshire came to live in
Torre Cinque[1]. Heathcliff, as his name so readily hinted,
was an Old English sheep dog. In reality, the four-legged
bundle of fur and canine personality was treated, and
responded, as though he were the favored family son. Tenth
floor condominium living contributed to this innocent
unawareness on the part of the loveable gray and white pet.
Walking and exercising their 'son' on the beach became a
daily routine. Becky and Heathcliff went alone if Dan was
flying. Wintertime now, there would be long walks, no one
in sight, just long stretches of sand and water.

Pinetamare, a seaside village located twenty miles north of
Naples where the Browns had resided since arriving
overseas, is still chilly in April. Brisk breezes demand winter
bundling, especially for shoreline strolling. For as far as the
eye can see, the beach is usually devoid of people or activity.
Here, as in many parts of the world, the coming of spring
brings dramatic changes to the local environment. In
southern Italy, the effect caused by change in seasons is even
more striking. The month of May will see overnight
transformation. A contributing factor to that
metamorphosis is the local practice of renting specific spots
on the beach to paying families. In support of this economic

---

[1] Tower Five

enterprise, large amounts of supplies begin arriving in early April. Stacks of lumber that will become kiosks show up by truck and are piled neatly on the sand above high water marks. Folding chairs and giant umbrellas will follow in lock step. Over the next two or three weeks the prefab boards will be assembled into little one-operator vendor stands for beverages, ice cream, sunglasses, and beach paraphernalia. Families will stake out their piece of beach real estate, approximately five feet square, by row and umbrella color. Visitor activity will begin to increase until the sleepy little village of forty-five hundred reaches the mind-boggling total of sixty-five thousand tourists and inhabitants for the month of August.

For now, it is still mid-April. Only the organized piles of siding and doors, folded director-type chairs, and collapsed beach umbrellas mar the tranquility of the serene seaside. No one is to be seen among these silent, canvas covered monuments dedicated to the god of summer and sun. Anyone walking or jogging would do so on either side of the long line of stacked materials.

Bundled against the wind, Dan and Becky walked hand in hand along their usual path. They sauntered south, the beautiful, deep blue water of the Tyrrhenian Sea on their right with the Island of Ischia hazily visible to the southeast. Heathcliff had fallen behind to investigate a dead crab washed ashore by the tide. Twenty or so yards later, a passing cargo ship diverted Becky's attention at sea. Dan noticed the four-legged member of the family had not rejoined them. Turning to his left, he looked back up the beach for the shaggy pet. Initially, he didn't see the man and the woman, but eventually the undulating motion of the man's bared buttocks caught his eye. Virtually hidden, seen only because the walkers were directly abeam an opening between a stack of lumber on their left and a crate of beach chairs on the right. There, a large overly fed couple was so actively engaged in what they were doing they had no idea anyone else might be on the beach. The woman was lying on her stomach, her dress bunched up around her neck, her back and backside exposed. Dan could see her coal black hair contrasted against the pale skin of her lower back and right hip. He could see that she was a big woman. The even larger man was on his knees behind her, his trousers dropped to mid-thigh, his heavy, large buttocks shinning white in the afternoon sun. As the man rocked confidently back and forth, it was more than apparent that they were engaged in coital bliss. Behind him, Dan heard Becky gasp in absolute shock and disbelief when she finally turned away from the sea and discovered the unlikely scene taking place before them. She whispered, "Let's keep going and Dan, *STOP* looking at them!"

He frowned acceptance with a nod of his head. Then he remembered the missing dog. Turning and looking back again, he saw Heathcliff bound away from the lifeless form in the sand and start running in a straight line for their position. The animal would pass within fifteen yards of the secluded couple who were still unaware their presence had been detected. Once abeam the action in the sand, the dog suddenly veered left. It may have been an ancestral bloodline or a keen sense of smell that called to animal instinct. Or perhaps it was simply the undulating movements of lovemaking that dictated the dog head directly towards the two unsuspecting lovers. Mesmerized, the dog's owners watched the scene unfold.

The Italian lovers were so engrossed in their coupling they knew nothing of the impending tragedy. Finally, when it was evident that the dog had every intention of greeting the man with a wet lick to the backside, Dan was forced to call out: "Heathcliff, *NO!*" The dog obediently veered off to the right to return to his masters.

The woman reacted swiftly and predictably. Already facing away from the commotion behind them, she immediately put her hands over her head, her arms and elbows hiding her silhouetted face. The man turned his head to look sheepishly at Dan and Becky as he pulled his jeans over the nakedness of exposed flesh. As her companion pulled back, the woman pushed at the dark blue skirt bunched around her waist to cover her lower body. She then scooted forward on hands and knees for a few feet before standing and running. Never looking back, she hurried to a black automobile parked conveniently up the slope. The man did not run, but walked quickly in the same direction, tightening, then buckling his belt as he departed. Dan thought he could see a self-conscious, embarrassed grin cross the man's face as he looked back at them one last time. Upon reaching the Fiat, the couple sped away.

"Heathcliff, you weren't the only one playing doggy today," Dan laughed aloud.
Becky tried to chastise him for his callousness but in the end, both laughed heartily at the unlikely scene they had just witnessed. She continued looking at the Fiat becoming smaller and smaller in the distance, "I confess I would love to be a fly on the ceiling in that car and hear what they're saying. I wonder if they are married?"
Dan: "Italy is for lovers, isn't that what they say? Who knows?"

Heathcliff continued to enjoy his run on the lonely sandy beach. He didn't care if they were married or not.

Re-telling and reliving the amusing event in later years, he sometimes wished he had not shouted for the dog to turn away from its intended course towards the unsuspecting couple. Dan remembers the astonished look on the man's face when he turned and saw two people and a good-sized dog watching their intimate activity. Dan could only imagine what the reaction would have been, had that person, so busily engaged in the passion of the moment, with no warning whatever, been the recipient of Heathcliff's warm, wet tongue between his buttocks.

*****

What if.......?

Chapter 49

THE END CROWNS ALL

May, 1976
Age: 41

Work and play are words used to describe the same thing under differing conditions. Mark Twain

What's past and what's to come, is strew'd with husks
And formless ruin of oblivion. The end crowns all,
And that old common arbitrator, Time,
Will one day end it.
Trolius and Cressida Shakespeare

Three Naval officers in working khaki looked out at a lone T-39 *Sabreliner,* side number 362, parked on an expanse of macadam at Capodichino Airport. All three wore telltale gold wings above their left shirt pocket. The trio of aviators probably could not have described their feelings accurately. First, there was a strange emptiness matching that of the bare parking ramp stretched out before them. Under normal circumstances, the sleek nine-passenger executive-type jet would be parked among twelve to fifteen other shiny silver birds. Not today, not ever again at the Naples, Italy, airport. The older C-1A *Trackers,* the newer C-2A *Greyhounds,* and two sister *Sabreliners* were missing, not there, absent as in *gone for good.*

Spaces, formerly buzzing with activity typical of aviation workhorse squadrons, were deserted. One working telephone hung on the wall. An old, beat-up government-issue desk was the only furniture that remained to identify a former squadron duty office. A cardex file of phone numbers lay precariously on a window ledge near the phone while paperback flight planning publications, many now outdated, lay haphazardly and perceived as trash in a corner. Almost a full week had passed since VR-24 moved its base of operations from Naval Air Facility, Capodichino, Naples, Italy, to Naval Air Station, Sigonella, near Catania, Silicy. Officers, enlisted, civilian technical representatives, dependents and families were now residents of *Cosa Nostra* land, or simply "Sig" as they liked to shorten the name. At the same time, a few hands had been left behind in Naples. Personnel with change-of-duty orders effective within the next forty-five days were not included in the permanent move. Imminent detaching orders obviated any rationale for incurring the expense of moving personnel and their families to Silicy for a short tenure.

Still, most of the enlisted "short-timers" were in Sigonella temporarily helping establish squadron readiness as quickly as possible. Admiral Timothy Mason, COMMANDER, SIXTH FLEET, wanted the *Juliette Mike* transports back in the air as quickly as possible. The C-1's and C-2's were crucial, indispensable cogs in the scheme of carrier aviation. Those were the COD's (Carrier On Deck) aircraft that ferried mail and personnel to and from the carriers at sea and the beach. Study after study showed that mail was the single greatest morale factor affecting men at sea; give him his mail and he could get by. No mail - and you had an unhappy sailor. And of course, people and parts had to come and go, so the CODs were always in urgent demand. The '39's did not land aboard ships but supported the fleet by carrying dignitaries, personnel, and small repair parts station-to-station, base-to-base. Rounding out the diverse capabilities of VR-24, a detachment was stationed at Naval Air Station, Rota, Spain. The "Det" flew C-130 *Hercules* aircraft which could deliver huge loads of men and/or material to bases all over Europe.

A touch of remorse, yes, but Dan Brown, Joe Hamiliton, and Mitch Williams could identify other, more positive, feelings about the scene before them. They continued to watch as a skeletal crew fueled the *Sabreliner*. These three considered themselves the lucky ones as they would not be making the transition to new digs. While the other fifty-odd officers and pilots were necessarily optimistic about their new home base, Dan, Joe, and Mitch felt fortunate to have stateside orders in hand. Each of the three command pilots had landed numerous times at *Sig* during the past three years. The squadron's new home base didn't offer quite the appeal of "home", home as in *McDonalds*, *Kentucky Fried Chicken*, the Atlanta *Braves*, college football Saturdays, and operating telephones. Back in the colonies, why kitchens came with cabinets, apartments came with toilet seats and ceiling lights installed. What Italian housewife would believe such things?

Despite an air of solitude and finality around them, their mood was light. They were living the good life and would not be moving to *Mafia-ville*. *Per Diem,* the military's way of dishing out extra allowance money, helped fatten paychecks to pay for life in comfortable, convenient hotels. Household goods had been shipped back home approximately two months ago, in advance of departure. That necessitated short-term accommodations, thus the per diem perk. Dan and Becky were in Hotel Pinetamare, a modest establishment just eighteen miles north of Naples in the resort community they had resided for the past three years. Joe and Mitch and wives were holed up in fancier quarters, downtown Naples in Hotel Vesuvio. The Browns would be flying home in less than a week; Joe and Jacklyn had a departure date of June 15th, while Mitch and Tori wouldn't leave until the last day of June. If asked, they would have spoken as one in agreement: it had been a great tour. Three years overseas in *Napoli*, flying a super little jet, wonderful friends, vacation opportunities all over Europe, but the *colonies* were calling!

There was a more than subtle difference between the orders of Dan Brown and those of Joe Hamilton and Mitch Williams. Dan's were his final set of orders; he would be retiring June 30th after more than twenty-one years active service. Joe and Mitch were simply moving on to new duty stations. The prospect of retirement, of freedom, and of unemployment after so many years of following orders, made for ambivalent feelings deep in the senior officer's gut. He seemed totally absorbed by the now desolate acres of concrete.

That morning, he had arrived first and checked with the scheduling authority for any changes to the day's flight. Joe and Mitch arrived soon thereafter, and now the three gazed on the empty ramp remembering.......*how it used to be*. But those days were gone. The reality was that the three short-timers with one T-39 were expected to meet any priority or emergency transport requirements that might be deemed necessary and laid on by higher authority. While efficiency and readiness were being created out of chaos at *Sig*, the small detachment of three pilots, one jet, and a handful of enlisted maintenance types stood ready to respond to COMMANDER, FLEET AIR MEDITERRANEAN tasking. COMFAIRMED always had people and/or parts that needed to be moved from one place to another. The CODs were already flying out of their new home to keep the carriers happy. The single T-39 at Naples and C-130's of the Det at Rota would take care of non-shipboard requirements.

The phone rang, Mitch Williams answered. "VR-24 Detachment Naples, LT Williams speaking, sir." "Yes, sir. He's here. Dan, it's Captain Hilton for you."
Dan reached for the black handpiece. "Hi Skipper. You got a hot priority run for us?"
The voice on the other end of the line was more lighthearted than expected. "Dan, things are going great down here, much better than I envisioned. Our spaces are really going to work out well. We're starting to get organized and we just realized something. In the helter-skelter activities surrounding this mammoth move, we forgot to throw you a retirement party. And as well, a farewell party for Joe and Mitch."
Dan: "Ah, Skipper, we understand, no big deal. It's been hectic around here for several weeks. No one had time to party."
Captain Hilton: "Well, we're not letting you three guys leave without a bash. Here's the skinny. While family members were not permitted to ride in Navy aircraft while we were stationed in Naples, VR-24 dependents can ride in military planes now that our homeport is Sigonella. That's because we are now stationed at a base designated as

"remote". Naples was not a remote facility. Sigonella, Silicy is. That makes you three fellows and gals special folks. On one hand, you're assigned to Naples but technically, you're still a part of VR-24 and your parent squadron is now in Silicy. I'm going to take a chance and bend the rules a little and let you fly all six of you down here tomorrow evening. I know Joe and Mitch have a flight to Athens tonight and will return tomorrow. About mid-afternoon, let our few sailors there go home early so they are not involved in any manner. After 362 lands from Athens, have the base people service it. While that's going on, I want the three girls to meet you in the hangar. Keep them inside in the ready room out of sight until the last minute. When 362 has been gas'd and oiled, tow the plane into the hangar, and get those good looking babes of yours into the cabin as quickly as you can. Tow it back outside, start and taxi and come on down here to *Sig*. Party starts at 1900[1] hours tomorrow night! The X.O. is working up a roast for each of you right now. I haven't seen the scripts, but I know you're going to remember this retirement party! Joe and Mitch may be fried alive, but you, sir, because it's your last one before putting out to pasture, you will be skewered! Anyway, what do you think of my plan?"

Dan was smiling ear to ear, and could hardly contain his enthusiasm. "It's great! And I know the guys will love it, too. They're looking at me with big quizzical looks on their mugs right now. Wait till I tell them the news! I think you have one large set of cajones, Skipper, but I agree it will work. I know I can get the wives taken care of with no problems here in Naples and since we'll be landing there after dark, I really don't anticipate anybody asking questions at your end. We'll be landing about 6:30 your time tomorrow night. See you then. Ciao!"

The three women were boarded quickly. Dan as senior, was command pilot, and had filed the flight plan earlier. Joe Hamiliton, in the copilot seat, called NAF Naples Ground Control for taxi. A few minutes later, Dan eased the sleek twin-engine plane onto the runway. "O.K., Joe, takeoff

---

[1] 7:00 p.m.

check-off list complete. Remember our plan. As soon as we're safely airborne, unbuckle and send Becky up here as copilot. I wish I could see all the faces back there when you get up out of your seat like you're going somewhere!"

Throttles advanced, the T-39 quickly accelerated to flying speed and Dan rotated for takeoff. As wheels retracted, Joe Hamiliton moved from the cockpit to the cabin and switched seats with Becky Brown. At a safe altitude, Dan turned the climbing craft towards Mt. Vesuvious, dead but so dominant to the Neapolitan skyline.

"Well, Captain Midnight, you're full of surprises today, aren't you?" remarked his surprised and happy wife. She was wide-eyed and smiling as Joe Hamilton helped buckle her seatbelt around seven months of baby *in the oven*. When she was securely strapped in, Joe returned to the passenger cabin and eased into an empty seat.

"Eyes right!" Dan called and banked steeply over the famous mount. Everyone looked out and down, the three wives seeing craters and crevices for the first time from the unique aspect of directly overhead.

"Gosh, there's Pompeii, too" one of the women in back called to the others.

Another wing dip, this time to the left over Vesuvius, gave his passengers a second look at the craggy volcano, and then Dan headed the plane southerly on course for the Isle of Capri. Becky looked out her side window and was treated to a panoramic bird's eye view of the Bay of Naples defining the teeming city of two million, and off to the west, the island of Ischia.

Straight and level, engines purring, Dan let his mind wander for a moment as he contemplated his very pregnant wife eagerly taking it all in, looking out the windshield, apparently loving every minute of her time in the cockpit. He was amazed by the simple fact they were in the air together, seated side-by-side at the controls of an aircraft he was flying. Oh, they had ridden airliners together as passengers several times, but *non-compare*. Because of the aforementioned Navy Regulations prohibiting dependents flying on operational Navy aircraft (except under special or emergency conditions) this was the first time Becky had been able to fly in a plane piloted by her husband. Well aware this would be one of his last flights as an aircraft commander, it was a very special moment for Dan. He hoped – and he was pretty sure - it was just as meaningful to Becky. As Naples disappeared behind them, he held a thought for a few precious moments. "This is a great way – no, a fantastic way - to end a career. Could I have hatched a script any better if CNO[1] had given me *carte blanche* authority to write my own ending?"

Dan let Becky fly the airplane for a few miles, coaching her on holding altitude, then had her ease into a turn to feel the response of the controls. Soon they were back on course for Capri. Short of fifteen minutes, the island was disappearing beneath the nose of the *Sabreliner*. Dan wanted his female passengers to see as much of the *Blue Island* as possible. Because Becky was in the copilot's seat on the right side of the cockpit, he asked Joe to move Jacklyn and Tori to seats on the right side of the cabin. He then put the craft into a tight right hand bank, and took a sight seeing turn around the island. The ladies were again appreciative of a rare and spectacular view of the rich and famous Mediterranean landmark.

Dan rolled out on course for Stromboli, one of the Lipari Islands north of Sicily, the *football* being kicked by the *boot* of Italy. Becky moved to the back as Mitch Williams came forward and took the copilot's seat. As soon as Mitch was comfortably in control of the bird, Dan went to the rear and sent Tori forward to his seat. The Williams' now had the one hundred-twenty mile over-water leg out of Capri direct to the island of Stromboli, enroute Catania, Silicy.

Upon arriving over Stromboli, Mitch eased into a circuit of that lonely and remote volcanic island. The husband pilots had seen Stromboli often over the past three years, but the wives were astounded to find a tiny fishing village on the north shore, situated at the base of the volcano which had been in eruption almost continuously for at least the past

---

[1] Chief Naval Operations, the Navy's equivalent of a CEO

2,400 years.[1] As the aircraft completed the circle around the volcano's peak, they could see that the island was the volcano, the volcano was the island. Dan had recently read a travel article about the desolate, isolated village. He briefed the others in the cabin: "Believe it or not, Stromboli is a tourist attraction destination. Actually there are six other islands in this group besides Stromboli. Remarkably, there is regular ferry service out of both Sicily and Naples for these small places. They export some sort of heavy wine, and as we know, the Italians like heavy vino."

Mitch Williams leveled the wings on course for Catania. The double-swap was worked again for Joe and Jacklyn Hamiliton to occupy the pilot and copilot seats.
On this leg of the flight, the sun died slowly in the west painting the sky with a glorious blaze of beauty. At a snail's pace, the orange sphere dropped ever downward as if God had hit the slow motion button, then fast-forwarding as it appeared to suddenly dive into the sea. All eyes were transfixed on the horizon which slowly blended into a muted, golden array of clouds, sea, and aftermath of sunlight. Darkness enveloped the cabin as the plane continued on course for Silicy. Shortly, the Hamilton's had the flight approaching Mt. Etna, the highest mountain in Italy south of the Alps. With about twenty miles to go to the base of the 10,876 feet high mount, Joe Hamiliton called over the intercom for "All eyes forward, the whole mountain is burning alive!" Dan stepped forward to look out the windshield between the pilot and copilot.
Undeniably, Mt. Etna was active! Fiery eruptions were occurring all over the volcano's upper north face. The eruption episodes were not huge explosions but simply short blasts releasing incandescent molten lava gases into the air. The red and orange fireworks extravaganza was reminiscent of flame-thrower bursts seen in World War II movies. During the run to and subsequent climb up the mountain, Dan estimated that he saw at least fifty different eruptions of colorful burning gases released into the air. Many appeared to be repetitive from the same source site, then new,

---

[1] Stromboli was not erupting on that particular evening.

additional sites would shoot fireballs into the air. He estimated the height of the blasts at two to five hundred feet. The spectacle was almost ceremonious, memorable in every aspect except the absent cacophony one associates with fireworks of such magnitude. Inside the aircraft cabin, only the hum and drone of the engines broke the silence. The spectacular show before them was like watching a muted TV screen – visually beautiful, thrilling, impressive – yet surreal in the absence of sound.

Joe Hamilton asked Dan, the Mission Commander, for permission to fly up the side of the mountain at 800 feet above terrain rather than the 1500 feet normally observed. Dan concurred, telling the pilot to climb higher if the mini-eruptions intensified. As the aircraft climbed to 12,700 feet, always remaining less than a thousand feet above ground, the three couples were afforded unforgettable views of a volcano belching and spewing gas laden with minute particles of lava. It seemed the volcano was burping, perhaps in readiness for blowing its top.[1]
Topping the volcano peak, the city of Catania illuminated the night and filled the windshield view. Dan re-assumed the aircraft commander's seat with Joe Hamilton remaining in the cockpit as copilot. The *Sabreliner* was on the ground fifteen minutes later. Captain and Mrs. Hilton met the group with two Navy sedans. The three couples were quickly escorted to the waiting vehicles and taken to pre-arranged quarters in Officer's housing. Thirty minutes later, the party began.

Joe and Mitch were honorees but soon-to-be retired Daniell Brown was *the* Guest of Honor. He donned flight gear worn by Navy pilots circa 1940's to showboat his advanced age of 41! Dan was flying airplanes for Uncle Sam when Joe and Mitch were just getting out of diapers. The party proved to be festive and lively, the speeches thankfully short and

---

[1] The gaseous eruptions we saw lasted 406 days! The mount finally did blow its top in 1979 killing 9; lava destroyed a cable car hut in 1983; more summit eruptions caused ash problems for cities in 1999-2000; add a flank explosion in 2002.

generally forgettable. Still, memories were generated that day and night for three guys and three gals to last a lifetime.

Appropriately feted and roasted, three very happy and sated officers flew JM 362 back to Naples the following morning. Unfortunately, COMFAIRMED lay on high-ranking officials as additional passengers, so the flight was *by the book*: Flight Level 230, routing direct Catania, direct Naples; pilots Brown/Hamilton/Williams. Authorized (?) passengers included Mrs. Brown, Mrs. Hamilton, and Mrs. Williams.

As the reader might expect, the Hail and Farewell Party was anti-climatic after the once-in-a-lifetime experience of flying alongside your spouse in the cockpit of a million dollar jet aircraft. First, enjoying the panorama of Southern Italy on a near perfect summer afternoon, including such famous sites as Mt. Vesuvio and Capri. Then the "discovery" of a fishing village in the shadow of a forever active volcano on the forsaken isle of Stromboli off the Calabria Coast of Italy. And finally, highlighted by a low altitude climb up an active volcano spewing fire and lava particles at night like 4th of July or New Year's Eve! All are great memories, super memories, fantastic memories, never to be forgotten. Thank you, Captain Hilton, you made Mark Twain right again – work and play can be synonymous.

Shakespeare sure had it right for Dan Brown. "The end crowns all." This flight climaxed a Navy career of over twenty-one years.

The dazzling nighttime display of explosive fireworks on Mt. Etna was Strombolian eruptions. Oddly and coincidentally, the non-stop small-scale eruptions were named for the volcano/island the crew of six had seen just twenty minutes earlier.
Typically, Stomboli eruptions are characterized by the release of volcanic gases which occur every few minutes or so, sometimes rhythmically and sometimes irregularly. They are usually short blasts, separated by periods of less than a tenth of a second but can become temporarily inactive only to reoccur after several hours. Each burp represents the bursting of a rising bubble of gas within

the magma (lava) column as it approaches the surface. Strombolian eruptions involve release of much larger proportions of gas to magma than other types of activity; in some cases, the magmatic material may not escape from the vent at all, <u>and is recycled.</u> In comparison, the Mount St. Helen's eruption of 1982, a real top blower, was a Plinian eruption, named after the elder Pliny who lost his life while at Pompei investigating the Mt. Vesuvius eruption of ad. 79.

*****

A true mountaintop experience! Anytime I read about Mt. Etna, it all comes back again.

Chapter 50

SUNDAY'S CHILD

August, 1976
Age: 41

*......a child born on the Sabbath day,
is fair and wise, and good and gay*. Unknown

She was healthy and whole. And beautiful. At first sight of
her little body lying there in the ward bassinet, he knew he
loved her in a way, to a degree, that he could not have
explained. Standing alone in the semi-darkened hallway,
looking into the nursery, he asked aloud of himself, "How
can you love someone so much when you don't even know
her yet? He knew it was not because she was a part of him.
His contribution to her young life, to her very creation, had
only to do with physical pleasure. Perhaps it was love at
first sight with the little kid because she was an extension of
her mother. Facial features and eye and skin coloration like
a Becky in miniature would come, and she would soon
emulate many of her Mom's unique mannerisms. But
tonight he saw the newborn as a legacy of her mother's inner
self: Becky's giving personality, her goodness, her love for
him, her feminine mystique.

His wife had not had it that easy the past two days. Oh, the
pregnancy had gone OK up until these last hours, no big
deals, just the routine morning sickness at first, and then the
slow but sure addition of pounds and inches so that finally
she was miserable in any position, day or night, awake or
sleeping. She was a week over an incubation time of nine
months although both her doctor in Italy and then the Fort
McClellan obstetrician had given her a good chance for
early delivery. That had not happened. Visibly, she
appeared ready two or three weeks prior to full term. She
had carried the baby right out front and up high. There was
no doubt that she was "P.G." (a term commonly used then)
early on in the first stage of pregnancy. The first nine
months and three days had been normal in all respects as far

as he knew, as far as physicians had expounded. But the last forty-eight hours had been tough. Two or three false starts, then when the contractions began, they persisted for thirty-six hours before the little bundle of joy finally arrived. The prolonged delay had caused the obstetrician to attach a fetal monitoring machine to the baby's head through the mother's vagina. Then began the long hours of monitoring vital signs shown by little pulsating lights in conjunction with rhythmic, green vertical zigzags on a monitor screen.

Nine hours earlier the delivery room doctors and nurses had gone to CODE STAT when the fetal monitor abruptly indicated that the baby's heart rate had been seriously impaired. Later information revealed that staff members materialized quickly from several directions. Within moments they had determined the umbilical cord was wrapping itself around the baby's neck. The team worked quickly, varying positions of the prostrate mother, feeling the fetus by massaging the extruded belly. As quickly and as unexpectedly, the baby acted on its own accord and situated itself comfortably within its warm, cozy world. The monitors soon displayed normal readings.

After the cord incident, he had gone into the labor room and looked down at her grotesque, misshapen body. Pale and perspiring, hair askew, gown loose and dampened from sweat, her mouth covered with a green surgical mask.

He tried to sound upbeat, "Hi, gal. How's it going?"

She hardly acknowledged his presence. Taken aback, he realized he had expected her usual cheery welcome. She had been so positive about the baby throughout the pregnancy that he had just assumed she would push down when the doctor said it was time, and it would all be over. Looking down on her discomfort, he felt a rush of feelings that ran the gamut from dumb to stupid to selfish. He felt helpless and ...."useless" was the term that kept coming to mind. Perhaps inadequate was a better description. He had not ceased looking at her. He stood, shook his head, and admitted, "I'm not up to this. The waiting and watching is too much for this ole country boy. I've got to find something to do."

He found his father-in-law in the waiting area. He had always liked Mr. Knight. They had many interests in common. Both loved professional baseball, Southeastern Conference football, and the Boston Celtics. Earl Knight then hit both a home run and scored a touchdown with his son-in-law: "I know it's Sunday but let's go fishing anyway - I can't stand it anymore either. When we get back, surely the baby will be here." They left an anxious Mrs. Knight at Becky's bedside.

Returning to the Knight residence, they changed into grub clothes and loaded light fishing tackle. Very little conversation passed between the two men that afternoon. Both were absorbed in private thoughts of which Rebecca Farrow Knight Brown was the centerpiece. The elder fisherman undoubtedly remembered a dad's little girl grown to full womanhood. The younger man focused on more intimate memories and shared dreams. They fished for bream in the thirty-acre pond about fifteen miles out of town. In the heat of the day they caught few fish. The ever present and always hungry turtles wanted the crickets far more than any blue gill or shellcracker. In truth, the catching of fish was irrelevant. Being there, the simple act of fishing was the key to easing anxiety. It was a time for thinking.

They had a good marriage. He was outgoing, a good mixer, loved travel, jokes of all sorts, folk music and *Star Trek*. Once divorced, he was the jet pilot who had seen and experienced a lot of the world. She was the serious part of their twosome act, the quiet one, a voracious reader, fun once you broke her privacy shell, never married before. Her world was her husband and soon-to-be family.

Switching his bait to red wigglers, he cast again to his favorite fishing hole. The fish continued to sleep or whatever they do on a hot August afternoon in Alabama to elude a loaded hook meant to tempt their gullet. As memory followed memory, he recalled that he had always kidded her about marriage versus bachelor hood: The old argument: "Which was better?" He had constantly reminded her that his vote was fifty-one percent to forty-nine percent. Fifty-one that marriage was better contrasted to the forty-nine for being single. Why? Married got the slight edge because it was nice to come home to a prepared meal, a clean house, made beds, Spic and Span bathrooms, and knowing a warm body was there on a cold night. And any other night! These amenities were on a scale versus the forty-nine percent positive vote for being single and available when that cute new face with the big hooters and the hot bod came along. "Now if the wife works and makes over thirty-five thousand dollars, then I alter my vote to sixty-forty, marriage winning!" was his usual comeback to any comments defending the institution of marriage. Wearing her cute, crooked little grin, the one that told him she knew he was kidding but realized there was more than an ounce of truth in his jests, she usually played the game.

He knew he had gotten lucky when he found her. Four tours of duty aboard aircraft carriers, all in excess of six months each, plus the numerous at-sea exercises required prior to deployments, all occurring during a five-year stretch had undoubtedly contributed to his previous marriage falling apart. His son and adopted daughters would become a rarity in his life as they lived half a continent away with their mother. He remembered the thrill of the girls asking, "May we call him daddy now?", once the adoption was complete. They were both beautiful girls. And of course, the birth of a healthy, handsome son is an unforgettable event in any father's life. For a moment he relived the exhilaration of seeing Bobby the first time. His birth had been late, too, almost a ten-month baby. For a long moment, Bobby, Teresa, and Gayle filled his thoughts. Then he reminded himself, 'Well, that was my other life, a story for another day. For now, let's concentrate on this one and keeping it together.'

Almost five hours later they returned to the hospital. Disappointed, they found the baby still safe inside its warm and watery womb. The mother's contractions remained rhythmic and steady with no increase in frequency. He visited her briefly to make sure she knew he had returned for the big moment. The nursing staff encouraged the two men to wait in the visitor's recreation and snack food area.

Sometime later the doctor came by personally and advised that if the baby didn't come on it's own by 8 p.m., a caesarian section would be performed. No big deal, Dan realized, it was just that all during the pregnancy she had told him time and again that she had wanted to have the baby by natural childbirth methods. Nine months had nearly ruined her once slender and beautiful body. She deserved to have it any damn way she wanted.

At 7:50, he walked down the corridor past the nursery *one more time* for at least the thirtieth time since he had returned. As he peered in, he noticed new activity. Two nurses were there, one seated, the other returning to the supervisor's desk from the bassinets. As he looked through the nearly spotless viewing window, there was a bundled, moving form in one of the cribs in the middle of the room. Hoping, hoping, but not yet knowing for sure, he raced to the delivery room sixty feet down the same hall. As he hesitated momentarily, debating whether he should intrude, the obstetrician opened the door from the reverse side and stepped out into the open space. Removing his surgical mask, and wiping his hands on the pure white cleanness of a hospital towel, he said, "It's a girl and we didn't have to take it - Congratulations. She looks like a good healthy baby. And 'Mom' did fine - she's a lady to be proud of."

Dan Brown felt 10 feet tall! And he felt 2 feet tall. Excited, rapturous, over that little body lying inside the room behind closed glass. New life! Unbelievable! And yet brought down to earth by the knowledge that for other than a moment of passion, he had nothing to do with it. For the remainder of his life he would remember two moments of joy in awe of the miracle of birth, thankful for a happy, healthy boy those thirteen years ago and now a perfect, beautiful daughter.

He turned and walked back up the hall to stare through the picture window into the nursery. She was arching her little reddish, wrinkled neck, pushing her small chest upwards while her arms moved outward, inward, downward, and up and around like a doll. She had not yet made a sound that he had heard. Light brown, fuzz-like hair topped her head and she tilted her face towards the big clear window that opened into the nursery from the corridor. He saw her look directly at him and even though he knew she could not be seeing him through newborn eyes, he could imagine the latent beauty behind her features. He knew he was the luckiest person on earth. Years later in fifth or sixth grade, she would write a story about him: "My Heavenly Hero" and chronicle some of his minor attributes in the realm of fatherhood. Thirteen or fourteen years from now he would be just another jerk, a know-nothing father trying to keep her from experiencing life and freedom as teenagers feel they should. But for now, for this night in history, she was simply a precious child, his daughter. For some unknown reason, he remembered a book and while the plot was not about infants nor was it even a children's story, the title met this moment for him perfectly, *"The Precious Present".*[1]

He checked on Becky and kissed her wet cheeks. She was pale and enervated, but happy. His wife looked into his eyes and spoke with a note of sadness. "The reality is that you're right, one child is enough. I don't think I could go through thirty hours of labor again. I'm still shaken over that wrapped cord. We could have lost her." Dan felt that no response was his best response. She always said she wanted two or three children, perhaps even a basketball team, but he had held his ground that one was all he could handle as he approached middle age. Now she was agreeing. He was thinking, 'Let's leave it at that' and said nothing.
Soon, he returned to the nursery window to gaze at the small form, seemingly content in her new environment. He thought of things he might tell her. "Well, Mary Elizabeth Brown, you are named after your mother's mother and grandmother. You were made in London, incubated in Italy, and born in Alabama. I guess that makes you a *redneck Limey ragazza.* Your mom is sleeping. You sure wore her out, scared us all to death with that rope around the neck trick. I guess you weren't sure you wanted to be out of the cozy confines of Mommy's tummy. But here you

---

[1] Spencer Johnson, author

are. You made it with all your fingers and toes, thank goodness. All that *Sunday's child* stuff aside, you are one special baby girl. So special, your mother is taking five or six years off from work to be with you, to enjoy you. Me? Well, your daddy is a retired Navy pilot as of a couple months ago. You'll never see me as a hero, I guess. Heck, you won't even see me in uniform, dress whites or inspection blues or workday browns. I wish you could watch me go roaring down a runway with a twenty million dollar jet airplane strapped on my back. I sort of hate that you won't know *Commander Brown* but at least you won't have to worry about me leaving home for six to seven months at a time. I flunked the job of daddy the first time I had it. I sure hope I can do better this time around. I promise to try. Now that you're here, I guess I had better get my act together and make arrangements for some bread for this family. You'll probably need a dress or a toy or something one of these days. Tell you what, tomorrow I'll send in the first team to look for a job. Hey, it's your fault I don't already have a position, you know. I sent out some resumes but that's about all the job hunting I've done. I was afraid to really get serious about finding work. What if I had gotten a great offer but immediate training was required in some weird place like Oklahoma? Your mother would have raised holy hell with me if I had not been here for today's big event. Which reminds me, I wonder if she knows her dad and I went fishing today? I guess I'll be saying 'Goodnight, Miss Brown'. Tonight your granddaddy and I are going to celebrate with the biggest steaks we can find. Nanny says she's going home and crash, she's tired out after watching your mom all day. Your straight-laced granddad doesn't imbibe, but I might even have a rum and coke, or two or three. Just in your honor. Tomorrow, *domani,* I promise to get us the best job Jacksonville, Florida, has to offer. See you in the morning, little kid."

On the way out to the parking lot, Dan reflected on the changes about to take place in his life. He understood his neat, organized, and orderly routine was about to be altered drastically. Parenting would be wonderful, but from experience he knew detours and potholes lay ahead in the road of life. There would be tears and disappointments, hopefully far fewer than joys and discoveries. The fun and games that total freedom had afforded the first five years of marriage had just been superseded by a little seven-pound bundle of joy. He loved the little *bambina* lying back there in the crib, but there was a hanging sense of remorse in letting go those wonderful years that he and Becky had alone. Then he remembered Becky's thirty-six hours of labor and was ashamed of such self-indulgent thoughts. The new father continued toward the exit.

Somewhere between the hospital door and the parking lot, he remembered Mike Allison telling him, "Brown, you are one lucky son-of-a-bitch. Me personally, I've been a salesman for over twenty years and I'll be a salesman for life. I've lived in one city all my life, I'll die here. But you, you're going to live two lives. Country boy from nowhere, twenty-one years in the military, saw the world, flew fast airplanes, landed on ships for Chris' sake. Crashed an airplane and walked away from it, then went off to Vietnam three times and came back without a scratch. You've lived one life with an attractive redhead, adopted two daughters and had a son. Now you're in the big city, you'll have a new career in the civilian community, you're married to a second beautiful woman and going to have a new baby. Count your blessings, pal."

Dan paused before opening the door to his car and turned for a last look at Becky's room. He found it, second story, second window in from the west. Light from a desk lamp glowed dimly in the window; all other rooms nearby were dark. It was after nine and night had fallen. A starry, immense sky seemed to envelop the hills surrounding the little medical center. He spoke aloud as if someone were listening, "Sorry, Mom, it's a figure of speech, no reflection on you, but it's true. I'm just counting my blessings. *I am a lucky son-of-a-bitch!*"

*****

Yep.

Chapter 51

THE THIRD OPTION

Summer, 1979
Age: 44

......the diagnosis

The physician turned away from the patient. Standing over the stainless steel sink, he prepared to wash his hands. He squeezed a tube and green gel oozed into his palms. The doctor expertly activated the over-the-faucet lever with his left elbow to begin the flow. Dan Brown could hear the water as it began cascading over the doctor's hands. He expected the urologist would wash vigorously for the full thirty-five seconds recommended after intimate physical contact. And this one had been intimate. "Finger waves" are very intimate.
With his back still to the patient, the urologist began telling him of the findings from the examination just completed. "Your prostate is hard as a rock. I don't want any misunderstanding about the fact that something is definitely wrong. It can only be one of three things. First, it could be scar tissue from a previous infection, but I don't think so. In my many years of experience I know how scar tissue normally feels. You didn't have any lumps or ridges or anything to make me deduce scar tissue. The second possibility is prostate stones, similar to kidney stones in a way, but in the prostate, they are situated between the sac covering the prostate and the organ itself. But I don't think you have stones because you are only forty-four years old and I've never seen prostate stones in anyone younger than fifty." At the end of that dialogue, the doctor dried his hands and then began to write in the patient's chart. He had not yet looked into the face of the patient.

"What's the third option, Doc?"

Doctor Miller now turned and looked at him. In telling the story later to friends, Dan would try to explain the expression - actually the lack of some definitive visage - on the doctor's face as the third possible explanation was given. "Try to imagine someone looking at you with a totally blank countenance on their face. They speak words to you while their eyes are saying 'You are so stupid for asking such a ridiculous question', and at the same time you can feel them wanting to reach out and say, "I'm so sorry for you". 'Arrogant compassion' - a real oxymoron but it's the best way I can describe it."

Pausing for just a moment, the doctor finally answered the query. Dan felt his face flush with embarrassment as the doctor uttered one word. Only one word comprised of six letters but a more devastating word for an ostensibly healthy person in the prime of life cannot be found in *Webster's*. "Cancer."

He felt as though a sledgehammer had slammed into the center of his chest. He felt his tear ducts well up and he knew there was no force on earth that could keep back the tears. He'd have to worry about manly appearances later. For now, for this moment, he knew immediately that he had read correctly the meanings behind the doctor's eyes. Indeed, he was empty headed not to have guessed, not to know that *carcinoma* would be the third and most probable diagnosis.

As his brain brought him back to the reality of the small room and the situation at hand, the doctor was talking in clinical terms, yet genuinely concerned tones:

"Now don't leave here thinking or hoping I may be wrong. I've just seen too many cases like this and I think your family doctor referred you to me because of my reputation and experience. You know what cancer does. It causes radical and uncontrolled growth in the tissue cells. In my opinion, the malignancy is already distorting the prostate with tumorous growth. If we don't act and act quickly, it will spread into the lymph glands and become uncontrollable. Now keep in mind, this is not the end of the world for you, but we do have to think and act without delay. First, we'll get a biopsy next week and confirm my diagnosis. Then we can and will talk in far more detail. For now, I want you take this little pamphlet home and read about cancer of the prostate. Read everything you can in any medical books you have at home or can borrow. Go to the library if you have time. Talk to other men whom you know has had this cancer. And be thinking about your wife. She will still be a young woman of what, thirty-six, thirty-seven? She will have physical love needs for a long time into the future. You will have to decide on one of the two different types of prostheses to satisfy those needs as you will be unable to have an erection. All the information is included in the pamphlet and you can ask me questions about both models after the biopsy. Any date next week OK with you? If you agree, I'll schedule us into *St. Joseph's* for first available."

Leaving the medical complex parking lot, Dan glanced at his watch. He could hardly see the hands of the watch because of the glaze in his eyes and on his cheeks. 3:30 p.m. traffic entering and departing the city would make the drive back to work a potential disaster. In retrospect, after leaving and heading back to his office, he realized he should have called someone to come for him. As he drove along the city's streets just starting to be over-crowded in advance of the afternoon rush hour, he was conscious that his speed was far slower than the usual rushed pace displayed in everything he did and everywhere he went. He also realized that he was still emotionally charged, that he could not stop his tear ducts from continuing to drain down his cheeks. 'Should I just cancel my meeting and turn around for home? No, there is no choice. I have to go back to work and write that schedule for tomorrow.' As he turned the bright red vintage Jaguar onto the upramp leading to the interstate bridge that would carry him back to his office, he tried to sort out his feelings. 'Does the water look any blue-er? No. Does it look any less blue? No. Do I love this twenty-year old Jaguar anymore than I did yesterday? No. Am I suddenly more aware of everything going on around me than I was before I went in the doctor's office? No. If I had to describe my feelings right now, what would I say?'

288

"I don't know, I really don't know," he answered aloud his own question. Then thinking, 'I just know that I have never felt this way before, not when my dad died, not even when the lawyer called me half way around the world to tell me I was being divorced.' Until now, those were the unhappiest moments of his lifetime. 'Those were bad times, real low points, but totally different from anything I am feeling now. One thing for sure, in all of them you feel like someone just kicked your ass.' Then he asked himself if he were scared.

'Yes. Sort of like that long night before my first combat mission, not knowing what to expect, not knowing how I'd perform under fire. Wondering how I would stack up compared to my peers. Worried that I wouldn't measure up in some manner. I guess this is the same thing. Just like 'Nam - they told me what it would be like but still you never know what combat really is until you see it up close and personal. Here, a lot of people will tell me what it's like to have cancer, but I won't know for sure until I've had the knife and the chemo and the radiation. And more of that terrible pain. Hell yes, I'm scared.'

It had started about three weeks before. After making love, he had lain back on his pillow basking in the warm glow of mutually satisfying physical and mental enjoyment. Only a few seconds, perhaps twenty, had passed, when it hit him. The excruciating pain started inside his lower backside like a hot, searing knife cutting raw flesh. His body would immediately and involuntarily recoil into the fetal position as the pain racked his entire body. He would eventually describe the feeling for physicians as "Someone blowing up a balloon filled with sharp elongated tacks pointing in all directions with the pain growing to a crescendo just short of fainting." By that time, his body would be drenched in perspiration, large sweat beads showing dramatically on his contorted facial features. Try as he may, he would be unable to endure the pain silently, his groans and obvious hurting would thoroughly upset a devoted wife. He was fearful that his outwardly show of tortuous pain, immediately following moments of previously shared passion, would severely dent his wife's confidence in her femininity. Following three successive, painful occasions after making love, he had relented and called their family doctor for an appointment. The dreaded finger exercise completed, Dr. Ledford was alarmed to the point he had · personally called a well-known urologist for further tests. Dr. Miller had scheduled him for consult within twenty-four hours to determine the origin of pain.

Now he could look forward to an overnight hospital stay. In his lifetime, biopsies would become far more routine without requiring in-patient hospitalization. That day had not yet arrived in 1979 when Dan Brown needed the procedure.

He knew he had to speak with God. He wasn't all that religious although he had been *raised right* in the Methodist Church by very Christian parents. When he left home, as with many young men of that generation, he virtually forgot all about worship. Even in the war, he had kept his distance from God, feeling it would be hypocritical to suddenly get devout when faced with danger. Two days remained until the short hospital stay would confirm the dreaded disease had invaded his body, or refute Dr. Miller's preliminary diagnosis. He labored with words to the Almighty. "Lord, I remember being told there is no specific, correct way to pray. I hope that's true because I don't know how to pray properly. Why am I here in the Chapel today? I didn't pray much before combat. I didn't cry on Your shoulders about my divorce. I did beg you to help Becky with the birth of Beth. Perhaps I should have prayed at other times, too. What makes this time different? I'm not sure, maybe it's because I'm older now. OK, you know the truth anyway - because this time I'm really scared. I do know that I must ask You for help. My basic prayer is there will be no malignancy, that instead I will have some treatable disorder. We know something is wrong, but please, don't let it be cancer. Oh God, please don't make me a eunuch. My next prayer is just as important. If cancer is found, I ask You to help me be man enough to accept it, to handle whatever comes. If I do have the 'Big C', I beg You to give me strength to manage the pain. I do not want to embarrass my girls or myself. I'm sure there is a lot more I should say but

I think You know my heart. If You are the God that my
father believed in, then You know everything before we ask
it. If You are the God I believe in, then it is not Your will
that I have cancer. I just don't think You work that way.
Whatever the result, I ask Your Holy Spirit to be there for
me and for Becky and for Beth.   Amen."

*He was standing at a gate, a replica of the entrance gate to the
White House. The gate was swinging open slowly. He then saw
the sentry-type gazebo and next to the small enclosure stood an
older, stately gentleman in flowing white robes. His hair and beard
were the color of his robes making it difficult to distinguish the
outline of the beard from the toga-like clothing. The older man
seemed preoccupied as he studied the computer printout in his
hands. Finally, he acknowledged the younger man's presence. "I
am St. Peter", and continuing, "It appears that you are expected
today. How did you pass into the spirit world?"*

*The puzzled candidate for heaven answered. "I don't know, sir. I
was admitted to the hospital for a biopsy procedure and the last
thing I remember is being stuck in both arms by an Indian."*

St. Peter glared. "An Indian? As in Geronimo of the wild west?"

*The candidate was more than a little nervous. "No, no. I mean
'Indian' as in guru, Ghandi, Union Carbide, close to Pakistan,
'The Jewel in the Crown'. Yeah, all the anesthesiologists down in
Jacksonville are Indians these days. In Miami, they're probably
Cuban, but in Jacksonville, definitely Indians."*

*St. Peter nodded. "Oh, I see. Well, never mind, I see you are listed
here on the data sheet as INCOMING 09/18/79. Evidently, down
there on earth you passed the supreme tests. Welcome to heaven,
Daniell Brown. Let's go inside."*

*He had made the cut! O.K., I'm dead but at least I don't have to
worry about going to hell anymore. Now he could see the imposing
gold and emerald, jeweled city in the distance beyond the pearl-
white Corinthian gate. So the old joke, three-questions-before-
entering-heaven, was not true. But there was a thought troubling*

him. *"Uh, just a minute, your holiness. I'd sort of like to be briefed on procedures and options up here. Do we really get wings? And how about air conditioning?"*

The Saint admonished him. "Evidently you didn't listen to the sermons those Sunday mornings you spent in church, Daniell. Heaven is paradise. Here, it's always 78 degrees and perfect weather. Your only other choice for residency in the spirit world does not come with climate control. You'll learn the ropes naturally and the wings come later. Shall we go in?"

Dan: "Well, OK, Father Peter, but I sure hope they don't do a lot of singing up here."

St. Peter: "Why is that, Mr. Brown?"

Dan, sheepishly, "Because my wife always told me I sang like I snored, loud and awful."

St. Peter touched his arm in a fatherly way. "Well, we do some singing but I'm sure you can look down at your song book or something like that so as not to inflict your voice on others nearby. Come on, I think you'll see a lot of old friends you haven't seen in quite a while. In fact, here comes Johnny Richards from your youth. Didn't he die of pneumonia during your high school senior year?"

Dan could not believe his eyes! "It sure is! Johnny, it's Danny. I can't believe it. Remember me? Gosh, it's good to see you. You haven't changed a bit! You're still 17 years old. Hey, you remember that cheerleader with the big boobs and hot pants?"

*His senses were suddenly flooded by sound and light. Bells clanged, piercing strobe lights flashed brightly as in Disney World sound and light shows or Times Square on New Year's Eve. **DING DING - DING DING - DING DING** and he heard a strong deep voice over the noise and confusion: "Daniell Brown, this is God speaking. References to carnal knowledge are forbidden in Heaven. This evening after vespers you will report to Cloud 17 to march and sing for one hour to atone demerits for this grave infraction."*

292

"Shit! Johnny, why didn't you tell me ...." Dan began.

DING DING - DING DING - DING DING. FLASHING LIGHTS. *"Daniell Brown, this is God again. Neither is profanity permitted here. Make that two hours of marching and singing demerits."*

There was nowhere to run. He was dead meat. *"Yes, sir. I'll be good. Johnny, what do we do here in heaven?"*

Johnny: *"Well, Danny, we go to church a lot. See the big onion spires over there? That's cloud number 10. We go to church there every day from 7 a.m. to 5 p.m. And then we attend vespers from 7:30 till 10 p.m."*

"I think I am beginning to see why it's called 'eternity'," the newcomer commented. *"I guess I can't go looking for the Moslem's seventy-two virgins either?"*

Johnny continued. *"No, no such welcome for Methodists. Actually, Dan, I'm afraid you haven't come at the best time. This month, it's Brother Charles Wesley who is preaching day after day. I know you remember who he was, and while he was a great hymn writer, you may not have known that his public speaking qualities leave a lot to be desired. In fact, he's pretty boring."*

His mind was beginning to wander. *"John, do you reckon they'd mind if I just beamed on over to 17 and started marching and singing right away? I figure I'm going to stay in the hole on demerits anyway. Say, did you notice that St. Peter looks a lot like Billy Graham with a beard. And God sure sounded a lot like Charlton Heston. Johnny, how will Becky know how to find me when she shows up at the gate? And listen, it's always bothered me back on earth - when both the batter and the pitcher cross themselves, how does the Lord know which one to bless and help? Oh, another thing, how often do we get lobster for dinner? Johnny, you're fading, you're starting to disappear, come back and ...."* Somehow he felt trapped. He had made the cut for heaven but even in heaven he had to pee and there was no where to go. If he urinated there on that billowy puff of cloud, would it fall to earth? Did rain come from angel pee? It didn't matter, he had to go. *"I've got to take a leak," he muttered groggily, tried to speak more plainly, but found his mouth so dry he could only murmur. He struggled to sit up.*

"No, you don't," came a soft delicate voice in reply. A vision in white not unlike the heavenly beings just encountered was beginning to come into focus. The angelic voice continued: "You just think you have to go to the bathroom. You really don't. After surgery, you always feel that way. Go back to sleep."

His brain was starting to comprehend his surroundings. Finally the white form materialized into a neatly uniformed nurse hovering over him. So he wasn't dead. He hadn't really made the cut for heaven. Again his anesthetized brain was filled with ambivalent turmoil. He wanted to live, yet he feared that day to come when he really would have to face that final judgment the Baptists are always talking about. 'Well', he thought, 'Like Scarlett, I'll have to worry about that later'. Right now, his head ached, his penis throbbed, and he had to piss. 'That nurse is full of it,' he rationalized, and tried to raise up and argue. Through the shadows of his dulled mind he could see Becky staring at him from a chair in the corner. She was starting to stand now, to come toward him. She wasn't smiling, nor was she crying. He wondered why he thought she would be, one or the other. Even in his stupor, he sensed her love and concern for him and the biopsy procedure. The urgent state of his bladder was totally disconcerting as he tried to concentrate on her face. Restless, yet blissful sleep came instead.

Four days later they were on the patio, she was having a rum and tonic, he had to wait one more day before alcohol could pass his lips per instructions from Dr. Miller. As he sipped his cranberry juice and 7-up cocktail, they watched "little kid", now three, playing with a friend in the evenly mowed green St. Augustine grass. The tall azaleas that rimmed the back yard were not in bloom this late in the year, but still their fullness and foliage gave a healthy and pristine appearance to the back yard. The patio was neat

294

and colorful with buckets and planters of impatiens, hibiscus, mums, begonias, and the mandatory ficus tree.

Dan surmised, "Peaceful, hon, peaceful. If we could just get that call from the doctor's office to tell us YES or NO, POSITIVE or NEGATIVE, what or whatever." The doctor had told him to hold out no hopes for a negative finding. But Becky had tried to remain optimistic. And she had attempted to raise his spirits. However, try as he might, he was becoming more and more apprehensive and convinced he should prepare for the worst. He was probably going to lose his ability to have sex. Other men would secretly talk about him and perhaps, even laugh about it. Becky could want him in the sack, need him, and he would be useless. Now, he was becoming miserable. He noticed the late afternoon shadows were starting to think about becoming evening. The results were supposed to be back from the lab today. Pretty soon the lateness of the day could no longer be called afternoon.
Becky saw his psyche sliding downhill. "I called a little while ago but they didn't have anything. If we don't hear something soon, I'm afraid we'll have to wait until Monday knowing nothing over the weekend," she said wistfully, as she lifted the frosty, moisture-beaded glass to her mouth.
"RING-G-G-G!"
"I'll get it," she said, as she stood up and moved quickly to the French doors. He sat there in deep anticipation, trying to visualize what he would say or do when she told him the results were indeed positive. At that moment he was convinced his body had been invaded by killer cancer. That the test might be negative was no longer a hope. 'Don't well up and cry, Brown, dammit, she will need for you to be strong and ....'

"IT'S NEGATIVE," she screamed through the open doors. "You don't have it - it must have been a severe infection is all they can come up with! Oh, honey, you don't have cancer!"

He had his booze twenty-four hours early. She had called their fondest friends and neighbors to come over and

celebrate. In the excitement of the happy news, someone had popped a bottle of champagne. After a couple of glasses of better than average New York grape with corresponding toasts for his longevity and happiness, he reverted to his normal *Barcardi and Coke* even though he knew elimination two hours from now was likely to burn like crazy. As he sipped the cool wetness of his drink, he remembered his ride across the bridge as he returned to work after receiving the original unconfirmed diagnosis by Dr. Miller. He had asked himself if the water was blue-er, if that moment was more precious than the previous. His answer then had been, "No", but as he stood there in the middle of his den, he could see her, his lovely wife, the gracious hostess among their closest and dearest friends, and he knew his beautiful, *perfect* daughter lay asleep down the hall. He could feel the genuine concern his friends had for his well being. Suddenly, he realized that in some manner the answers to his previous questions were now different. *'Yes, the grass is green-er, the water will be*
blue-er the next time I see it. Life is more precious than I ever thought."

They were in bed. Everyone had finally left a little before midnight. Becky and Dan had eventually made it to the bedroom after cleaning up leftovers, glasses, chips, dips, and the usual after-party mess. He felt fatigued, exhausted. Like all "highs", when the mountaintop experience is over, the slide into the valley can be rapid and tiring. Just before sleep overtook him, he remembered thinking about the *bird*, the gun and the vision in Daytona, and the crash on FORRESTAL. He reached out and brushed a hand against Becky's body. Confirming her closeness always warmed him with inner peace as did thoughts of the *"little kid"* sound asleep in her room. Now he had survived, technically, he had dodged, a bullet called *cancer*. He didn't understand it, he probably never would, but he could sure accept it. He wasn't going to be a eunuch after all. *Thank you, God.*
He slept soundly, no dreams at all.

It was sometime later, perhaps weeks, when he realized that while he had worried about being less a man and dreaded the pain that would come if he did in fact have cancer, there had been no thoughts of the cloaked, faceless old nemesis with scythe. Perhaps hard to believe, but true, believe me.

*****

I guess we imagine some things worse than death.

Chapter 52

"JUST WAITING ON MY CAR TO RISE"

May, 1981
Age: 45

A quick jab to his side awakened her husband. The red-eyed numerals of the GE digital on the bedside table read 6:15 a.m. "Was I snoring?" he mumbled sleepily.
Nervous and agitated, Becky whispered, "No, there's someone in the house. He's in the other bedroom. I saw him through the bathroom doors." The master bedroom of the beach house had access to two bathrooms. A private bath with tub was situated in one corner of the oversized room while a shower cubicle could be entered through doors that opened into a second bedroom. Probably built for monitoring small children, the Browns had not used the extra bedroom. On special occasions, vacations, and trips, Dan and Becky routinely let Beth sleep in their room. The five-year old was asleep on the small chaise lounge next to their bed.
Dan eased his feet over onto the floor. His wife spoke softly into his ear, "Maybe we should call 9-1-1. I'm afraid for you to go out there with no weapon." He shook his head but did speak softly, just above a whisper. "Honey, he's in the house. I've got to see who it is. He hasn't harmed us to this point so take it easy for a few more minutes."

Dan pulled on his pants and walked down the long hall to the large Florida room that looked out onto the Atlantic Ocean. He replayed in his mind the conversation of the previous day with their hosts, Mike and Jennie Allison. Dan and Becky and Beth had enjoyed the beach house for the weekend and were scheduled to leave Sunday afternoon after lunch. The Allison's original plans called for arrival back in town Sunday between four and five o'clock and would immediately head for the beach to get in a walk before sunset. But they had called from Atlanta early Sunday morning with news that their plans had changed and they would not be returning to Jacksonville until the next day, Monday. "Why not stay another night?" their good friends insisted. The Browns had readily accepted. Dan would go to work and return for his girls just before the Allison's were due to arrive. It was now Monday morning.

As Dan entered the large living area, he saw a man of slight to medium stature standing with his back to the fireplace. His shoulders were hunkered over like he might be cold. His hands were behind his back as if warming before a fire. This was puzzling because the ashes in the fireplace had been cold for hours. He and his wife of ten years had sipped wine as the fire burned out around midnight. Now only dark ashes remained. Perhaps the power of suggestion was warming the uninvited guest.

The man turned his face toward Dan and seemed to await Dan's first words. His facial features telegraphed nothing of what he was thinking or what his intent might be. The sight and presence of an intruder had quickened Dan's senses. No longer half-awake, his mind was racing for a plausible explanation for a stranger standing in the den, somehow entering through locked doors. A scan of the room invited a possible and plausible solution. Through the large den window he noticed the outside sprinklers were on and watering the lawn. Perhaps this was the yardman or caretaker of the property. They, the guests, were supposed to be gone this morning. Was it possible the man standing before him was to check hot water heaters and air conditioning settings for the owners once guests had departed? Of course, the Allison's were supposed to be here this morning. Would they give a caretaker free reign to enter their home as he pleased? Anyway, Dan asked: "Are you the yard man Mike Allison has told me about?"
The man just looked at Dan as he answered, "Naw man, I'm here just waiting on my car to rise."
It was not an expected response. Dan was sure his face registered surprise and doubt. He tried to keep his voice normal and natural as he repeated, "Waiting for your car to rise?"
The intruder took a step forward and motioned toward the large window and the blue sea beyond. "Yeah, I was doing

wheelies on the beach last night and got stuck in the sand.
After awhile, the surf came in and covered up my car. I'm
just waiting for the tide to go out so I can get it."

Dan resisted the urge to smile at the nonsensical statement.
His inclination was to ask, "Are you going to drive it off
after it's been in salt water all night?" Under the unusual
circumstances, he curbed any attempt at light-hearted
humor. He looked out at the ocean but there was no
automobile in sight, either in the sand or stranded in the
water.

Watching Dan scan the shoreline, the man was insistent.
"It's still under the water but the tide's going out fast. We'll
see it soon."

Dan moved into the kitchen as he continued to dialogue.
"How did you get in the house? And where did you sleep?"

The stranger perched on a stool at the see-through counter
as he answered, "I came in through that window over the big
chair. Then I slept on the sofa."

Dan turned back to the den and saw the screen missing from
a window. They had left that window ajar the night before
as they listened to the surf of an incoming tide. And he
could see a wet spot on the couch about the size of the
fellow perched at the breakfast bar. Dan played a sympathy
card. "Well, listen, my wife is pretty upset about all this.
Would you mind waiting for your car to rise down on the
beach? I'll bring you a cup of coffee when it's ready."

The man slid off the barstool and answered matter-of-factly,
"I figured I scared her pretty good when she saw me through
those open doors. I was just looking for a cigarette. Yeah,
I'll go wait on the beach but do you mind if I leave through
the door? When I go out, I'll put the screen back in."

Dan began walking toward the back door. "I'll open the
door for you and I'll put the screen back before I go to work.
Don't worry about it - just get down there on the beach and
find your car."

Dan had opened the door but the visitor was not quite ready
to leave. He said, "I owe you for two beers, Mr. Brown.
Yeah, I know your name. You left your wallet on the
kitchen counter and I looked in it to find out your name but

your forty-seven dollars are still there. I broke in 'cause I needed a place to sleep but I ain't no thief."

Dan was beginning to feel comfortable that no harm was to come of the highly irregular - and illegal - visit. "Don't worry about the beers. And sorry I don't have any cigarettes." Dan opened the door and the uninvited guest walked out onto the porch, down the steps on to the concrete patio. He stopped for a moment, gazed out at the ocean, then ambled lazily down the path. He disappeared behind the dunes for a moment and then Dan saw him standing at water's edge.

Becky had been listening in the hallway. When the man was safely off the porch, she entered the room. Still dismayed, she said to her husband, "Can you believe this? He slept with us all night. Honey, you've got to call the police."

Dan had no inclination to do so. "Becky, he's gone. He didn't hurt us. He didn't steal our money. He's got enough problems facing him about that car in the water without the cops involved. Let him watch for his car in peace. Then he'll leave."

Becky was not buying any excuses. "But what if he doesn't? You'll be gone to work. Beth and I will be here if he comes back. And what if he had broken into the home of some elderly person. They would be terrified about now. Call the police."

Dan could not argue with reason – he knew she was correct. "O.K." He picked up the phone and asked the operator for the local law enforcement office. On the line, he explained the circumstances for the call to the Sheriff's Department dispatcher.

The officer was as impatient with Dan as his wife had been. "Mr. Brown, you are in Ponte Vedra, Florida. We can't have beach bums breaking and entering homes at will, just because they need a place to sleep for the night. I'll send a squad car out right away to get your statement and talk to the man. You say he's still there on the beach?"

Slightly chagrined at being chastised, Dan took the portable phone to the window. "Yes, I can see him down at the water's edge, picking up shells."

A car with two deputies arrived at the beach house within minutes. The first officer through the door walked over to Becky. Unsmiling, he asked curtly, "Do you realize how lucky you are that you're not laying in the bed with your throat cut?" Her features paled as she realized the dire consequences of what might have occurred under different circumstances.

Dan again explained the morning's events, beginning to end. While Dan talked, Becky and the second deputy watched the subject through the large picture window. Suddenly, she exclaimed, "I can see the top of a car in the water." Dan and the first officer joined them at the window. Sure enough, the flat roof of a small blue sedan was now visible in the breaking surf. Wanting a better view, Becky moved to the sofa, sat on her knees, her back to the room. As she positioned herself in this manner, she noticed something between the overstuffed seat pillows. She picked the two items up. "Look, here's his driver's license and a paycheck." Sergeant Evans moved quickly to take possession of the items. "Well, we know his name and that he works for CSX Railroad. It's time to go down to the beach and talk to him."

Dan and Becky remained in the house at the picture window, watching the scenario develop. The two uniformed men followed the sandy path through the dunes and oat-topped sawgrass. The man in question stood near the water's edge, and remained still as they approached. At first, a normal conversation appeared to be taking place. Then suddenly, the night's uninvited guest started running south, down the beach. The deputies gave chase and tackled him after about fifteen yards. All three men picked themselves up as a fight ensued. Surprisingly, for a moment or two, the smaller man held his own with two larger adversaries. The fight lasted for approximately a minute and a half before the two-trained lawmen could subdue the small figure. Finally, one officer locked his arms around the subject's legs. When the smaller man fell, the second deputy handcuffed him.

302

All the commotion and the highly unusual sight of a dark blue sedan parked about fifty yards out in the ocean surf had summoned several neighbors into back yards and onto the grassy knoll overlooking the beach. As the three men came back up the path, the prisoner screamed obscenities at anyone and everyone.

A second Sheriff's Department vehicle arrived about the time the prisoner and his captors reached the back yard. The second sedan was equipped with a backseat lockup. The prisoner was locked inside while the three deputies conversed with the Browns in an attempt to complete necessary paperwork. A fourth deputy was left with the cars to watch the prisoner. Standing between the two cars, the young law enforcement officer was to keep his eyes on the backseat of the sheriff's cruiser.

Inside, Deputy Turner went through the routine questions with Dan. Suddenly, the rapid BEEP BEEP BEEP BEEP of an automobile horn interrupted them. All occupants inside, the three officers along with Dan and Becky rushed to the kitchen window. They could see the outside officer was in the first squad car blowing the horn for their attention, pointing at the second car which held the prisoner. Inside the locked car, stuffing could be seen flying in the air. The very upset and angry prisoner had used his handcuffs to rip the seat covers. As everyone watched, the prisoner turned around, lay on the seat with his head in the floorboard area and his feet in the air. He then began trying to kick out the rear window.

The senior deputy turned to Dan and said, "Mr. Brown, do you mind signing a blank statement? We've got to get this character to jail before he ruins my car."

As the cars pulled away, Becky breathed a sigh of relief. "Thank goodness Beth slept through the entire encounter." Dan nodded, then added. "Yes, but we'll never hear the end of it" – "Daddy, why didn't you wake me up for all the excitement? I would have helped you with the bad guy."

Over the years, Dan and Becky have enjoyed telling this story to friends. Both realize how fortunate they are to be able to do so. Under different circumstances, the events recounted above could have gone very wrong. A few weeks later, the intruder was given a year in prison for possession and use of illegal drugs and other various charges, including resisting arrest.

*****

The car did "Rise" – about 11 am, by way of a tow truck.

Chapter 53

THE REUNION

June 1982
Age: 47

The Austell High graduates of 1952 had not had a reunion
during the twenty-nine years that followed graduation. For
whatever reason or combination of circumstances, a
homecoming event was never organized. Many of the
classmates still lived in or near Austell, and presumably felt
no compulsion to arrange a celebration for members who
had fled the area for greener pastures. Dan Brown had
really hoped for a twenty-year get-together, had even made a
few calls to guys whom he thought might be up to the task of
organizing the return of approximately 50 graduates. No
volunteers stepped forward. Then twenty-five years came
and passed with no word on plans for such an event.
Finally, as the thirty-year anniversary approached, the
hoped-for letter arrived with details for a grand reunion.
Dan was elated and anticipated a wonderful weekend of
memories with old classmates. According to the
information provided, sixty of the sixty-two graduates were
still living and major efforts were being extended to get as
many as possible back home for Reunion Weekend.
Enthused over seeing old buddies again, Dan filled out and
returned the form with deposit the same day the information
arrived. Over the years, he had managed to keep in contact
with six or seven of the group, but as in every class, many
members seem to just drop off the face of the earth.
Two weeks before event weekend, Dan pulled out old
photograph albums. The class had opted not to have a 1952
yearbook so a picture resource of that nature was not
available....no one had wanted the extra-curricular
responsibility required for such a huge project. Maybe that
was a clue to no reunion for thirty years?
Would he recognize anyone? He was certainly 30-35
pounds heavier than the 155-pound weakling they would
remember from the early '50's. How in the world did Coach
Johnson talk him into playing tackle on the football team?

"I guess that's one reason we went 0 and 10 that year."
Then mimicking Frank Sinatra, he belted out, *"It was a very small year."* And then added, "But we went to State in basketball." He finally found five or six snapshots of school chums from thirty years past.

Perhaps the long awaited social function was ill fated from the outset. Just two weeks before event weekend a letter arrived notifying attendees that the Friday Nite Festivities had been canceled due to unforeseen circumstances. Subsequently, members learned the reason for the cancellation. The Friday night Host family had separated pending divorce. Dan was disappointed to lose a night of conversation and reliving old times, but there was still Saturday night even though he didn't really understand reasons for driving to a motel twenty-five miles away in Marietta for an Austell reunion. But hey, he wasn't in charge, he was one of the returning prodigals who had gone away and basically stayed away.
As they drove north from Florida to Atlanta, he said to his wife: "Becky, how many of your reunions of yours have I attended? Four or five? I've always enjoyed seeing you interact with your friends from yesteryear and I'm sure you will enjoy meeting some of mine. I hope the class responds and the turnout is good. I can't think of anyone in Class of '52 that I wouldn't like to see again."

Finally Saturday night came and Dan and Becky were on their way to the Marietta *Marriott*, arriving at exactly six o'clock. Very excited in anticipation of a great evening, he wanted to max socialize over drinks with as many classmates as possible before dinner. He hated sit-down dinners that curtailed visiting and chatting. Navy reunions were often of the pickup food variety – all sorts of hors d'oeuvres and lots of them, with plenty of liquid refreshment as well. This was to be a sit-down dinner at seven p.m. so he was there to visit early and often. "Call me a table-hopper if you want to but I like parties for visiting, telling jokes, and getting to know people better. For sit-down eating, I go to restaurants."

306

He had just given his order for a glass of wine for Becky and a rum and coke for himself, when a man in an official Marriott uniform came up to the bartender and advised him to shut down the bar. "Why?" was the cry from several classmates just arriving who had not yet ordered liquid refreshment. The *Marriot* official responded: "Your class president just told me that the ministers in your class object to alcohol being served. Hey, I don't like it either. Your cost for using the room was calculated on bar drinks being sold."

The group turned away, disappointed but amiable to keeping peace "in the family."

Dan and three friends relived old times over dinner while four wives listened attentively. Too soon, Dan thought, the night's program started. Class president Jimmy Seward introduced the school's principal and two teachers who were still living and in attendance. They offered short remarks. Class officers from 1952 were recognized and applauded. Thankfully, no speeches from them. Organizers of the event were named and stood for applause. Only one of the group said anything, asking for addresses for a few members whose whereabouts were unknown. Then president Seward asked the valedictorian of the 1952 Class at Austell High to say a few words.

Sara Bell Hardy walked to the podium with a sheath of papers in her hand. "I didn't know what to say tonight so I just started looking through an old trunk with lots of stuff from high school days. Guess what? I found my commencement speech. I read a few lines of it to my husband and he said that's it was so good that I should do it tonight – just give my speech all over again. So here goes." The attendees were stunned. For thirty-five minutes, a room full of fifty-year old men and women listened to a speech prepared by a teenager thirty years before. Does a boring speech get better with age, like spirits in a cask? Not on your life! And so the captured audience sat there without alcohol, without iced tea, heck, without even water – the waiters/waitresses had disappeared. This was probably due to the fact the *Marriot* was going to lose money on the gig. They wouldn't have wanted to hear parts of the damn speech anyway. The only good thing that can be said about the experience is that the class members acted with class and dignity. No one got up and left. The room was very quiet, like a mausoleum.

When Sara finished, the class president stood and said simply, "Thanks for coming. That's it folks." Within two minutes the room was empty and deserted. There was next to no conversation as couples left hurriedly, probably afraid of injuring feelings if they enunciated their thoughts.

Dan was totally exasperated but not one to be totally quiet. As he stepped through the doors into the lobby, he said aloud to no one in particular, but not caring if someone, anyone might hear, "I hope you'all enjoyed the first and last high school reunion Austell '52 will ever have."

He was wrong. There was a fifty- year reunion with open bar. The two ministers and Sara Bell Hardy did not attend.

*****

And of course, the author attended. And had fun.

Chapter 54

MRS. JOHNSON

July, 1985
Age: 50

The small family of three was enjoying their home on Arbor
Lane, a dream coming true. Dan and Becky and the little
kid, now nearly nine, enjoyed the neighborhood, their
neighbors, and loved the big, plentiful water oaks anchoring
the corners of the front yard. Dan had managed to find the
teenage son of a family who lived around the corner to cut
and edge the lawn for a reasonable fee. So maintenance of
the grass and routine landscaping were solved problems for
the time being. The rose garden was his domain, his little
parcel of earth over which to toil. Most afternoons he found
time to spend with *Mr. Lincoln, Peace, Color Magic, Granada,
Queen Elizabeth*, and his favorite, *Double Delight.* Much of the
time, Beth helped him with the spraying, fertilizer, weeding,
pruning, and cutting. She loved catching the fat, wiggly
earthworms transplanted from a bait store to aerate the earth
around the roots. The rose garden had become a mutual
joy, one of many bonds between father and daughter.

Often, across the chain link fence that separated the two
yards, Mrs. Johnson would be mowing the grass. Mrs.
Johnson was a wonderful neighbor in every respect.
Widowed, she was older, probably seventy or more. Young
for her years, "Healthy as horse" was the clichéd description
she awarded herself. She enjoyed taking care of her yard
personally. Beyond being a great neighbor and keeping a
luscious green manicured lawn, she had two traits that Dan
found intriguing. She had an affinity for jewelry and often
told of a husband who had loved buying it for her before his
demise. At functions of any and every nature, she invariably
wore beautiful, expensive, eye catching jewelry. Rings,
bracelets, pins, earrings, necklaces, she enjoyed them all and
wanted those in her company to enjoy them with her. The
other interesting thing about Mrs. Johnson was that she
loved to work in her yard wearing comfortable culottes'

shorts and a near-bikini halter-top. Conversationally stimulating under any condition, Mrs. Johnson's appearance in her outfit for yard work was inordinately impressive to see. Mrs. Johnson was extremely well endowed, truly blessed in frontal chest development. Dan loved to paraphrase from an old joke; "She definitely was not behind the door when the Lord passed out knockers." If or when someone approached Mrs. Johnson while she was working in the yard, so dressed, she kept an old long sleeved white shirt of her late husband's nearby which she would immediately fetch to cover her upper torso. Dan and Mrs. Johnson had often talked over the back fence; Mrs. Johnson always attired and covered in her loose fitting, floppy white shirt.

Mrs. Johnson's mother died in May of that year. Among her inheritance was a magnificent diamond pendant. The stone was two and a half to three carats, marquise cut, enhanced in a solitaire mounting. Brilliant, flawless, at least an E on the coveted colorless scale by which diamonds are evaluated and appraised, the gem was exquisite in every detail. Mrs. Johnson usually wore the prize possession on a gold choker.

In July, Dan was working in the rose bed near the back fence. Mrs. Johnson was cutting the back lawn. She had made several lengthwise sweeps across her yard, nearing completion of the portion close to their mutual fence line. Dan innocently stood, turned and walked over by the fence to say hello. As he approached, Mrs. Johnson shifted the green and white *Lawn Boy* to idle, and called out. "Good morning, Dan. How's my good neighbor?"

"Oh, we're fine, Mrs. J--.............Mrs. Johnson, I don't think I would wear that while cutting the grass!"

Apparently the realization that her massive bosoms were exposed except for the miniscule cups of red cloth - that she had forgotten to retrieve her white cover-up - totally confounded and befuddled Mrs. Johnson. Her mouth set, her face framed in exasperation and bewilderment, she clasped her arms across her chest in an "X" pattern, and exclaimed, "Dan Brown, I can't believe a good Christian man like you would say something like that!"

Hurriedly, defensively, he reacted verbally, his right hand drawing a semi-circle around his neck, "The diamond, Mrs. Johnson, the diamond!"

*****

Great story – wonderful lady

Chapter 55

TWO VERY YOUNG PILOTS

September, 1990

This is my token 'Wifey' story, but hey, it's neat, too

Becky inherited a grammar school library in sore need of
new blood and innovative ideas. The former media
specialist retired over a year earlier leaving behind a barely
adequate program that had grown increasingly tiresome and
boring without a designated media specialist on staff.
Missing books and outdated inventories set the tone for a
lifeless, lackluster library. The challenge of learning
appeared non-existent. Becky understood her first, and
probably her most difficult task, was to create an atmosphere
that would make the children want to see and experience the
media center. She was determined to find a way of
increasing student traffic in the library. Then she could
work her special magic in helping the students develop a
love for reading. She was confident that once she had their
interest she would win their minds, maybe even their hearts.

First, a thorough cleaning of the room, windows and shelves
was accomplished over a summer weekend with the help of
her kind husband. She purchased with her own funds
colorful, vibrant curtains that added personality to the
inherently bleak gray room. Bookshelves were re-arranged
and learning centers appeared. Then off to *Reddi-Arts* to
purchase several posters that would brighten and liven the
room even more. Animals and places and landscape scenes,
of course, but she also tried posters of contemporary
subjects: dancing and dancers for the girls, and for the boys,
Batman's car (the movie was popular then) and a picture of
a life-size Lockheed L-1011 *Tristar* aircraft cockpit
instrument panel showing two throttles and all associated
gages and switches.

At the beginning of the second year at Justina Elementary School, Becky Brown was voted Teacher of the year. The library had come alive!

But this story is centered around two young men who fell in love with a corner poster in Ms. Brown's overhauled media center. After only a few weeks, a routine developed for two young second graders. Every free moment before school and during, the two boys headed to the library and placed two chairs in front of the cockpit poster. There they would become pilots and "fly" the airplane in their young fantasy world. One afternoon the two young aviators were doing their thing when a third youngster approached Becky in tears.
She asked: "What's the matter, Jonathan?"
The young lad answered through tears and sniffles: "Phillip and Devaughn won't let me play with them in the cockpit."
Becky walked over to the boys and told them they had to let Jonathan play also.
Both perplexed *pilots* turned and responded in unison, "But Mrs. Brown, we've already taken off."
The librarian admonished them sternly. "Well, right now, you're passing over the airport at Jacksonville, Florida. Land that airplane and let Jonathan on board!" Inwardly, her heart smiled.

About the same time the above story was developing, the author found the following essay, written by a young 'wannabe' pilot:

> *I want to be a pilot when I grow up because it's fun and easy to do.*
> *Pilots don't need much school, they just have to learn numbers so*
> *they can read instruments. I guess they should be able to read maps*
> *so they can find their way if they get lost. Pilots should be brave so*

they won't get scared if it's foggy and they can't see or if a wing or

motor falls off they should stay calm so they'll know what to do.

Pilots have to have good eyes so they can see through clouds and

they can't be afraid of lightning or thunder because they are closer

to them than we are. The salary pilots make is another thing I like.

They make more money than they can spend. This is because most

people think airplane flying is dangerous except pilots don't because

they know how easy it is. There isn't much I don't like, except girls

like pilots and all the stewardesses want to marry them and they

always have to chase them away so they won't bother them. I

hope I don't get airsick because if I do I couldn't be a pilot and

would have to go to work.

A fifth grader

*****

The writer is, or was, one sharp young fellow. He's probably a Delta pilot now.

314

Chapter 56

<u>HOME ALONE</u>

August, 1994
Age: 59

The Chevy Astro rolled along at seventy miles per hour, devouring miles and minutes between Tallahassee and Jacksonville. Dan stretched his legs and relaxed deeper in the driver's seat. Interstate10 and monotony were synonymous, the dual lanes of concrete stretched straight across eastern Florida. The steady hum of the engine, the shadowy outline of pine trees lining both sides of the median, the quiet companion beside him, all accentuated the heavy silence in the van. Becky had not uttered a word since leaving Tallahassee, now about an hour behind them. In reality, there was little need for conversation since both driver and passenger knew – perhaps 'felt' is the better word - the singular subject dominating the inner thoughts of the other. Today was a red-letter day in three lives, not just an ordinary dot on the timeline of life. This landmark date would not be forgotten. Paramount in the couple's reverie was a special eighteen-year old girl who had remained behind. This day in her life was a mammoth step toward young womanhood and independence. For the van's occupants, father and mother, husband and wife, the day was overly important as well. Another test along the path of parenthood was now history.

On that hot, humid, mid-August day in 1994, Dan and Becky Brown had moved their only child into a freshman dormitory room at Florida State University. Their precious, beautiful butterfly had emerged from chrysalis. She was this day a college student. For all intents and purposes, the umbilical was severed.

The van continued eastward, an omnipresent white line always unraveling on the concrete before them. Memories, oh, a plethora of memories of their darling daughter dominated the thoughts of the father and mother team returning home alone. Infancy, pre-school/grammar school/high school, family vacations, highpoints over the past eighteen years as well as miss-adventures along the way, all played on mind rewind for the nearly ninety minutes since pulling onto I-10 eastbound.

Dan broke the silence. "That's another 'X' in the block; kid in college." Twenty-one years of Navy procedures had a way of creeping into the ex-pilot's vocabulary on occasion. In Navy lingo, a checkmark denoted progress achieved towards a project, an 'X' in the box signaled completion. Once financial considerations had been solved, the grade point and SAT dragons that devour parent's dreams of a university education for their offspring had not been detractions in the Brown family. Beth's studies had never been suspect. One of Dan's oft-quoted stories concerned his daughter's late night study hours. There were friends and acquaintances that might think he and Becky were *pushers*, goading Beth into intensive, unrealistic study habits. In fact, Beth was her own motivator. Depending on her age, seven, ten or fourteen, she cried, begged or demanded to stay up later than scheduled bedtime to study "just a little longer." In the early years, more tears were shed over extra study time versus bedtime than any other issue. Finally, somewhere between age fifteen and sixteen, the parents acquiesced (a high priced word for 'gave up'), went to bed when they were ready, and let "the kid" study into the wee hours. Of all the thoughts coursing through the minds of Dan and Becky Brown on the return home, scholastic concerns were almost non-existent. As to the other pitfall that denies deserving kids a higher education, he had worked and reworked their budget. A downsizing of discretionary spending would hurt for a little while, but all in all, money did not appear to be an insurmountable factor. Dan nodded, agreeing with his thoughts, 'Yes, today marked another "magic moment" in their respective lives but by golly, the Brown trio – the Brown family - had not only passed the test, they aced it. He and Becky got an "A" in parenting; Beth got kudos for being such a wonderful, responsible child. Now he smiled, mocking himself as if Beth were there: 'Dad, I'm not a child. I'm a college girl!'

As the van passed beneath the concrete behemoth of the I-75 and I-10 interchange, Becky finally spoke, interrupting the parade of memories past. "Just the two of us, home alone. Other than the obvious super hero solution you have to any question, seriously, what's the first thing you want to do after all those years having a little girl in the house?"

He pondered a response. 'What would it be like without "little kid"?' The first five years of childless marriage were certainly wonderful but that was a long time ago. They had been a threesome, a close family unit for eighteen years. They would adjust – every family did eventually but it wasn't going to be easy. Absentmindedly, his right hand went to his head as he brushed back salt and pepper locks in disarray after a long day of moving and driving. Opposite direction traffic splashed light over the windshield and illuminated their faces in the darkness. Glancing at the silhouetted form beside him, he marveled again that such a beautiful woman had picked him for a husband, to be the father of her child. 'So beautiful,' he thought, 'even with teary mascara.' Smiling wickedly, his reply was more a question than an answer, "Eat pizza naked?"

*****

I invoke the 5th yet again.

Chapter 57

THE NURSING HOME

July, 1995
Age: 59

Terry Brown walked out of the Temple Terrace Nursing Home into Atlanta's ungodly July heat. Leaving the patio area, he found a well-defined path winding under a forest of foliage. A myriad of trees and dense shrubbery surrounded the complex. Stopping in the shade and looking back up the incline towards the tall two-story brick building, he enjoyed a quiet and calm moment. Birds chirped among the branches adding to the serenity of the scene around him. Appreciative of the luscious greenery, he felt that their mother could easily come to love a place like this.
Terry had been appointed by his brother and sister to find a continuing care facility for their aging parent. He was thinking that his brother and sister, Dan and Sylvia, would like this place for Mom. This particular facility had been recommended by several friends and enjoyed a strong reputation as one of the first in the south to offer extended care to the elderly.
Quietly accessing the grounds and view, he became aware of a walker coming towards him. The man walked rapidly, his arms swinging to and fro. Attired in dark exercise shorts and grey shirt touting "TECH", he appeared to be listening with rapt attention to a Walkman radio attached to his left arm by a Velcro band. As he came closer, Terry figured the gentleman's age to be about seventy to seventy-five. A graying mustache complimented silvery, but not white, hair. Only a little over five feet tall, and slender, he was evidently fit and in excellent physical condition.
Terry held up a hand and queried, "Sir, may I bother you just for a moment?"
The walker stopped and pulled the headset from his ears, leaving the yellow plastic horseshoe shaped device hanging loose around his neck. "Yes, of course. How can I help you?" He reached for the on/off switch to the radio.

Terry began his spiel. "Hi, I'm Terry Brown from Lithia Springs out near Douglasville. I'm looking at Temple Terrace as a potential home for my mother. She's over eighty now and has Parkinson's. I was wondering if perhaps you are a resident and could give me first hand knowledge of how it is to live here."

The older man looked at the younger man with an amused grin. "Well, Mr. Brown, you must understand the Temple Terrace total care concept. That's the Nursing Home you're seeing there on the hill. I don't know a whole lot about life in the nursing home or the assisted living community. Just down the lane you can see the outline of an eight-story building. That's the retirement community where I reside. There's fifty-three of us: forty-nine women and four men. I love it! There are ladies at my door day and night with cookies and cakes and pies and invitations to dinner. Frankly, I've never had so much **(DELETED)** in my life."

*****

Trying to stay "R" category, but you get the picture.

Chapter 58

I THINK I'LL WRITE A BOOK

October, 1995 – September, 1999
Age: 60

> *Play out the play!*
>
> *King Henry, Part I* Shakespeare

......The 'Bard' paraphrased loosely, Write out the Story

Sitting at the Yacht Club bar, Dan Brown nursed a second
rum and coke and enjoyed the wide-open view of blue
water. The *St. Johns* was calm today, only two white sails
dotted the horizon. Still, the lonely duo of boats enhanced
the picturesque beauty before him. Alone at the bar, the
serene moment seemed to coax deep, inner thoughts of self-
identity. 'Sixty now – officially a geezer, had he done it all?
Their only child was in her second year at Florida State
University. His "little kid" was doing great. Better'n great –
heck, she was on the honor roll. He didn't have to worry
about her. Then, Becky too, sure seemed happy in her work,
so don't go there. Next – himself. He certainly wasn't going
to fly anymore. Hell, he hadn't flown in nearly twenty
years. He never got that bridge cap with scrambled eggs he
had coveted, but who knows, maybe he was the lucky one.
Another promotion would have meant a fourth deployment,
perhaps a fifth, to WestPac and Becky wouldn't be in his life
which meant Beth wouldn't either - even if he had returned
from all missions safely.' Another rum and coke and he
remained the bar's only patron. So he continued this line of
self-examination – life beyond sixty. 'He was definitely still
working hard and planned to keep going until Beth was out
of college. Except for high blood pressure that was proving
persistent, his health was hanging in there. The little bout
with possible cancer seemed to be a thing of the past.'
Sipping his drink and reaching for peanuts, "Let's see, what
else do I consider? He was chairman of the board at church
and taught some Sunday School. There was a small
mortgage, relatively new cars in the garage, and they
enjoyed moderate vacations, even skiing occasionally. But

had he done all that he wanted to do?" The boats on the water held his attention for a moment. More self-introspection: 'A dog, a cat, and a rose garden didn't seem to fill his inner needs. The empty nest syndrome had been overcome and the married duo was finding time outside work to rekindle patterns idle for so long: tennis, reading, computer-eze, day tripping on Saturdays, long bike rides, extended walks. He wasn't addicted to television and cared zilch for golf. But was he missing a bet? Was this his life for the next twenty years?'
And then from nowhere, like a bolt of lightning, an idea hit him hard. Up to this point, he had been as calm as the river. Suddenly, he could no longer sit still. Now, he was enthused and excited. He signed his bar bill and left hurriedly.

Entering the back door, he called out to Becky. "I have just had a great idea. Listen up. You won't believe it." As he entered the kitchen, she looked at him quizzically. Her husband explained, "I think I will write a book." His wife's face still registered a question mark as he continued. She could see he was more animated and energized than she had seen him in a long time. He definitely had a thing on his mind. He put down his brief case and kept talking. "You know when I was in the Navy, I helped formulate and write several task Force Operation Plans and Orders. Over the years in my civilian jobs, I've written or rewritten OSHA and Hazardous Waste compliance manuals for small companies. I have single-handedly authored two different firm's Safety Manuals. Last year I wrote our plant's first Standard Operating Procedures booklet. Admittedly, the OSHA, Haz Waste, and Safety manuals didn't call for original thinking. It was basically a matter of picking and choosing excerpts from federal, state, and/or local guidelines that applied to the situation at hand. Then all I had to do was tie them together in understandable English. On the other hand, the SOP Manual showcases sixty pages of my creative talents. But even the compliance manuals offered an opportunity for developing writing style. I had to make bureaucratic bullshit readable and convert techno-geek-eze into understandable fifth grade English. That's the comprehension level for most employees when it comes to work-related regulations. Back to the Navy Op orders – those helped me develop skills, too. Large operation plans call for clear, concise, and correct written plans and instructions. Doesn't that all add up to lots of experience writing? Yep, I think I could author a book."

Becky was channel surfing when Dan went to the computer, turned it on and waited for it to boot. "Where to start? First, maybe a glass of iced tea." He strolled down the hall towards the kitchen. Passing by the den, he looked in to see Michael Douglas and Sharon Stone filling the screen in one of their steamy scenes from an old thriller. He paused for a moment to watch erotic images of the sexy actress as she crossed and re-crossed her legs. While pouring Tetley into a goblet, he continued to watch the sexy movie over the breakfast bar. A mischievous glint showed in his eyes. 'Maybe I should have a little fun with this. Let's see what Miss Prim and Proper Librarian thinks of a hot love scene that could be right out of an HBO script.'

He slipped into bed beside her naked, warm body. Moonlight reflected off the blue water of the pool through double doors, outlining, just for a moment, her pointed breasts. His bride shivered as her nipples pressed into his chest when he pulled her close.
The scent of her hair, mingled with a lingering hint of French perfume, intoxicated his senses. 'Joy' he thought, the bottle I gave her last Christmas. She sighed deeply and sissored a knee between his legs. He could feel the growing heat of her inverted "V" on his upper thigh. She did not resist as his lips moved to enjoy her nipples at the end of perfect globes. Then he reached to caress the soft skin of her lower stomach. A forefinger toyed with the indentation of her navel. Their lips met in mutual hunger; warm, moist, and exciting. His tongue found hers and her breath quickened. He wished he could taste her mouth forever. Now he felt her body undulating, responding to his touch. His hand began its downward trek to the epi-center of her being. She.........

*For two and a half pages, the lovers pleasured and satisfied each
other's sexual dreams and desires. Sweating, touching, kissing, they
exchanged words of excited endearment, whispering heartfelt
exhortations meant solely for the privacy of their bedroom.*

Finally the aspiring author let them fall asleep and ended his
initial attempt via written word into the world of carnal
fantasy.

"Hon, I want you to read this and tell me what you think of
the writing style. You are to be the critic. Tell me if you like
it or if it's strictly trash. Don't read it like it was some
pocket porn novel but consider it more like an excerpt from
Grace Metalious' *Peyton Place* or Harold Robbins' *The
Carpetbaggers*. Maybe like Rhett making love to Scarlett, not
Debbie Does Dallas. Tell me the truth, good or bad writing."
She took the pages and moved closer to the light. She began
reading the short treatise, her legs tucked beneath a long T-
shirt nightgown. He watched her face for any sign of
approval or distaste. Her facial features remained stoic,
intense, serious. Once, he thought he saw the first stages of
a frown begin to form but the facial lines disappeared as
quickly. Suddenly, she stopped abruptly, looked up and
proclaimed matter-of-factly: "Honey! You can't write that
in a book. People will think it's us!"
Laughing, he chided, "Beck, it is us!"

She laid the printed sheets aside. "I'm still a little confused
over this new focus of yours. Why, all of a sudden, do you
feel the need to start a writing career? You know how I love
books - I'm a librarian. But in nearly twenty-five years of
being married to you, you have never mentioned a desire to
author a book. You don't keep a diary, and I don't think
you've kept notes as we traveled. What kind of book are
you contemplating anyway? I certainly hope it won't be
anything along the lines of what I just read? I'm not
interested in sharing my sex life with the world."
He understood her doubts. He had some, too. But he tried
to explain. "First of all, I'm thinking of short stores, not a
love triangle or a Whodunnit. And remember, Grandma
Moses didn't start painting until she was seventy-eight. And

get this. Did you know Hank Williams, Sr., read romance comic books to get ideas for country songs? It just seems to me that the memories of a lifetime are as good a reference pool for writing short stories as comic books are for songs. Anyway, there's another fire burning inside me. All of us tell our favorite stories over and over again at cocktail parties or dinners or family reunions. If stories are worth telling, aren't they worth jotting down on paper? I'm just afraid my interesting experiences are going to die with me. Some are great, some are funny, some are sad, all too good never to be told or heard again." He looked at her intently. "So why not write them down for posterity? One of the best ever is when your dad decided he and I should go fishing while you had the baby. How about that holographic, three-dimensional vision I had when that jerk kid pointed a gun at me in Daytona? There's always my carrier landing accident aboard FORRESTAL. Or the circumstances on that trip to Cairo to see Sadat. On the lighter side, remember Heathcliff and those fat Italian lovers screwing in the sand? How many times have I told that story? I'll be the first to admit I don't envision any big deals of major import, no international intrigue, nothing to make a movie about. Just entertaining and/or interesting occurrences, I might even call some of them adventures, that I think should be remembered by somebody, sometime, somewhere and passed on down the line. Wouldn't you like to have some notes on how your family came to be in Chattanooga and Alabama? My mother's genealogy shows both a horse thief and a governor in our family tree. I wish we had their stories to read about, to talk about. Well, if I can manage this writing bit, I will leave a permanent chronicle for my great-grandkids that I will never know. They say you can't take it with you. But you know what? You do take "it" with you – you take your memories, your stories, your jokes, your anecdotes right down into the ground with you. Babe, am I talking ego? I guess I am. But does that make it bad? Nope, I don't think so – only if the writing itself is poor. Tell you what - I'll let you be the judge of that."

He knew exactly where he wanted to start. The keyboard came alive with *The Boy and The Bird*. Oh, there was lots of

324

backspace time on the keyboard, numerous edits and rewrites. But soon he felt better and better about the sentences that were appearing on the screen. Words began to flow, but he was always thankful for how easy the computer made editing, and for help *Reader's Digest Word Finder* gave him with synonyms. He wrote the stories exactly as he remembered them. He wished he had kept a diary but there would be no Jay Leno incidents of plagiarizing someone else's story.

FAST FORWARD FOUR YEARS TO SEPTEMBER, 1999.

Thousand of words disappeared one evening in a computer crash. Dan had certainly heard of "backing up" and he always intended to do it, but just never seemed to get around to putting in a disk, formatting it and learning how to dupe his files. It was such a devastating psychological loss that it was another year before he could force himself back to the keyboard. But once at it again, words seemed to appear on the screen like magic. Short story after short story was written, edited, and saved to disk. Then he hit 'The wall'. How to end it? The aspiring writer faced an impasse. One night he sat, hands in lap, staring at words on the screen that no longer made sense.

His better half walked by, sipping a cup of steaming tea. "What's the problem? Writer's cramp? You look dejected." Her husband nodded his head. "I'm stuck for an ending. I taken my hero from A to Y but I can't seem to get him to Z. I've alluded all through the book to questions that Aristotle, Plato and Socrates couldn't answer. 'Why me? Jeez, Why me?' I know I can't solve that question if all the great thinkers from the time of Adam and Eve couldn't and can't, but I would like to offer some insightful thoughts as to why I've been given so much time to enjoy good health and a loving wife and daughter, live through 415 carrier landings, have two great careers while other guys got the short end of the stick. So many of my friends – all the way back to my buddy in first grade, are only memories – they're all gone. 'Gone' as in being dead."

He leaned back in the chair and continued. "I know I can't solve the riddle of the unstoppable force meeting the unmovable rock, but I want to finish this future bestseller by saying something worthwhile. The reader will have been with me through thick and thin and deserves something, anything of substance as an ending. And remember, it has to be a true story that happened to me, a family member or a close friend."

Absent-mindedly running his hands through disheveled hair, his mind still seemed blank with no answers. Then he remembered an almost forgotten quotation that could solve the situation, at least temporarily. Becky watched as he inserted a disk and copied, then saved the information on the screen.
He stood, rolled the chair under the desk and raised his hands in surrender. "I know what I'm going to do. I'll do what that not-so-famous Greek philosopher suggested, Henry or Harold or something like that. No, that's not right but it's definitely a name that starts with an 'H'.[1] He said 'Put it in a drawer for a while' or words to that effect. I'll just leave it here in Mr. Dell Computer, backed up on a disk, for as long as it takes."

*****

And that's how we've come to 2005.

---

[1] *"let it be kept till the ninth year, the manuscript put away at home: you may destroy whatever you haven't published; once out, what you've said can't be stopped".*

Horace, 65-8 B.C. Actually, he was a Roman poet

326

Chapter 59

MY HOME'S IN ALABAMA

Late summer, 1997
Age: 61

......My home's in Alabama, no matter where I lay my head. My home's in Alabama, Southern born and Southern bred.
ALABAMA, Award-winning Country Music Band

...Always have your bags packed; you never know where life's journey is going to take you.
Old Appalachian saying

Surprise! And life is full of them. Dan and Becky Brown now live in Anniston, Alabama. For those readers who believe in fate, certainly an ironclad case can be made for arguing the point in the Brown's decision to relocate in 'Sweet home Alabama'.
January of this year saw unexpected events like dominos toppling one by one to disrupt the Brown's placid, routine lifestyle. Twenty-one years of fun and sun and casual Florida living were about to be pre-empted by unforeseen circumstances.

The first domino fell when Dan lost his long held position as general manager of *Sterling Publishing Company*. The company changed direction and decided on a new, younger, bullish oriented management team for tackling 21st Century competition. Perhaps providence did play a hand in the game of life, and if so, at this point pitched in a trump card. For several months Dan had been battling dangerously elevated high blood pressure. Readings were routinely 205/100, sometimes 210/110 while taking three different physician ordered prescriptions. As #2 management executive, all aspects of employee relations, manufacturing schedules, deadlines, and deliveries, as well as OSHA and hazardous waste compliance fell under his purview of responsibility. His doctor repeatedly advised a change in vocation, a change of scenery. At sixty-one and a half, Dan debated the pros and cons, ifs and buts, of switching careers so late in his working life. In January, the company made the decision for him.

Other factors were in play as well. Mrs. Knight, Becky's mother, had suffered a severe heart attack two years earlier and now mini-strokes were complicating the picture surrounding her health. This fact combined with a small school library opening in the Anniston area provided Becky ready-made impetus to favor the move. Mrs. Brown's health too, was failing steadily. The double whammy of Alzheimer and Parkinson's was taking its toll. Re-location to within an hour's drive of his family's home outside Atlanta would give Dan an opportunity to see her more often.

On a positive note, the hot housing market in northern Florida greatly favored the Browns as housing sales in Anniston (primarily due to Fort McClellan being on the BRAC[1] list the previous year) were depressed. This was a defining factor in the decision to move. Their Ortega Forest home in Jacksonville would sell for a price that permitted outright purchase of home on Choccolocco Mountain (locals call it '10th Street Mountain) in Anniston. And Dan had a trump card of his own to play. Retirement became a viable option as age sixty-two rapidly approached and he studied Alabama's reduced cost of living index. Military retired pay and early social security benefits would "cut the mustard" and make budget. Actually, Becky working made money for the time being a non-issue. Someday when she left the library for good, they might have to watch their dollars more closely but would never have to count pennies. His conscience hurt him about two seconds after making the decision to "hang it up". *Well, maybe two minutes.* He had begun writing a book of short stories about his experiences and misadventures along life's way. Perhaps he could finally finish *Eating pizza naked*, the temporary title he called his manuscript. He would certainly have the time.

Leaving Jacksonville was not easy. *The Bold New City of the South* had become home to them. Beth had planned to be

---

[1] Base Realignment And Closure

married one day in Ortega United Methodist Church, the
church in which she grew up. Her plans would have to
adjust. Always a realist, Dan finally saw the choice as a
Godfather type offer, one that simply could not be refused.
Too many *doors* had opened inviting the Browns to return to
Becky's hometown. It was as if the move was ordained by
cosmic decree. In view of all the positive factors at play, the
Anniston house was purchased immediately and Becky
moved north. Her husband would commute as necessary
until 4214 Arbor Lane sold. To salve his pride and ego as
Becky went off to work each day, he forsook his vow to
never cut grass or shine shoes. Mrs. Knight moved into the
downstairs apartment and became Dan's daytime charge
while his wife was at school. The yard, weekday lunches for
Mrs. Knight and himself, after meal cleanup (all meals), the
dishwasher, and yes, the shoeshine kit, became his new
responsibilities. Fifty-five employees, delivery deadlines,
safety, training, OSHA, HAZWASTE, hiring, firing, were
all headaches of the past. Dividends were immediately
apparent. His latest annual physical, just completed, saw a
new blood pressure of 138/80 on only two medicines of light
dosage.

Sale of the Arbor Lane home had taken almost six months
but the papers were finally signed. A final load of furniture
and household goods was loaded on a twenty-four foot
U-Haul rental truck. The large truck extended the normal
eight-hour driving time from Jacksonville to Anniston via
Atlanta to a little over ten hours. Alone, no radio, Dan had
lots of time to think and remember. The truck was stuffed,
every inch top to bottom packed with something. He
remembered the first time he had driven a truck like this.
Moving Becky, Atlanta to Jacksonville, had been a snap.
The truck had been hardly half full and loosely packed. As
he drove, he thought of the friends they were leaving, always
a downside to moving. How often had he done this in
twenty-one years in the service? He mused, "Well, the
Christmas card list just grew by a bunch." Passing an old
and closed service station just north of Valdosta, he recalled
the station in 1971 as the stop for fill-up with cheap gas, 29.9
cents a gallon. Those were the days when he was tearing up

I-75 to date his favorite librarian, down I-75 trying to get back to Jax in time for a decent night's sleep before test hopping an unforgiving *Vigilante* the next morning.
One's thoughts often take uncharted paths. As Dan rolled north on the busy super highway, he passed an exit near Cordele that held painful memories for him. His favorite commanding officer had died just a few miles west when the plane he was flying inexplicably exploded in mid-air. The skipper had ejected but the fireball consumed his parachute and he had fallen seventeen thousand feet to his death in a Georgia cornfield. (The RAN had ejected only a second earlier and was injured but survived).

The door was open and Dan stuck his head in to see if the CO was ready for him. The sign on the desk in front of the slender, handsome officer read "Commander Les Lincoln, USN". "Dan, come on in and close the door. There are two important subjects we need to talk about: your rotation date and assignment of pilots and navigators as permanent flight crews. First, you're due to transfer out of the squadron back to shore duty only four or five days after we go on line as part of the Tonkin Gulf Yacht Club next May. I need you, pal. I'm asking you to extend your sea duty for the duration of that tour, about seven or eight months. If you don't feel so inclined, I'm going to have to ask the Bureau to replace you right now so your relief can be getting as much practice and experience as possible before we ship out. For you to remain with RVAH-12 just for the voyage over doesn't make any sense and would actually hurt the squadron; you would be taking valuable training time from your relief who needs it for the full deployment. Besides the month's ride over with no flying would be boring as hell for you. But I really want you to remain as my Operations Officer. I'm going to sweeten the pot. I promise to get you promoted and make you a full commander. When the selection board sees the fitness report I'm going to write for you, they will think you're the second coming of JC! What do you say?"
Dan had known this discussion was imminent. He and Eleanor had talked at length about the pros and cons of a third tour to WestPac. Without a college degree because he was not permitted to attend Post Graduate School when he made the prospects list in '64, his chances for selection before the next promotion board were diminished. A combat tour could definitely help overcome that

hurdle. "I'd like to stay on as your Ops O, Skipper. I've made two deployments over there already as ship's company supporting the operational guys. This will be my first real combat tour. It just doesn't seem right to have all that photo recon training and experience and then not take pix of the gooks. And of course, I'd love to wear scrambled eggs on my cap."

The Commanding Officer seemed pleased. "Great. I had an idea you would to stay. I'll call Washington as soon as we settle the next topic. Now, we've got to finalize crew assignments that will remain in effect through the Vietnam deployment. As I mentioned in the All Officers Meeting, you, as Operations Officer, and I will make the team pairings and there will be no discussion or arguments once the list is posted. Now, basically, I want to put an experienced pilot with an inexperienced navigator. And vice-versa, we'll put experienced RANs with newer pilots. Don't you think that's the way to go?"

Dan: "Absolutely. That way we have no absolutely weak teams."

CDR Lincoln: "Now, who is the best, most experienced pilot?"

"You are, sir." Dan answered matter-of-factly. The Operations Officer was no sycophant. CDR Lester Abraham Lincoln had several hundred carrier landings in his aviator's log (about twice as many as the next highest pilot). He had extensive experience aboard carriers, and was known throughout the Vigilante community as one of the smoothest 'sticks' around. An unusual claim to fame that bolstered his reputation was that he had flown the U-2, the spy plane made famous by the Gary Powers shoot-down incident.

CDR Lincoln smiled. "O.K., I accept that. Now, Dan, I'm going to pull the old 'rank has privilege' trick. Mark Carrier is my guy. I know he's not the least experienced navigator, but goshdarnit, I am the C.O. I've worked fifteen years to get to this point. It likely will be my last and only command and I want to enjoy the short one-year that I have the squadron. Do you think I'll get any grief over selecting Mark for myself? I don't want a morale problem before we even start out."

Dan thought for a moment before responding. "I think it'll be O.K., Skipper. As a matter of fact, I think most of the guys had an idea you would want LT Carrier all along."

CDR Lincoln jotted a note on the lined pad before him. "It's settled then. I know that makes me a little hypocritical but Lincoln/Carrier is crew number one. Now, who's the next best pilot?"

Unsmiling and serious, Dan looked directly at the C.O. There was no hesitation in his voice when he answered confidently: "I am."
Nodding, the man behind the desk agreed. "You're right. As Ops O., you're number three in the chain of command but our executive officer has spent a lot of his career ashore and has very little carrier experience. That's why you and I are deciding the crews rather than the normal C.O./X.O. bit. Now the bad news. You're a damn good pilot, Dan, and I hate to do it to but you said it yourself, we can't have a weak-sister flight crew. I've got to put the better pilots with weaker RANs and average pilots – thank goodness we don't have any real weak aviators - with good RANS. You're going to have to take LTJG James in your back seat. How do you feel about that?"

The younger man's face remained impassive as he replied, "Skip, I ain't happy about it but I guess I would do the same thing if I were in your shoes. LTJG James was evaluated by not one, but two performance boards. How he got past them is beyond me. He's not only the least capable navigator we have; he may be the worst in the entire Vigilante community. My wife is going to scream to high heaven when she hears I'm flying combat with LTJG 'dingleberry'[1], as she calls him, but what's that old General Sherman saying? 'War is hell'. Flying with Mr. Numbnuts James will be my private hell, I guess."

CDR Lincoln leaned back in his chair and smiled broadly. Unable to contain his mirth, he jokingly chastised Dan. "C'mon, Ops O, say something nice about your RAN."

A moment of humor surfaced in Dan's reply. "Well, as far as I know, he's not queer."

The C.O. playfully raised an eyebrow as if to speak, then smiled again and said nothing. Dan thought, 'you should be smiling. You've got yourself the Operations Officer you wanted for an additional eight long months and you've solved your worst crew member problem – all in one fell swoop. Daniell Brown, bend over and grab your ankles. The Navy's sticking it to you again – without vaseline!'

They returned to the business at hand. The four remaining reconnaissance flight crews were 'married up' to be announced later that day.

---

[1] Definition censored; having to do with the anus

Two weeks later Les Lincoln was dead. The executive officer "fleeted" up to command and a new exec was quickly reassigned. Except for the addition of the new X.O., flight crews remained unchanged for the duration of the nine months deployment to WESTPAC. Dan Brown and John James flew more missions than any RVAH-12 crew, even beating out the new commanding officer by one flight.

A silver *BMW* whizzed by, passing the slower truck, and breaking the spell of long ago memories. Checking the gas gauge, Dan noticed the need to fill up soon, and began watching billboards for the next *Shell* station.

Back on the road, thoughts of Les Lincoln lingered. Dan knew I-75 and Florida would be in his future time and again over the years. He would pass that same exit which would key memories of his favorite C.O., a super pilot, a fun drinking buddy, and a great friend. Miles continued to tick off on the odometer and Les Lincoln was once again relegated to the subconscious.

He thought of the book he was writing. Did the *deaths* of so many close friends tie neatly into the storyline? Was Les Lincoln an integral part of the story? Would injecting the pilot/RAN match-up incident into his book be strictly an ego trip? It was sure to piss-off Rich Martin if he ever got his hands on the book. He ran mental images through his mind of his old X.O. who became C.O. through default when Les Lincoln was killed. Then he said aloud, "Screw him. Truth is truth."

And how would Alabama fit into the book's story, if at all? From day one he had always pictured the final chapter ending in Florida. "Well, Scarlet, you're right again. We'll just have to wait and see. The next adventure is about to begin. It is going to be nice to see stars at night. The city lights of Jax have all but hidden the night sky from me for over twenty years now. You know, it looks like Mike Allison was wrong. I'm going to live *three* lives, not just two. Airplanes and oceans for twenty-one years; management exec and Florida for twenty-one years; and now retirement on an Alabama mountaintop for X - who knows how many years? *Ain't* life something? You just never know what's over the rise. And I guess it's a good thing we don't. I suppose Somerset Maugham said it best."

There was a merchant in Bagdad who sent his servant to market to buy provisions and in a little while the servant came back, white and trembling, and said, "Master, just now when I was in the market-place I was jostled by a woman in the crowd and when I turned I saw it was Death that jostled me. She looked at me and made a threatening gesture; now, lend me your horse, and I will ride away from this city and avoid my fate. I will go to Samarra and there Death will not find me." The merchant lent him his horse, and the servant mounted it, and dug his spurs in its flanks and as fast as the horse could gallop he went. Then the merchant went down to the market-place and he saw me standing in the crowd and he came to me and said, "Why did you make a threatening gesture to my servant when you saw him this morning?" "That was not a threatening gesture, I said, it was only a start of surprise. I was astonished to see him in Bagdad.....for I had an appointment with him tonight in Samarra."

Appointment in Samarra   Somerset Maugham

*****

Chapter 60

CANCER vs. BROWN, round 2

April, 1999
Age: 64

......'adenocarcinoma' is a scary word

Dan looked at the clock on the wall: 9:27 a.m. Becky had
spent the night in the recliner next to his hospital bed but
had been called to school to solve a minor computer glitch
in the library. Muted TV, door closed, the room ultra quiet,
for nothing better to do he picked up a magazine left behind
and within reach on the chair. Flipping through the pages
he found a short article on *"January 1, 2000/2001 – which
begins the new millennium?"*
He browsed the short article and mentally agreed that 2001
is the real date of beginning the next thousand years. 'I
won't be surprised if we celebrate it twice, just to make
everybody happy.' With the millennium article fresh in his
thoughts, his mind returned to a memorable New Year's
Eve. *It was December 31, 1957. He and Anne were two of the
thousands who thronged to Times Square for a new decade's
celebrations. Sometime after midnight they were finding their way
on side streets around the crowds, hoping to find a late night eaterie.
Shortly they rounded a corner to a lighted but almost deserted street.
Under the streetlight stood a lonely old man, warmed by a faded
and tattered coat. He held a basket full of little toot-toot horns. A
homemade pasteboard sign read, "New Year's Horns, 25c." He
still had several left after the evening's sales and appeared to be
getting ready to call it a night. Suddenly, from around a corner the
street was filled with young boys, perhaps seven or eight in their
early teens or even pre-teens, playing a street brand of "pop the
whip". The boys were all joined in a long line by holding onto each
other with one hand. The leader would then run one way or
another and the "tail of the whip" tried his best to hang on. As the
tail passed abeam Dan and Anne, two boys on the end lost their
grip and barged into the old vendor. The man, who had to be
seventy at least, perhaps more, was knocked to his knees and several
red and white horns scattered hither and yon. Dan now saw that the*

beggar was blind as he reached out patting the cement with his hands trying to find his wares by touch. The old man was desperately trying to save his merchandise. Dan and Anne were helping the old man salvage what he could when the leader of the 'Pop-the-whip Gang' came over and started stomping the tin horns into unrecognizable pieces of flattened metal.

Dan shouted: "Stop, you assholes! This old man is blind. That's his only living you're destroying."

In a flash, the leader pulled a knife. "Click" and Dan saw a five-inch switchblade for the first time in his life. Almost as quickly, the other boys held weapons of some sort: knives, sticks, one picked up a broken bottle from the street. Anne stepped backward, too terrified to scream. Dan was in awe of how quickly the lead boy had brandished a knife when suddenly the consequences of what was about to happen filled him with a fear he had felt once before. He was thinking 'It's Daytona Beach all over again.' He yelled to Anne, "Run like hell!"

Luck, fate, providence, whatever you want to call good fortune, intervened. Two uniformed policemen, both swinging nightsticks, rounded a third corner of the intersection. "What's going on? Any trouble?" One of the beat cops asked. As quickly as the boys had materialized, they were gone.

There was no kissy-face for LTJG Brown that night. Anne lectured him all the way to Connecticut on the absurdity of country hick "honor" on the mean streets of a big city, especially New York. An unhappy Mr. Dixon echoed derision the next day when Anne told her family of the night's adventure. Mrs. Dixon said nothing about it but Dan caught her looking at him while Mr. "D" was talking. She was shaking her head in disbelief, occasionally staring at him as though she was seeing right into his soul. Dan liked the lady who was to be his future mother-in-law and usually she gave every indication that the engagement met with her full approval. But this day he imagined her thinking he was some kind of backward ploughboy from the Confederate south.

'Well,' he thought as he lay back on his pillow in Anniston Regional Hospital. 'Truth be told, I guess I've always been a redneck. I was born so far in rural Georgia that the community had no name, I now live in Alabama, I love country music, my next vehicle is going to be a truck. Dammit, cowboy jeans or dress whites, I did the right thing that night on Times Square. After forty

*years, I think maybe Anne knew it too. And while we're on the
subject of the South, all the Dixon's friends used to tease me about
my Southern accent. They were always asking me to talk in front of
their friends. "Say something for us in that cute Southern accent."
At the time he didn't mind being the butt of their northern humor
but remembering it now irked him. Then a question popped into
his mind highlighting a proposition he had never evaluated
previously. Has anyone from the South ever asked a Yankee "to
talk, to say something," for their friends? Hell no! No one wants to
hear cacophonous gibberish.'*

Dan noticed the urine bag was near capacity – and that the
contents were bright pink. Dr. Fuller said there would be
bleeding for a few days but had guaranteed him that "It"
was going to work just fine again after healing. He had told
Dan that he had not taken the entire walnut shaped organ,
that basically he had *shaved* it. Now Dan spoke aloud to no
one there just to hear his voice, perhaps to convince himself,
"Doc better be right." As his mind dwelt on future romantic
activities at home with his wife behind closed doors, he
remembered the young woman who had appeared at his
bedside in pre-op. Just as the anesthesiologist stuck a needle
into his left arm, a pert, cute young thing spoke to him from
the opposite side of the bed. "Mr. Brown, I'm Janet Combs.
I'm a student nurse in my senior year at Jacksonville State
University and if it's O.K. with you, I'd like to observe your
surgery this morning. Dr. Fuller said it was all right with
him if you didn't mind." The drug was beginning to work
already. Dan could feel his eyelids growing heavy. "Well,
Janet Combs, senior student nurse; do you know they are
going to operate on me in a very private and intimate area of
my body?" She smiled. "Yes, but if I'm to be a good nurse I
have to learn about such things."

He attempted to return her smile as he tried to verbalize an
impish response. He wasn't sure he got all the words out but
perhaps he did because he thought he saw her blush just
before blackness prevailed. "Well, you show me yours and
I'll show you mine…….."

A nurse arrived with a little cup of medications. Swallowing
them, he was thinking 'Wonder where little Miss Nurse
Trainee is today? Maybe she'll come by before I'm released.
I'd like to know what she thought as she watched me being

sliced and quartered.' Thoughts of the prostate's vital functions in all things carnal revived another memory, and precipitated a genuine smile. The first twelve to fifteen catapult shots sending his jet fighter into the air at 200 miles per hour had produced immediate tumescence. Of course, it was the excitement and adrenaline of those first, real fly or die, solo launches at sea that did the trick. Sexual fantasy had nothing to do with it. Taxiing onto a catapult and waiting for the kick in the ass that will send you and 60,000 pounds of aerodynamic metal off the end of a flight deck at a few knots over stall speed leaves no time for thoughts of seduction or *T & A.*[1] And of course, so much is happening right after launch that the swelling subsides immediately. But oh! What a feeling! Those first few cat shots! To be 25 again!...............

Supine and resting, his mind wandered until the pain pills kicked sand in his eyes. Then labored sleep and jumbled, confused dreams invaded his drugged mind. *Someone was talking to a person half-hidden in shadows. The facial features favored those of Les Lincoln but the body outline, the pear-shaped belly, was closer to a Woody Miller. For a moment he couldn't identify the voice talking with the apparition. Then recognition came through the hazy dream. It was <u>his</u> voice verbalizing, telling a war story. "Well, I sure didn't have a hard-on for my first mission over 'Nam. First of all, it was the Skipper's flight but I was launched instead......" He was rudely interrupted by another speaker – who was it? The muted voice spoke again and now he recognized the Southern accent of his old roommate, Pete Driscoll. He was saying, "Where do you go to puke?" But it couldn't be Pete. He died three years ago with cancer.'*

"Mr. Brown, you're talking in your sleep. I couldn't make out the words but it sounded serious, like maybe a nightmare. Anyway, it's time for a round of exercise and walking." He opened his eyes to find the floor nurse hovering over him. She continued, "Let's get you out of bed and out into the hall."

---

[1] Colloquial-*speak* for women's breasts and rears. Very famous in a Broadway musical, *Chorus Line.*

Dr. Jason Fuller reviewed the patient's history. *Chronic prostatitis in excess of twenty-five years; had undergone a previous biopsy approximately twenty years earlier when a hardened prostate found by digital examination was mistakenly thought to be cancerous.* Unsmiling, the urologist re-read the pathology report. Moments later, he donned a white lab coat and caught the eye of his nurse. "I'll be at the hospital making rounds. I'll finish up in Mr. Brown's room around three p.m."

The new patient had been referred to him for excessive urination urges, a severe reaction to pain medication following extensive sinus and throat surgery two weeks earlier. Mr. Brown's lengthy bout with repeated prostatitis over many years had undoubtedly exacerbated the urinary dysfunction. Just forty-eight hours ago the urologist had performed a trans-urethral resection of the prostate to relieve urethra distress. The removed tissue had been sent as a matter of routine to the pathologist for diagnostic examination. Dr. Fuller walked briskly from his office in the Doctor's Building to the hospital next door. How many times had he walked this way with bad news for his patients? For patient Brown, the news was not good but it could be much worse.

The physician found his patient connected to a tri-wheeled I.V. cart, walking gingerly, slowly, in the east corridor near his room. The urologist seemed pleased. "I'm glad to see you exercising. That's good because we're going to release you from the hospital this afternoon. As expected, you're recovering right on schedule for the trans-urethral resection procedure. I'll discuss your medicine and what to expect over the next few days in a moment. First, let me remove your catheter and then I want to review the pathology report with you."

Dan eased onto his bed in a sitting position as Dr. Fuller cut the balloon valve that let the catheter fall free from the intimate connection with his body. A nurse removed the hose apparatus along with the nearly full urine pouch. Dan sensed the ugly red fluid in the bag somehow presaged ominous news.

"Mr. Brown, I have bad news followed by not-so-bad news. The pathology report is positive for cancerous chips. That's the bad news in a nutshell. The better news is that we've found the disease in its earliest stages. I don't think it could have been detected any earlier, especially because your PSA is a low *point* 25. Your case is a bit unusual since we don't usually see cancer with a PSA under 3.0. Since we know the problem, we can monitor it, check it, keep tabs on it. I would think now that you know you have cancer, you'll make every appointment I schedule for you so that we can take corrective steps if there's any increase in PSA or any other indication of more diseased chips. I think you have every chance in the world of dying from something else in the far off future, rather than prostate cancer. And new scientific discoveries are coming every day. The other part of good news is, as we've discussed before, your sexual performance should not be affected, or if so, to a minimal degree."[1]

Dan had known there was a real and distinct possibility the biopsy finding would be positive. Still, he had hoped for a repeat of the negative report issued nearly twenty years before. Now, he simply nodded and asked, "May I see the sheet and read it for myself?"

"Certainly."

He found the accursed line at the bottom of the page. '*Adenocarcinoma,*' possibly, probably the most feared word in modern English language. "Cancer versus Brown, round 2. And the winner is… cancer. So this time I have it. Thank goodness for the twenty intervening years. O.K., doctor. You schedule the appointments and I'll be there."

Soon Becky eased the door open, peeked in and entered. "What did the doctor say about the biopsy?"

---

[1] Again, advancements made in treating prostate surgery during the nearly twenty years between the author's first and second biopsies are nothing short of incredible. In 1979, any proven diagnosis of prostate cancer was cause for immediate radical surgery. In this new millennium, the dread factor associated with prostate cancer is minimal when detected early

Dan was ready for her question. "Well, he didn't put it exactly like this but here's my take on what he said. *I don't have the Big C but I do have Little C."* He reiterated Dr. Fuller's positive outlook *re* the determination that cancer cells had dwelt deep within his body but very possibly were not of immediate or future concern.

Just inside the automatic doors the orderly waited with the patient in a wheel chair while Becky went to reclaim the van. The pain medicine was wearing off. He'd want a new batch of magic juice when they got home but for now he could think clearer. Two diverse incidents – New Year's Eve '60 and his first twenty-five cat shots - from the past had surfaced in his afternoon 'reflecting'. Two experiences that had faded into the shadows of his mind over the years but like spring flowers had blossomed in the last few hours. The GMC van pulled up. Inside, he pulled on the seat belt and said, "I think I got two more stories to liven up *Eat Pizza Naked,* the 'saga of my life'."
Becky: "Where did you find more stories?"
Dan: "Thinking and dreaming this morning. They're good ones."
Becky smiled at her pajama-clad passenger, "If you keep coming up with more stuff to put in that book, you may wind up with another *War and Peace!*"

Note: As of publication date, the author has been cancer free for six years.

*****

Chapter 61

THE WEDDING

October 29, 2000
Age: 65

The bride was beautiful. Radiant, her smile exuding the joy
of the moment, she exited the bride's dressing room while
the soloist belted the last stanza of John Lennon's *Grow Old
With Me*. Dan had seen her in the dress a month earlier –
photographs, expensive and lots of them are a part of the
ritual - but this was the real thing. Staring at her, so proud
of her, he wondered if he had that same shit-eating grin on
his face that seemed to inflict and manifest itself in the
darndest situations. Thankfully, the Wedding Hostess broke
the spell and said to him matter-of-factly, "This is the last
opportunity you'll have to call your daughter 'Miss Brown',
if you're so inclined."
Dan could not have taken his eyes off his daughter if he
tried. Was this terrific young woman really his little girl all
grown up? Yes, the female before him was Mary Elizabeth
Brown, but she wasn't 'little kid' any longer. He was still her
dad but their relationship was about to undergo imminent
and permanent change. No time for pondering such
thoughts, time was of the essence. The organist began the
wedding march. For himself, a simple thought: 'O.K., let's
get on with it.' To his daughter, he posed the timeless
question that fathers have uttered for ages, "Ready to go?"
Then he straightened, and asked more formally "Miss
Brown, may I escort you down the aisle? I believe we have
a young man waiting."
Hand-in-arm they paused as the double doors opened into
the sanctuary. The narrow inlaid stone aisle yawned
invitingly. The hostess tapped him on the shoulder and they
were on their way. He checked to insure they were in
military step, noticed with satisfaction that the church was
nearly filled on both sides. Then he managed a quick glance
at the young woman on his arm. Memories flushed upon
him as he moved robot-like in joint step with his beaming,
beautiful partner down the long center aisle.

*The little girl was nearly three years old, the predictable apple of his
eye, the core of his affection. Her vocabulary was increasing
exponentially each day. He didn't realize how much his own speech
and mannerisms were influencing hers. Until one
afternoon.........Becky called from the kitchen and asked him to
check the mail. He lowered the paper he had been reading, stood,
and walked barefooted to the front door, his little feminine shadow
and her bouncy puppy tagging along. Holding the door open, he
reached for the letters and pamphlets in the brass box. Seizing the
opportunity, the young dog dashed outside, off and running across
the front lawn. Shoeless, the father stepped gingerly into the yard to
watch the direction the animal would take. Thankfully, no
automobiles were in the street and he saw the little furry creature
scurry into the Harper's yard, disappearing beneath the tall hedge.
He turned back to retrieve his shoes and was met by a determined,
scowling little girl. "Goddamned dog runned away, didn't he,
Dad?"*

*Two large, green- striped watermelons lay in the grass near the
patio's edge. The two of them, father and daughter, were on their
stomachs gliding as silently as possible, through the dense forest
portrayed by potted plants, flowers, bushes, and patio furniture.
The man carried small binoculars around his neck. They rose just
enough to sight-in their objectives. The eight-year-old girl
whispered, "Has anyone seen us yet?" He hushed her with his
finger across his lips and whispered even more softly in her left ear.
"I don't think so. Mom and Nanny are in the swing and
Granddaddy is still reading his paper. Careful now, quiet, we don't
want them to catch us." Like infantrymen moving stealthily
through an enemy field, the two propelled themselves forward using
their elbows for leverage, pushing with toeholds in the soft mulch.
Finally, they were within five feet of the melons. She watched for
his sign, he nodded his head. They suddenly jumped up in full view
of the three adults; each picked up a melon and ran to the edge of the
yard. The father dropped his onto the ground, the rind breaking
wide open, displaying the red, ripe heart of the fruit. The little girl
followed suit. He quickly grabbed a handful of heart meat and
showed her how to scoop out the center delicacy. Then they ran
around the side of the house, laughing at the fun of it all. The
knowing grandparents and Becky delighted in their unorthodox*

recreation. With juice dripping from the corners of his mouth, the dad was explaining, "And that's what we did to Mr. Roberts' watermelon fields when I visited my cousin Darrell in the summers. I'm sorry you will never get to taste a stolen watermelon. It's so much sweeter when taken straight from the field. Let's go back and see if Granddaddy wants some of that murdered fruit."

The phone rang shortly after midnight. Dan and Becky had been asleep since just after eleven.
"Mr. Brown?" The voice on the other end inquired.
"Yes." Sleepily, Dan rose up on an elbow.
"This is the Jacksonville Sheriff's Department. Do you have a daughter Mary Elizabeth driving a Honda Accord?"
Grogginess disappeared. His heart felt heavy in his chest but he was wide-awake in a moment. Was his daughter dead or dying? He managed to answer, "Yes" before turning to find a wide-eyed Becky sitting up in bed staring at him expectantly.
The voice went on. "Please come to the Lakewood area, corner of San Marco Boulevard and Largo Place. Her group has been drinking. She is all right but we need her parents to come down and get the car."
Within minutes, Dan and Becky were dressed and driving towards town. Becky drove and offered no comment. But Dan was angry. The "perfect" kid had lied to him, she had been drinking. The trust relationship was gone. Fifteen minutes later, the parents arrived at the given address. Dan could see several boys and girls standing around Beth's Honda as well as the Toyota of a friend. In front of the two vehicles was a police car. Dan could see one kid in the back seat lockup of the black and white cruiser. His heart became even heavier when he saw the lone juvenile in the car was Beth. He was astonished when she slid across the seat, opened the door and ran to her mother without apparent opposition by the attending officer.
The policeman exited the front seat and strode toward the Browns. He explained that in situations like this, minors had to be separated from adults. Beth was the only one in the crowd under eighteen so he had kept her in the car and played the radio on her favorite station. "She wasn't drinking, Mr. Brown, but three of the boys were. The Sheriff's Department has a rule that after an incident like this, young people cannot drive their cars home. We always call the parents to come for it." Dan felt imagined devils of deceit and

deception fly off his shoulders as Becky and Beth hugged, tears streaming down happy, lovely faces. There they were again – those two-faced feelings of ambivalence: happy that his wonderful daughter had not failed him; embarrassed that he had doubted her. On the way home, he would lecture on the improprieties of underage guys and beer but he would remember he had been young once, too.

She found Mr. Wonderful, *Doug Darlin',* at Florida State. Dan had liked the kid from the moment Beth introduced them. The two of them seemed to be so compat......... They had arrived at the altar. A tall, good-looking young man, smiling ear-to-ear, eagerly stepped forward. The minister asked the scripted question, "And who gives this young woman in matrimony?"

The proud father recited the traditional response, "Her mother and I." He gave her hand to Doug and returned to sit beside Becky. His part was over but for just a moment he remembered an evening almost twenty-nine years ago when he was the fellow wearing the happy smile that Doug Hubrich presently wore. Becky turned her eyes away from the ceremony for a second, looked directly at her husband and silently mouthed, "Penny for your thoughts." He took a pen from the church pew and scribbled on the wedding program, *Jimmy Doolittle,* and slipped it into her fingers. Becky read the two words, then stared at him blankly, her brow wrinkling, her frowning countenance clearly confused and questioning. Dan penned again. *His quote about leaving the world a better place.[1] Look at those kids. We've done it.* He glanced toward the altar and then nodded as if agreeing with and confirming for himself the Doolittle quotation.
Becky read the words, the frown rapidly disappearing into a happy, widened smile. She tenderly, lovingly squeezed his hand. Her eyes softened and he could see a tear trying to form but she dabbed her eyes quickly. Soon the ceremony was completed. Dan and Becky Brown's *little kid* was now Mrs. Douglas Hubrich.

---

[1] *We were put on this earth for one purpose, and that is to make it a better place.* General James H. Doolittle, USAF

To the host's minds, the reception was slightly short of fantastic. Three hundred of the Brown's and Hubrich's closest friends attended the grand occasion at the Brown home atop 10th Street Mountain. A perfect, cloudless, 70 degree evening awaited them. The last Saturday of October ended daylight savings time and provided an extra hour of gaiety. An excellent combo sang and played all the bride's favorite songs. The many young folks dancing the night away put the twenty by thirty foot dance floor, erected just for the evening, to good use. Tasty and plentiful food and drink was enjoyed and praised by one and all; large, gorgeous cut flower arrangements adorned every table. Pots of colorful mums, some built into six-foot mountains around tiers of unseen straw bales, along with blue and red salvia and zillions of multihued pansies greeted the guests at every turn. A ten to twelve foot Confederate Rose bush laden with pink and white *Tifton* blooms dominated one corner of the fenced backyard. Ablaze in vivid glory, the lighted grounds might have challenged a millionaire's sculptured garden.

All too soon the cake was cut and newly weds Mr. and Mrs. Hubrich were on their way to Saint Maarten.

*****

Chapter 62

THE THIRD TIME AROUND

November, 2000
Age: 65

I can't put my hands on the reference but several
years ago I read in the Grit Magazine newspaper that the average
person, in a lifetime, will walk a distance equivalent to three times
around the earth's equator. My insurance agent tells me the
industry's current average life span for a man is 79 years. Three
times around, that's an orbit every 26.4 years. Realistically, a
human isn't walking all that far the first 4 years nor, let's say, the
last 9 years. That leaves a nice round 66 actively walking years to
divide by 3. So let's divvy up the revolutions as the first between
birth and 26 years (4 + 22), the second circle of Mother Earth
between 26 and 48 years (22), the last time around slower and
longer, ages 48-79 (22 + 9). In this final chapter, Dan Brown is
well into the third time around.

Physical examination time again. The Navy planted the
seed for a full-blown physical on or around birthdays. This
was standard military procedure that he still tried to follow
nearly thirty years later. The wedding had delayed the
examination on or around September 28th, but last week had
seen him reporting for duty at the medical complex. Today,
he was back to review results of blood and urine tests with
the doctor. His physician of three years, Dr. Turner, seemed
pleased with the data he was seeing on the printed sheet.
Oh, the doctor always wanted that last twenty pounds (or
more) taken off, but Dan figured it was too late to change his
ways. Cheese Danish maybe twice a month; one, only one,
quarter-pounder with cheese a month; heavy desserts only
on special occasions, were rules he already lived with.
Decree set down and religiously checked by the graduate
school dietitian in the family. Yes, the cute little kid had
grown up to become a nutrition specialist. Her father found
it oddly curious that Beth's private school and college
education that cost a small fortune had recently culminated
with lectures on how he should eat healthy. She had no

patience, no sense of humor at all when it came to his waistline. For fun, he once quoted for her a doctor's comment out an old *Ladies Home Journal*: *'If you do everything you should do, and do not do anything you should not do, you will, according to the best available statistics, live exactly eighteen hours longer than you would have otherwise'*.[1] She didn't think it funny at all. He thought it hysterical but inwardly knew, 'I can't really gripe. Hell, she's just like me. Gets an idea and runs with it all the way. She's a pain about eating right, but damn, she is right, and on top of that, she's beautiful. Besides that, she's neat *people*. Doug Darlin' will think he's died and gone to heaven with an angel for a wife – well, that is, as long as he eats right!'

Arriving back home on Ayers Drive, he pulled into the driveway of an upper-middle class home. Built in the 60's, the moderately sized brick home wasn't prestigious but certainly respectable in an older, desirable neighborhood. Dan was especially fond of the curved red brick walkway ambling downhill from the street, inviting one and all to the front door. In fact, Dan loved almost everything about their home. Becky had worked wonders with the landscaping, especially with the side and back yards. A new fishpond added a melodic peace to the area as water cascaded dutifully down seven-drop levels from the bog pond to the main waterfall. 'Oh, yes, I'm supposed to call it *a water garden*. Well, heck, it does have fish in it.'

He parked the van and went into the house through the garage. Becky was not home, of course. She would be at school, doing her thing as media specialist or fiddling with the library's computer system that seemed to always need tweaking. The downstairs apartment was quiet too, as his mother-in-law was out for the afternoon. She'd reminded him as he left that morning she had a noon Garden Club luncheon and an afternoon meeting. She'd also reminded him she had proofread some more of his manuscript. Again, she asked him to change the title. "My friends just won't like a book on their coffee table that says, *Eating Pizza Naked.*" Relenting, he had promised to find one a little less provocative.

---

[1] *Ladies Home Journal*, Dr. Logan Clendening, March, 1944

A radio in the study was on and playing elevator music. He switched the *select* indicator from RADIO to CD and pushed the corresponding button. An old Billy Joel disc began playing *Piano Man*. Picking up the morning paper, he· moved out to the screened porch. Pale yellow pillows decorated in muted hues of various natural colors on wicker furniture greeted him as he surveyed their small kingdom: a perfectly manicured lawn with all Becky's plants and flowers and shrubs neatly pruned and recently watered. As he looked and appreciated her efforts once again, his eyes were greeted by numberless hues of green on leaves and branches belonging to full and healthy plants. Some were still flowering. The giant blooms on the perennial Hibiscus, so different from the Florida variety, were especially beautiful. Fall was here but warm days persisted.

As *Piano Man* ended and *Captain Jack* began, he about-faced and went into the kitchen to fix a solitary lunch, deciding upon iced tea and a sandwich. Returning to his favorite chair on the porch, he sipped the refreshing amber liquid and nibbled on the hot pita sandwich. Tasty, it reminded him of days long ago in South Florida. 'Ham and cheese, pan toasted, then add crushed potato chips between the meat and cheddar. An old Cuban trick passed on to me years ago in Key West. Of course, the cook there used real Cuban bread, I have to use an Arabic Frisbee. That makes it a little different but still definitely delicious.' He would have liked more chips but remembered the high caloric and sodium content he was supposed to avoid, and resolutely clipped the bag tight.

Lunch over, he moved to the den and perused the local paper for articles of interest. *BJ* was crooning the final CD selection, *Always a Woman*. Finally, wearying of day-old news, he relaxed and let his body dig deep into the pillows of the comfortable sofa. He lay there, mulling again the physical examination just completed. As thoughts do, one triggered another until he was contemplating his immortality. 'Well, birthdays are always a good time to reflect on one's life,' he decided, 'particularly a MEDICARE birthday'. Gosh, I remember doing this at the Club when I turned sixty and got the yen to write a book. The introspective train of thought he was riding took him deeper into his psyche. 'Where was he at sixty-five as opposed to five years ago?' A numbing thought caught him off guard when he realized he was ten years older than his dad had been when Julian Brown had died of massive heart attack. Surely - with a pulse of 80, blood pressure of 125/78, cholesterol less than 200, he wasn't in bad shape. Well, maybe the *cardura* and *ziac* helped hold the blood pressure down and he would like to fit into a size 40 instead of 42's being a bit tight. Walking two miles a day now that the sizzling summer was ending would help that goal. Anyway, he was still good enough behind closed doors to keep Mrs. Becky Brown off the streets! What was that old saying, "Not as good as I once was but as good once as I ever was" or something like that? Well, he was holding his own in that department, thank goodness. And he could damn sure pee a lot better after the prostate trans-section a year ago that turned up cancerous. A new PSA of point 7 was up a little but still well below worry level. That thought reminded him that he did have cancer down there but the urologist had told him he would probably die of some other cause. On the minus side, he was blind in his right eye from a bout with high blood pressure some years back. The left ear was mostly deaf while the right ear was still about fifty-percent effective. Siding up to those damn jet engines for twenty-one years had dealt his auditory senses quite a blow. He knew hearing aids were in his future. Still taking stock of the wear and tear on the body issued him many moons ago, he listed 'Sleep apnea' as another ailment but the effects were essentially diminished by use of *c-pap,* the little black machine that pumped air into his mouth cavity so that he could breathe normally while sleeping. The little nose pillows were not a bother and he definitely slept better. The worse thing for *c-pap* users was the necessity of negotiating their love life before turning out the lights – the headgear was definitely a put off. Finally came his latest diagnosis, *'idiopathic-hypersomnia'.* A distant cousin of *narcolepsy,* this sleep disorder of unknown origin caused random daytime drowsiness. He enjoyed telling his friends that the best doctors in Birmingham had declared him "legally lazy" but that problem, too, wasn't a real bother as oral medication helped alleviate daytime sleepiness. He could continue to drive automobiles safely.

So five entries on the minus side of health but he knew the credits far outnumbered the debits. His left eye was twenty-twenty, his hearing really hadn't dissipated much in the last several years, he might put off hearing aids indefinitely. It wasn't a problem as long he stayed out of crowds. Cancer? He never thought of it outside the doctor visits. And the sleep apnea, plus the *'idio'* whatever it is, was under control. He felt good and decided he was satisfied with his physical health, even content, as he entered *Medicare* rolls. He was sure that a man of the cloth, any denomination, would say that he was *blessed*. And Dan would not disagree. Dan Brown was an American. A Southerner. A Georgia boy by birth, a Floridian at heart, a cheerful Alabamian by default. A husband. A father. Younger, a Navy pilot. Combat experience. Air medals. Older, a vice president and management executive in small business. He was married to an angel who, for some strange reason, apparently thought he had proved to be a decent catch. He was the father of a happy, well-adjusted daughter now taking on the world and married to "Mr. Wonderful". Materially, there was adequate retirement income and they would be O.K. even when Becky retired which was still sometime in the future. The disparity in their ages meant she'd have to work a few more years before giving up her job, but she loved the library, so, no conflicts there. Dan remembered a paragraph from a Christmas letter he had sent along with cards two or three years earlier. "I have found the secret of life: military retirement plus social security, *and* a ten-year younger working wife." Happy with his own original humor, he found all this thinking was tiring and let his eyes zero in on the ceiling fan. He watched the never-ending circular voyage to nowhere for only a few minutes before his eyelids closed. Sleep came quickly.

Eighteen months after their wedding, Dan and Becky Brown found themselves living a different lifestyle, abroad, compliments U.S. Navy. Dan had been assigned to Naples, Italy, as the T-39 pilot for Admiral Rance Smith, Commander, Fleet Air Mediterranean. Their seven-room apartment in a high-rise condominium a few miles north of Naples overlooked the blue-green and ever-changing Tyrennian Sea. An eastward view from their tenth floor balcony was picture perfect in the mornings topped only by stunning sunsets in the evening.

One Saturday morning, he jogged along the sandy shoreline. Passing abeam Tower Five he looked up to their rooms and saw Becky standing and watching, her elbows resting on the safety rails bordering the open porch. She waved as he passed. The thought hit him like a rock. 'She's not just pretty, she's beautiful and she loves you, Brown. Just you. Just me.' He returned the greeting and continued his run southward with the open water on his right. The Island of Ischia was visible to the southeast. As he ran, countless memories flooded his mind. It occurred to him that they had met two years ago this month. She had ended his solitary self-deprecating dates with himself while lounging in front of a crackling fire. He readily acknowledged his indebtedness to fate (and his mother's introduction) for a second opportunity at happiness. He had gotten lucky again. Suddenly he stopped, looked back to see if Becky was still outside and visible. She was, she waved again. As he looked at his attractive wife leaning casually against the iron railing of the balcony, he felt it was time to be rid of the heavy anvil of guilt he had carried for so long. He said aloud to the warm morning, to the endless grains of sand on the beach, to the open sky, "I am the luckiest person alive. I'm the happiest guy I know. Eleanor, please forgive me. I'm sure the divorce was primarily my fault. I hope you're as happy in your second life as I."

For a moment he almost awoke, but turned on a side and soon entered dreamland again.

He was a young boy of seven or eight. His dad had purchased a used bicycle for $5.00 and Danny was teaching himself to ride. He would push it up the sloped hill next to the side of the house and then try to ride it on the way down to the back yard. His grandfather was splitting firewood near the back door steps. The elder Mr. Brown yelled encouragement to his grandson as Danny pushed the bike up the hill for still another try. Once more, he pushed off and jumped on the seat. This time he was on for good! He was riding the bike! He balanced the cycle for the length of the house and suddenly realized he didn't know how to stop. As the *rider and vehicle neared the fence surrounding the chicken coop, Danny forced himself to jump off the bike and tumble away to the side. Exhilarated at having ridden the bicycle down the hill, he was still disappointed and surprised that he had failed to find the brakes in time to stop. He heard the bike crash into the fence and abruptly, he came to a sudden stop against something round and hard. For a moment he was disoriented but then realized he was lying against his grandfather's splitter log. His head was thrown back, his neck taunt and stretched. He was looking up into the eyes of his grandfather who was poised with the ax over his shoulder ready to swing the blade downward. Terrified, Danny yelled and thought for an instant that his grandfather might not be able to stop in time. Still frozen in fear and shock, the boy finally saw him relax and drop the ax to his side. Mr. Brown said nothing but slowly shook his head in wonder at what might have been, then walked away to salvage the bicycle. Breathing normally again, the flustered boy lay in position for several minutes looking at the scenes around him. He realized that for just a second he had come close to never seeing these images again.*

  Waking, he stood and stretched and walked to the sliding glass door. Dense woods beyond the perimeter fencing enhanced the solitude of the afternoon. The mountains Becky loved which were so visible in winter were just peaking through fall foliage. Pensively, he recalled his dreams. The memories were vivid and real, no shadows or weird situations like so many dreams. Undoubtedly the Italian beach scene was precipitated by his 65th birthday recount of life's debits/credits pondered so vigorously before napping. He could only wonder at the sequence of the two dreams. Evidently making an inward peace with Eleanor after several years, and his first brush with death were somehow imbedded together in his sub-conscious. This introspective state of thinking wandered haphazardly to memories of the movie, *It's a Wonderful Life*. Mental images of Jimmy Stewart as the character George Bailey began to take shape. The storyline was a Christmas TV favorite of many, featuring a young man coming to grips with the knowledge that his presence had made a giant positive difference to the town of Bedford Falls. Dan Brown's serious mood entered the next logical progression.

He remembered the Doolittle quote used just a week or so ago about our purpose in life is to make the world a little better place during our allotted time. Yes, they, he and Becky, had raised a wonderful young woman who picked a heckava guy to fall in love with. But had he, Dan Brown, made a difference in his sixty-five days in the sun? Of course, his life had directly impacted, for better or worse, the lives of Becky and Beth and now Mrs. Knight. He imagined they would give him a passing grade with kudos. But had his life influenced, in a positive manner, other people or the world around him? He spoke to the inanimate objects on the porch, "Dammit, always questions, never answers." What was that he had read about *honor* versus *honors*? 'Honor' was to be pursued, 'honors' per se were not. 'Have I met that simple criterion? The old cliché, *Do the right thing*. Did I do the right thing in difficult decisions?' He wished he could confess only to the pursuit of honesty, integrity, character. He thought of his lifelong idol, a dying Lou Gehrig making the inspirational *Luckiest man on the face of the earth* speech at Yankee Stadium. 'You were a bona-fide hero, Lou, and I'm just an ex-Navy pilot, an ordinary guy, but I think I know exactly what you meant, how you felt.' His ego wanted to shout, 'Yes! You have made a difference! Think of the friends and contemporaries, enlisted sailors and former employees whom you have helped. You were there for them. You're not overly selfish and you try to tithe. You give time to the elderly through a volunteer program. You coach reading for the disadvantaged at a local grammar school. You………'

He could hear his alter ego yelling, 'But you could have done so much more!'

A disturbing thought flashed into his thinking. 'Is this how people wind up on the couch listening to some shrink utter psychobabble? Left side of brain at war with right side brain? Conscience arguing with reason? One part of you wanting to do the right thing at odds with human primal urges to be base and selfish?'

His mind was stuck on one track as though it wore blinders. 'Had he contributed anything of consequence to the world?' He answered himself within his thoughts. 'Truthfully? I guess not. Well, when I was a kid I always wanted to come up with a great line, a saying that would live on forever, like *I have just begun to fight. The buck stops here,* or *Pilots who hoot with owls by night should not fly with eagles by day, There is no free lunch*, stuff like that. About as close as I came is the *Holding Hands Theory.* Over the years, I've told anyone who would listen my *Holding Hands* theory. The theory has stood the test of my lifetime as far as I'm concerned and I know the premise to be one of the real truths of life. In a nutshell, *everyone always wants more and never expects less than they had.* When you first hold a girl's hand, you don't ever expect not to and you want more next time. When you kiss her, you don't ever expect not to and you want more the next time you see her. When you get a little feel, you don't ever expect not to and want more on the next date. When you get a lotta feel, you don't ever expect not to and you really want more than feel. When you go all the way, you don't ever expect not to and you'll want it more often. Simply stated, that's the *Holding Hands Theory.* I tell it as an oversexed teenage parable but it's applicable to everything, every situation in life. No one wants to step *down* the ladder of success.

'I didn't invent the idea of always wanting a little more and never wanting to go backward, but as far as I know, my title is original and I've never heard a better, more descriptive one. The *Holding Hands Theory* really should be made famous. Brown, you're on a roll. Go for it, where to next?' He walked to the left side of the porch and looked down again at the little fishpond, 'But maybe I do have a new saying. I've been trying out a new line on some friends and getting pretty good reactions. When I think of 9-1-1, *Roe vs. Wade*, and things like senators and representatives in Congress voting themselves stratospheric pay raises and retirement benefits, not to mention traffic tie-ups and computer crashes, I feel like *There are some things about getting old that ain't bad.'*

He then realized that he had been thinking and answering himself. 'Maybe talking to and with yourself is one of the clues that send you to the casting couch for nuthouse auditions. Well, I've been doing it all my life. I don't think that makes me crazy – maybe a little different. Hey, Tevye sure talked to himself in *Fiddler* and folks loved it. So, up yours, you finks who think I'm a little weird. To continue, O.K. your *Hands* and *Getting old* theories aren't quite up to the level of *Three score and seven years ago* but Brown, the point is don't beat yourself up over not being perfect. At the same time don't break your arm patting yourself on the back because you passed out a little 'tea and sympathy', i.e., *Jacksons and Grants*[1] and compassion, along the way.'

He watched a squirrel jump, tree to tree. Birds flittered away. 'For a moment, forget the debits, look at your personal credit ledger. Wonderful wife. Perfect daughter. Great guy for a son-in-law. Good friends here, there and everywhere. Minor physical problems, relatively little indebtedness.' Now he spoke aloud to the porch, the birds, and the squirrels. "You're a lucky son-of-a-bitch. Just accept it."

A lone blue jay flew into one of the pine trees beyond the back fence. "Hello Mr. Bird." Dan spoke to the bird as though it could hear and understand. Frowning now, he continued dissecting his life and life in general. "Damn!" he said aloud. Then thinking 'How in the world would an average person like me ever know to what degree, or if at all, he or she had impacted the little part of their world known to them? I don't have a Hollywood script. I'm not Jimmy Stewart playing George Bailey in a happy ending movie. I have questions, when do I get answers?' The dialogue inside his mind continued. 'Hell, I don't even have all the questions. Now they tell us that we can see stars that exploded, I think *nova* is the word they use, millions of years ago. Because they are so far away, it has taken eons for the light made by a big blast to get close enough for the Hubbell to see it. To cap off scientific discoveries, we are now cloning living animals. They're even talking of cloning a mammoth by using DNA preserved by the ice age. Man-oh-man, if that doesn't complicate the meaning of life, what does? And where in the world does hitting that bird in a tree, looking down the barrel of a .38 in Daytona, and 415 carrier landings fit into all this?'

---

[1] Twenties and Fifties

He was exasperated with himself for again going down that old road that has no end, no answers. He was back where he started. Consternation deep within colored the tone of his meditation. Relaxing into the nearest faux wicker chair, he admitted to himself, 'I know the real problem. I'm wrestling with myself over a conclusion for my foray into the world of written literature. The stand-alone stories are fine, I think, I hope, but several chapters dealing with life have been about my wondering about the *why* of things. I've boxed myself into a corner, and right or wrong, I've got to put into words my take on the meaning of life. I have to tell the world – at least my little world of folks that will read my manuscript – what I think about life, its meaning, its consequences. Well, *Turkey*, how are you going to get out of this one? That 99% complete manuscript has been in the drawer long enough, don't you think?' He threw his hands up in the air, 'I might as well be trying to figure out who God is.' His next thoughts were even more berating and sarcastic. 'Wait a minute. Forget all that happy horseshit and mammoth manure. Great minds of the ages have searched each and every millennium for the meaning of life. Do you think you're going to find it on a sunny afternoon in Alabama? Are you going to sit under a fig tree to be *enlightened* like Buddha? There's your tree just sixty feet away in the corner of the yard. Perhaps you'd rather *hear voices* in a cave like Mohammed? DeSoto Caverns are only fifty miles southwest. Maybe you'd prefer a voice out of the sky sending you to Cheaha Mountain to confer with Moses and Elijah?'

His serious contemplation continued. 'Is there another slant, a different vein I can approach this thing from? All right. So I've admitted again I can't untangle the meaning of life, but what if, just what if, I was asked for my thoughts on the subject. What road would I take, where would I go, what would I say if David Letterman asked me such a question? I can just see the famous host saying, "Now, Mr. Brown, you're the star of our ordinary people segment. It's your fifteen minutes of fame. Here's your subject and it's a toughie. Tell us what you think about the meaning of life." Dan rested a shoe on a bench beneath the picnic table as he pictured himself stammering and making a fool of himself

on late night TV for the entire world to see. 'Not a pretty
sight', as he forced the annoying images from his mind.
He was making no headway in a fruitless quest and
remained agitated with his failure to do so. Yet it seemed
like his mind was nibbling at something important. 'Why
can't I come up with an answer to satisfy yours truly –me,
myself, and I - about life's meaning?' Then an unanticipated
revelation, much like the one that challenged him to write a
book, quickened his thoughts. 'You know, maybe that – me,
myself, and I - *is* the key .....not to look for answers that
pleases everyone, not for answers to meet the needs of the
world, not for answers that would make *Mensa International*
happy, but approach the question on a much smaller scale.
Turn the premise around, Dan. Instead of 'What is the
meaning of life?' Make it, 'What does life mean to me?'
"All right, Mr. Letterman, I'm ready to begin my
dissertation on life."
A realization that he might be on the right track energized
him to stand and pace to and fro across the porch. Not only
was he on the verge of grasping an ending for his book, but
perhaps he was going to make peace with his inner self
about being here and alive for his many *in absentia* friends.
And maybe, just maybe, he would leave readers liking his
book and writing style. Now his thoughts were racing.
'Danny Boy, you're on to something. Slow down and think
of a good starting point that will set the parameters for what
life means to you.'
He stopped pacing and assumed an even more serious
demeanor. 'How to begin?' He needed to talk to someone.
With that thought, another new idea was born. Why not
talk to himself? No, not just reasoning with himself, or
verbalizing occasional expletives to birds and trees. A real,
formal conversation was the answer. Dan Brown chatting
with and interviewing Dan Brown. David Letterman was
not available, so he would host a debate with himself after
creating two new personas, each with good and bad qualities
he recognized in his own personality. He became convinced
that two identities arguing with each other, was innovative
and an excellent plan of attack.

Dano was the name selected for a solemn, impatient, almost angry Dan impersonator. A happier, gregarious personification, who at times could be inquisitive and questioning, would be named *Danny*. To help keep the two imagined creations straight in his mind, *Dano* would always stand along the longer side of the picnic table. *Danny's* place when speaking was to be at the end of the table. Dan himself would move back and forth between the two positions at the table as each duplicate identity spoke his respective thoughts. He would try his hardest to be positive or negative, pro or con, as the conversational situation developed and dictated.

Dan moved to a point beside the table, facially assumed a very serious countenance, and the show was on. *Dano,* not bothering to mask an air of superiority in his voice, asks, "So, Mr. *Danny* Brown, you're going to solve life's greatest mystery, at least to your personal satisfaction. Well, what does life mean to you? One hundred words or less – no more."

Dan moved towards the head of the table. His face exploded into a wide grin as he assumed the role of *Danny*. Confidently, he began, "First, I'll expound on what it should not mean. Life should not be a pursuit of free love or casual sex. Life should not be an eternal quest for youth. Life should not be about a pretty face or a perfect body. Life's focus should not be on making a lot of money."

Stepping quickly around the table edge, now tight lipped and tense, *Dano* returned to his original position to interject sternly. "Just answer the question, Mr. Brown. What does life mean to you?"

Back at table end again, this time sitting, Dan almost laughs aloud at the farce of conversing aloud with himself. Composure regained, the compulsory smile re-appeared and *Danny* was back in action. *Danny* attempts to offer a satisfactory answer for his alter-self. "O.K., O.K. Life *to me* is both for _the_ living - and _for_ living. Life means growing up a Georgia country boy. Life means going off to college without a penny in my pocket. Life means flying a ten million dollar airplane at fifteen hundred miles an hour. Life means productive *and* satisfying vocations. Life means a million stars overhead zillions of miles away. Life is a walk on the beach. Life can be a rainbow, a sunrise, or a sunset. Life is all about experiences. Life means sharing. Life is making the most of second chances. Life means friends. Life means children. Life is ...."

Dan goes again to a side position around the table corner, his mouth tightens, and as *Dano,* he interrupts. A furrowed brow telegraphs severe agitation. "Whoa, Mr. Brown. That's a lot of *pie-in-the sky*! Are you telling me that life *for you* is only good stuff? That bad things don't happen to good people? That little kids don't die from horrible diseases? That people aren't starving in third world countries? That Jim Jones didn't really pass out Kool-Aid? It appears that you consider you and yours immune to the rottenness rampant in the world."

Stepping to a neutral position between the two imaginary adversaries, a pensive, almost rueful Dan Brown nods in agreement as he declares a non-verbal time-out. 'First', he thought, 'this is working out well. And it's fun to argue with myself.' For a few more moments he contemplated a response for *Danny* to rebut the logic offered by *Dano*. Very little time passed before he assumed a more cheerful countenance and moved into *Danny's* chair at the end of the table. The more upbeat persona answered his serious protagonist. "You're right. Life is more than Mom's apple pie, Roth IRA's, the Atlanta Braves or the NFL. There are always bad things to deal with. Mass murderers, slaughter on the highways, aircraft accidents, terrorists, earthquakes, volcanoes; if we don't have floods we get drought. Heart attack and cancer are out to get us. Alzheimer's and Parkinson's are waiting for everyone to get older. Depression in all ages and both sexes is now a major health care problem. Corrupt politicians and war, not to mention AIDS, are more evils released from Pandora's Box. And those are just a few of the really bad ones. The ingredients of unhappiness, suffering, and death will have to be reckoned with when someday a great thinker finally offers a solution to the meaning of life. But I don't have to mix those sour apples into my recipe for *what life means to me.* I'm not missing your point, though. Part of living life is knowing that auto accidents do occur, planes do fall out of the sky, disease spreads, the seven deadly sins are always around us. *Shit happens* and we may step in it, but by golly, we can wipe it off! We don't have to walk forever in the stench."

The speaker then shook his head, shrugged his shoulders, and again assumed a neutral stance at the far corner of the table. He considered *Danny's* impromptu response more than sufficient to counter the injection of malevolence into the debate by *Dano*. He decided to let *Danny* continue stating the case from a positive point of view.[1]

Returning to his place at head of the table, *Danny's* countenance was a study in sobriety. Words that followed were bathed in persuasive sincerity. "You could say that life is a game, a game of give and take since it requires adaptation to changes. We must deal with cards that are dealt, whether aces of success or jokers of adversity. Life is making the best out of any crappy situation that comes your way. 'Lemonade out of lemons', someone has said. An old platitude but true: deal with it, get over it, get on with the living of life. The asshole kid with gun in Daytona is an old man now, might even be dead. The divorce, the crash on FORRESTAL, passed over for full commander. Those were important hurdles along the way to overcome, but keep going, Pal. Keep going".

Taking a deeper breath, *Danny* continued. "Back to an optimist's take on life. Very important, and we're nearing the bottom line. Life is a gift. Why a gift? Because gifts do not open themselves, we have to reach out, accept the gifts, and tear off the wrapping paper to see what we have received. I believe with all my heart that Muslims, Orientals, Jews, Blacks, Christians, sports stars to garage mechanics to waitresses, all can accept the gift of life and live it to the fullest. *Homo sapiens* had to learn to walk upright on their own but we were blessed with power to reason. We think, we discern, we aspire. White, black, red, yellow, brown, we all have the intelligence, the desire, the initiative, the drive, and the inquisitive nature to open the

---

[1] Did the narrator realize he tainted the validity of a two-way discussion by siding with *Danny*? In retrospect, yes; at the time, I don't think so.

gift of life. When people don't unwrap the gift, we are vulnerable to false prophets, other charlatans and politicians who speak with forked tongue. Then the focus of lives is misdirected. Ultimately, the gift is rejected and distorted views of bigoted leaders is accepted."

Dan as Danny paused for a sip of tea and began his soliloquy again. "Then in yet a totally different tangent, life is like a train ride, always traveling to destination but stopping occasionally at places we would not have selected. Another parallel, life is like a jungle. Lions and tigers and snakes disguised as death and taxes and the IRS - all out there to get you. A good military analogy is looking at life as a 'foxhole'. First you dig it by making mistakes, then you have to climb out using your own experience, knowledge, and internal fortitude. There's a saying in aviation: 'Good judgment comes from experience and experience comes from bad judgment'. Seeds of truth seem to be sowed therein."

Another swallow of tea – the ice cubes mostly melted - and the discourse continued. "Let's not forget that life is a miracle. All life, not just human life, but of course we *Homo sapiens* are the pinnacle of life's pyramid. Scientists are still adding planets to the known universe but haven't found a single indication of life in the galaxy – not a weed, not even the tiniest amoebae. I'm not sure if man's reasoning ability comes to us through Adam and Eve[1] or Cro-Magnon Man[2] or even 'Lucy'[3]. In either event, we are unique, we are not animals living by instinct, we have been given freedom of choice. Life is indeed a miracle. Evolutionist or Creationist, or combinations thereof, surely there's no argument to that statement."

Standing, Dan realizes that, unconsciously, he has dismissed his imitation personas. Both *Danny* and *Dano* have vanished from the folds of his mind and he is speaking once more as himself. He nods in understanding and proceeds to finish the discourse only in the valleys of his mind. 'It's very

---

[1] Estimated four to five thousand years ago *by creationists*
[2] About twenty-eight thousand years ago *by evolutionists*
[3] Probably three million years ago *by evolutionists*

important to remember life is love: my love for Beck, for Beth, for country, for God, even my love for Meg Ryan, our Sheltie. Lastly, one more way of summing it up: to me, life is a code you have to decipher, one letter, one word at a time. Since we don't know the future, we simply cannot be prepared for what's coming next. Like the man says, *Life is just one damn thing after another*, i.e., one damn surprise after another. Mostly good surprises, I hope, but some won't be joyful. Some will be downright bad, but always a surprise.'

Content, actually more than content, pretty damn well satisfied with his explanation of life's meaning for Dan Brown, he sat again, this time on the white wicker sofa. No, he had not solved any world problems. Many, perhaps even close friends, might laugh at his treatise on life, demean his explanation as feeble or even harebrained. But Dan was happy. He knew he had made a significant breakthrough in both his search for a model to describe, and for words to convey, his feelings on a wonderful thing called *life*. And pretty much, he had done it without theological references or extensive research into orators and philosophers. The little computer chip in his brain that points out shortcomings tried to kidnap that moment to take some of the wind out of his sails. "You've still got some *whys* that are looking for answers." He refused to let his mood degenerate. 'Looks like I've got a little of *Dano* hanging around in the back of my mind. And you know what, *Dano,* you're right again. I've tiptoed around the meaning of life, somewhat successfully I think, but I've yet to give words to my understanding why I am enjoying life on a beautiful mountain when so many close friends and contemporaries are gone. I have tried my damnedest to keep this book secular, devoid of religious overtones. On this point though, I have to break my own rule. If there is any satisfactory answer or reason to the *whys* of life when death is the other option, then a force above and beyond that of man must be conceded. Whether that being is called God or Allah or One or Buddha or whatever, I refuse to debate today for the same reasons already noted in the preface. The point is I believe there is a *Plan.* I hope my readers won't turn off. I ask, I want them to follow me on this. Daniell Brown is still here because I feel that I will affect someone's life, someone who is destined to accomplish some sort of feat for humanity's good. Perhaps I will save a child from drowning, rush an injured woman to a hospital after an accident, any of a thousand scenarios. The act may be simply influencing a person's attitude or thoughts in one way or another. It may be indirectly where I know nothing of the occurrence or influence. But the person whose life is affected or saved will do something-somewhere - sometime that is in *the Plan*. This does not mean that the person I'm theorizing about is to become president or find the cure for cancer or hit 100 homeruns – he or she might do nothing that catches the public's eye but somehow contributes to *the Plan*. That's my take on why I'm still around: happy and healthy. Certainly this take is not scriptural and anyone can argue all they want. In any event, that's what I think, that's what I believe. And by the way Mr. O'Malley, yes, *life is just one damn thing after another.*[1] And, by golly, it's also one <u>*wonderful thing*</u> after another! And sometimes, it's one terrible thing after another. But you know what? I wouldn't have it any other way. Reader, would you? The surprise is the spice, the hot sauce, the salt, the fireworks, that adds zest to the flavor of living.'

This had been a good *Come-to-Jesus* session. Some hard issues were becoming clearer in his mind. A tape recording of the conversation between *Dano* and *Danny* would have been fun to have. He wished he had at least the last ten minutes of his soliloquy for posterity, but key elements he would remember. Pluses and credits in his life far outweighed the unhappiness of debits and maybe he had not hit a homerun on the subject of life's meaning and/or deciphering its *whys*, but doggone it, he had tried and tried hard. A new idea punctuated the accepted success of the moment. He needed 'Closure'. The 1990's had produced this popular by-word for coming to grips with tragedy. *Closure* was the new end-all concept for achieving peace of mind in any crisis. Tom Cruise found it in *Topgun*. Pilot 'Maverick's' radar intercept officer, 'Goose', died in an

---

[1] Frank Ward O'Malley (1875-1950)

ejection sequence gone bad. After agonizing through much of the film, Cruise's character finally pitched the dog tags of his backseat buddy into the ocean and then got on with his life. Dan smiled a satisfactory, knowing smile. Something good was cooking in his thoughts again. Perhaps, in similar fashion, he might find closure to the deaths of so many close friends through the years. He would return to Flinthill Church and find Jimmy Frazier's tombstone. Jimmy was the first of his close acquaintances to die and could proxy for those who followed. Eulogizing a goodbye to Jimmy would symbolize finality for all the others as well. Putting fresh flowers on the grave, perhaps one for each friend might help with the closure process. Maybe he would sit on the marble stone or in the dirt and recall first grade times and then tell Jimmy about Tommy and Woody and Buzz and the others. He'd talk to Jimmy's memory as though he was there in person beside him. Then he would get up, walk away, and never look back 'just like in the movies'. Dan spoke aloud again, "They're gone but for whatever reason, I'm very much alive. I will accept my good fortune and be done with it. On the one hand MEDICARE-age *sux* but on the other, sixty-five and beyond isn't going to be all bad! Everyone has to take that final ride to *Valhalla* someday, but I will do my damnedest to make sure I meet the *fourth horseman* on my terms." In his mind's eye, a young Naval aviator in a crisp white dress uniform materialized. Bright gold wings shimmered above the left pocket on his breast. Not surprisingly, the uniformed officer's image looked a lot like himself at twenty-five. In that moment the aspiring author found the long awaited name for his book. Happy to have his new title in mind, the image slowly faded into nothingness. Suddenly he shouted up at the tree-dotted mountains beyond his property, "Screw you, Death, and the horse you rode in on!"

Impatiently, the novice writer waited for the word processor to bring up Chapter 62. When the bluish screen appeared, Dan began reliving and typing the thoughts and solo conversations of the past half-hour. In another forty minutes, the book was history. Ten years of searching his memory and his soul were safely tucked away inside the computer's hard drive along with backup disks. In Florida, he would have headed for the Club and a congratulatory drink. In Alabama, he opted for a glass of chocolate milk and a bench seat in the side garden. Tranquility prevailed. It seemed the trees were greener, the birds happier, the sounds of water cascading into the fishpond even more peaceful than he remembered.

Soon, sounds of an automobile easing into the garage were heard and he returned to the den by way of the porch. Shortly, Becky came up the stairs from the lower rooms. As always, she was wearing a broad, 'I missed you today' smile. They sat on the sofa where he had napped earlier and she told him of her day. She asked about her mom and Dan reminded her of Mrs. Knight's afternoon social. Before he could spring his news on finishing the book, Becky began thumbing through and scanning afternoon mail. Reading one, then another, discarding some, she was preoccupied for the moment. Her husband took the opportunity to look carefully at the woman who had given him twenty-eight years of her life. She had aged so gracefully. He knew she hated her gray hair that the Farrow genes had decreed upon her. Like all the women and some of the men of her family, she was prematurely graying, more salt than pepper, by thirty-five. By fifty, the pepper was gone. Thankfully, her hair color was an *alive* natural slate rather than hated drab gray or shimmering silver out of a bottle. "Gray" just the same as far as she was concerned but her ashen hair was beautiful in his eyes. He continued to gaze at her profile and hoped that he had left no doubt in her mind as to his love, his devotion, his appreciation for her love and support for the past quarter-century. Finally, she laid the mail aside and went to the kitchen to prepare the evening meal.

Shortly, Dan joined Becky as she set the table for dinner. He tried to be casual as he said; "I finished my book today." Becky turned and smiled at him warmly, almost with a start of surprise. "And how does the next best seller end?" "Something like this." His arms encircled her and he softly kissed, then nuzzled her neck. He whispered in her ear.

"Me *Tarzan*. You *Jane*. May be play house now? Celebrate?"

She teased. "Oh, a splash of spice to end your masterpiece, a dirty old man trying to seduce a prim and proper librarian. Are you sure your readers will respond to a bit of erotic innuendo?"

He pushed his lower torso closer against hers. "Hey, it works for me. Feel this, *I'm* responding."

She tilted her face for his kiss. His hands found and released her zippered shift. She took his hand and pulled him toward the hallway leading to the bedrooms.

He stopped momentarily and with his free hand pointed back at the kitchen. "*Tarzan* thinking of using table."

She didn't even look back. "In your dreams. This dime-store novel ends under the covers."

He was right behind her. "I sure wish you had said 'this Bestseller' instead of 'dime store novel'."

She turned and put her arms around his neck. "Dime-store or best seller, it's a good book. I'm proud of my ex-Navy super hero author. Now, is this the point where I'm supposed to look into your eyes, breathe hard, and say, 'Take me'?"

*****

Yep.

EPILOGUE

September, 2005
Age: 70

*Only a little more to write. Then I'll give o'er and bid the world
goodnight.*

                  His poetry, his pillar   Robert Herrick

Evidently, I lied.

I have just proofread the final manuscript for publishing,
therefore re-read *en toto*, **Dress Whites, Gold Wings** from
beginning to end and much of it sure looks like stuff heroes
are made of. Perhaps, contrary to all my claims otherwise,
writing these thousands of words has been a self-
aggrandizing journey to *Egoland*.

Regardless, the book stands as written and as stated in the
preface, that while I hope everyone enjoys my stories, the
primary target audience is family, friends, and future
descendants. I stand by my declaration the events and
stories related herein are true to the best of my knowledge
and memory, and searches of the Internet.

I think it relative to the story you've just read to know that I
did return to the place of my youth and found Jimmy
Frazier's burial site. I was surprised to see plastic flowers in
a stone vase adorning the grave. I had no idea who placed
the bouquet there; perhaps family descendants or possibly
the church provides such service (Later, I was told Jimmy
had a brother that I did not remember at all). Anyway, I
squatted down beside Jimmy's tombstone and wished he
were there. You won't be surprised to hear that I talked to
the tombstone as though it was Jimmy. I tried to remember
everything I ever knew about him. After awhile I stood and
spoke the names of Tommy Dixon, Woody Miller, Buzz
Settles, Les Lincoln, Pete Mitchell, and Tom Brooks (for
the record, those were aliases – I spoke their real names).

Then I read aloud two lines from a Pearl S. Buck book[1]: *"I see him this minute, as he was alive, because we were friends. As long as you remember somebody, he's still alive – in you, if nowhere else…….."* My eyes did not water as I looked skyward but my pulse beat a little faster. I think maybe my heart was crying for me. I muttered, "Guys, as long as I'm alive, you're alive. I'll never forget you."

Then I simply walked away. Did I find closure? I hope I did. Only time will tell for sure. I don't have plans to visit the little grave at Flinthill again but the quiet cemetery is always there if needed. I probably will return to the graveyard on occasion since my paternal grandparents are there. Perhaps I will say "Hello" – or "Goodbye" to Jimmy if and when I go back. For now, I'm at peace with myself. I've shared with present and future generations, to the best of my ability, my thoughts on the meaning of life.

I quoted *Horace* in Chapter 58 about putting the manuscript away for nine years. Some of these chapters were actually conceived that long ago (computer crashed but retyped pretty close to originals). The last few chapters matured during the past five years. My goal was always to complete this project by the time I was seventy. I just made it.

Before the word processor is shut down, let me say I learned something, heck, I learned a good bit, along the way. First, I found life is not black and white –it's mostly grays. I guess the book could have been titled, *Ambivalence*. I seemed to always be running into situations where right and wrong, good and bad, funny and sad, were inter-laced.

Most importantly, I found a lot of good clues to the ***real*** meaning of life. Look at the following five *Oxford* quotes and they're just the best of many I happened upon. Take these to the bank, take them to heart. Somebody, someday may explain the meaning of life in better terms, but for now, these are keepers:

---

[1] *The Christmas Ghost*, a children's book

First, the full and complete Doolittle quote mentioned in a previous chapter. *We were put on this earth for one purpose, and that is to make it a better place. We should, therefore, be contributing members of society. And if the earth, as a result of our having been on it, is a better place than it was before we came, then we have achieved our destiny.*

General James Doolittle, U.S. Air Force (1896-1993)

The PURPOSE of life is to discover your gift. The MEANING of life is giving your gift away.

David Viscott, Psychiatrist and Writer

There is no power on earth that can neutralize the influence of a high, pure, simple, and useful life.

Booker T. Washington, Educator and Writer (1856-1915)

And in the end it's not the years in your life that count. It's the life in your years. Abraham Lincoln

And life is what we make it. Always has been, always will be.

Grandma Moses

The Final Postscript. *I am very foolish over my own book. I have a copy which I constantly read and find very illuminating.*

J.B. Yeats

My feelings exactly!! Another thing I learned along the way is how hard it is to end an autobio. But now, this book finally comes to a close even though it's not the end of the story. The bird, the gun, the aircraft accident, the romance, the child, the cancer, and now, the book, all are part of and give meaning to Daniell Brown's life. While I try to live up to the challenges enunciated by the five wise and learned folk above, the search for "And They Lived Happily Ever After", continues.

Daniell M. Brown

ABOUT THE AUTHOR:

Daniell Maurice Brown, now 70, wife Becky, and Sheltie, *Meg Ryan,* continue to live in and enjoy Becky's home town of Anniston, Alabama. Dan volunteers his time with the homebound and elderly of their Church. Dan has found a new love in life – Hostas, plants that love shade. He presently has over 100 varieties. Occasionally he performs one-man, one-act dramas as *The Centurion at the Crucifixion* and *John Wesley.* When asked about a second book, he remains uncommitted but smiles.

ISBN 141206762-6